Sail's Last Century

Sail's Last Century

The Merchant Sailing Ship 1830-1930

Editor: Robert Gardiner

Consultant Editor: Dr Basil Greenhill
CB, CMG, FSA, FRHistS

CHARTWELL BOOKS, INC.

Series Consultant   Dr Basil Greenhill
                      CB, CMG, FSA, FRHistS

Series Editor   Robert Gardiner

Consultant Editor   Dr Basil Greenhill

Contributors   Peter Allington
                 Dr Basil Greenhill
                 Per-Ove Högnäs
                 David MacGregor
                 Captain W J. Lewis Parker
                 Dr David J Starkey
                 Dr Simon Ville

Frontispiece: *In general the nineteenth-century trend in sailing ship development was towards ever larger ships, built of iron and later of steel, with canvas spread over increasing numbers of masts and yards. However, in some parts of the world the traditional wooden ship survived in a form that would have been recognisable to sailors of two or even three centuries earlier. An example of this more traditional vessel is seen here in the form of the barque* Ellen. *Built at Grimstad, Norway, in 1893, the 509-ton vessel is under tow by the Clyde paddle-tug* Flying Huntress. (CMP)

© CONWAY MARITIME PRESS 1993

This edition published in North America in 2001 by
CHARTWELL BOOKS INC.
A Division of Book Sales Inc.
114 Northfield Avenue
Edison, New Jersey

ISBN 0-7858-1416-7

First published in Great Britain in 1993 by
Conway Maritime Press,
a division of Chrysalis Books Plc
9 Blenheim Court, Brewery Road
London N7 9NY

Printed and bound in Spain by Bookprint, S.L., Barcelona

Contents

Preface

THIS title marks the halfway mark in an ambitious programme of twelve volumes intended to provide the first detailed and comprehensive account of a technology that has shaped human history. It has been conceived as a basic reference work, the essential first stop for anyone seeking information on any aspect of the subject, so it is more concerned to be complete than to be original. However, the series takes full account of all the latest research and in certain areas will be publishing entirely new material. In the matter of interpretation care has been taken to avoid the old myths and to present only the most widely accepted modern viewpoints.

To tell a coherent story, in a more readable form than is usual with encyclopaedias, each volume takes the form of independent chapters, all by recognised authorities in the field. Most chapters are devoted to the ships themselves, but others deal with topics like 'shiphandling' that are more generally applicable, giving added depth to the reader's understanding of developments. Some degree of generalisation is inevitable when tackling a subject of this breadth, but wherever possible the specific details of ships and their characteristics have been included (a table of typical ships for each relevant chapter includes a convenient summary of data from which the reader can chart the evolution of the ship type concerned). With a few historically unavoidable exceptions, the series is confined to seagoing vessels; to have included boats would have increased the scope of an already massive task.

The history of the ship is not a romanticised story of epic battles and heroic voyages, but equally it is not simply a matter of technological advances. Ships were built to carry out particular tasks and their design was as much influenced by the experience of that employment – the lessons of war, or the conditions of trade, for example – as purely technical innovation. Throughout this series an attempt has been made to keep this clearly in view, to describe the *what* and *when* of developments without losing sight of the *why*.

The series is aimed at those with some knowledge of, and interest in, ships and the sea. It would have been impossible to make a contribution of any value to the subject if it had been pitched at the level of the complete novice, so while there is an extensive glossary, for example, it assumes an understanding of the most basic nautical terms. Similarly, the bibliography avoids very general works and concentrates on those which will broaden and deepen the reader's understanding beyond the level of the *History of the Ship*. The intention is not to inform genuine experts in their particular area of expertise, but to provide them with the best available single-volume summaries of less familiar fields.

Each volume is chronological in approach, with the periods covered getting shorter as the march of technology quickens, but organised around a dominant theme – represented by the title of the book – that sums up the period in question. In this way each book is fully self-sufficient, although when completed the twelve titles will link up to form a coherent history, chronicling the progress of ship design from its earliest recorded forms to the present day.

This volume deals with the merchant sailing ship, which by a particular irony of history was reaching the apogee of its centuries-long evolution as the new technology of steam began to replace sail on the world's oceans. However, the nineteenth century was far from a simple struggle between old and new in which sail represented the past and steam the future. Although steam rapidly took over routes where speed and reliability were needed at any cost, for decades there was no viable alternative to the sailing ship for most commercial activity. Some of the shortcomings of the new technology have been pointed out previously in the volume on early steam vessels, but a full understanding of the complex developments of the period also requires knowledge of parallel changes in the world's navies. As a result the reader will find numerous references in the following pages to both *Steam, Steel and Shellfire* and *The Advent of Steam*, the companion volumes in this series. All volumes are generally similar in their approach

and organisation, but these three were designed as a particular unit and accordingly depend more on one another than the rest of the series.

The history of the sailing ship is particularly difficult to summarise in that huge numbers of vessels and a myriad variety of types are involved. In order to keep in the foreground the essential driving forces – technical, economic and social – that were common influences on the evolution of all, it has been necessary to depart somewhat from a chapter structure based on specific ship types. In this case division by rig or trade makes little sense for the kind of overview intended for this series; instead the main developments of the century are seen as the changes in hull construction and form, responding to industrial and commercial opportunities offered by such diverse factors as improved tonnage regulations, the increasing economy of iron and steel production, or the liberalisation of trade legislation. These affected sailing ships of all types and, in different ways, of all nations. Not only do they explain why sail continued to be chosen over steam as a commercial investment, but these considerations also reveal that apparently retrograde phenomena, like the lingering American preference for wood over iron, were actually based on sound decision-making. Even the twentieth-century twilight of sail can be described in terms of hard economics rather than nostalgia.

Although shaped by the above theme this volume has found room for a few studies of particularly significant types and trades. The evolution of the relatively small European schooner forms a contrast with the chapter on its American cousin, a class which included some of the world's largest sail traders. On a regional basis, the Baltic provides an example of a local type, its development and its significance to the community that employed it. There are many others that might have been covered, but while the broad sweep is most important these chapters enliven the general themes of the volume through specific examples.

Robert Gardiner
Series Editor

Introduction

THIS is the second of two volumes in this series dealing with the history of the merchant ship in the nineteenth and early twentieth centuries. This volume deals with the sailing vessel and, because cargo-carrying sailing vessels in one form or another lingered on in a 'long goodbye' far into the twentieth century – even well into its second half, and have in that second half undergone a small renaissance as commercial passenger carriers – we have included a chapter on sail in the twentieth century.

As I wrote in the introduction to the volume which deals with the history of the merchant steamship (*The Advent of Steam*), the division of the history of steam and sail propelled vessels into two volumes is artificial, but, given the way in which the study of merchant shipping history developed in this century, probably at this stage inescapable. The history of the merchant ship is one aspect of the history of a great industry, itself only a part of the industrial history of Britain, as Simon Ville makes clear in his chapter in this volume. Moreover, merchant sailing vessels existed in infinite variety in the nineteenth and twentieth centuries. For example, a proper ex-amination of the development of pole-masted sailing vessels – polaccas – in the Baltic, the Mediterranean, and the port of Bideford in Devon, among other areas, would itself occupy several chapters. A comprehensive history of the

For most of the nineteenth century sail and steam co-existed. Until the 1880s most seagoing steamers carried auxiliary sail and sailing vessels, although not as regularly fitted with auxiliary power as their twentieth-century descendants, made use of steam in the form of tugs. This view of Yarmouth shows a trading schooner and fishing ketch being towed to sea, while another paddle tug brings in a fleet of fishing boats. (CMP)

The archetypal sailing ship of late nineteenth-century America was the large wooden multi-masted schooner. This is the four-master Albert F Paul. *(CMP)*

sailing vessel at this period alone could well occupy several volumes. It would have to encompass the development of local types all over the world and would involve ethnographic as well as historical studies. In a single volume we have had to confine ourselves to the mainstream of development of comparatively large vessels in western Europe and North America, with a final brief salutation to those remarkable survivors of the early nineteenth century, the Indian and Sri Lankan square rigged merchant sailing vessels, which, in the 1950s and perhaps even the '60s, really ended the long continuous history of the cargo-carrying sailing vessel – and did so not with motor sailers but with vessels which, in the words of Sir Alan Moore, were 'in the blaze of the old tradition',[1] with wooden hulls, fibre rigging, single topsails, high seamanship and primitive navigation, and a form of communal life on board which was, in north European terms, perhaps more reminiscent of earlier centuries than the nineteenth.

But, to show the sort of detailed local study which would be necessary many times over in a fully comprehensive history of the merchant sailing vessel in the nineteenth century, we have included one chapter, Per-Ove Högnäs' study of the development of the local vessels of the mid-Baltic archipelagoes, which shows what can be done. We hope this will encourage more studies of this kind.

The remarkable variety in which merchant sailing vessels existed in the nineteenth century is demonstrated in terms of the largest classes of tonnage by the divergent courses taken by developments in Britain and North America in the second half of the century. In the 1850s, though there were many differences of detail, broadly speaking the merchant shipping industries of both societies were dependent on wooden square rigged vessels of up to 1500 tons, though the majority were smaller. But among British shipowners larger iron vessels were already coming into use while in the United States, as Jeffery J Safford has argued, there had already begun the move away from investment in merchant shipping in international trade into other forms of industrial and financial development, which was to gather speed after the War Between the States.[2] While in the larger classes of tonnage the typical British merchant sailing vessel was shortly to become the iron ship or barque and later, in the 1880s, the steel square rigged vessel, and in due course, in the last decade of the building of big merchant sailing vessels, the steel four-masted barque, on the seaboard of North America the development of the large merchant sailing vessel took a completely different course. As Captain W J Lewis Parker shows, the industrialisation of New England, the legal restrictions on the employment of foreign-built tonnage in the coasting trade, and the poor loading

facilities of the coal ports of Virginia, among other factors, led to the development of the big multi-masted wooden schooner. On the West Coast the Pacific lumber trade had much the same influence. The square rigged wooden sailing vessel, except in the form of the barquentine – this rig being especially favoured on the West Coast – played a relatively small part in North American merchant shipping in the latter part of the century.

In Britain and Europe, as David Starkey shows in this volume, the history of the schooner was quite different. The evolution of the rig began in Europe, progressed in North America, and then came back to Europe to develop into a class of small tonnage employed in rather specialised deep water trades and in European local trades. As the century advanced the schooner rig was more and more widely adopted for smaller vessels. Only in the early years of the twentieth century at the end of the history of the merchant

1. A Moore, *The Last Days of Mast and Sail* (Oxford 1925), p241.

2. Jeffrey J Safford, 'The Decline of the American Merchant Marine 1850-1914: An Historiographical Appraisal', in L R Fischer & G E Panting (eds), *Changes and Adaptation in Maritime History: The North Atlantic Fleets in the Nineteenth Century* (St Johns, Newfoundland 1985).

sailing vessel were large schooners built in Europe: small four-masters in Denmark and Holland; four-masters in Finland copied from the West Coast of North America in style and size; and steel five-masters, the largest European-built schooners, in Germany.

David MacGregor's chapter dealing with the development of the larger wooden vessels over the period covered by this volume is a study of the later period of the tool of mankind which had existed since the early 1400s, if not before – the sailing vessel capable of prolonged ocean sailing with substantial loads – the earlier history of which is recorded in other volumes in this series. This was the mainstream of shipping development until the practical application of the compound engine (for the history of which see *The Advent of Steam*) and the availability of iron and later steel at prices and in quantities which made it a potential proposition for the merchant shipping industry. These events took place in the 1860s and '70s. It is perhaps useful here to repeat – as I said in the introduction to *The Advent of Steam* – that the sailing vessel and the steamship have too often been presented in popular history as rivals in an organic sense. In fact, as this series makes very clear, the nineteenth century 'battle' between sail and steam, presented by so many pseudo-historians, simply did not exist. The merchant ship, however propelled, must be considered as part of sea transport as a whole. A merchant vessel exists, like any other piece of machinery, for one purpose only – to produce a reasonable return on capital invested. Subject to a number of qualifications, which I mentioned in the introduction to the *Advent of Steam*, the market will determine the class of tonnage built and employed. Until the mid-1860s the steam vessel, though she had made great technical progress, could be profitably employed only in very limited trades. She tended to be a fully-powered vessel with, sometimes very sophisticated, sail-assist, employed on relatively short routes with valuable light cargo and passengers, and operating, on longer routes, often with government subsidy for carrying mail. Except for some limited trades – such as that to and from Australia with passengers and light cargo – the steam auxiliary square rigged vessel, for reasons explained in detail in the chapter on sail assist in *The Advent of Steam*, was simply a nonstarter. The sailing vessel was the commercial proposition for the world's carrying trade until the compound engine and cheap readily available iron for hulls as well as boilers, and then steel

Continued, page 16

The British steel four-masted barquentine Westfield *(1108 tons gross, built in 1896) was typical of the last generation of commercial sail. The barquentine reduced the labour-intensive square canvas to the fore mast alone, and* Westfield *even had booms at the heads of the main and mizzen masts to save effort dipping the gaff topsail tacks and sheets over the stays when tacking.* (CMP)

A Guide to Merchant Sailing Vessel Rigs in the Late Nineteenth Century

All drawings are to the same scale (Drawings by Lionel Willis)

Masters' qualifications

At the end of the nineteenth century, the Masters' certificates issued by the British Board of Trade were of three types:

(a) *Ordinary Master* – entitling the holder to go to sea as the Master of any vessel, steam or sailing, square rigged or fore-and-aft.

(b) *Master, fore and aft* – entitling the holder to act as Master of a fore-and-aft rigged vessel, but not to act as a Master in any case in which a certificate for a square rigged vessel was required. Square rigged vessels were usually considered to be full rigged ships, barques (barks), brigs, barquentines (barkentines) and steamships carrying square sails.

(c) *Master, steamship* – entitling the owner to go to sea as the Master of a foreign-going steamship only.

These certificates remained in use until 1 January 1931, when a revised system of certificates with endorsements came into being.

Under the old system, the only way to obtain the Ordinary Master's certificate was to have had wide experience in square rigged ships. In the communities whose maritime capital was largely invested in schooner rigged vessels such experience was becoming rare by the end of the nineteenth century because the small square rigged ship had been dropping out of use for many years. In consequence, the shipmasters of these ports mostly had the second kind of qualification – the fore-and-aft certificate.

Small vessels clearing from a port in mainland Britain for a port within home trade limits, that is, another port in mainland Britain or a continental port lying between Brest and the Elbe, were not required to have certificates of competence and there were very many highly efficient uncertificated Masters employed in the home trade.

The rigs illustrated are those which were common in northern Europe and North America. There were many variations of detail at different periods in different countries, particularly among smaller vessels; no attempt has been made to cover the rigs of small craft in other regions

1. *A full rigged ship*

2. *A barque or bark*

Square rig

1. A full rigged ship, normally referred to simply as a ship, all other sailing vessels customarily being described in the later nineteenth century by their rigs, is illustrated here. A ship was square rigged, as defined in the text of this book, on all her three masts. She set a gaff sail, called the spanker, from her mizzen lower mast. The ship in this drawing has double topsails, double topgallants, and royals on all her three masts.

2. A barque or bark. The barque also had three masts but the mizzen, instead of being square rigged with a spanker, was fore-and-aft rigged, that is, it was in two parts, lower mast and top-

mast, and from it the gaff sail and a gaff topsail were set. The barque in this drawing has double topsails, double topgallants and royals on fore and main. The building, maintenance and manning costs of a barque were less than those of a ship and there was very little difference in performance between the two rigs.

3. A brig. A brig was square rigged on both her two masts, and, like the ship, also set a spanker, in her case on her main lower mast. Quite often this spanker was actually set on a small mast stepped immediately abaft the main lower mast and secured to it at the top, that is, the small platform at the lower end of the doubling where main lower mast and topmast overlap. Vessels rigged in this

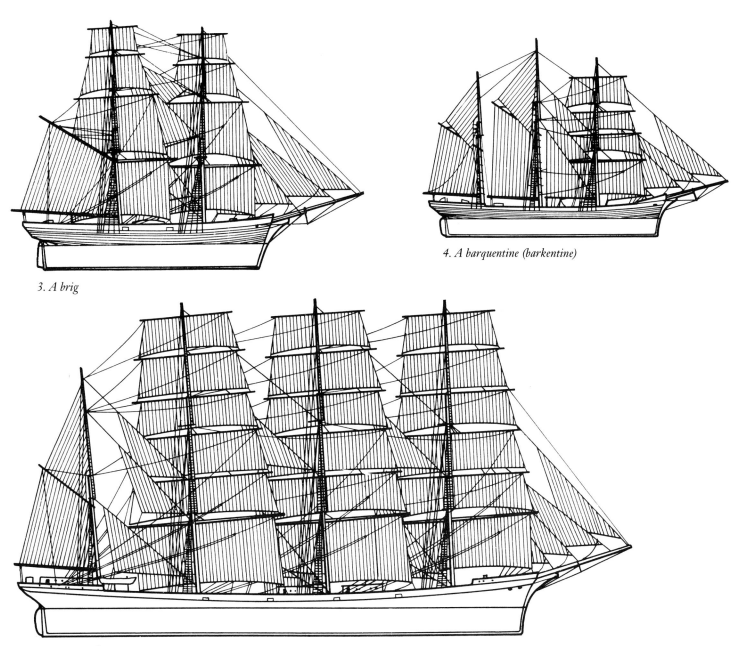

3. A brig

4. A barquentine (barkentine)

5. A four-masted barque (bark)

fashion were known as snows. This brig has single topsails, single topgallants and royals.

4. In her modern form a product of the first half of the nineteenth century, the barquentine (barkentine) was equipped with a fully square rigged fore mast, as defined in the text of this book, while her main and mizzen were fore-and-aft rigged. This was a very efficient, weatherly, economical rig, for smaller vessels. This barquentine has double topsails and a single topgallant on her fore.

5. A four-masted barque (bark). The four-masted barque was essentially the product of iron and, in due course, of steel shipbuilding and became increasingly common in the 1880s with the

falling price of iron, and the demand for larger vessels. In the last days of the building of large square rigged merchant sailing vessels in the 1890s the four-masted barque became more and more popular with the shipowners concerned and some vessels of this rig survived in commercial employment until the middle of the twentieth century.

6. A four-masted barquentine (barkentine). The success of the barquentine rig, like that of the big schooner, depended on breaking up the fore-and-aft canvas into manageable units. In big barquentines this could be done by increasing the number of masts in relation to the vessel's size. Four-masted barquentines of 1000 tons or so, like the

four-masted schooners of the same size, were very successful merchant vessels, though the fore mast with its yards and complex rigging cost as much as the other three masts added together. The rig was particularly popular on the west coast of North America where barquentines were used in the Pacific trade.

7. A late twentieth-century barquentine. In modern barquentines in the passenger cruise trade, which are much bigger than their forebears, the problem is solved by using the staysail rig advocated by the American, Captain R B Forbes, in the late 1880s for the wooden schooners in the coal trade to New England, at a time when ever larger vessels were being built for this business.

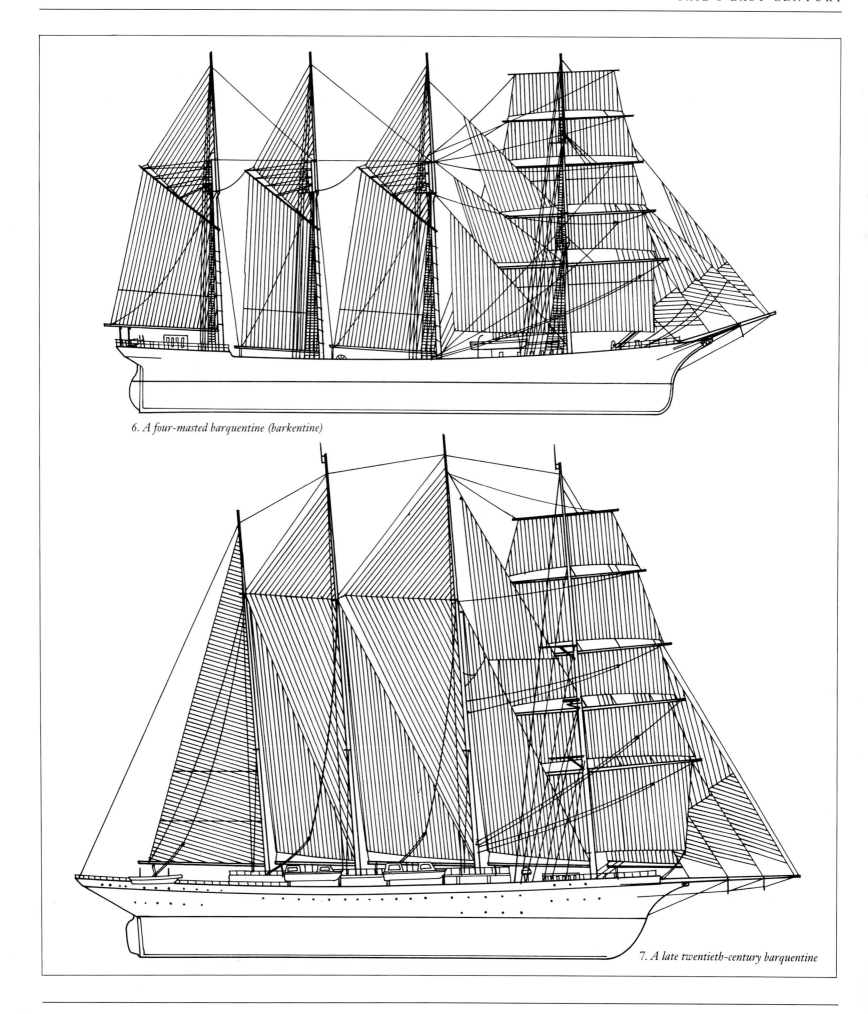

6. *A four-masted barquentine (barkentine)*

7. *A late twentieth-century barquentine*

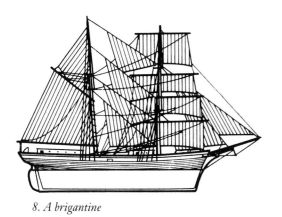

8. A brigantine

9. A Bideford polacca brigantine

Fore-and-aft rig

8.   Brigantine. The brigantine in late nineteenth-century British usage was a two-masted vessel with a square rigged fore mast and a gaff rigged main. Despite the fore mast she was usually treated administratively as a fore-and-aft rigged vessel as far as Masters' qualifications were concerned. Many brigantines, like many British schooners, operated largely in the home trade in which it was not legally necessary for the Master to possess a certificate of competence. The brigantine shown here has double topsails and a single topgallant.

9.   A Bideford polacca brigantine. Polaccas, in which one or more masts comprised a single pole without tops or crosstrees, were common in the Mediterranean and in the Baltic, surviving in the

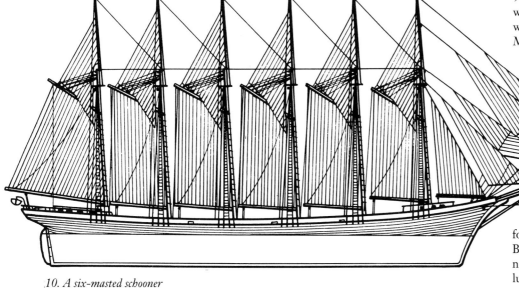

10. A six-masted schooner

former sea until well into the twentieth century. Brigantines with pole fore masts were built in north Devon in some numbers and sailed in the lumber trade from Canada as well as to the Iberian peninsula and widely in the home trade.

10.   A six-masted schooner. The six-masted schooner was essentially the product of the coal trade from southern ports to New England, and of the twentieth century. Although developed after the merchant sailing vessel elsewhere had become obsolete, some of these huge wooden vessels were among the largest merchant sailing vessels ever launched and were able to carry a bigger cargo than some four-masted barques.

11. A four-masted schooner

11.   A four-masted schooner. Although employed in many trades all over the world, the four-masted schooner was again a product of the coal trade 'down east' from southern ports in the United States, and of the Pacific lumber trade. In the late nineteenth and the early twentieth centuries four-masted schooners were built in large numbers on both coasts of North America and in smaller numbers in Denmark, Finland, Germany, Holland, Great Britain and elsewhere. The North

American-built vessels were predominantly of wooden construction but many of the European-built four-masted schooners were of steel. Although because of the wear and tear on the gear in ocean sailing conditions the four-master was not entirely suited to all trades, a well-designed four-master of not more than 1000 tons or so was considered to be among the most efficient of merchant sailing vessels.

12.   A Swedish or Finnish *slättoppare – slettop skonnert* in Danish – more usually perhaps with her masts all at the same height, as her name suggests, was one of the later types of merchant sailing vessel to evolve in the late nineteenth century. This efficient and seaworthy rig became very popular in the Baltic countries and especially Danish vessels of this type were employed in the Newfoundland and Mediterranean trades.

13.   The Nova-Scotian round-sterned 'tern schooner'. The tern, a three-masted schooner with her masts all set at the same height and often with much of the gear on fore and main interchangeable, was another late development of the merchant sailing vessel. Terns were widely employed on the east coast of North America and in the transatlantic trade. The tern illustrated here, with round stern and forefoot, represents the final development of this type into one of the most efficient of small merchant sailing vessels.

14.   Swedish or Finish *galeas*. The galeas in the form illustrated here was another product of the nineteenth century. The rig, highly suited to operation among the heavily wooded islands of the Baltic archipelagoes, became very common in that sea. *Galeaser* continued to be built in Finland into the 1960s and a number were employed in the 1990s in the passenger cruise business in the Gulf of Finland.

15.   A Breton schooner with roller-reefing square fore topsail. In the North Atlantic Banks fishery off the coasts of New England, Nova Scotia, Newfoundland, Greenland and Iceland and in the trade with pit props, vegetables and other cargoes from Breton ports to Britain, schooners were employed which were equipped with square topsails which could be taken in from the deck by rolling them up under the fore topsail yard. This system was adopted in only three' British schooners, probably because the necessary ironwork was not readily available in British schooner-building ports, but it was undoubtedly highly successful. Roller-reefing topsails are carried today by the French training schooners *La Belle Poule* and *L'Etoile*.

16.   A New England fishing schooner of the 1870s.

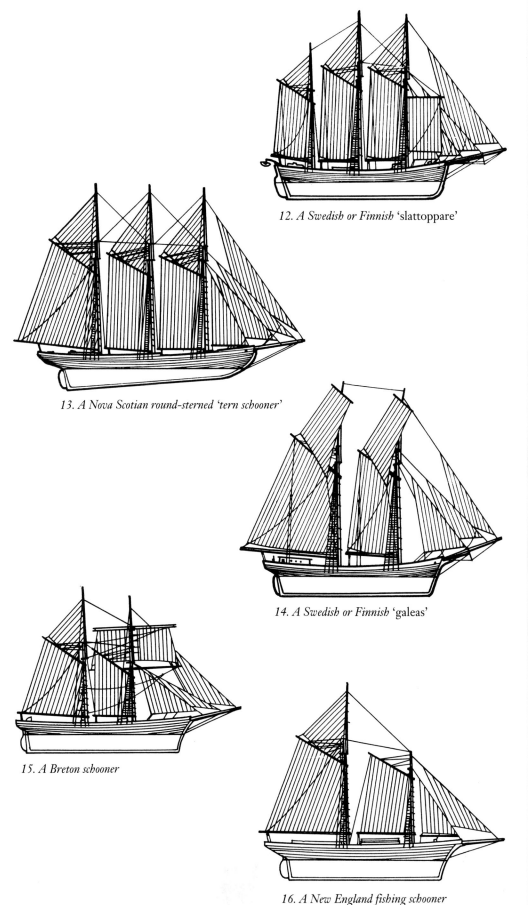

12. A Swedish or Finnish 'slattoppare'

13. A Nova Scotian round-sterned 'tern schooner'

14. A Swedish or Finnish 'galeas'

15. A Breton schooner

16. A New England fishing schooner

British fore-and-aft rigs

British schooners usually carried square topsails set from yards on the fore topmast. So common was this practice that the term 'topsail schooner', sometimes used to describe vessels so rigged, was not used by seamen. The term 'schooner' in Britain was taken to encompass square topsails unless otherwise specified. The use of square sails on the fore masts of small two- and three-masted schooners in America was so rare that the reverse held true. A schooner, without qualification, meant a vessel with no square canvas and often, with small vessels, with no fore topmasts.

There were a number of different combinations of square sails used in British schooners. Four of these are illustrated.

17. A schooner with single topsail and flying topgallant.

18. A schooner with double topsails.

19. A schooner with single topsail and standing topgallant.

20. A three-masted schooner with double topsails and standing topgallant. Such a vessel, when equipped also with a flying square sail set from the fore yard, had many of the advantages of a small barquentine off the wind and of the schooner on the wind and in some schooner-building ports may have been the product of an attempt to combine the advantages of the barquentine with a sail plan which enabled the vessel to be commanded in foreign trade by the holder of a fore-and-aft certificate. The three-masters launched at Porthmadog in north Wales between 1890 and 1913 were rigged in this fashion and were considered by many seamen involved with this class of tonnage as the finest of all British schooners.

21. The ketch. The ketch rig was very widely adopted in Britain and Denmark for small vessels in the home trade and also the trade to Newfoundland and back to Europe with salted fish, after 1870. The rig was very economical to man and maintain. A ketch can be regarded as a small American schooner with the masts reversed. The main boom was all inboard, unlike that of most American two-masted schooners which projected far over the stern. An inboard main boom was a very desirable factor in the more taxing conditions which, generally speaking, were liable to predominate in British waters. Motor ketches (a ketch was known in Denmark as a *galease*) persisted in trade around the Danish islands until the development of roll-on roll-off ferries and linking road bridges in the 1960s. A number sail today as cruise and training vessels and as yachts in Danish waters, some of them very fine examples of their type.

22. The cargo smack. The term smack tended to be used in the later nineteenth century, at least in the west of Britain as far as merchant vessels were concerned, to describe a single-masted sailing vessel. Such little vessels were very common until they were gradually supplanted by ketches after 1870. Cargo smacks equipped with auxiliary engines persisted in trade on the south Devon and Cornish coasts until after the Second World War.

17. A schooner with single topsail and flying topgallant

20. A three-masted schooner with double topsails and standing topgallant

18. A schooner with double topsails

21. A ketch

19. A schooner with single topsail and standing topgallant

22. A cargo smack

in the triple expansion engine, made the steamship, with her three voyages to the sailing ship's one, the better proposition for investment.

But even then, as the chapters of this volume show, the sailing vessel's goodbye was going to be very long drawn out. This was for a number of reasons. The industrialised world disposed of the big sailing vessel, when she had ceased to provide a reasonable return on capital, with great rapidity. This process took place in Britain after the mid-1890s and in the United States after improved loading facilities of the Virginia coal ports in 1909 made the big schooners less competitive in the coastal coal trade. The process of disposal of the obsolete tonnage rapidly gained impetus in what Georg and Karl Kåhre in their great work on Åland shipping called 'The Worldwide Abandonment of Sail'.[3] Consequently, prices of sailing tonnage fell to the point at which, particularly in countries in a less advanced stage of industrial development than Britain, where labour costs were lower, lower standards of living were still acceptable and necessary skills were still available, it was still possible to make money with sailing vessels. The shipping boom of the First World War led to the construction of much new sailing tonnage, most of it of wooden construction in countries where wood and woodworking skills were still available relatively cheaply. This subject is dealt with in the chapter on the last period of sail in the present volume. When the boom rapidly collapsed in the very early 1920s, sailing vessels in considerable numbers, some of them nearly new, became available at rock-bottom prices. Some Nova Scotians, some New Englanders, Ålanders, Breton and Portuguese fishermen, were able to work sailing vessels in ever-decreasing numbers at a profit into the middle of the twentieth century. Meanwhile a new small industry developed: the cruising business under sail. It appears to have begun on the coast of the state of Maine in New England and to have spread all over the world. It has led to the rehabilitation of old tonnage, the construction of new small vessels for the business, and ultimately to large-scale investment in multi-masted motor schooners and in auxiliary barquentines in the 1980s and '90s. So the large commercial sailing vessel, even the square rigged sailing vessel in a form visually familiar, but technically unrecognisable to earlier generations, has undergone a minor renaissance at the end of the twentieth century.

As far as small vessels were concerned, the development of the cheap, reliable and compact diesel auxiliary engine gave a new lease of life to the schooner and the ketch operating in coastal and island trades. Thus, for example, new wooden motor schooners and ketches, some of them heavily rigged, were built for the trade among the Danish islands into the 1950s. It was not until 1960 that the last auxiliary sailing vessels ceased to work in the British home trade.

Technicalities

In this book we have had to use technical terms because it is quite impossible to write even in the simplest way about the development of the sailing ship in the nineteenth century without doing so. The technology of sailing vessels was extremely complicated and there is a large number of books on the subject. Some of them are listed in the Bibliography under the appropriate chapters in this volume, but perhaps particular attention might be drawn here to the work of Harold Underhill, whose two books *Masting and Rigging: The Clipper Ship and Ocean Carrier*, and *Deep Water Sail* are an invaluable layman's guide to the complex technicalities of merchant sailing vessels of many kinds at the time of their ultimate development.

To aid the reader who may not be familiar with such terms as barque, barquentine, brig, and so on, the classic sailing vessel rigs of the nineteenth century are illustrated diagrammatically here. During the nineteenth century it be-

Auxiliary diesel engines gave a new lease of life to the sailing ship in European coastal waters, but a few vessels continued to make do without mechanical power. One of the last pair of sail-only schooners in British waters was the Belfast-built Mary Miller *which traded out of Fowey in Cornwall until the Second World War.* (CMP)

came the general practice to describe sailing vessels by the disposition of their masts and sails rather than by their occupations or the shape of their hulls, as had in general been the practice in earlier centuries. The rigs became standardised, more or less.

To go into further detail it is perhaps necessary to define what is meant by the terms 'square rigged' and 'fore-and-aft rigged'. A square rigged mast was one divided by its supporting rigging into three distinct parts, a short lower mast, a topmast, and a topgallant mast. From each of these masts sails were set from yards, athwart the mast, which would be trimmed on the fore side of the mast only, so that the wind always acted on the same surface of the sails, the after surface. The fore-and-aft rigged mast was in two parts, a long lower mast and a short topmast. A gaff and boom sail which could be trimmed only abaft the mast was set from the lower mast and a gaff topsail, or sometimes one or more square sails, was set from the topmast. A gaff sail received the wind on either side according to its direction, relative to the direction in which the vessel was sailing.

Legal and administrative practice in the nineteenth century in Britain defined the square rigged vessel as one having at least one square-rigged mast, as described above. A fore-and-aft rigged vessel had all her masts fore-and-aft rigged as defined above. In the later nineteenth century certificates of competence were granted to masters and mates under the Merchant Shipping Acts which qualified them to be employed in charge of fore-and-aft rigged vessels only, or steamers only, or to take charge of all types of vessel, including square rigged vessels.

A square rigged vessel was therefore a ship, a barque, a brig, or a barquentine. A fore-and-aft rigged vessel was a schooner (even though she had square topsails on her fore topmast), a ketch or a smack, that is, one of the numerous varieties of single-masted gaff rigged vessels. The brigantine appears to have occupied, in legal and administrative practice, a kind of twilight world between the two classes of rigging. The master of a barquentine had to have a certificate of competence qualifying him to take charge of all types of vessel including square rigged ships, but the master of a brigantine in circumstances in which she was required to have a qualified master – that is when she was sailing beyond the limits of the home trade – could take charge of her even though his certificate of competence was one for fore-and-aft rigged vessels. The reasons for this situation were probably partly so-

3. G & K Kåhre, *Den Åländska Segelsjöfartens Historia* (Mariehamn 1988).

The barquentine Waterwitch *under full sail. When originally built in 1872 she was rigged as a brig with double topsails, and single topgallants and royals above, but the three-masted rig was adopted in 1884. The barquentine was regarded as square rigged and as such* Waterwitch *was the last UK-registered square-rigger to carry commercial cargoes on a regular basis. (CMP)*

cial. A heavily rigged schooner with square topsails could carry almost as much square canvas as a brigantine. In local communities operating both types of vessel the distinction became unreal and was probably blurred over in terms of certificates of competence.

The basic terms, ship, barque and barquentine refer to vessels with three masts. Thus the term 'three-masted barque' was not customarily used by seamen or in the industry since by definition the barque had three masts. Similarly the term schooner referred to a vessel with two masts. The qualification of number of masts only became necessary as vessels grew bigger in the later years of the century. Thus to indicate that the barque had more than three masts she was referred to as a four-masted barque. A schooner which had more than two masts was referred to as a three-masted or four-masted schooner, etc. If a vessel was referred to without reference to the number of her masts it was assumed that she had the basic rig as defined above.

The illustrations in this book, studied with reference to the foregoing and to the rigging diagrams provided here, will provide numerous examples of the different types of vessel in use in the nineteenth century.

Square rig seamanship required skills which are now almost entirely lost: the crew of the three-masted barque Garthsnaid *(ex Inversnaid, 1842) on the fore yard struggle with the fore sail. (By courtesy of David MacGregor)*

A cultural fracture

This question of technicalities leads to a very difficult subject, one touched upon at least by inference by Captain Peter Allington in his chapter on the changing problems of shiphandling in the nineteenth century, that of the complete break in historical tradition which has taken place with the demise of the sailing vessel in the forms in which she had developed over the centuries. The merchant sailing vessel has sometimes been romanticised, almost as if she had

some abstract, but undefined, moral worth in her own right. In fact she was inefficient and dangerous and working conditions on board her were frequently utterly intolerable by modern standards. She was a vehicle of an earlier stage of human development and latterly a tool of underdeveloped societies. Her purpose, as with all merchant vessels, once again, was to make money, return on capital invested, and she had no other. But she is, nevertheless, an historical fact, a principal tool of mankind for centuries of the development of modern society. In this, the volume of 'Conway's History of the Ship' that deals principally with the last sailing vessels, it is perhaps appropriate to comment on some of the implications of her demise.

These volumes comprise the history of the ship. This means that of the complex of elements, financial, political, social, industrial, strategic and technical, which make up the sphere of human activity, seafaring, in which the ship, mercantile or naval, operates, the ship herself has been selected for particular attention. This is rather unfashionable. The current trends in mainstream historical studies are away from the particular to the wider field. The study of the particular is neither encouraged nor likely to gain much repute for the young historian. Thus it is normal to examine, for instance, the prob-

A big sea coming over the portside rail of the Inversnaid. *Life at sea in the age of sail was always perilous, often uncomfortable and frequently squalid. To survive at all required a high degree of co-ordinated skill, preferably practiced from an early age, and this total commitment to a peculiar way of life set the seaman apart from his shore-going brother.* (By courtesy of David MacGregor)

lems of management and finance of early steamship companies, but the study of the performance limitations of the paddle steamers themselves and the effect that this had on what was possible in the way of commercial operations would, perhaps, not be thought relevant. This kind of situation can lead to imbalance and even downright misunderstanding in forming conclusions. Similarly, in considering the strategy of naval operations, it is really necessary to understand the limitations imposed by the grossly inadequate navigational techniques and by the fact that the square rigged ship was a poor performer to windward – and the naval square rigged ship as she developed in the eighteenth century particularly so, so that in bad weather she became very difficult to handle. Thus the Hon Victor Montagu, later a Rear-Admiral, wrote, 'A three-decker in a gale of wind is rather a curious being. Under close reefed topsails you could not lay her near enough to the wind to enable her to meet the seas properly. The effect of the wind on her huge sides was to drive her bodily and very fast to leeward: in fact, you simply drifted.'[4]

To some extent, if I am right in the assumption that it exists, the resistance to the study of the particular, the ship and her world, may arise not only from incomprehension of that world,

and a perhaps subconscious belief that it is just all too difficult, but from a deep strand in our Judeo-Christian culture, biblically derived, which sees the sea as chaos, a very alien world.

To acquire the skills physically to survive as a seaman in sailing vessels it was, after all, necessary to begin very early in life and undergo a training – work experience if you like – so totally absorbing as to deprive the individual concerned of much ordinary human experience. As Thucydides wrote, more than two thousand years ago of the seamanship of oar and sail, 'Seamanship is a skill just like anything else, and it is impossible to perform it proficiently as a haphazard, spare time activity. In fact it leaves no spare time for anything else.'[5]

As with the men of Thucydides' world, so the nineteenth-century seamen tended to be a society within a society with their own way of life, their own language, their own peculiar attitudes and ways of thought, all conditioned by their all-absorbing 'total occupation'. To the landsmen

they were very alien. They had little to share with him, for lack of common experience. The ancient mariners of Coleridge survived as long as there were survivors of sailing vessels' crews to be met with – but there was a vast deal to be learnt from them: of the understanding of sea speech, of shiphandling, of the social systems on board vessels and affecting the seamen ashore, of the technicalities of the sailing vessel and her limitations, all of which information helped the historian with respect for these men to enter to a degree into the lost world of the sailing trade. Sir Alan Moore summed it up, foreseeing what was to happen, for though in 1924 there were still thousands of sailing vessels of all kinds in the world, very few were being built, so that their end was then predictable – indeed Moore would have been surprised to know how long they were to linger on. Moore wrote:

In all classes of ships and boats sails have already been given up, are in the process of abandonment, or exist under threat of being supplanted. ... No man can follow the naval campaigns and battles of the past or understand the development of the ship unless he realises the limitations of sail and the difficulties with which the seaman of former ages had to contend.

It is true that men who are not sailors have

4. Rear-Admiral the Hon Victor Montagu, *A Middy's Recollections, 1853-60* (London 1898), pp32-33.

5. Thucydides, 1. 142. 9. I believe the words are John Morrison's translation – see *The Age of the Galley* in the present series.

The last deep water commercial sailing fleet was owned in the Finnish Åland Islands. This photograph was taken on 14 August 1932 in the outer roads of Mariehamn's West Harbour and shows the barques (left to right) Viking, Killoran, Penang *(arriving from London, and about to let go her anchors) and* Herzogin Cecilie. *(CMP)*

One of the last trades conducted under sail was the Grand Banks fishery, and the most famous of all the vessels employed was the Canadian schooner Bluenose. *(CMP)*

studied these subjects and have written admirably upon them, but they lived in the blaze of the old traditions. ... we group men in our thoughts according to their political divisions. It is possible to separate them by occupations instead of countries, and the classes so formed are realities and their members have a kinship of method and outlook that makes them different from other men. One of the greatest and most ancient of such brotherhoods is coming to an end.

We would not, in the closing years of the twentieth century, wish any human being to live the life of physical hardship, danger, sometimes squalor, often impoverishment, and above all of social and intellectual deprivation which was all too often the life of the merchant seaman in sailing vessels. But, historically, we have lost dimensions of understanding of what was perhaps the most complex and demanding pattern of skills ever acquired by ordinary men.

It is certainly true that the study of the maritime aspects of history today is flourishing in many ways as never before. Maritime and shipping themes are the subject of numerous theses for higher degrees, especially in economic and social history, in universities the world over. The work of the late Professor Keith Matthews, and of Professor Lewis Fischer, both of them of Memorial University of St Johns, Newfoundland, has encouraged, among other media, through the *International Journal of Maritime History*, studies into merchant shipping history of a depth and diversity not attempted at earlier periods. As far as Britain is concerned a new generation of naval historians, Nicholas Rodger, Andrew Lambert of King's College, London, D K Brown, Michael Duffy and others are blowing away old myths and folklore to reveal the political and technical realities behind naval policy. Conferences, symposia, discussion groups and lectures on maritime historical and archaeological themes are organised regularly by universities and other institutions all over the world. Moreover, the world is full of sail training vessels of every size, rig, purpose and organisation.

But for all this the ship herself, the heart of the matter, and her rigging, handling, pilotage and navigation have received less attention, as has the way in which men were conditioned into sailing her, their attitudes and outlooks. They had, for example, a preoccupation with the exact meaning of words within their own terminology

which arose from the sheer necessity for absolute precision. The sailing vessel, especially the wooden sailing vessel, operated commercially under nineteenth-century conditions, was a very dangerous work place. Modern sail training vessels, whatever their merits, offering a brief group experience under (in the best of them) carefully controlled conditions and with full motor power available at the touch of a button, do not exist in the same world. If your life, scarcely less importantly the livelihood of yourself and your dependants, depended on the immediate understanding of transmitted instructions, then exact terminology became a matter of life and death. Remember how Long Jack, as told in Kipling's rather misleadingly titled *Captains Courageous* (which is in fact a first-class piece of professional research and reportage), made it his business at the first possible moment, and by the method likely to be quickest, to teach young Harvey Cheyne

'things at the sea that ivry man must know, blind, dhrunk, or asleep.' There is not much gear to a 73-ton schooner with a stump foremast, but Long Jack had a gift of expression. When he wished to draw Harvey's attention to the peak-halyards, he dug his knuckles into the back of the boy's neck and kept him at gaze for half a minute. He emphasised the difference between fore and aft generally by rubbing Harvey's nose along a few feet of the boom, and the lead of each rope was fixed in Harvey's mind by the end of the rope itself.

It was dangerous to have on board the *We're Here* (which, never forget, actually existed and fished out of Gloucester, Massachusetts) somebody who did not know. This grammar of the ship, as of her handling, pilotage and navigation, is basic to merchant shipping historical studies. There was a time when maritime museums could be looked to for standards in these matters, but with the erosion of government finance museums increasingly retreat from curatorship and precision in scholarship. It is up to the individual to seek to master, as far possible (and enough has now been published to enable the student to go a long way in the right direction), the intricacies of the ship and how she was conducted about her business, the terms her people used in describing her and her handling, to understand something of these people and how they looked at the world, to be meticulous in their terminology as these people were, and to respect the ship and her people as the very heart of their studies. We hope that this series of volumes will help.

Dr Basil Greenhill

6. A Moore, *op, cit*, pp241-2. It is to be remembered that Moore, a Baronet and a distinguished medical practitioner educated at Eton and Trinity College, Cambridge, in his approach to his subject of 'Nautical Comparative Anatomy', was breaking through class barriers which are still, unfortunately, strong at the end of the twentieth century. The history of the sailing vessel owes much to old fashioned élitist education. Basil Lubbock and David MacGregor are of the same background.

1

The Wooden Sailing Ship: over 300 Tons

THE ravages of war were finally brought to a close by the defeat of Napoleon at Waterloo in 1815, and the shipping industry had the momentous task of trying to acclimatise itself to an era of peace, in which the need to be ever on the defensive could be forgotten. Admittedly, there were still pirates to be encountered on all the oceans of the world, and in certain trades and in eastern harbours the need to defend a ship still required a modest armament. Shipbuilding costs had risen steeply during the long years of war, as witness the prices at the Blackwall Yard on the River Thames: here the price of an East Indiaman was £12 per ton in 1774 for a ship of 723 tons; it had risen to £20 per ton in 1801 for a ship of 818 tons; and by 1812, a ship of 950 tons cost £27 per ton. However, peace had no sooner been declared than prices for the larger Indiamen of 1315 tons fell by £4 to £5 per ton.[1]

The demands to replace tonnage lost due to capture or enemy action continued to give shipyards adequate business, and the lifting in 1813 of the monopoly to trade with India resulted in a surge of exported goods. Many privately owned ships in the 300–500 tons range were built to take advantage of this and there was a further boost provided in 1823 by the freeing of trade to anywhere in the East, with the exception of China. The Honourable East India Company's right to exclusive trade with China was finally revoked in 1834. Other European countries, such as Sweden, France and Denmark, were also abolishing the trading monopolies of comparable companies at much the same time.

As regards the British shipping industry, it was largely protected from external competition and exploitation by the Navigation Acts which remained in force until their repeal in 1849.

This lithograph by John Ward (1798-1849) depicts a merchant ship of about 500 tons running before the wind with stunsails set. Although a relatively few East Indiamen were far larger, this ship would be regarded as large in her day, and her appearance is typical of such vessels between 1820 and 1850. (By courtesy of David MacGregor)

These Acts ensured that goods from certain countries could only be imported into the United Kingdom in British vessels, and it is claimed that the Acts may have had the effect of producing stagnation in ship design. However, new laws for measuring tonnage had come into effect in 1836 and a loophole had been discovered by a shipyard at Aberdeen whereby a longer and finer-lined vessel with raking bow and stern profiles could achieve a smaller tonnage figure. Extreme versions of this new design appeared in the 1840s and were copied abroad, notably in Holland, and elsewhere in the United Kingdom, although nearly all were built of wood, so that when the Navigation Acts were duly repealed in 1849 there was a good flow of new ideas concerning ship design already in force. In addition the constant meeting with American ships in Eastern waters urged British designers to provide ships that could match the speed and sailing qualities of these competitors.

During the period of the industrial revolution in Great Britain, iron was used extensively, not only in machinery but increasingly in the structural members which supported the machines. At first, wooden trucks had wooden wheels that ran in grooved wooden rails, but soon metal wheels were to run on metal rails, and as the century advanced the use of wood constantly de-

1. David R MacGregor, *Merchant Sailing Ships 1775-1815: Sovereignty of Sail* (London 1985), appendix 2, p210.

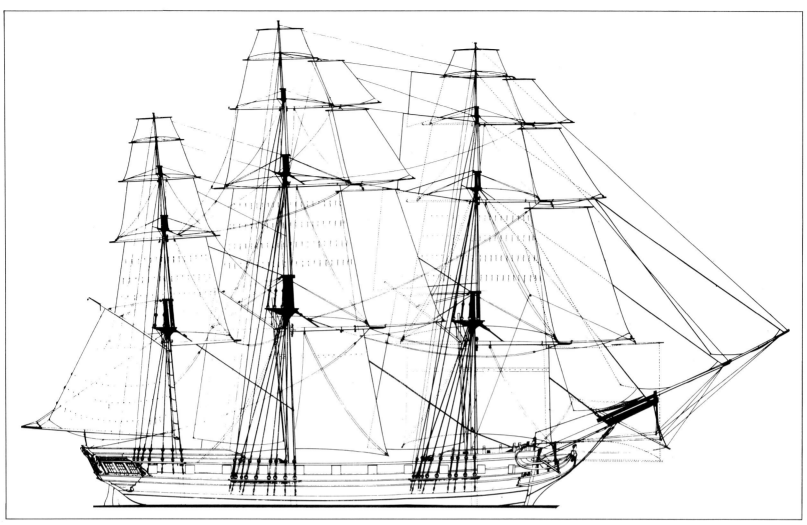

creased in all forms of life and work ashore. But afloat, wood remained supreme until the second half of the nineteenth century for large vessels and through the entire period for smaller craft. Many shipyards specialising in smaller vessels lacked the facilities to build a hull in anything but wood, and when owners asked for an iron or steel hull it had to be refused. Often these yards were obliged to close down or concentrate on building wooden fishing boats and repairing wooden hulls.

One way to indicate the quantity of wooden shipbuilding is to isolate construction in iron and steel by outlining the progress it made in various countries. In Great Britain, canal and river craft were being built of iron from the 1820s and so were a few small oceangoing vessels in the 1830s and 1840s, with an occasional larger sailing vessel of 550 to 700 tons. After 1850, shipyards in Scotland and the North of England adopted iron shipbuilding to an increasingly greater degree. By contrast, construction of iron vessels in America was minuscule, partly owing to the vast amounts of timber available and partly due to the tax levied on iron, which rose from 24 per cent in 1857 to 168 per

cent in 1868. In America, very few square rigged ships or barques were ever built of iron or steel. In Germany, five named sailing ships were built of iron in the years 1844–1861, and the industry began to expand only after 1875. In Holland, a few iron ships were built in the 1860s.[2]

In 1830, the total registered tonnage of shipping in Great Britain was approximately 2,350,000 tons and in America it was approximately 1,150,000; for America there were virtually no iron vessels in this total, and only an exceedingly small fraction in the British tonnage. By the middle of the century, the total for the United Kingdom was 3,396,000 tons for sailing ships alone and 168,474 for steamers.[3] Compared with the totals of twenty years earlier, there would have been more iron construction included in these figures, especially for steamers.

The period from 1850 to 1880 saw great changes in shipbuilding in Great Britain, and the costs of producing iron ships had an effect on the survival of wooden construction. Knick Harley has attributed the amount of these costs to three main factors: the course of iron prices, the level of wages and the degree of technological change. His calculations indicate that by 1880

A rare contemporary masting and rigging plan, from Peter Hedderwick's A Treatise on Marine Architecture, *published in 1830. This ship measured 117ft 2in for tonnage by 31ft 0in x 22ft 0in, giving 503 tons om. The heavy head and elaborate quarter gallery parallel naval practice, and the lofty rig, with separate fidded royal mast stepped abaft the topgallant is worthy of notice (the same rig is shown in the Ward engraving above). (By courtesy of David MacGregor)*

the price of iron had declined to half what it was in 1850 while the level of wages had risen by 50 per cent. In addition, improved techniques in metalworking had resulted in savings for the iron shipyard.[4]

At Aberdeen, some ships of up to 1000 tons

2. David R MacGregor, *Merchant Sailing Ships 1850-1875: Heyday of Sail* (London 1984), pp10-11.

3. Adam W Kirkaldy, *British Shipping: its History, Organization and Importance* (London, 2nd impression 1919), Appendix XVII.

4. C Knick Harley, 'Aspects of the Economics of Shipping, 1850-1913', in Lewis R Fischer & G E Panting (eds), *Change and Adaptation in Maritime History: the North Atlantic Fleets in the Nineteenth Century* (St Johns, Newfoundland 1985), p174.

From the 1830s the barque rig grew in popularity. One reason may have been the increasing length of ships, responding to the new tonnage laws; short, deep vessels might be rigged as brigs but the new longer vessels could step a third mast, which if only carrying fore-and-aft canvas did not require a larger crew. This painting shows the Anna Robertson *of 317 tons nm (built at Sunderland in 1842) sailing from Malta in 1849. She has trysails on the fore and main which are more effective than the square courses when close-hauled.* (Private Collection)

were still being built of wood as late as 1870, although iron was gradually supplanting the use of timber. On the River Clyde, sailing ship construction was nearly all in iron, and the larger shipyards often took orders to build schooners, brigantines and barquentines in iron. Sunderland had a long tradition of wooden shipbuilding, in spite of its proximity to coalfields, iron ore and blast furnaces, but it becomes increasingly difficult to find examples of timber construction after 1870.

In order to survive, shipyards in the Canadian Maritime Provinces – where so much wooden tonnage was exported to Great Britain and other parts of the world – were obliged to cut their prices to remain competitive with iron shipyards, and the shipwrights had accordingly to accept lower wages. Shipbuilding entirely in timber continued into the 1870s and it was only the falling prices of iron ships that forced Canadian shipyards to abandon the sale of wooden tonnage abroad. From the 1880s onwards, these shipyards mostly built only for the home market. In the 'Down East' state of Maine, wages for shipwrights had remained almost unchanged during the thirty years from 1850, although rates in other trades and generally in America had risen by 50 per cent. The shipbuilders here

The 920-ton American ship New England *being dismasted, as depicted by Venetian artist John Luzro. The ship belonged to the Regular Line of packets sailing between New Orleans and Liverpool, and was built at Bath, Maine, in 1849. The deck layout of this big passenger ship shows a long quarterdeck and a midships deckhouse that extends into the forecastle; there is a gangway between the two over the small waist amidships.* (Peabody Museum of Salem)

were still benefiting from the American Navigation Acts which restricted the coasting trade to American-built vessels. Large wooden square rigged ships continued to be produced in this state until the early 1890s.[5]

Although official statistics separate the totals of sail and steam tonnage, wood and iron or steel are rarely dealt with so conveniently. One way is for the researcher to work laboriously through the pages of a volume of *Lloyd's Register of Shipping* to determine the tonnage according to the material of construction. However, this work has occasionally been carried out by officialdom and Sarah Palmer was able to utilize

such an analysis for the years 1886 and 1910, and the table she produced separates sail from steam, with sub-headings of wood, composite, iron and steel for each mode of propulsion. The table commences with 'United Kingdom' and 'British Possessions' followed by eleven other countries.[6]

This table is derived from *Lloyd's Universal Register* in respect of the year 1886, which includes vessels of 100 tons and upwards; after 1890 they were regularly listed in the main register book. Sailing vessels of less than 300 tons will unavoidably be included, although for this volume they are specifically covered in a separate chapter.

For the year 1886, wooden sailing ships in the United Kingdom add up to 946,000 tons which represents 13.2 per cent of the total tonnage for sail and steam; for British Possessions, the respective figures are 1,315,000 tons and 82.3 per

5. *Ibid*, pp173-74.

6. Sarah Palmer, 'The British Shipping Industry 1850-1914' in Fischer and Panting (eds), *op cit*, pp96-97.

For Sale by Private Contract,

THE SPLENDID FAST-SAILING SHIP,

PRINCESS ROYAL, A I

$637\frac{467}{1000}$ Tons N. M. and $564\frac{23}{94}$ Tons O. M.

Inside & 30ft outside

Length 132 ft. $\frac{6}{10}$—Breadth 27 ft. $\frac{4}{10}$—Depth 20 ft. $\frac{6}{10}$; built at Aberdeen in 1841, of the best seasoned Materials, under particular inspection. This fine Vessel was built expressly for the India Trade, and has beautiful Accommodations for Passengers; she has made Two Voyages, and has just completed the second out and home to Madras and Calcutta in less than nine months, eighty-three days of which were expended in port. She is well found in Stores of every description.

Now lying in the St. Katharine's Docks.

Hull, Masts, Yards, Standing and Running Rigging, with all faults as they now lie.

INVENTORY.

ANCHORS.

1 best bower
1 small ditto
1 sheet
1 stream
2 kedges
1 grapline

CABLES.

1 best bower chain
1 small ditto ditto
1 stream
1 hawser
1 towline
1 warp

SAILS.

1 flying jib
2 standing ditto
1 fore staysail
2 ditto topmast staysails
3 foresails
2 ditto topsails
2 ditto topgallant sails
1 ditto royal
1 fore spencer
1 fore and aft mainsail
3 main topsails
2 ditto topgallant sails
1 ditto royal
2 mizens
2 ditto topsails
1 ditto topgallant sail
1 ditto royal
2 square mainsails
1 wind sail
2 lower steering sails
4 topmast ditto
3 topgallant ditto
3 ditto royals
3 jolly boat's sails
1 quarter deck awning
1 poop ditto
6 bolts canvas
12 bundles twine

CARPENTER'S STORES.

1 pump hook
3 ditto brakes
3 ditto spears
3 lower boxes
6 pump bolts
1 sounding rod
2 spare topmasts
2 ditto lower yards
3 ditto topgallant masts
1 ditto topsail yard
1 ditto jib boom
2 lower steering sail booms
4 topmast ditto ditto
4 topgallant ditto ditto
3 royal ditto
10 steering sail yards
1 piece pump leather
300 ditto tacks
6 bags nails
1 cross cut saw
1 pair copper scissors
1 pitch pot
1 grindstone and trough
Hatch bars complete
Tarpaulin ditto
Handspikes ditto
Capstan bars ditto
6 padlocks
6 hen coops
1 oak plank
2 bundles oakum
1 ship's skeet
24 chain hooks
7 spare sheets of copper
2 pair grains
2 shank painters
3 pair boat's gripes
Quantity old iron
2 crow bars

BOATSWAIN'S STORES.

2 cat blocks
3 top ditto
3 iron-bound snatch ditto
1 signal halyard
2 fish hooks, runner, and tackle
1 fish pendant
Belaying pins, complete
6 double blocks
6 single ditto
2 bumkin ditto
2 burton ditto
1 spunyarn, winch, and bolt
1 winch handle
Mats for rigging
2 serving mallets
1 dozen scrapers
½ dozen marline spikes
24 hooks and thimbles
2 tar brushes
2 ditto buckets
½ cask tar
½ barrel black varnish
4 pair can hooks
1 ditto man ropes
1 ditto side ropes
3 cork fenders
6 ballast shovels
2 deck stoppers
2 cathead ditto
6 pair handcuffs
12 leg irons

SHIP CHANDLER'S STORES.

2 brass compasses
1 brass hanging compass
1 wood ditto
1 deep sea lead
1 ditto line
1 deep sea lead reel
1 hand lead
1 ditto line
1 log
1 ditto reel
1 ditto line
3 ditto glasses
1 hour ditto
1 speaking trumpet
1 signal lanthorn
2 hand ditto
1 ensign
1 jack
1 burgee
1 set Marryat's signals
1 ditto Telegraph Vocabulary
1 spy glass
2 copper pumps
2 brass binnacles
1 pair steelyards
1 set weights and scales
1 bread sieve
4 paint brushes
1 ship's bell
6 paint pots
6 oil cans
2 shark hooks
2 patent filters
1 medicine chest, with medicine

COOPER'S STORES.

3 butts
27 puncheons
2 harness casks
1 oil cask
1 vinegar cask
2 steep tubs
3 mess kids
1 nun buoy
18 buckets

COOK & CABIN STORES

1 patent troop's hearth
1 Winchester's patent cabouse house
1 shovel
2 frying pans
2 tormentors
5 saucepans
3 stewpans
1 cook's axe
2 steamers
1 tea kettle
2 baking pans
1 copper ditto
1 dripping pan
3 cabin tables
3 table covers
3 trays
2 swinging ditto
2 chairs
4 stools
4 curtains
1 looking glass
2 sets of castors
4 candlesticks
1 cabin bell
2 pair snuffers
1 foul plate basket
2 bread baskets
10 table knives and forks
12 desert ditto ditto
1 knife box
30 cups and saucers
10 table spoons
12 tea ditto
17 desert ditto
12 egg ditto
24 plated forks
26 ditto desert ditto
2 ditto gravy spoons
2 ditto ladles
29 tumblers
8 decanters
37 wine glasses
7 champagne ditto
36 claret ditto
16 liqueur ditto
8 salts
2 pickle glasses
1 water decanter
75 table cloths
1 tureen and ladle
4 sauce tureens ladles and stands
132 plates
8 dishes
2 corner dishes
2 pie ditto
56 towels
2 funnels
1 brass cock
8 dish covers
1 wash hand bason
2 black jacks
1 water jug
2 coffee pots
1 pepper mill
2 tea pots
6 milk ditto
1 coffee mill
4 butter boats
2 cabin lamps, with 10 chimnies and 2 shades
1 cork screw
1 hearth brush
1 dust pan
set of spirit measures
1 meat safe
1 steel

BOATS.

1 long boat
1 pinnace
1 skiff
1 gig

The Ship and her Stores to be taken with all faults as they now lie, without any allowance for length, weight, quality, quantity, or any defect whatever.

For further particulars, apply to

HENRY & CALVERT TOULMIN,

8, *George Yard, Lombard Street.*

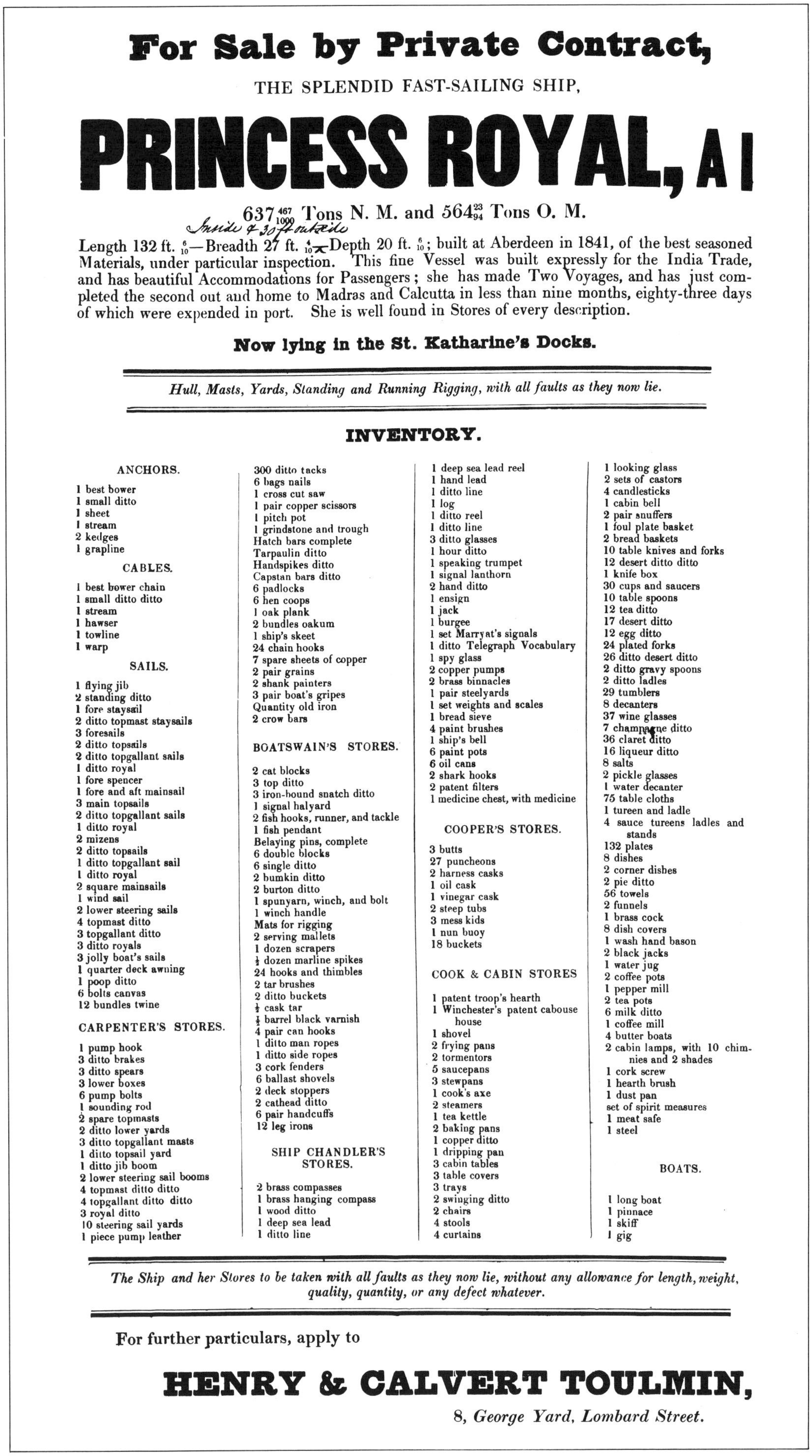

A handbill advertising the sale of the East India trader Princess Royal *built by Alexander Duthie at Aberdeen in 1841. The inventory gives some idea of the furniture and fittings of a large wooden merchant ship.*
(By courtesy of David MacGregor)

cent. This gives a grand total of 2,261,000 tons for wood construction, ignoring composite ships. Iron and steel sailing ships in the United Kingdom total 2,211,000 tons and British Possessions raise the amount to 2,265,000.

There was only 7000 tons of iron construction in America in 1886 but 1,579,000 tons of wood, which is 81.2 per cent of the total for sail and steam (Great Lakes tonnage is excluded). The totals can best be compared in tabulated form, arranged after the two British totals, in descending order of size for 1886. The corresponding totals for 1910 are tabulated beside them. The following figures are extracted from Sarah Palmer's table and are confined to wooden sailing ships, the figures for iron, steel and composite sailing ships and all those for steamers having been omitted.[7]

Table 1/1 *Wooden sailing ship tonnage for the major maritime nations registered in 1886 and 1910*

	1886	*1910*
United Kingdom	946,000	63,000
British Possessions	1,315,000	149,000
United States of America	1,579,000	*984,000
Norway	1,348,000	175,000
Italy	703,000	125,000
Germany	674,000	13,000
Sweden	329,000	119,000
France	277,000	72,000
Russia	270,000	141,000
Holland	188,000	2000
Spain	153,000	14,000
Denmark	125,000	47,000
Japan	31,000	2000

* Great Lakes tonnage excluded

The tonnage totals for the year 1910 indicate, as might be expected, the fairly rapid decline in the number of wooden sailing ships still registered, although the total for America remains on the high side. Great Britain and its Possessions

7. *Ibid.*

The Eleanor Dixon of 454 tons nm was built at Belfast in 1848 as a full rigged ship. Like many ships later in the century she was cut down to a barque, as shown in this photo, but was also equipped with Cunningham's patent roller-reefing topsails – on the main topsail yard the chafing spar around which the sail was rolled can be just made out. Crew numbers were reduced inexorably as the century wore on, in an attempt to stay competitive, and roller-reefing was one of many work-saving devices employed. (By courtesy of David MacGregor)

had by far the largest amount of composite construction in 1886, with a total of 96,000 tons; Holland was next with 19,000 tons, followed by Germany with 6000 tons; all other countries had less than 1000 tons each, and several, including America, had none.

By 1910, Great Britain still possessed a large fleet of iron and steel sailing ships, most of which were more than ten years old, but Germany and France had fleets of newer sailing ships, mostly built of steel.

Advantages and disadvantages of wooden construction

Shipwrights required specialised knowledge of the properties of timber in order to perform their craft to the best ability. Not only did they have to possess the skills to cut, work and shape the wood, but they needed to be able to judge the suitability of any timber and how best to utilise it in the construction of a hull. Shipbuilders might buy a load of timber from abroad, or they might send men into a forest to mark trees for cutting which could then be sent to the yard. Moulds, made of rough pieces of timber of light scantling and shaped to a frame or knee, would be taken by shipwrights to the piles of timber that were seasoning in the yard and the most suitable baulks of wood were selected to be shaped according to the mould. This 'conversion', as it was termed, required the minimum of wastage for a shipbuilder to make a good profit.

In the earlier days of shipbuilding in Canada and America, the forests lay close to the shipyards, so that transport of the logs was relatively easy, but as the shipbuilding industry increased, timber had to be brought from further afield. It was a common sight on lakes and rivers in all countries to see large rafts of logs lashed together and being floated to the shipyards. In his report on the shipbuilding industry in America, issued in 1882, Henry Hall comments on how timber was obtained for the shipyards:

Changes also took place in the kinds of timber used for building ships, as about 1835 the supply of oak timber began to grow scant in New England. Two hundred years of occupation and settlement, with the pursuit of shipbuilding and other industries, having nearly cleared the primitive forests from such parts of the country as were accessible from water-courses, southern timber was now finding its way plentifully to the northern markets, and between 1830 and 1840 was introduced into the shipyards. The peninsulas of Delaware, Maryland, and Virginia were overgrown with splendid forests of towering white oak, and the getting out of

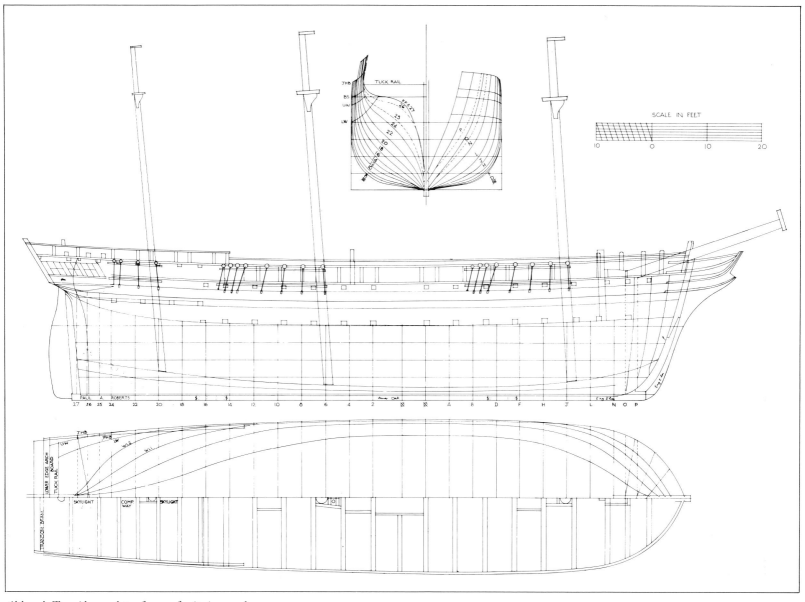

Although Tyneside was later famous for its iron and steel shipbuilders, many yards built only in wood - and relatively small vessels - well into the iron era. One such was J & J Hair of Newcastle, the Parsee *of 1851 being a typical mid century product. The ship measured 412 tons om and 437 nm. Even at this late date the ship still features full quarter galleries and a heavy stemhead arrangement. (By courtesy of David MacGregor)*

the timber for the frames of vessels in that region soon became a regular industry. A complete set of patterns, or molds as they are called, having been made for the timbers of the vessel, they were turned over to contractors, who went out into the woods in the winter time with a party of men armed with axes. The party encamped in rough board or log huts, and remained until the trees had been felled and the complete frame of the ship hewn from them. Each piece was then marked, and the whole was hauled to the nearest water-course

before the snow disappeared in the spring and put aboard a coasting schooner and sent north. This industry of getting out frames on these peninsulas is still a marked feature of shipbuilding as now pursued on the north Atlantic coast, nearly all the frames of the large New England ships being now obtained from the region named.

Southern pitch-pine timber was also introduced, the sticks of which could be obtained of such great lengths that they strengthened the ship. This timber was first used for beams and decking and the various longitudinal ties, such as waterways, clamps, keelsons, etc.; but as soon as the insurance companies were induced to approve of pitch-pine its use also became general for the ceiling and planking of ships, its great length making it desirable for both purposes. Pitch-pine remains the favourite wood for all the parts of a vessel of over 100 tons except the stem, keel, sternpost, and frames, for

which oak, hard wood, and hackmatack are preferred. For the masts and spars preference is given to white pine and spruce, but a great many lower masts are made of strips of oak or maple and yellow pine, doweled, bolted, and hooped over with iron. Topmasts and bowsprits are frequently made of pitch-pine sticks.[8]

Similar ways of obtaining timber must have been practised in all the shipbuilding countries of Europe, although some of the timbers used would have had different names. In France and other countries, books on naval architecture frequently contained plates illustrating different trees and the ways of cutting trunks and branch-

8. Henry Hall, *Report on the Ship-Building Industry of the United States* (Washington, DC 1884; reprint New York 1970), p87. This book originally appeared as the final section of Vol 8 of the Tenth Census published by the Department of the Interior, Census Office.

es to obtain the needed timber with the least possible wastage.

Whereas iron or steel was ordered specifically for a vessel under construction, with only some basic amounts of material held as stock, a wooden shipyard would have large piles of timber littering the premises which could be available for any orders that might be obtained. The greater ease with which wood could be worked was a great advantage for the smaller shipyard, and in its basic form it was human muscle rather than mechanical tools that provided the power to build a hull of timber. The ease of working in timber was equally important in an older vessel where repairs could be conveniently made, and on an ocean voyage the carpenter was an important member of the crew. If a wooden vessel was dismasted, the wooden spars could be repaired or replaced, but if they were of iron or steel plates, then it was a shipyard job. This meant that costs were that much greater and the prob-

lem of getting to the repairer's yard might aggravate the situation. When metal masts buckled, steel wire rigging twisted or stretched, and ships' crews could only cut it away. Shipyards in remote ports took many years to get themselves properly equipped to repair an iron vessel, and prior to about 1875 this problem confined iron vessels to trades which took them to the larger commercial entrepôts. Thus wooden vessels were well adapted to handle a variety of cargoes to anywhere in the world and could confidently be placed on the berth to accept any freight that was being offered.

When the London Missionary Society required a new vessel in 1867 to sail amongst the outlying islands in the Pacific, they approached the Aberdeen shipyard of Alexander Hall & Sons, who recommended that a wooden hull be built as it would be far easier to maintain and repair in such areas.

Another advantage of timber construction was

the ease with which antifouling could be applied to the underwater part of the hull in order to deter barnacles and weed from attaching themselves. All vessels venturing outside the home trade areas required protection, and copper sheathing was the answer. It was applied in sheets nailed on to the wooden planking over tarred felt, and the letters 'Y.M.' – standing for 'yellow metal' – would appear against the ship's name in *Lloyd's Registers* to indicate vessels so treated. This sheathing remained clean for up to ten years or as long as it was exfoliating. By the 1840s, Muntz metal (a mixture of copper and zinc) began to replace pure copper; it was cheaper and more effective. The paints and patent applications applied as antifouling to iron hulls were for many years moderately ineffective, and dry-dock owners must have earned regular employment scraping the bottoms of iron ships. Composite construction, in which iron frames were planked with wood, did provide an answer, as will be described later.

But all-wooden construction had its own problems. There was the growing shortage of timber, particularly of hardwood of the recognised species, and this resulted in large numbers of softwood ships being constructed in boom years. Timber merchants were scouring the world for suitable wood and Lloyd's Register of Shipping was obliged to examine and recast their grading systems. The softwood ships, launched in America and Canada in response to the demands for more tonnage, were often classed at only 4 or 5 years A1. This meant only a short life but the owner hoped to profit by the high freight rates available, and when the ship's original classification expired it was probably too expensive to repair her, so she was sold or broken up. Many of these softwood ships met their fate at the end of the 1850s or early in the next decade, and perhaps the good profits made enabled the owner to order a higher classed ship on the next occasion.

Large wooden vessels used up prodigious quantities of timber in their construction and huge logs were required to provide longitudinal strength. A coloured plan in the Peabody Museum, Salem, depicts the structural timbers for the 'American packet ships *Star of Empire* and *Chariot of Fame*. They measured 220ft 0in length on deck, 43ft 0in breadth, 27ft 6in depth of hold and 2050 tons. The midship section shows very little rise of floor with the bilge kept low and the sides then tumble home right up to the bulwark rail. The keelson was composed of eight logs, each some 15in square, with two rows of three each, placed one above the other, and then two more above each other on the centreline. Each beam in the lower and middle holds was supported by three wooden pillars; all the hanging and lodging knees were likewise of timber; there were massive bilge stringers and the ceiling planking at the turn of the bilge was some 12in thick. Much space was occupied by these structural members, and the protagonists of compos-

ite construction would claim that considerable cargo space was being wasted, and that an iron frame did an equally good job, even though its size appeared diminutive by contrast.

For ships of over a certain length, Lloyd's Register of Shipping required diagonal iron trussing let in flush with the outer face of the wooden frames, and this had the effect of allowing the use of planking with smaller scantling.

Shipbuilders and shipbuilding ports

As pointed out in the previous section, shipbuilders fared best if their yards lay in close proximity to the sources of the principal materials which were employed in constructing the hull. In the case of wooden shipbuilding, many of the virgin forests in Canada and North America that lay close to the shore were in the process of being consumed during the first quarter of the nineteenth century, so that shipbuilders had to look further inland for timber or establish new shipbuilding centres. As the size of vessels increased, the Chesapeake Bay area became less suitable and shipbuilders moved northwards. New York and Boston had always been important shipbuilding centres and now ports in the states of New Hampshire and Maine were rapidly obtaining orders as foreign trade expanded in the 1830s.

A thriving shipbuilding industry was established at Bath, Maine, with such firms as Clark & Sewall and the Houghton Brothers, both of which built for themselves. The Sewalls' first ship of over 1000 tons was the *Rappahannock* of 1133 tons, which was launched in 1841 as a full-bodied carrier for transatlantic trades. In spite of her light scantling, she survived for twenty-one

years. The majority of their vessels from then until 1880 were full rigged ships; this was likewise the case with the vessels turned out by the Houghton yard. After the Civil War, many shipbuilding centres which had specialised in the construction of clipper ships found that orders dried up entirely, whereas in the state of Maine, the orders for ordinary cargo ships continued to arrive. Thus it was that Bath became America's principal shipbuilding port by 1880. Large sailing ships of wood were also built at Thomaston, and Edward O'Brien built six ships of over 2000 tons each between 1875 and 1882.[9]

Portsmouth in New Hampshire was an important shipbuilding port and many fine clippers were built there. In Massachusetts, shipowning had made Boston an important centre and from this had developed a shipbuilding industry, even though all the timber had to be brought there by sea. The deep water harbour possessed natural advantages, and with the demand for larger ships some builders moved their business there, such as Samuel Hall from Duxbury and Donald McKay from Newburyport. They laid down their building slips at East Boston, and thither also came shipbuilders from Medford on the Mystic River, who were cramped for space. Paul Curtis, Robert Jackson and A & G T Sampson were other prominent shipbuilders there, and most benefited by the boom in orders during the fifteen years from 1845 which were drastically curtailed by the Civil War in 1861.[10]

From 1845 to 1860, Donald McKay built many packet ships, about a dozen extreme clippers, and numerous clippers and medium clip-

9. *Ibid*, pp70-71, 98-99, 101.

10. *Ibid*, p110.

A typical scene off the French port of Granville. In very light conditions a topsail schooner to the right sets all possible sail, while the barque (centre) is towed to sea by a steam tug. The nearest vessel is the barque Charles *of 596 tons, built at Granville in 1871. (By courtesy of David MacGregor)*

One trade that required specialist vessels was whaling and between about 1820 and 1850 it was dominated by the New England states of the US. One survivor from this period is the Charles W Morgan, *which was built at the famous whaling port of New Bedford in 1841. The 351-ton ship worked as a whaler until 1921 and is now preserved at Mystic Seaport, Connecticut. (David MacGregor)*

pers. The clippers included the ships *Staghound* (1850), *Flying Cloud* (1851), *Sovereign of the Seas* (1852), *Great Republic* (1853) and *Lightning* (1854), to name but a few. He claimed that he studied the hull form of clippers designed by others and then formulated his own designs; certainly his designs varied from ship to ship.

At New York there had been a shipbuilding business for many years, and here again it was the Atlantic packet and Far Eastern trades which provided an important boost to business. Probably some twenty shipyards were operating in the port during the boom years of the 1840s and 1850s. Amongst these were to be found the yards of Smith & Dimon, Brown & Bell, Jacob Westervelt, and the famous William H Webb. From 1840 when he built his first vessel until the last in 1869, 138 craft were built by him, of which approximately 100 were sailing ships built of wood. No vessels were launched from his yard in 1859, 1860, 1862, and 1865–1868, which indicates the effect of the financial crisis of 1857 followed by the Civil War. After 1858 only two more sailing ships were built.[11]

Webb's most extreme clipper, the *Challenge* (1851) was a disappointment, perhaps because she was over-sparred; he was more successful with the ships *Comet* (1851) and *Young America* (1853), which made some fast passages, although none of his designs achieved the degree of fame which has been assigned to McKay's clippers.

Tonnage measurement remained similar to the British 'old measurement' (om) rule until 1864 and by this rule the depth of hold was assumed to be half the maximum breadth. This resulted in deep, flat-floored and full-bodied ships with wide square sterns for the general cargo-carrying business, but with lofty masts on which were narrow sail plans. By the end of the 1830s there were many vessels of up to 500 tons constructed in this form. Ships exporting cotton from southern American ports to Liverpool or Continental ports found such hull forms ideally suited to this trade, as did most of the freighting business around the world. Only a few trades wanted something different.

One of these was the establishment of regular packet ship sailings across the North Atlantic as from 1818, and this proved a great incentive to New York shipbuilders. The ships had to be heavily built to withstand the rigours of the trade; they required a reasonable turn of speed as well as good cargo capacity; and a splendid class of vessel was developed over the years, while the masters and officers who manned them gained valuable experience in adverse conditions.

11. *Ibid*, pp116-117.

The launch day of Donald McKay's highly successful medium clipper Glory of the Seas *in 1869. All the staging around the ship has been removed in preparation for launching, but the absence of any industrial infrastructure is a notable feature of wooden shipbuilding; all that was necessary was access to timber, a workforce and deep water. This last attracted McKay and a number of other builders to Boston from the smaller ports as ships became larger in the second half of the nineteenth century. (Peabody Museum of Salem)*

Another fast-developing trade was that to China and the East, in which a finer-lined version of the transatlantic packet was employed. Some of these vessels produced remarkably fast passages for their hull form and they were the progenitors of the clipper ships of the late 1840s. William Webb of New York built a China packet in 1841 (*Helena*, of 598 tons) and he and other builders were able to fulfil the orders placed by eager shipowners who saw a good profit to be made in this trade.

But harbour facilities were not yet capable of coping with anything much larger than 500 tons, nor had the process of collecting goods for shipment been improved to the state that was in existence by 1850. So the over-large *Washington* of nearly 1000 tons, completed about 1825, was not a success. William Webb's first ship of over 1000 tons, was the packet ship *Yorkshire*, of 1165 tons, built in 1843.

In Canada the ports of Saint John and Quebec were the principal shipbuilding centres and the latter contributed the two monster four-masted barques *Columbus* (3690 tons) and *Baron Renfrew* (5294 tons) in the 1820s. They were really long flat-bottomed shells, crudely shaped in the form of a ship and filled solid with timber for sale on arrival in England. George Black operated one of the yards in Quebec for thirty years from 1819; the majority of his ships were square rigged and fifty out of the firm's fifty-four vessels were acquired by British owners.

At Saint John in New Brunswick, the ship-builders William and Richard Wright built thirty vessels in the years 1830–1855 with an average tonnage of 972. The 1372-ton *Dundonald*, which was built in 1849 and was the largest ship they had constructed prior to 1850, was sold at Liverpool in 1854 for £11,500, which works out at £8.38 per ton. The Wrights launched some large well-known clippers in the 1850s, such as *Star of the East* (1219 tons), *White Star* (2339 tons) and *Morning Light* (2377 tons). The forty-one ships and two barques constructed by the brothers Francis and Joseph Ruddock prior to 1868 exceeded the Wright Brothers' average by 30 tons. The port of Saint John boasted several shipbuilding families named Smith: one of them, James Smith, built the famous *Marco Polo* and other vessels; another was John W Smith.[12]

The Canadian shipyards launched much larger wooden ships than could be built in Great Britain, and their comparative cheapness assisted British shipowners in containing the threat of American ships dominating the world-wide shipping business in the 1850s. Due to the demand for ships to participate in the Australian gold rush, Canadian vessels reaching Liverpool in 1852 often received a class of 6 or 7A1 and a price of £6 to £8 10s per ton, and 120 of them were sold there that year. In 1853 prices had advanced for 7A1 ships to £10 to £11 5s per ton. These low-classed ships would have been the first to be sold or laid up, once the trade boom of the early 1850s was finished. Great Britain

was still purchasing wooden ships from Canada in the 1870s, while the Maritime Provinces themselves continued to build fine wooden ships and barques throughout the nineteenth century for use by their own shipowners.

In the period up to 1849, when the Navigation Acts were repealed, British shipbuilders ensured that their hulls were for the most part well built and capable of obtaining a good classification at Lloyd's Register. A ship built of hardwood to class 12 or 13 years A1 and measuring some 750 tons might be on the stocks for a year. This was all very well if times were slack, but in the days of the Australian gold rush or if freight rates were rising, then an owner might want a ship in a hurry. In the middle of the century came the demand for a large increase in tonnage to meet booming trade requirements, and the shortage of native timber in the British Isles forced shipbuilders to import vast quantities.

Alexander Stephen Jr estimated that 100 tons of old measurement tonnage consumed twenty-five loads of teak. Prices for British-built ships were some £4 per ton above Canadian ships, making the former £14 or £15 per ton for 7A1. Alexander Stephen's wooden ship *Tyburnia* of 1012 tons om and built in 1857, cost £20 8s per ton according to contract. The larger ship *Eastern Monarch* of 1849 tons om, built at Stephen's Dundee yard, cost £20 12s 5d per ton as completed.[13]

In the first half of the century, shipbuilders were still very active at numerous yards on the River Thames and Lloyd's Register often awarded such 'River-built' vessels a higher classification than a 'country' or provincial-built ship. The Blackwall Yard, owned by the Green and Wigram families, constructed nine East Indiamen between 1815 and 1825 of a nominal size of 1315 tons, although they may have been larger.[14] However, merchant sailing ships of this size were hardly ever again constructed in Great

12. David R MacGregor, *Merchant Sailing Ships 1850-1875*, pp47-51.

13. *Ibid*, pp59-61.

14. David R MacGregor, *Merchant Sailing Ships 1775-1815*, p210.

Britain owing to the expense of importing so much timber, and because iron construction was cheaper. The number of wooden sailing ships registering more than 1200 tons is surprisingly small and is limited to Blackwall Frigates and ships built for the Australia trade. Basil Lubbock has listed these passenger frigates and many measured 1000 tons or more.[15] By far the largest of these were the *Monarch* of 1444 tons built in 1844, the *Marlborough* of 1402 tons built in 1846, the *Agamemnon* of 1431 tons built in 1855, and the *Eastern Monarch* of 1631 tons (new measurement) built in 1856.

Shipbuilders in England capable of building the larger wooden ships consisted of T & W Smith at Newcastle, who constructed many big Blackwall Frigates, and James Laing and William Pile at Sunderland. Hilhouse, Hill & Co at Bristol constructed ships of up to about 650 tons, and so could some of the other yards, but the majority of shipbuilders around the country found it a strain to build vessels in excess of 500 tons. In Scotland, Alexander Hall had built only one vessel of above 500 tons prior to 1840, but Robert Steele & Co had built several at Greenock. Shipbuilding on the Clyde around Glasgow was only getting started in the 1840s and many

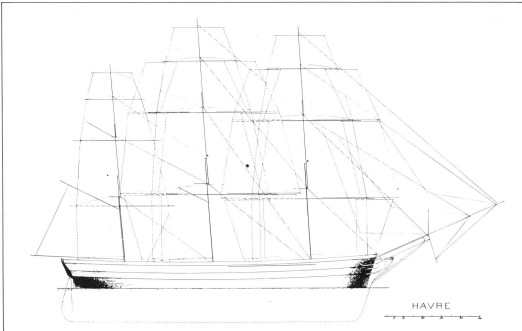

HAVRE

15. Basil Lubbock, *The Blackwall Frigates* (Glasgow 1922), pp300-302; see also David R MacGregor, *Fast Sailing Ships, their Design and Construction 1775-1875.* (2nd ed, London 1988), p137.

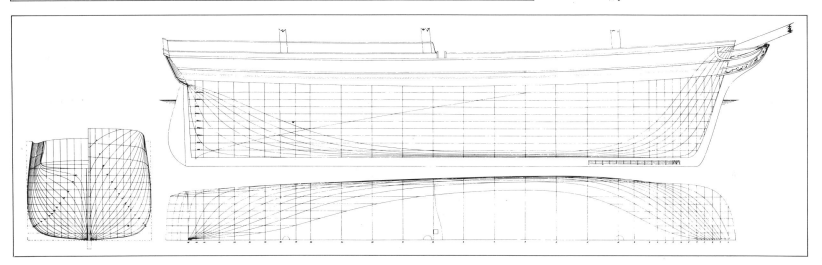

For much of the nineteenth century the British merchant marine made great use of ships built very economically in the Maritime Provinces of Canada. An example was the barque Fairy Belle, *a 519-ton ship built at Clifton, New Brunswick, in 1863. She is seen here at Dover being re-caulked; unlike many wooden ships she does not appear to have been coppered – confirmed by her Lloyd's Register entry which has no 'YM' against her name. (By courtesy of David MacGregor)*

of the yards there commenced by specialising in iron construction.

During the 1850s and 1860s, many wooden ships were under construction in Great Britain, even though the changeover to iron was gathering pace. During the clipper ship boom of the 1850s some larger than usual wooden ships were built, of which Alexander Hall's *Schomberg* of 2600 tons om and 2284 tons nm was by far the largest. Her dimension were 247.7ft × 42.2ft (internal breadth) × 28.9ft, and she cost £14 per ton on 2492 'contract' tons om. Hall's last wooden

One of the largest Blackwall Frigates, the Parramatta *of 1521 tons, is shown on the stocks at James Laing's Sunderland yard. Launched on 29 May 1866, she was the last wooden ship built by this yard, which went over to iron construction as so many British yards were doing at that time. (By courtesy of David MacGregor)*

square rigged wooden vessel was the barque *Samoa* of 200 tons, launched in 1868. Other shipbuilders at Aberdeen which built large wooden ships at the end of the period were Walter Hood with the *Aviemore* of 1091 tons in 1870, and John Humphrey & Co with the *Invercauld* of 1311 tons in 1874. The last-named ship was probably the last wooden ship of over 1000 tons to be built in Great Britain, because although wooden square riggers continued to be built here after the mid-1870s, they were all of under 300 tons. The rigs commonly adopted for these vessels were barque, brig and barquentine, as will be related in the next chapter.

Although schooners of over 300 tons were probably never built in Great Britain, they were very common in America, Canada and Continental Europe right up until the end of the period covered by this chapter, and reference will be made to them in the next section. In northern

The largest ships in the British merchant marine were East Indiamen, at the beginning of the century rated at 1200 tons although actually larger when measured by any of the recognised tonnage rules. These were succeeded as passenger carriers by Blackwall Frigates, so called from their general resemblance to naval cruisers. This photograph taken after the Calcutta cyclone of October 1864 shows the wreck of the Southampton *of 971 tons, built at Blackwall in 1841. (By courtesy of David MacGregor)*

Europe, iron construction was still a rarity by 1860 and timber construction continued apace in all the various shipbuilding centres. At the Bremerhaven yard of R C Rickmers, their first iron ship was not launched until 1890. At Hamburg, however, iron construction was commenced in some yards in the mid-1870s. In Holland, the last large wooden ships were built in 1879. In that year a barque and two full-rigged ships were launched, the largest being the *Graafstroom* of 1359 tons net.

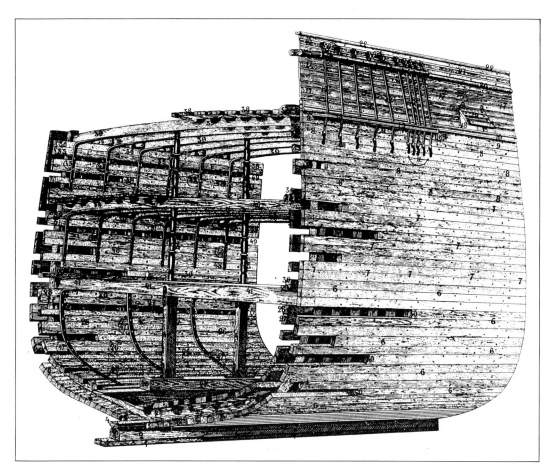

Some idea of the complexity of wooden ship construction can be gleaned from this section drawing from Paasch's well-known marine dictionary From Keel to Truck. *The principal weakness of a wooden ship was the lack of longitudinal rigidity, since it was necessarily composed of numerous relatively small individual pieces. This drawing represents later practice with iron straps and brackets replacing wooden riders and knees, but the percentage of internal volume taken up by the structure is still far higher than for an iron ship of the same external dimensions; softwood ships, which required timbers of larger scantlings were even less economic in this respect.* (By courtesy of David MacGregor)

Design and construction

The art of the shipwright is really a lost art. True, the tools are preserved, the instruction books are preserved, and even timber is available. But the skills needed to fashion timber of large scantling is surely absent. The long hours of apprenticeship under the watchful eyes of an exacting master, the growing up of men in a world dependent on timber, the constant feel and smell of it in the shipyard are gone for ever. Although a few skills remain in old ship restoration, the printed word can hardly convey the full range of wooden shipbuilding techniques.

However, some slight impression of the qualities of timber construction can be gained by the fulsome reports of ships described from time to time in the pages of the *Atlas* of Boston, as written by Duncan McLean. We are indebted to the late John Lyman for having collected a number of these reports and reprinted them in facsimile form. One of these accounts, describing the *Mastiff*, was published in 1856, and a few extracts are quoted below to show the somewhat flamboyant style of writing and the detail given:[16]

This vessel has been designed for the California and China trade, but as she is very capacious and buoyant, she might be profitably employed in any trade, which requires a light draught of water, with good carrying qualities. ...She is 169 feet long between perpendiculars, has 37½ feet extreme breadth of beam, 22 feet depth of hold, including 7 feet 8 inches height of between decks, and registers 1030 tons. ...A full figure of a well-fed mastiff, on the lookout, ornaments the bow, and the head of his brother peers from among the gilded carved work on the stern. The sheer is truly graduated the whole length of the vessel, with just enough forward, to throw an air of lightness over the bow. Her stern is light and rounded, and tastefully ornamented with gilded carved work, over which are her name and port of hail. Her bottom is sheathed with yellow, above it the hull is painted black, and inboard her houses are light pearl color, and the waterways are blue. ...

The hanging knees are sided from 12 to 10 inches, have three feet arms, 5 feet bodies, 16 bolts and 4 spikes in each, measure from 18 to 22 inches in the angles, and their lower ends rest upon a lap-strake or stringer, which extends fore and aft. ...

She is rather heavily sparred. Her lower masts and bowsprit are built of hard pine and hooped with iron, and her topmasts and standing jib-boom are also of hard pine. She has a main sky-sail yard rigged aloft, but carries nothing higher than royals on the fore and mizzen. Her rigging is of Russia hemp; and she has all the chain and iron work aloft and about the bowsprit, now in general use. All her masts are bright, and her yards and bowsprit black. From the royal yards to the deadeyes, she looks quite neat and clipperly. ...

Such a piece as quoted above is unusually well detailed and McLean's work as a seaman fitted him ably as a reporter. The interiors of the deckhouse accommodation are described and he then gives details, with dimensions, of the timbers and scantlings. No British narratives are so thorough in their descriptions nor do they give a list of the spar dimensions which usually accompany McLean's text, although they happen to be absent on this occasion. The *Mastiff* was undoubtedly only a medium clipper with fairly flat floors, as 9ft out from the keel the deadrise was only 1ft; the lines are termed 'decidedly convex'. Donald McKay had designed her to carry cargo because the great wave of clipper ship building was over and extreme clippers were uneconomical to operate with falling freight rates.

To judge from the comparatively few surviving plans of ships in the first half of the nineteenth century, design had changed but little since 1800 according to the plans published in 1830 by Peter Hedderwick in his work on shipbuilding and naval architecture. This book and its plates indicate that hulls were still short, deep and broad with heavy headwork, broad square sterns and quarter galleries. There were two important contributions made by this book: first, it had three sail plans consisting of a full rigged ship, a schooner and a cutter; and second, the plans were of merchant ships, so that for once ships of the line were absent. The sail plan of the full rigged ship depicted a lofty vessel with skysails on each mast and a large suit of stunsails. Ship design in Great Britain must have been greatly influenced by this publication, and yet al-

16. John Lyman (ed), *Boston Merchant Vessels 1851-1856: As written by Duncan McLean for The Atlas of Boston* (Chapel Hill, NC 1975), pp35-36.

terations in design concepts cannot have been advanced by it.[17]

At the same time, Hedderwick's work is almost certainly the last large work in Great Britain to be devoted exclusively to wooden ship-building. Subsequent books, such as W J M Rankine's *Shipbuilding, Theoretical and Practical*, published in 1866, include both wood and iron together. Of course, David Steel's books on masting, rigging, naval architecture and ship-building remained in print as standard works, probably until the 1840s, even though they were first published in the period of the Napoleonic Wars. Yet the force of circumstances inevitably brought innovation and alteration to the accepted order of things. A change in tonnage measurement rules in Great Britain in 1836 encouraged longer hulls by measuring the depth of hold for the first time, and demands of trade required faster ships to be built.

Previously, fine-lined ships had been built for a few very specialised trades, and then the vessels concerned were often of less than 300 tons as the commodities carried, such as fresh fruit, mails, opium or smuggled goods, were not bulky cargoes. Suddenly the discovery of gold required the movement by sea of vast numbers of people to California and to Australia, with passengers and cargo taking up considerable space. Great ingenuity had to be displayed to design and construct ships to make a fast passage and still to

earn a good profit. The various builders referred to in the last section were able to fulfil the orders of the owners with various degrees of success: whereas Donald McKay varied his design from one clipper to another, William Webb tended to employ a somewhat similar hull form with varying degrees of sharpness. The clippers only represented a small proportion of the ships annually constructed, but they consumed an immense amount of time and energy, and far more was written about them than the ordinary merchantmen. However, the design of the latter fell under this influence; never again could they be so bluff-bowed as formerly, because competition was now the catchword. They copied the clippers above the waterline, discarding the heavy headwork and stern galleries and providing a more graceful appearance to the hull. Their sail plans were not so large and their spars were somewhat shorter, but the science of hydrography had advanced and their passage times were often as good as those of the clippers.

In Great Britain the change of tonnage measurement in 1854, to what became known as the Moorsom system, measured a ship's hull internally by a number of cross-sectional areas. America did not adopt this method for another ten years and so the tonnage of all their clippers was virtually calculated on the old British pre-1836 rule in which depth was not measured. However, this did not prevent them from designing ships that could sail well and which were no deeper than their British counterparts. This older rule or 'old tons' had the effect of making their ships appear somewhat larger than their British contemporaries, and it is instructive to

compare them with the 'new tons' figures which were first applied in 1864.

For example, the tonnage of the American extreme clipper *Challenge* is 2006 'old tons' and 1375 'new tons'; the large *Great Republic* (as rebuilt) is 3356 'old tons' and 2751 'new tons'. In *Greyhounds of the Sea*, Carl Cutler gives the 'new tons' for a few ships, presumably if, after 1864, they had to be re-measured.[18]

In the account of the building of the *Mastiff*, referred to above, there was very little mention of iron being used in the wooden construction, all the lodging and hanging knees, the breast-hooks and the hold pillars being of timber. By contrast, many ships built in Great Britain by 1850, and even earlier in some cases, would have had all these structural members in iron; some selected vessels even had iron beams. During the remaining years of wooden construction in Great Britain, ways of economising in the use of timber in large vessels were tried. Diagonal iron trussing, consisting of iron stringers let in flush with the outer faces of the frames, gave added stiffness and was required by Lloyd's Register for vessels that were long in proportion to breadth or depth, and for large ships built of softwood.

---

17. Peter Hedderwick, *A Treatise on Marine Architecture*, 2 vols: text and plates (Edinburgh 1830).

18. Carl C Cutler, *Greyhounds of the Sea: The Story of the American Clipper Ship* (New York 1930), Appendix I(c), pp412-447.

As the nineteenth century progressed information on wooden ship design and construction became far more widely available, in contrast to the way in which such data was jealously guarded by shipwrights in earlier eras. This longitudinal section and deck plan of a barque of about 360 tons is taken from a portfolio of plans by N C Kierkegaard published at Gothenburg in 1862 as Plancher till Praktisk Skeppsbyggnaskonst. *(By courtesy of David MacGregor)*

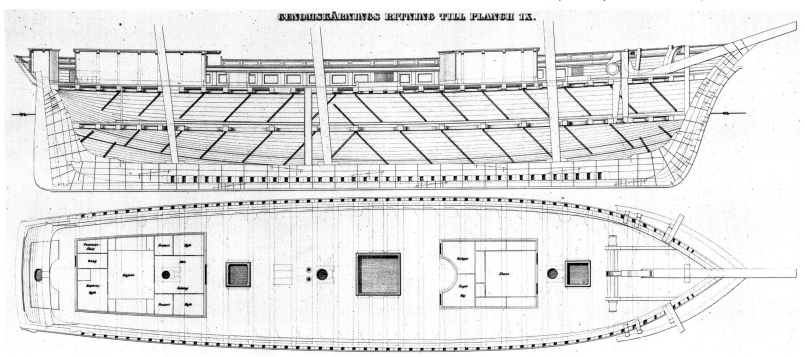

GENOMSKÄRNINGS RITNING TILL PLANCH IX.

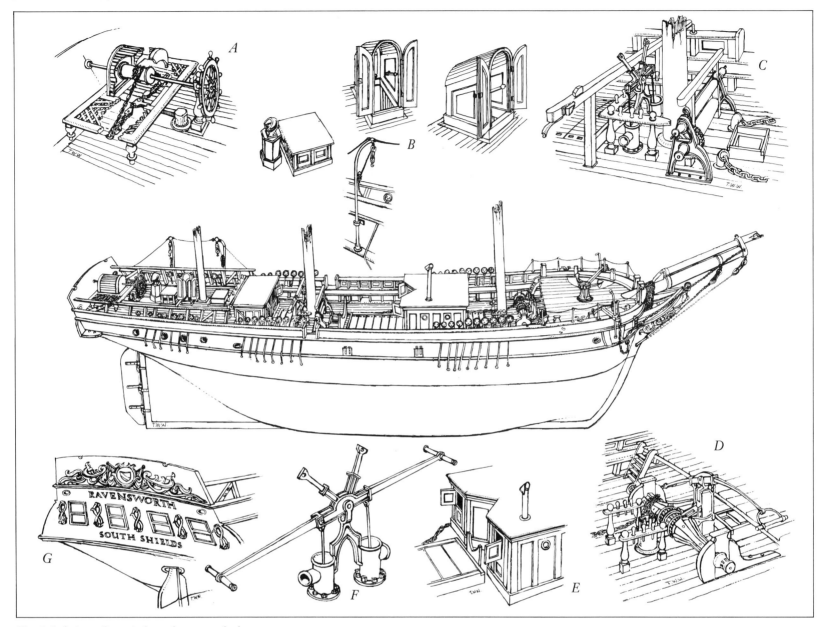

The deck fittings of a typical merchantman, the barque
Ravensworth of 508 tons nm built at Newcastle by
Gaddy & Lamb in 1856. The drawing by T W Ward
is based on an unrigged model in the National
Maritime Museum at Greenwich.

A. The steering gear, with cover cut away to show lead
of chains to drum.

B. Binnacle and skylight; two views of the companion;
and detail of a davit.

C. Foot of main mast with pumps inside fiferail; cargo
winch beside small hatch.

D. Armstrong patent windlass, with pump handles
shipped and several turns of chain cable around the port
windlass barrel

E. After end of the forward deckhouse; the V-shaped
notch is designed to take the bow of the longboat which
would otherwise be too long for the available space.

F. Close-up of the pump in (C); the handles are
shipped but ropes could be rove through the upper arms
to add additional hands to the pumps when required.

G. The decorated stern with name and port of registry.
(By courtesy of David MacGregor)

Several shipbuilders in Great Britain adopted
diagonal construction during the 1850s. J & R
White of Cowes built ten vessels on the principle of three layers of diagonal planking and the
minimum of frames, but with long iron hanging
knees. Two of these ten were schooners and
three were paddle steamers. Alexander Hall &
Sons at Aberdeen built three ships and two
schooners on their own diagonal system in
which the skins of external planking were secured to the widely spaced frames with screw
treenails. Although it was very strong, it was
more expensive than the conventional method.
In the case of two of his clippers, both classed
7A1 – the conventionally built *Cairngorm* and
the diagonally built *Vision* –the former cost £14
per ton and the other £16 15s per ton. On the
River Thames, Bilbe & Perry of Rotherhithe
built three ships and two barques on their own

diagonal method, and builders in other parts of
the country were experimenting in various ways.[19]

There was another form of construction
which began in an experimental way but later
developed into something really substantial, although short-lived: composite construction,
consisting of an iron frame covered with wood
planking. Various builders experimented with it
during the 1850s, of which Jordan & Getty of
Liverpool had the greatest success with their
patent process, and launched a ship, two barques
and two schooners.

Meanwhile Alexander Stephen Jr, who was in
charge of the Glasgow yard of Alexander
Stephen & Sons, obtained the approval of
Lloyd's Register to build an iron frame planked
with wood, in accordance with models of the

19. David R MacGregor, *Fast Sailing Ships*, pp140-141.

framing, supported by detailed specifications and drawings, which he submitted to the Committee. Their approval in October 1861 entitled him to obtain a class as high as 15A1, and the first ship on this principle was the *John Lidgett*, which was launched on 29 August 1862. The building time had occupied only 5 months and 24 days since laying the keel, and the work was rushed ahead as it was feared that Alexander Hall would get a composite ship launched before them. However, they won by a comfortable margin of six months. The new ship was expensive, costing £18 18s per ton, which gave Stephen a profit of approximately £3 per ton. In spite of the suspicion with which Lloyd's Register viewed composite construction, it immediately became popular with shipowners engaged in the China tea trade and elsewhere, because the wooden planking could be sheathed with copper sheets, and the thinner shell of the iron framework increased the cargo capacity. All the vessels so built had long lives, the *Cutty Sark*, preserved at Greenwich, being a good example.[20]

During the 1850s, ships were being built at Nantes and Bordeaux of composite construction. It was also very popular in Holland, where it first appeared in 1864, and hardly a year went by without at least one such vessel being constructed. Latterly the construction consisted of an iron framework plated with iron but having wooden planking from keel to waterline, and over this copper sheathing could be laid on. The

Internal section and deck plan of the composite clipper Sir Lancelot, 885 tons nm, built by Robert Steele of Greenock in 1865. One of the most successful composite ships, she was supposed to have once made a day's run of 359 miles (an average of nearly 15kts) and was said to be capable of 16kts in the southeast trades.
(By courtesy of David MacGregor)

last composite vessel appears to have been the barque *Thorbecke VII* of 928 tons net, built in 1885.[21]

The construction of American ships has already been referred to above, in the second section, and also earlier in this section in respect of the medium clipper *Mastiff*. Because she was built on the verge of the financial panic which gripped America as 1857 approached, she was not built on such sharp lines as McKay's clippers of earlier years. In the first year or two of the California gold rush, fancy prices were being paid for ships. Henry Hall stated that 'in ordinary years' ships were built at New York at a cost of $55 (£11.36) per ton, but that ships built for the packet, tea or California trades cost more, and from the lump sums he gives it can be estimated that prices ranged from $60 (£12.39) to $75 (£15.49) per ton.[22] The conversion is calculated at an exchange rate of $4.84 = £1, which is the rate set by the United States Treasury on 19 September 1851, for the benefit of customs officials.[23]

Henry Hall provided some other interesting comparisons of prices for shipbuilding:

In 1825 a 300-ton ship cost from $75 [£15.49] to $80 [£16.53] per ton in the United States, from $90 [£18.59] to $100 [£20.66] per ton in Canada, and from $100 [£20.66] to $110 [£22.73] per ton in England. In 1847 a large ship, first class in every respect, cost from $75 [£15.49] to $80 [£16.53] per ton here, against $87 [£17.97] to $90 [£18.59] in England.[24]

After the Civil War, wages rose steeply in New York and Boston, which sent shipbuilding prices rising and this had the effect of driving shipbuilding away to ports where costs were less,

leaving the once thriving areas with mostly ship repair business. The cost per ton of building new vessels in the yard of Houghton Brothers at Bath, Maine, was as follows: 1825 – $45; 1835 – $50; 1845 – $45; 1855 – $60; 1865 – $70; 1875 – $45. These prices are in respect of large ships.[25] While square rigged vessels cost on average $45 per ton in Bath in 1882, the price for building schooners was higher at $55 to $60.

Commenting on shipbuilding in Maine after 1870, the late John Lyman wrote in his inestimable publication *Log Chips*:

With only the meanest grade of lumber locally obtainable, Maine shipbuilders continued to assemble Virginia oak, Georgia pine, Michigan hackmatack, Oregon pine spars, Pittsburgh iron, Manila hemp, Connecticut copper, and Massachusetts canvas into the largest sailing vessels ever set afloat.

The reasons for this were in the large part geographical. Maine is cut up with fjord-like rivers that restrict land transportation paralleling the coast, but permit logs from the hinterland to be floated readily down to salt water. ...

The climate, too, is conducive to the heavy exertion involved in converting timber. The summers are insect-free, and in the winter heavy logs can be skidded over the frozen

20. *Ibid*, pp143-144.

21. John Lyman (ed), *Log Chips* (Washington, DC), Vol 1 (May 1950), pp143-46, and Vol II (July 1950), pp11-12.

22. Henry Hall, *op cit*, p116.

23. J R McCulloch, *A Dictionary, Practical, Theoretical, and Historical, of Commerce and Commercial Navigation* (3rd ed revised, London 1854), pp1445-46.

24. Henry Hall, *op cit*, p87.

25. *Ibid*, p103.

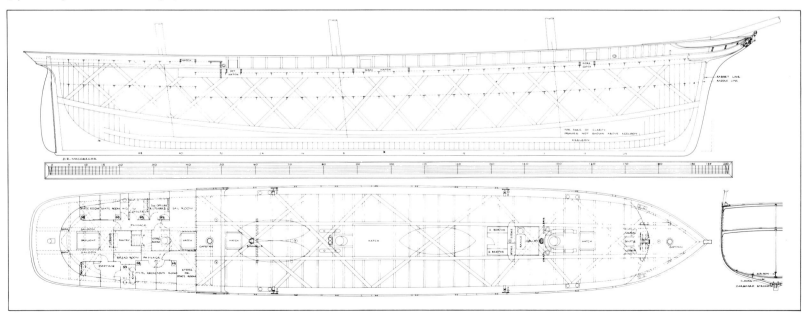

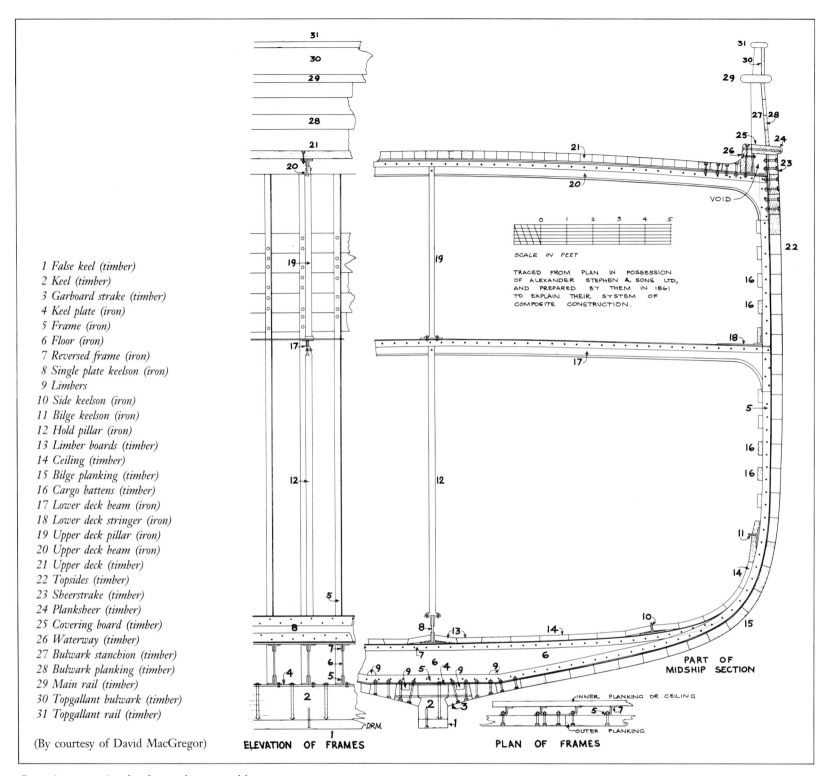

1 False keel (timber)
2 Keel (timber)
3 Garboard strake (timber)
4 Keel plate (iron)
5 Frame (iron)
6 Floor (iron)
7 Reversed frame (iron)
8 Single plate keelson (iron)
9 Limbers
10 Side keelson (iron)
11 Bilge keelson (iron)
12 Hold pillar (iron)
13 Limber boards (timber)
14 Ceiling (timber)
15 Bilge planking (timber)
16 Cargo battens (timber)
17 Lower deck beam (iron)
18 Lower deck stringer (iron)
19 Upper deck pillar (iron)
20 Upper deck beam (iron)
21 Upper deck (timber)
22 Topsides (timber)
23 Sheerstrake (timber)
24 Planksheer (timber)
25 Covering board (timber)
26 Waterway (timber)
27 Bulwark stanchion (timber)
28 Bulwark planking (timber)
29 Main rail (timber)
30 Topgallant bulwark (timber)
31 Topgallant rail (timber)

(By courtesy of David MacGregor)

ELEVATION OF FRAMES

PLAN OF FRAMES

TRACED FROM PLAN IN POSSESSION OF ALEXANDER STEPHEN & SONS LTD, AND PREPARED BY THEM IN 1861 TO EXPLAIN THEIR SYSTEM OF COMPOSITE CONSTRUCTION.

Composite construction, based on a plan prepared by Alexander Stephen & Sons in 1861 to explain their system of construction.

ground by ox-power, where a similar shipyard farther south would be churned into a morass.[26]

Shipyards in Maine were responsible for almost all the wooden ships, barques and barquentines built until the early nineties. In 1893 the last wooden full rigged ship was launched; she was the *Aryan* of 2124 tons. Barquentines with three and four masts continued to be built until the end of 1902, when no more appeared until 1917. Some pure sailing vessels as well as some auxiliaries were built during the First World War and also in 1919; those with five masts were in the region of 2000 to 2500 tons.

After the Civil War, schooners with three, four, five and six masts were built of wood in great profusion on the Atlantic and Pacific coasts, and likewise many with two masts; although the three-masters were often of 500–700 tons, those with two masts were usually under 300 tons. Schooners had been growing in popularity throughout the nineteenth century, and gradually had been discarding their square canvas on the fore mast. During the 1850s, some three-masted schooners of about 300 tons or more were being built without any square canvas

26. John Lyman (ed), *op cit*, Vol 2 (September 1950), p14.

and with masts of equal height; they became known as 'tern schooners' or simply 'terns', the word meaning three of a kind. They were simply rigged and the absence of square canvas enabled them to manage with a smaller crew.

Tern schooners were particularly popular in the Maritime Provinces of Canada – in Nova Scotia, New Brunswick, Prince Edward Island, Quebec and Newfoundland. Between 700 and 800 three-mast and four-mast schooners were built and operated in these Provinces. None appears to have had centreboards fitted, and all were designed to sail deep water; with their fairly flat floors, many could sit on the bottom beside a quay that had dried out at low water. They were built from the end of the 1850s until the early 1920s, and traded to both sides of the North and South Atlantic oceans.[27]

Denmark appears to have been the only country outside America and Canada where four-masted schooners were built in any number. From a list compiled by Jens Malling, the first was built in 1913 and the last in 1924. The majority were auxiliaries and a number were built of steel, yet altogether sixteen pure sailing schooners were constructed of wood and some carried yards on the fore mast. In size they ranged from 300 to 360 tons.[28]

Mention should be made of the tern schooners built in Finland and the construction of a four-mast schooner about 1920 which had the raised poop and forecastle of the style to be found on the West Coast of America.

Voyages and the factors influencing passage times

The winds were blowing throughout the nineteenth century and those who knew where to find favourable ones could harness them to propel their vessels. Human nature tends to search for speed, and ships that could make a quick passage got reported, while the majority were sailing about on their lawful occasions. Wooden sailing ships that were carrying cargo at the start of the nineteenth century could reach a speed of 6 or 7kts if the wind was from astern, but they could hardly beat to windward and often had to wait for the wind to change direction before they could proceed on their passage. This delayed their progress considerably. For instance,

Compared with the big British iron and steel vessels of the period, the tall narrow spar plan of American ships gave them a rather old-fashioned look. The Hotspur, *seen here setting her royals, was a typical product of the 'Down East' state of Maine, having been built in 1885 at Bath. Of 1210 tons she had a life of only two years. (By courtesy of David MacGregor)*

there might be a strong south-westerly wind blowing up the English Channel against which only a few fruit schooners could beat but against which the fleet of outward-bound merchantmen were incapable of making any progress. So having got out of the River Thames, they waited at anchor in the Downs off the Kent coast for a change of wind. They might wait there a month while boatmen from Deal took out supplies and fresh vegetables daily. Once the wind had gone round to the north or east, the fleet would up-anchor and be off, and a shipping paper such as *Lloyd's List* would have a column of names of ships that had taken their departure for foreign ports.

The British Admiralty provided sailing directions to assist captains in choosing the best route to their destinations, according to the season of the year, and monthly publications such as the *Nautical Magazine* gave additional information in Great Britain. Later an American naval officer, M F Maury, began issuing sailing directions which were based on the collected log-books of countless ships from several countries, and by analysing these Lt Maury was able to recommend the best route to adopt. His directions were in their eighth edition by 1858 and were much respected and valued.[29] Many of Maury's routes were at variance with the Admiralty ones.

The factors influencing a passage were many and diverse, and the best manned ship which was

equipped with the best spars and rigging was as much at the mercy of the vagaries of wind and weather as an ill-found vessel that was not really seaworthy. The skill of the master was paramount in ordering the course to be steered and navigating the ship, with the assistance of the two mates, and in overcoming storm, fire, dismasting or any of the many hazards to be encountered at sea. But countless ships reached their destinations safely, frequently without meeting any of the gales which landsmen believed blew continuously out at sea.

By tradition, it was square rigged vessels which made ocean voyages, although some schooners with additional square sails were accustomed to cross the north Atlantic and enter the Mediterranean, while others traded regularly with the West Indies, but it was not until the 1860s that schooners of a size larger than 300 tons were really making longer ocean passages. The square rigged ship or barque carried single topsails and single topgallants until the 1850s,

27. See John P Parker, *Sails of the Maritimes* (Halifax, NS 1960).

28. John Lyman (ed), *op cit*, 'Four-Masted Schooners Built in Denmark, compiled by J Malling', Vol 3 (July 1954), pp119-120.

29. The 8th edition was in two volumes published in Washington. The full title was *Explanations and Sailing Directions to accompany the Wind and Current Charts*; Vol 1 dated 1858; Vol 2 dated 1859.

The crowded scene at Cossack Bay, Balaclava, during the Crimean War. One of a number taken by Roger Fenton – probably the world's first war photographer – this March 1855 shot shows the St Hilda, *identified by the '11' on the quarter (all hired transports were numbered and had been from at least the Napoleonic War). This ship was a typical product of Canadian yards; of 791 tons nm, she was built at Quebec in 1849. (By courtesy of David MacGregor)*

but then double topsails were first introduced in America and double topgallants made their appearance towards the end of the 1860s. Although it was probably left to the iron ships to carry seven yards on each mast, numerous wooden sailing ships carried studding sails (stunsails) and other flying kites to increase the sail area. The large crews of clipper ships would be changing the sails constantly to catch every shift of wind, and the studding sails on one side could be set and then taken in again in the same watch.

After the East India Company's monopoly with India was abolished in 1815, there was a minor rush to send out ships to participate in this trade, and after the entire monopoly to China was removed in 1834 trade increased considerably so that by 1847 it was estimated that the tonnage sailing out to India and the East was ten times greater than it had been in 1816. This meant that trade routes around the Cape of Good Hope were very busy and Cape Town needed good facilities to service ships that called there.

Ships were busy taking emigrants from Britain and Continental Europe across the Atlantic to America, but having to sail on a westerly course and not having the experience of the regular packet liners, they often took weeks to get across. Conditions aboard have been described as akin to the slavers from West Africa, only here people had *paid* for their passage. Trade routes to the Mediterranean, to South America and to Australia were burgeoning, and the staple

Sailing about as near to the direction of the wind that a wooden square-rigger could manage, the Norwegian barque Ocean *(490 tons, built 1861) is a fine sight under all plain sail. However, because the square rigged ship could make so little headway in the direction of the wind, even when tacking was feasible, the duration of voyages was unpredictable and could be very prolonged. During the nineteenth century considerable effort was expended on codifying information about winds and currents so that faster passages could be made by making better use of prevailing conditions.*
(By courtesy of David MacGregor)

trade to the West Indies remained. The times occupied by the passages were approximately twice or more longer than the times which the clippers took from 1850 onwards, and such a significant reduction can be ascribed to competition, gold fever and improvement of sailing dir–ections. Once the example of faster passages had been established, owners wanted their captains to emulate such records, and often provided them with larger sail areas, a freshly coppered hull, a set of Maury's sailing directions and appropriate instructions. A friendly rivalry between masters existed in most trades.

Prior to 1850, wooden sailing ships were taking an average six months on the outward passage from England to Australia or to China, and approximately the same length of time to California from New England. Without telegraphic linkage, months or even years went by before reports of their arrival became known. There is the well-known case of the former cotton carrier *Marco Polo*, sent out by James Baines to carry gold-hungry passengers to Melbourne, entering

the River Mersey on 26 December 1852 after a record voyage, with news of her own arrival in Australia and subsequent departure for home. It was even imagined by some, on first sighting her, that she had been obliged to put back in distress, the protracted length of a passage being only too well known. They could hardly imagine

Even though sail became less and less of an economic proposition as the century wore on, many shipowners continued to value training in sail as the best possible preparation for a life at sea. One vessel which took on a training role was Devitt & Moore's passenger frigate Sobraon, *the largest composite vessel ever built; these views of the life on board give some impression of shipboard activities.* (By courtesy of David MacGregor)

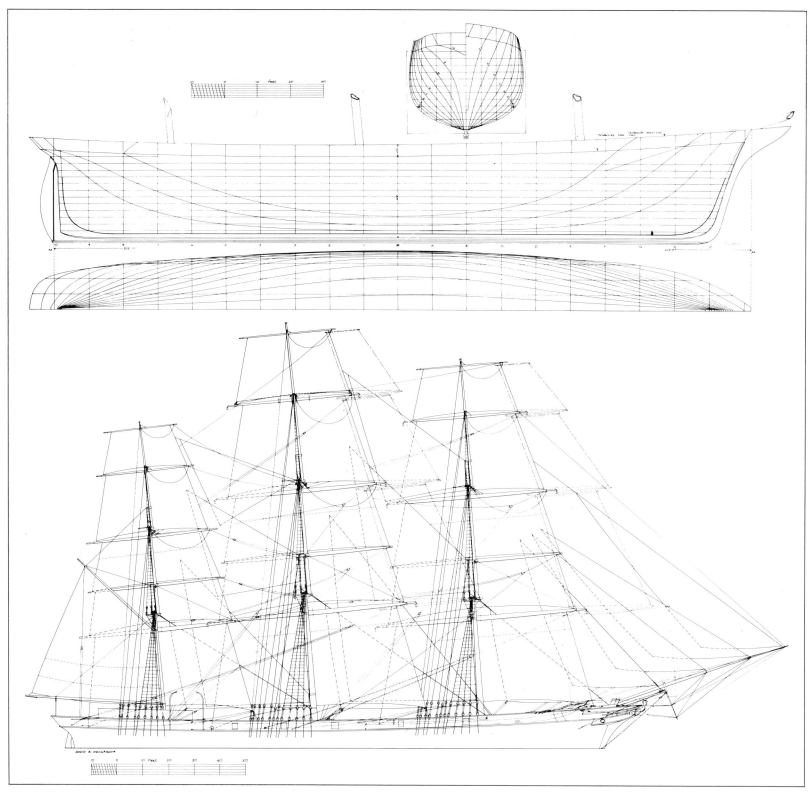

The British tea clipper Thermopylae, *composite-built by Walter Hood & Co, Aberdeen, in 1868. Fast on virtually all points of sailing, her best day's run was 348 miles but her average speed over long periods was, relatively speaking, even better since she could ghost in very light airs. (Plans drawn by David MacGregor)*

that she had circumnavigated the world in the short space of approximately 5 months and 3 weeks. Such were the sort of changes occurring

to maritime business ventures as the century progressed.

Record passages made by American and British ships have been listed in various forms, notably by Carl Cutler in *500 Sailing Records*,[30] by Basil Lubbock in *Lloyd's Calendar* (an annual publication) and by the present author in *The Tea Clippers*, for the China trade alone.[31] Many British captains pasted the track of *Thermopylae*'s

record maiden voyage of 1869 in their journals, and no doubt American captains did the same for one of their own clippers.

30. Carl C Cutler, *Five Hundred Sailing Records of American Built Ships* (Mystic, CT 1952); 114 pages of passage times, 24-hour runs and rates of speed.

31. David R MacGregor, *The Tea Clippers: Their History and Development, 1833-1875* (2nd ed revised and expanded, London 1983), pp244-246.

The British tea clippers such as *Ariel* and *Taeping* did not expect higher speeds than 14kts or 15kts and they rarely exceeded 300 miles in 24 hours, but it was their ability to keep going even in light winds that produced fast passages and was the real secret of their success. It was left to the larger and longer American-built clippers to achieve speeds through the water in excess of 20kts for a few hours and 24-hour runs of over 400 miles.

Fast speeds such as these were the exception and although they may have caught the imagination of successive generations, they were not the intrinsic spirit of what the wooden sailing ship consisted, nor of what it achieved in the last century of its existence.

David R MacGregor

Wooden Sailing Ships over 300 Tons: Typical Vessels 1830-1930

Name	Rig	Flag	Built	Launched	Hull	Tonnage Register	Dimensions (Feet-Inches) (Metres)	Remarks
'Ship of 500 tons'	3-mast ship	British	–	–	Wood	504 om	117-2 × 31-0 × 22-0 35.7 × 9.4 × 6.7	Design from Hedderwick's treatise of 1830
GLASGOW	3-mast ship	American	W P Pattee, Bath, Maine	1836	Wood	595 om	135-0 × 31-2 × 19-0 41.1 × 9.5 × 5.8	Typical full bodied carrier; for New Orleans-Liverpool cotton trade
SERINGAPATAM	3-mast ship	British	R & H Green, Blackwall, Thames	1839	Wood	818 om	152-6 × 34-6 × 22-0 46.5 × 10.5 × 6.7	Passenger frigate of the type that succeeded East Indiamen
YORKSHIRE	3-mast ship	American	W Webb, New York	1843	Wood	1165	174-0 × 36-8 × 21-6 52.0 × 11.2 × 6.6	Atlantic packet; Webb's first ship over 1000 tons
PETCHELEE	3-mast barque	British	T & J Brocklebank, Whitehaven	1850	Wood	357	118-10 × 22-9 × 17-6 36.2 × 6.9 × 5.3	Example of small barque of the period
FLYING CLOUD	3-mast ship	American	D McKay, Boston	1851	Wood	1782	229-0 × 40-8 × 21-6 69.8 × 12.4 × 6.6	Famous Donald McKay clipper
CHALLENGE	3-mast ship	American	W Webb, New York	1851	Wood	2006	230-6 × 43-2 × 26-0 70.3 × 13.2 × 7.9	Webb's most extreme clipper; was only 1375 tons by new measurement
MARCO POLO	3-mast ship	British	J Smith, St John, New Brunswick	1851	Wood	1625 nm	184-1 × 36-4 × 29-5 56.1 × 11.1 × 9.0	Well-known Canadian-built clipper
GREAT REPUBLIC	4-mast barque	American	D McKay, Boston	1853	Wood	4555 om	325-0 × 53-0 × 39-0 99.1 × 16.2 × 11.9	Largest wooden ship of the day; burnt out before maiden voyage and rebuilt smaller
MASTIFF	3-mast ship	American	D McKay, Boston	1856	Wood	1031	168-10 × 36-6 × 22-0 51.5 × 11.1 × 6.7	Less extreme form, of greater capacity than genuine clippers
EASTERN MONARCH	3-mast ship	British	A Stephen, Dundee	1856	Wood	1631	239-0 × 40-4 × 24-11 72.8 × 12.3 × 7.6	Large Blackwall passenger frigate
JOHN LIDGETT	3-mast ship	British	A Stephen, Glasgow	1862	Composite	770	178-8 × 30-1 × 20-5 54.5 × 9.2 × 6.2	First example of wood-on-iron-frame composite construction
JOHN WILLIAMS (ex-SAMOA)	3-mast barque	British	A Hall, Aberdeen	1868	Wood	200 gr	106-0 x 24-6 x 15-6 32.3 x 7.5 x 4.8	Easily maintained wooden vessel for the London Missionary Society
THERMOPYLAE	3-mast ship	British	W Hood, Aberdeen	1868	Composite	947	212-0 × 36-0 × 20-11 64.6 × 11.0 × 6.4	One of the best known British clippers
CUTTY SARK	3-mast ship	British	Scott & Linton, Dumbarton	1869	Composite	921	212-6 × 36-0 × 21-0 64.8 × 11.0 × 6.4	Famous tea clipper; now preserved at Greenwich
OCEAN KING	4-mast barque	American	Kennebunkport, Maine	1874	Wood	2526	250-6 × 42-4 × 30-1 76.4 × 12.9 × 9.2	First of an economical type of large 4-masted barque
OREGON	3-mast ship	American	W Rogers, Bath, Maine	1875	Wood	1431	205-11 × 30-11 × 24-0 62.8 × 9.4 × 7.3	'Down-Easter' of moderate form
THORBEKKE VII	3-mast barque	Dutch	A H Meursing, Neuwendam	1885	Composite	929	194-6 × 35-9 × 20-5 59.3 × 10.9 × 6.2	The last composite sailing ship
ARYAN	3-mast ship	American	C V Minott, Phippsburg	1893	Wood	2017	248-7 × 42-4 × 26-4 75.8 × 12.9 × 8.0	The last wooden full rigged ship
JAMES TUFT	4-mast barquentine	American	Hall Bros, Puget Sound, Washington	1902	Wood	1274	201-8 × 42-0 × 16-4 61.5 × 12.8 × 5.0	Example of last generation of Pacific Coast wooden shipbuilding

2

The Wooden Sailing Ship: under 300 Tons

BY the end of the nineteenth century, wooden vessels of less than 300 tons seemed quite small when compared with steel-hulled ships or barques of over 2000 tons, and the uninitiated would imagine that only the larger vessel was capable of making ocean voyages. Yet, in 1815, 300 tons was considered a fair, average size for a full rigged ship that was suitable to sail anywhere in the world. At a time when many books on naval architecture gave

scant attention to merchant vessels, David Steel, in *The Shipwright's Vade-Mecum*, reproduced three plans of a ship of 330 tons, which is not much larger than 300 tons.[1] This work was first published in 1805 and appeared again in 1822 in a second edition; it was accompanied by three folding plates of the merchantman and a further plate of a warship. It must have exerted considerable influence in small shipyards.

Using Steel's plans, the present author reconstructed plans of this ship and incorporated a longitudinal section and deck layout on the lines plan. Also reconstructed was a sail and rigging plan, and for this purpose a table in Steel's *Rig-*

ging and Seamanship was employed to calculate the lengths of the spars, as at that date such plans did not appear in book form. All this was set out in some detail in *Merchant Sailing Ships 1775–1815* together with the possible identifi-

The barque Sir John Beresford, *built at Liverpool in 1830, measured 295 tons. Although small by late nineteenth-century standards, such vessels were considered a fair size when built and perfectly capable of world-wide trading - indeed, this vessel went to Batavia (modern-day Indonesia) in 1840. Note the widely adopted convention in ship portraiture of depicting the vessel from more than one point of view. (By courtesy of David MacGregor).*

1. David Steel, *The Shipwright's Vade-Mecum: A Clear and Familiar Introduction to the Principles and Practice of Ship-Building &c*, 2 vols: text & plates (2nd ed, London 1822).

The schooner sail plan from Hedderwick's treatise of 1830. This vessel has been identified by the author as the Glasgow, *of 155 tons, built at Leith in 1826. With the other drawings available this makes the* Glasgow *the best documented merchant schooner of the period; it seems safe to assume that the example was chosen to typify a successful trader rather than to advocate a hypothetic design, so often the case in naval architectural works of the period. (By courtesy of David MacGregor)*

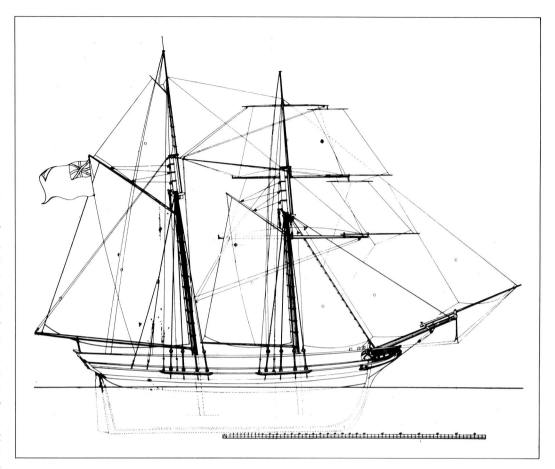

cation of the plans as representing an actual vessel.[2]

The various works originally published by David Steel continued to be reprinted for a number of years and became standard reference manuals in shipyards in the first half of the nineteenth century. At the same time, other works were appearing, such as Hedderwick's *Treatise on Marine Architecture*[3] and Richardson's *Mercantile Marine Architecture*.[4] Hedderwick actually gave three sail plans: a full rigged ship, a topsail schooner and a heavily rigged Leith smack. The author has identified the schooner as the *Glasgow*, which was built at Leith in 1826 for trading in the North Sea and was of 155 tons; the Leith smack was slightly larger at 173 tons and has not been identified. Both vessels had somewhat similar hull forms and confirm the hypothesis that all Hedderwick's designs exhibited a family likeness — namely a short, deep hull with small deadrise, rounded bilges, a full entrance and a hollow run, all of which gave good cargo capacity and enabled the vessel to sit upright in harbours which dried out at low water.

Richardson's book appeared three years after Hedderwick's and his plans would appear to have been influenced by the whaling trade; the hull form is a little finer than Hedderwick's in the waterlines, but the midship section and rise of floor are similar. He divided merchant vessels into three classes: the smallest he allotted to the 'coasting trade' with tonnages of 88 to 140; the middle size was for 'trade to Europe' with tonnages of 200 to 300; the largest was for trade elsewhere and with tonnages of 370 to 420 tons. He suggested that some published plans differed little from those of a century earlier, and the student of naval architecture has little difficulty in noting the repetition of plates in one encyclopaedia after another spanning the years 1775–1845.

On examining plans of many small vessels built in Europe in the 1850s, it is obvious that Hedderwick's designs have not been altered greatly for vessels built of wood: the shape of the midship section is similar and so is the headwork and square stern; the waterlines are a little finer; the chief difference is that the hulls are shallower

and longer. Thus cargo capacity is not lost and the vessels's speed potential is increased. The introduction of a rounded stern and a lighter bow improved appearance above the waterline, and, as the century wore on, the number of trailboards and headrails decreased. Brigs and schooners built of iron could vary their proportions considerably, but for wooden vessels the hull-forms had more or less been established by 1860.

In the United States, books on naval architecture were rare and in 1839 Donald McKay's elder brother, Lauchlan, wrote the only one that appeared before the middle of the century.[5] It contained seven folding plates among which were lines plans of a sloop, a trading schooner and a brig; there were no sail plans. All were full-bodied craft with little deadrise and a very bluff entrance; the sloop was broad enough to carry a 70–75ft mast. There is also the plan of a 'Pilot Boat' which is a schooner with steep deadrise and fine convex lines. The text, written by a shipbuilder, yields sensible practical information on how to design a vessel, how to utilise the drawing in the construction and how to build the craft out of wood.

The influence of this work is unknown, but it must have proved a useful tool to aspiring shipbuilders in regions where wooden craft were needed, but where the knowledge of how to construct craft was lacking. For instance, wood-

en vessels were being built at San Francisco soon after the first gold prospectors arrived. Were there amongst them thoroughly competent shipwrights who knew the art intimately, or would they have had recourse to McKay's work? Occasionally one comes across a note of books possessed by a shipbuilder and this is instructive. The Appledore shipbuilder Robert Cock possessed a copy of John W Griffiths' *Treatise on Marine and Naval Architecture*, which was first published in 1851;[6] Alexander Stephen Jr had the same title written down on the last page of a notebook which he had begun in August 1851.

2. David R MacGregor, *Merchant Sailing Ships 1775-1815: Sovereignty of Sail* (2nd ed, London 1985), pp109-114.

3. Peter Hedderwick, *A Treatise on Marine Architecture*, 2 vols: text and plates (Edinburgh 1830).

4. Thomas Richardson, *Mercantile Marine Architecture: or an Elementary Work on the Art of Drawing the Draughts of Vessels* (London 1833). There is a slim book of text and 7 plates.

5. L McKay, *The Practical Ship-builder: Containing the Best Mechanical and Philosophical Principles for the Construction of Different Classes of Vessels ... &c* (New York 1839; reprinted New York 1940; new reprint of latter, New York 1970).

6. John W Griffiths, *Treatise on Marine and Naval Architecture, or Theory and Practice Blended in Ship Building* (3rd ed, New York 1853); there is also an edition published in London in 1853 of 199pp of text and with plates grouped at the end and redrawn without the use of curves, and in a smaller type face; another edition was published in Glasgow in 1857.

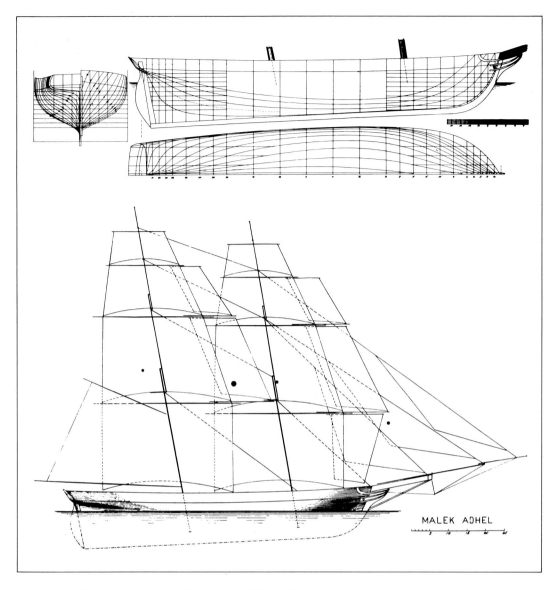

MALEK ADHEL

A very sharp brig by the famous American builder William H Webb, taken from his published book of plans. The Malek-Adhel *was constructed in 1840 for his own account with a view to trading in the Pacific. The hull form is derived from the Baltimore clipper model, which was adopted by New England builders for trades in which speed was an advantage.* (By courtesy of David MacGregor)

most anywhere, and the smaller the craft, the more inaccessible appeared to be the building sites chosen. Pictures often show a dangerously steep incline given to a slipway down which a vessel had to be launched, the construction having taken place in a shed on the wrong side of the road. Often a vessel was built on the open beach above the high water level; this was sometimes on a regular slipway or frequently on common land, and once launched, the vessel had to sail away because there may have been no port nearby and certainly no fitting-out berth. So she would have been launched completely equipped for sea, with her gear rove and her sails bent.

The entire process of building a wooden vessel is described by Basil Greenhill in *The Merchant Schooners*, his example in one particular case being the three-masted schooner *Katie*, constructed at Appledore in North Devon in 1903 by Robert Cock. He also describes the manner of building a wooden vessel on the open beach, as outlined above.[8] Although the pages referred to here specifically describe shipbuilding in a yard in the West of England, the principles did not vary greatly in other parts of the United Kingdom, whether the craft under construction was a sloop of 35 tons or a barque of 275 tons. Nor, in general terms, did the manner of wooden shipbuilding vary that much between one country and another. The method of design may have been different but full-size moulds had to be made, the frames assembled, and planking fastened to them; deck beams, decks, hatchways and deck fittings had to be put in place; and masts had to be stepped.

In Great Britain, accommodation was usually below deck and was similar to that of a larger vessel but on a smaller scale. The crew berthed in a small forecastle right up in the bows, entered through a scuttle close abaft the windlass and then down a steep ladder. The master and mate or mates slept aft; the only deckhouse would have been the galley, although sometimes the cooking was done below. In the billy-boy

In Great Britain, authors of books on shipbuilding began with long chapters on mathematics but in America the practical side was heavily stressed. John Griffiths considered that the 'new world' had nothing to learn from the 'old world'. In his *Treatise*, he does give plans of schooner yachts; also the sail plan of a 'three-masted fore and main topsail schooner' in Plate 1. Much of the prose is verbose and allows the author to indulge his own fancies, but perhaps the possession of this book gave the owner a secret pleasure in believing he held the panacea to all problems.

On the Continent of Europe, there were a number of works on shipbuilding published in several countries, of which that by N C Kierkegaard of 1862 produced the greatest number of vessels under 300 tons.[7] He gave a lines plan and sail plan and sometimes deck details. Brigs and schooners featured in most books on shipbuilding, because wooden shipbuilding techniques were still in the forefront of a shipwright's training.

Construction and rig

Throughout the nineteenth century and well into the present one, every port had at least one shipyard that specialised in handling wooden vessels, either by constructing them or in repairing them, and in numerous districts the well-being of the neighbourhood depended on that one shipyard. The premises required by a small yard were almost negligible, the counting house and office being almost the only requirement of covered accommodation for a small established yard. But for a craft built on speculation, sometimes on vacant ground beside a creek, only a shed would be needed. The timber could lie anywhere and improved by being outside; a sawpit could be dug out; a scrieve board could do duty in the open air for a mould loft floor; a steam chest for heating and making the planks pliable could be erected; the ironwork, sails, ropes and other items could be delivered when needed; shipwrights would provide their own tools. Vessels of under 75 tons could be built al-

7. N C Kierkegaard, *Plancher till Praktisk Skeppsbyggnadskonst* (Gothenburg 1862); the plates come separately in a long heavy portfolio.

8. Basil Greenhill *The Merchant Schooners* (London 1951), Vol 1, pp30ff.

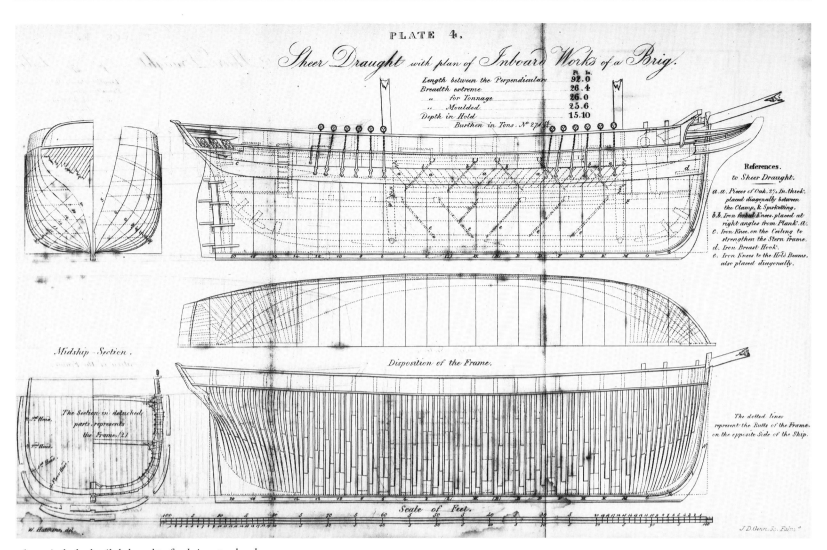

PLATE 4.

Sheer Draught with plan of Inboard Works of a Brig.

		Ft. In.
Length between the Perpendiculars		92.0
Breadth extreme		26.4
„ for Tonnage		26.0
„ Moulded		25.6
Depth in Hold		15.10
Burthen in Tons. Nᵒ 274 ¾		

References.
to Sheer Draught.

a.a. Pieces of Oak. 2½ In. thick. placed diagonally between the Clamp, & Sprketting.
b.b. Iron forked Knees. placed at right angles from Plank. a.
c. Iron Knee. on the Ceiling to strengthen the Stern frame.
d. Iron Breast-Hook.
e. Iron Knees to the Hold Beams. also placed diagonally.

Midship Section.

Disposition of the Frame.

The Section in detached parts represents the Frame (2)

The dotted lines represent the Butts of the Frame on the opposite Side of the Ship.

Scale of Feet.

W. Hutchins. del. *J. D. Genn. Sc. Edinᵒ*

A particularly detailed draught of a brig reproduced from a learned society report of 1842. Although adopting a typical full form, the design by one William Hutchins demonstrates originality in the shift of butts in the framing, a stern framed without transoms, and diagonal ceiling planking and iron knees forming a complete truss frame. The designer was awarded the society's gold medal, but there is no evidence that such a vessel was built. (By courtesy of David MacGregor)

Bluejacket of 57 tons, built at Wisbech in 1860, cooking was done in a 'caboose' on deck, which was too low for a man to stand in, so that he had to kneel down or stoop. Doubtless other craft resorted to similar means of food preparation. Crews were often quite small, five or six men, including the master, handling a brigantine, although square canvas in a brig or small barque

A drawing by T W Ward of the clipper schooner Scottish Maid *lying high and dry alongside a London wharf. Built by Alexander Hall in 1839, the ship introduced the sharp, overhanging and hollow-lined 'Aberdeen bow' which played an important part in British fast-sailing development. (By courtesy of David MacGregor)*

Despite the deep sea domination of steam, sail continued to be employed around the coasts of Britain well into the twentieth century. Many of the last survivors were small ketches like the Lady Agnes *seen here entering the Cornish port of Newlyn with the aid of a line taken out by a hoveller's boat. (By courtesy of David MacGregor)*

sometimes built into a raised quarterdeck. In America, deckhouses were also favoured for accommodation.

There was an immense variety of rigs put on vessels of under 300 tons, although the number of masts probably never exceeded three. The building of full rigged ships of this size began to die out after the 1840s, but a survivor, albeit with an iron hull, is the *Joseph Conrad*, formerly the Danish training ship *Georg Stage*, which was built in 1882. She measures 100.8ft × 25.2ft × 13.2ft and 203 tons, and is preserved at Mystic Seaport. She is of lovely proportions and exhibits the attractiveness of this rig on a small hull, and with her single topsail yards one glimpses the grace of a bygone era.

Three-masted barques of under 300 tons were still being constructed of wood in 1875, and in that year four were built in Great Britain, one in Denmark and one in America. Actually, the last vessel, the *Columbia*, was of 304 tons. The smallest was the *Bayadère* of 212 tons, built at Hylton on the River Wear.

At Aberdeen, Alexander Hall's last wooden square-riggers were the barques *Samoa* of 200 tons gross and *Helen Black* of 305 tons gross, both built in 1868. The latter cost £13.11s per ton which was on the cheap side; the former was a missionary ship for use in the Pacific and cost

did require more 'hands'. Although motor winches were to be seen in the cut-down ketches and smacks which still eked out a living around the British coastline in the inter-war era, there was no power aboard during the pre-1914 period when winch, windlass and pumps were all worked by hand.

In Continental Europe, by contrast, accommodation was usually in deckhouses, and berths were allotted in much the same way as in Britain, thus providing the maximum space below deck for cargo stowage. The after deckhouse was

Quite small three-masted vessels were built well into the latter half of the nineteenth century. This is the barque Isle of Beauty *of 286 tons net, built at Sunderland by Metcalf in 1865. The rig is not lofty, with no provision for royals, but the topsails are deep and fitted with Colling & Pinkney roller-reefing gear. (Colin Denny Gallery)*

The struggle to make sail pay became ever more evident as the nineteenth century progressed. Not only was sail area reduced, along with the crew to handle it, but the quality of the gear itself declined. In this late view of the barquentine Hilda, originally built in 1879, the patching of the sails is very clear; the poor fit of the jibs also suggests secondhand sails from another vessel. (By courtesy of David MacGregor)

mizzen is a pole mast. Although the rig was to be seen on steamers, twenty years were to pass before the next authenticated case of a sailing ship so rigged, which is the *Fanny* of Bremen, built in 1850. In 1853 the *Stockton* was launched at Manitowoc on Lake Michigan, and thereafter examples become gradually more frequent. The term 'barkentine' was probably coined in America at the end of the 1850s and this spelling was used in 1866 in Glasgow; however it took some

9. David R MacGregor, *Merchant Sailing Ships 1815-1850: Supremacy of Sail* (London 1984), pp78-80.

£25 per ton, which seems very expensive. As an indication of price, Hall's iron barque *Hokitika*, built in 1871 of 292 tons gross, cost £13.52.

Apart from the basic price of hull and spars, it was the quality of materials to obtain a certain classification with Lloyd's Register and the type of 'outfit' required which affected the price. The two basic outfits were termed Baltic and East India: the former was for the home trade area and cost from £1.50 to £2 per ton; the other was for deep sea voyages and cost £3 per ton or more. This sum covered the sails, rigging, boats, anchors, equipment and spares. The manner in which costs were made up applied to vessels of any size with the exception of very small ketches and smacks which only plied in a single tidal estuary or along a limited stretch of coastline.

The barquentine rig was first seen in Great Britain in the *Bonanza* which T & J Brocklebank built at Whitehaven in 1830, and a full description of her and a drawing of her sail plan appears in *Merchant Sailing Ships 1815–1850*.[9] Here the

The difference between a snow and a brig was largely forgotten by the end of the nineteenth century but this view of the Russian Aid (Thoraswarf 1873, 272 tons) depicts a genuine snow. The gaff is set from a trysail mast abaft the main and is loose-footed (ie it has no boom). Because of the absence of a boom the gaff sail could not be sheeted home beyond the taffrail so was smaller than a brig's main sail; as a result the snow tended to make more use of a square main course set from a proper main yard (as shown in this photo), although by this time brigs could usually set a similar sail from their main yards as well. (By courtesy of David MacGregor)

It was natural that the search for more efficient rigs should throw up some sail plans that did not fit traditional categories. With the sailor's conservative scorn for novelties these were generally dismissed as 'jackass barques', but one configuration that became relatively popular was a combination of barquentine and two-topsail schooner. Known as a 'barquetta' in the Channel Islands where a number were built, an example is the Matchless, *reproduced in this lithograph. She was built at Guernsey in 1859 and measured 241 tons. (By courtesy of David MacGregor)*

years before it was generally adopted. At first the rig had gone under the name of 'three-masted schooner' and latterly that of 'three-masted brigantine' and it was in this guise that the *Slyboots* was advertised for sale in 1880.[10]

Barquentines were classed as square rigged vessels in the Merchant Shipping Acts in Great Britain, which meant that they could only be commanded by masters with square rig tickets, whereas the brigantine was not so classed, which permitted masters with fore-and-aft tickets to take command of them. In America and Canada, large wooden barquentines with four, five and six masts were built, as referred to in the previous chapter.

10. David R MacGregor *Merchant Sailing Ships 1850-1875: Heyday of Sail* (London 1984), pp105-107.

The brig continued to be built for many years and there are a number of photographs of ones built in the 1870s in Great Britain, Scandinavia and Prince Edward Island. As the century advanced, some had the yards stripped off the main mast and became brigantines, and others, like the *Waterwitch*, were re-rigged as barquentines. Square rig remained popular in Europe, even in coasting vessels. As an economy measure, British brigs sent down their royal yards and shortened their topgallant masts, but many Continental brigs clung to their royals. Brigs often carried a trysail mast or 'snow' mast close abaft the main lower mast, but the term 'snow' was rarely used by then. In any case, such vessels had a long main boom which a proper snow did not carry. Both brigs and brigantines set four-sided staysails between the masts.

The schooner rig in Europe almost invariably carried square canvas on the fore mast, so that exceptions were labelled 'fore-and-aft' schooner. The reverse was the case in North America from about 1850, where schooners rarely had any square sails and those that did were described accordingly. In America, three-masted schooners were often considerably larger than 300 tons and so, too, were two-masted vessels. Two-masted schooners remained a popular rig throughout Europe during the nineteenth cen-

tury and frequently carried a topgallant above single or double topsails. When a square sail was set from the lower yard in light favourable winds, the similarity to a brigantine was unmis-

A remarkable photograph taken in 1870 of the Norwegian brig Ornen *with an impressive array of stunsails set. The use of such 'flying kites', as additional light weather canvas was called, tended to die out with the reduced amount of square sails and smaller crews of the late nineteenth century. (By courtesy of David MacGregor)*

Small trading vessels often had to take the ground in order to transfer cargo. This placed restrictions not only on size but also on hull form since they needed a relatively flat bottom. This scene of the ketch Pursuit *unloading into horse-drawn carts in an English Westcountry river about 1926 is typical of a scene that must have been familiar to waterside communities across the world until well into this century. (By courtesy of Ralph Bird)*

takable. On the main mast, a jib-headed topsail or one with a head yard was carried. Prior to about 1870, the main mast was stepped fairly close to the fore mast, so that when such vessels were converted to three masts, the main mast did not have to be moved; only the boom and gaff were shortened and an entirely new mizzen was then stepped. Examples of how this was carried out can be seen in sail plans of the *Express* (1860) and the *Rhoda Mary* (1868).[11]

Studding sails or 'stunsails' were still being fitted in 1870 to schooners, brigantines and brigs and remained in use for a number of years, particularly on Scandinavian vessels. There is the unique photograph of the brig *Ornen*, taken about 1870, with five of them set, including a triangular lower. No doubt, vessels bearing these rigs that traded in the Indian Ocean and China Sea continued to make use of these sails for a number of years. However other flying kites had probably dropped out of use by then.

Ketches were usually only fore-and-aft rigged although a yard was sometimes carried on the main mast for a square sail to be set below it. However, billy-boys were ketch rigged and yet their main mast was often like a schooner's fore mast, with two or three yards. A Danish galeas in the second half of the century might carry a single square sail on the main mast, with the lower yard secured to the mast below the hounds. The smaller vessels with the basic rigs of ketch or sloop might go under different names in different localities. In Great Britain, words such as trow, billy-boy, barge, keel, smack, flat, and wherry, were all to be found as well as others; all carried cargo. The lug rig was employed mostly by fishermen, yachtsmen and hovellers.

Some trades and occupations

Vessels of under 300 tons were engaged in a multiplicity of trades and occupations, and due

Built at Sunderland in 1846 the 152-ton brigantine Kezia Page *was employed in the coal trade. In this case she is approaching Folkestone harbour but other colliers often unloaded on to open beaches. (By courtesy of David MacGregor)*

to the small size of many of the craft concerned, they might never stray far from the land and so their continued presence near the coast subjected them to frequent hazards. A seaman in a larger vessel was happiest when away from the land but the coasters had to adopt a different set of

values. Colliers and other coasting vessels were numbered in hundreds, especially if they lay at

11. *Ibid*, p99 for *Express*; and pp211 and 214 for *Rhoda Mary*. For sail plan of *Rhoda Mary* as three-mast schooner, see Basil Greenhill, *op cit*, pp42-43.

A typical British 'Western Ocean schooner', the Little Minnie *seen in Mounts Bay. Built at Padstow in 1866 as the* Minnie, *she was renamed about 1890 after a change of ownership. She probably had a jibboom and topgallant as built.* (By courtesy of David MacGregor)

anchor waiting for a shift of wind. The headlands and harbours were familiar landmarks and the approach to them was a regular occurrence. But aiming for a narrow harbour entrance in a gale could be beset with great difficulties, and photographers and artists have often captured the moment when the vessel has been driven off course, either to be dashed against another vessel or swept away from the harbour mouth and driven ashore.

When there was no harbour available, the cargo had to be unloaded on the beach, and, in Britain, Hastings and Cromer were well-known places to view the unloading of coal. When this was a regular occurrence, moorings would have been laid well out to sea below the low-water mark, to enable colliers to haul themselves off the beach in an emergency. Photographs in the collection of the late Cmdr H O Hill show the brig *Lamburn* of Rye lying aground on Hastings beach in about 1865, discharging her coal into carts. Before the coming of the railway, 12,000 to 13,000 tons of coal was unloaded annually on to this beach and there were nineteen vessels, mostly of under 100 tons each, employed in this trade in 1852. In 1866 the *Lamburn* was driven ashore in a gale which must have risen before the tide rose to float her off.[12]

Of quite a different type to the heavy collier brigs were the schooners and brigantines used in the fruit trade with their sharp-bodied hulls and large areas of canvas. Ports in southern England built some smart vessels to bring back fresh fruit from the Azores, and this trade was at its height in the years 1840–1870. A size of 100 to 150 tons was popular and a voyage out from London to St Michaels and back home in three weeks was wanted. Others ventured into the Mediterranean and brought back dried fruit. A few of these clippers such as the *Time* and the *Hellas* were bought for the opium trade during the 1830s and 1840s. They would load the opium at ports and sail along the coast to smuggle it ashore. A large crew and a ready armament were required to repel boarders, but the rewards both for the owners and the captains were immense.

The barques, brigs, barquentines and schooners of under 300 tons carried vast amounts of cargo across the north and south Atlantic in the nineteenth and early twentieth centuries. The palm oil trade from West Africa required some smart ships with a good turn of speed, and the West Indies trade provided regular employment. Three-masted topgallant yard schooners from Portmadoc in North Wales, known as 'Western Ocean Yachts', took slates across to Canada and brought back dried cod from Newfoundland. One of these, the *M A James* of 124

12. David R MacGregor, *Merchant Sailing Ships 1815-1850*, pp49-51.

In European waters sail lingered longest in the Baltic and Scandinavian countries. This three-masted schooner, the Hans, *was built at Marstal in Denmark in 1907.* (By courtesy of David MacGregor)

tons gross, cost £2000 to build in 1900. She survived the Second World War.

In Continental Europe, schooners were engaged in many trades, and some of those from Denmark and Norway which sailed out to the West Indies or the Far East never returned home again, but spent their entire working life out there. Barquentines were also used. Three-masted schooners first began to appear in the 1850s and they were often built with straight stems and broad, square, 'Marstal' sterns. Such a one was the Danish *Hans* which was photographed becalmed off Le Treport when outward bound to the Rio Grande; she was of 161 tons net and carried three square sails on the fore topmast as well as five headsails.

The outbreak of War in 1914 changed everything. Steam power and the internal combustion engine combined to re-route traffic away from many of the haunts of the smaller vessels. Some of the wooden vessels survived, but usually their spars were cut down and diesel engines were fitted. In Scandinavian waters, remnants of these proud fleets still traded and the skills in building wooden hulls lingered on with them.

David R MacGregor

Wooden Sailing Ships under 300 Tons: Typical Vessels 1830-1930

Name	Rig	Flag	Built	Launched	Tonnage Register	Dimensions (Feet-Inches) (Metres)	Remarks
POCAHONTAS	brig	American	?, Newburyport, Mass	1830	268	113-0 × 26-4 × 17-6 34.4 × 8.0 × 5.3	Typical burthensome carrier of the time
BONANZA	3-mast barquentine	British	T & J Brocklebank, Whitehaven	1830	86 om	77-2 × 20-7 × 12-1 23.5 × 6.3 × 3.7	First recorded British barquentine
TIME	2-mast schooner	British	Fletcher, Son & Fearnall, Poplar	1832	139 om	85-9 × 19-9 × 10-9 26.1 × 6.0 × 3.3	A sharp schooner later employed in the opium trade
LAMBURN	brig	British	Thwaites & Winter, Hastings	1833	80 om	?	Employed in the Hastings coal trade, unloading on the beach
NEPTUNUS	brigantine	Danish	?, Christianshavn	1844	113	73-0 × 20-0 × 11-9 22.3 × 6.1 × 3.6	A common Danish type in mid century
ALVIN CLARKE	2-mast topsail schooner	American	J P Clark, Trenton, Michigan	1846	218	105-8 × 25-4 × 9-4 32.2 × 7.7 × 2.8	Wreck recovered from Lake Michigan and now preserved
VOLANTE	brig	American	William H Webb, New York	1853	300 om	112-0 × 26-6 × 11-3 34.1 × 8.1 × 3.4	Built for the Mediterranean trade by a leading US builder of wooden ships
ORNEN	brig	Norwegian	?, Stavanger	1857	57	97-5 × 21-0 × 11-9 29.7 × 6.4 × 3.6	Carried full suit of stunsails
ARRIERO	brigantine	British	Alexander Stephen, Glasgow	1862	167	105-0 × 25-0 × 11-9 32.0 × 7.6 × 3.6	Composite-built by a leading exponent of the technique
OTTAWA	brigantine (later 3-mast schooner)	British	Kelly, Parrsboro, Nova Scotia	1868	143	90-6 × 24-8 × 11-0 27.6 × 7.5 × 3.4	One of numerous wooden Canadian-built ships under the British flag
HELEN BLACK	3-mast barque	British	A Hall, Aberdeen	1868	305	132-0 × 25-4 × 14-0 40.2 × 7.7 × 4.3	The last wooden square-rigger built by Alexander Hall
SLYBOOTS	3-mast barquentine	British	Philip, Dartmouth	1868	178	104-0 × 23-6 × 13-0 31.7 × 7.2 × 4.0	Rig described in 1880 as 'three-masted brigantine'
WATERWITCH	brig	British	Meadus, Poole	1871	194	112-0 × 25-9 × 12-9 34.1 × 7.9 × 3.9	Later rerigged as barquentine
BAYADÈRE	3-mast barque	French	Gibbon, Sunderland	1875	212	102-1 × 24-9 × 12-9 31.1 × 7.6 × 3.9	A late example of a small barque
MARY	smack	British	H E Stephens, Devoran, Cornwall	1875	25	49-4 × 17-6 × 5-8 15.0 × 5.3 × 1.7	A Westcountry trading smack; one of the smaller single-masted types
HALDON	ketch	British	Hawke Bros, Plymouth	1893	77	88-0 × 21-6 × 9-9 26.8 × 6.6 × 3.0	One of numerous wooden-built British coasters of the period
M A JAMES	3-mast topgallant schooner	British	D Williams, Portmadoc	1900	97	89-7 × 22-8 × 10-7 27.3 × 6.9 × 3.2	Famous 'Western Ocean Yacht'
KATIE	3-mast schooner	British	R Cock, Appledore	1903	124	91-7 × 22-3 × 10-6 27.9 × 6.8 × 3.2	A late example of wooden shipbuilding in Britain
HANS	3-mast topsail schooner	Danish	H C Christensen, Marstal	1907	161	114-0 × 25-5 × 10-8 34.7 × 7.7 × 3.3	Typical Scandinavian wooden trader of the period

3

The Transition to Iron and Steel Construction

THE story of technological change in the nineteenth-century shipping industry is essentially that of the transformation of the small wooden sailing ship into the large steel steamer as the ideal embodiment of

In its early days iron shipbuilding was confined to a number of specialist yards, one of the most prominent being Robert Steele & Co of Greenock on the Clyde. One of their later products was the Parsee, *a 1281-ton full rigged ship whose crew are shown here proudly posing for the camera.* (By courtesy of David MacGregor)

the naval vessel and of the merchant carrier on most trade routes of the world. The prolonged nature of the secular decline of the sailing ship owes much to a series of efficiency improvements which enabled it to continue to offer effective competition across a number of ocean trades during the late nineteenth century and, in a few cases, beyond 1900.[1] Prominent amongst these improvements were changes in the matrix of sails, developments in mechanised handling gear and alterations in hull design. Most important of all, however, and impinging upon most

of the other changes, was the substitution of metal for wood in the construction of sailing ships. While the combination of steam and metal ultimately proved the best mix of technologies, this was far from inevitable in the middle of

1. B Greenhill, *The Life and Death of the Merchant Sailing Ship, 1815-65* (London 1980), p30 identifies the apparent paradox that the sailing ship reached its greatest efficiency in an era when it had become technologically obsolescent. N Rosenberg, 'Factors affecting the diffusion of technology', *Explorations in Economic History* 10 (1972-3), p28 rather prematurely suggests that sail had lost its dominance on even the longest routes by the 1880s.

The details of iron ship construction as applied to a barque of 440 tons gross. The scantlings are in accordance with Lloyd's rules for 100 A1 classification. By the time this illustration was published in A C Holm's Practical Shipbuilding *(1904) construction in iron and steel was no longer regarded with suspicion by shipowners, classification societies or seafarers. (By courtesy of David MacGregor)*

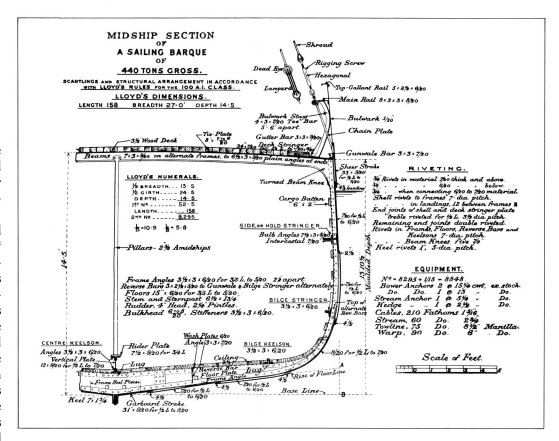

the nineteenth century. Indeed, as will be shown, some of the developments associated with the introduction of metal brought greater benefits initially to sailing vessels than to steamers.[2]

The use of iron in shipbuilding can be dated back until at least the late eighteenth century.[3] In the early nineteenth century iron was increasingly used in individual parts of a vessel such as the knees, straps, pillars and other small structural features.[4] In 1819 *Aaron Manby* was launched as the first prefabricated vessel. The use of iron as the primary construction material in a vessel, however, was not common until the 1830s and 1840s and it did not displace wood in this role until the 1860s and 1870s. Steel was used periodically for ship construction from the late 1850s and in particular components such as spars but did not supersede iron generally until the last two decades of the century. The transition from wood to metal in sailing ships occurred first and primarily in Britain: few other countries built metal sailing ships in any great number. The aims of this chapter, therefore, are to understand why metal replaced wood as the main shipbuilding material, to indicate the spatial diffusion of the transition process between the major shipbuilding countries and ports, and to account for this lagged effect.

Typical late nineteenth-century iron ship construction as illustrated in Paasch's From Keel to Truck. *Without the substantial width of frame timbers in a wooden ship, it is clear that the structure of an iron hull takes up far less of the revenue-earning internal volume. (By courtesy of David MacGregor)*

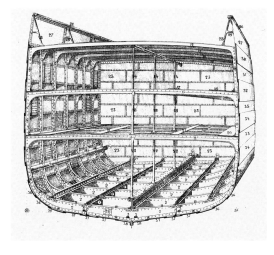

The advantages and disadvantages of metal in sailing ship construction

The formation of the Institution of Naval Architects in 1860 coincided with the main transition period from wood to metal in shipbuilding. Indeed, its members, who included many shipbuilders as well as naval architects, saw the discussion and promotion of technical change in the industry as one of its principal purposes. The publication of their papers and the ensuing discussions in an annual volume, the *Transactions of the Institution of Naval Architects*, has provided historians with an excellent account of the contending arguments for wood, iron or steel in contemporary shipbuilding. Regular papers were delivered by supporters of iron shipbuilding such as William Fairbairn, William White, Edward Reed, John Scott Russell and John Grantham. Each in turn published separate books extolling the practice in some detail.[5] As early as 1842 Grantham had published his annual presidential address to the Polytechnic Society of Liverpool on the merits of iron as a shipbuilding material.[6] This was followed up and expanded upon in a lengthier work, *Iron Shipbuilding*, whose success is indicated by the fact that it had reached its fifth edition by 1868. In this work Grantham sets out the main advantages and disadvantages of the use of iron in shipbuilding. The comprehensive and detailed nature of his comments can serve as an effective basis for our discussion of the factors

underlying the adoption of iron in shipbuilding. He identified the main benefits of iron as strength combined with lightness, greater stowage, safety, speed and durability but lower construction and repair costs. The main drawbacks of the new material he saw as magnetic deviation, susceptibility to fouling and lightning, and the inconsistent quality of the material. Alexander Stephens, whose Glasgow shipbuilding firm made the transition from wooden to iron sailing ships, cited cost, safety, capacity, durability and economy in upkeep as the main advantages of iron.[7]

Proponents of iron emphasised in particular

2. For example Clyde shipbuilder William Denny noted in 1881 that the saving in metal achieved by substituting steel for iron would be greater for sail than steam, 'owing to the greater amount of material employed structurally therein'. 'On the economical advantages of steel shipbuilding', *Journal of Iron and Steel Institute* (1881), p54.

3. The barge *Trial*, built by John Wilkinson of Coalbrookdale in 1787, is one of the earliest recorded examples.

4. E K Chatterton, *Sailing Ships: The Story of their Development from the Earliest Times to the Present Day*, (London 1909), p259.

5. For example, W White *A Manual of Naval Architecture*, (London 1877); E J Reed, *Shipbuilding in Iron and Steel* (London 1869).

6. J Grantham, *Iron as a Material for Shipbuilding*, being a *Communication to the Polytechnic Society of Liverpool* (London 1842).

7. Cited in D MacGregor, *Fast Sailing Ships: Their Design and Construction, 1775-1875* (Lymington 1973), p143.

The advent of iron and then steel allowed sailing ship hulls to be built longer without the traditional concern about 'hogging'. The longer hull required more masts if individual sails were not to become too big to handle, and had the additional benefit that the overall height of the masts could be kept down, reducing the risk of dismasting. The first four-masted ship of the period was the County of Peebles *of 1614 tons net, built by Barclay, Curle in 1875. This is the original sail plan of her sister, The* County of Cromarty. *(By courtesy of David MacGregor)*

its strength relative to wood. Iron possesses greater powers of resistance in all directions. Wood is very resistant in the direction of the grain but much less so across it. Wooden ships consisted of many interdependent parts which meant that weakness in one or the working loose of several parts might endanger the entire structure. Reed especially pointed to the superior longitudinal strength of iron vessels and this became a factor of increased importance as vessels became longer and narrower in the second half of the century. Already by the 1860s iron vessels were being built with a length eight or nine times their beam. A wooden vessel with a multiple greater than six might struggle to carry a heavy cargo, experiencing a tendency to 'hog' (an arching caused by the less buoyant ends falling in relation to the middle body) or its opposite, 'sagging'.[8] The survival rate among shipwrecked iron vessels was clear testimony to their greater strength. The most celebrated case occurred when the SS *Great Britain* went ashore off the Irish coast at Dundrum Bay in September 1846. When she was finally towed off nearly a year later she remained in good condition and able to float. Iron vessels were also less susceptible to fire and to breaking up while at sea, thus confirming the claim that they combined strength with safety. However, contemporary opinion was not unanimously of the view that iron was stronger. Charles Lamport, a keen advocate of composites, argued in 1864 that, weight for weight, any shipbuilding wood was stronger than iron. He calculated that the tensile capacity of teak was 6.74 tons per square inch with a weight of 47lb per cubic foot. The corresponding figures for iron were 22 and 486 suggesting that, weight for weight, teak was three times stronger than iron.[9] Grantham retorted that the critical factor lay in the different modes of construction, 'the iron ship becomes one ho-mogeneous mass, the wooden ship is composed of a thousand parts, imperfectly united'.[10]

In the fighting navies the strength of vessels in resisting attack was particularly important. The development of shellfire in place of solid shot by French General H J Paixhans from 1822 exposed the vulnerability of wooden vessels.[11] However, firing tests conducted on an iron vessel at Woolwich in 1840 indicated the inadequacy of the alternative material as well. This together with a further eight experiments convinced the Admiralty that iron was not suitable for warships, with the result that the incoming Whig government of 1846 decided that four iron frigates ordered by the previous administration be converted into troopships.[12] The major changes occurred during the Crimean War when the French successfully used armoured floating batteries. In 1858 the French combined iron plates with a wooden structure, thereby creating the *Gloire*, the first seagoing armoured warship. The British responded with the iron-hulled armoured frigate *Warrior*, two years later. However, the details of these events go beyond our story since by this time fighting navies had become predominantly steam-driven.[13]

Irrespective of the relative strengths of wood and iron, Grantham was able to observe that a much smaller volume of iron was required to build a vessel, thus yielding a significant saving in cargo space and material costs. He suggested that for a wooden sailing vessel stowing 200 tons, its iron equivalent could carry 250.[14] The gain of iron over wood in cargo capacity varied according to the type of wood used. George Moorsom, famous for his contribution to changing tonnage laws in mid-Victorian Britain, looked at vessels of 200, 500 and 1000 tons and calculated that the saving in cargo space for an iron vessel compared with an oak one was 14 to 18.6 per cent and compared with a fir one 21.5

to 28.6 per cent.[15] Charles Palmer drew attention to a substantial saving in weight, believing the iron sailing vessel to weigh 35 per cent less than the wooden one.[16] Based on evidence collected by the 1891 Commission on Measurement of Tonnage, Maywald estimated that the average carrying capacity of a wooden vessel was 1.8 deadweight tons per registered ton but the figure rose to 2.2 for iron ships.[17] Thus evidence from the 1850s, 1860s and 1890s all points to a substantially improved carrying capacity with the substitution of iron for wood. Finally, it is worth emphasising that these benefits were gen-

8. J Grantham, 'The strength of iron ships', *Transactions of the Institution of Naval Architects* (hereinafter *TINA*) (1860), p65.

9. C Lamport, 'On wood and iron ships and the advantages of the combined system of wood and iron in shipbuilding', *TINA* V (1864), p291. Although W Fairbairn believed that the strength of iron to a crushing force was more than seven times as great as wood. *Treatise on Iron Shipbuilding: Its History and Progress* (London 1865), p81.

10. C Lamport, *op cit*, p314.

11. G Naish, 'Shipbuilding', in C Singer *et al* (eds), *A History of Technology. Vol IV: The Industrial Revolution, c1750-c1850* (Oxford 1958), pp587-8.

12. J P Baxter, *The Introduction of the Ironclad Warship* (Cambridge, Mass 1933), pp36, 39.

13. By the 1860s sailing vessels in the Royal Navy were largely confined to harbour duties. Sail was used as auxiliary power though even this began to be abandoned in the battle-line by the 1870s with the introduction of turret guns, the improved efficiency of engines and the shortcomings of sail power for heavily armoured vessels. E H H Archibald, *The Metal Fighting Ship in the Royal Navy* (London 1971). See *Steam, Steel and Shellfire* in this series. The continuing debate regarding armour plating can be found in the pages of *TINA*. For example, H Douglas, 'On iron ships and iron-cased ships', J D Samuda, 'On the construction of iron vessels of war iron-cased', both *TINA* II (1861), pp2-7 and 8-17 respectively.

14. A similar experiment for steam would yield a 50 per cent increase in capacity. J Grantham, *Iron Shipbuilding* (5th ed London 1868), pp97-8.

15. G Moorsom, *A Brief Review and Analyses of the Laws for the Admeasurement of Tonnage* (London 1852), pp71ff.

16. J F Clarke, 'The changeover from wood to iron shipbuilding', *Occasional Papers in the History of Science and Technology* 3 (1986), Newcastle-upon-Tyne Polytechnic, p37.

17. K Maywald, 'The construction cost and the value of the British merchant fleet, 1850-1938', *Scottish Journal of Political Economy* 3 (1956), p47.

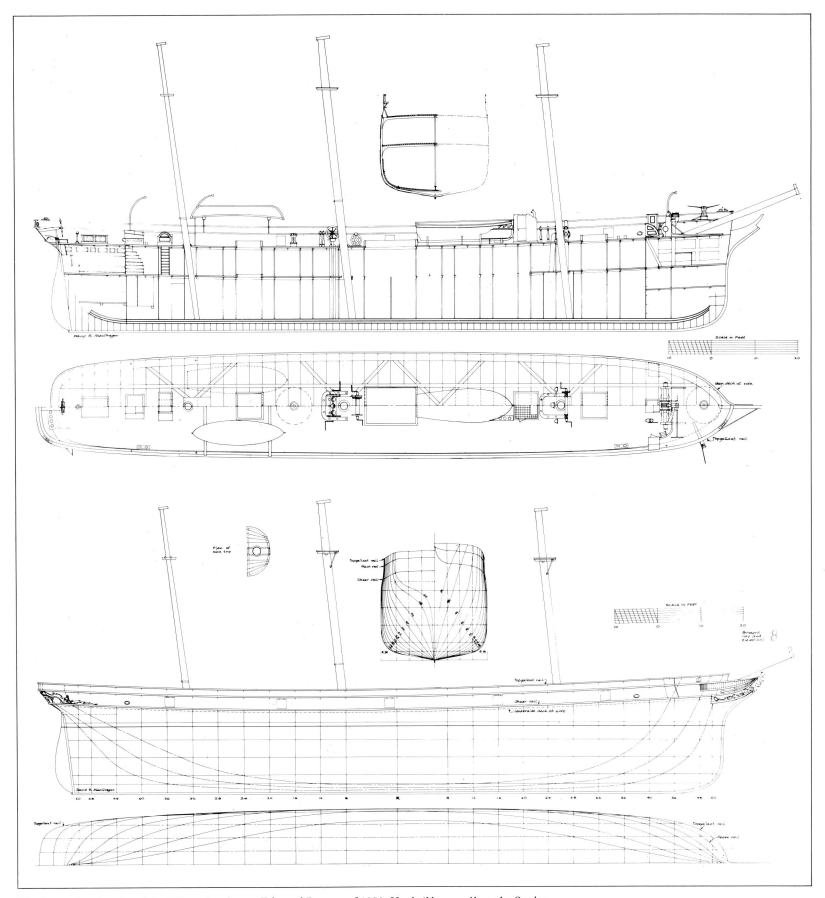

The lines and section plan of the 489-ton iron barque Edmund Preston *of 1858. Her builder was Alexander Stephen of Glasgow, an early convert to iron for the construction of sailing ships. The design shows some signs that the special properties of iron have not been fully appreciated (the tumblehome in the topside is unnecessary and a holdover from wooden construction). (By courtesy of David MacGregor)*

erally greatest for long and fine ships which were becoming more prominent in the mercantile marine of the second half of the nineteenth century. Indeed, a further benefit of iron over wood lies in its superior ability to be shaped to a particular design, a point not missed on London shipbuilder John Scott Russell who had once been a lecturer in geometry at Edinburgh University.[18] On the other hand, the use of cellular bottoms and bulkheads in some iron vessels to give greater rigidity and increased safety may have limited the gains in space and weight.

Finer designs for iron ships would have helped to increase vessel speeds although the trade-off between carrying capacity and speed was determined by the nature of individual trades. Given the malleable nature of wrought iron, builders attempted to achieve the best combination of both by building vessels of a spacious nature amidship but thinning to a sharp design in the bow. The output of vessels was determined not only by the trade-off between capacity and speed through the water but also time spent in port and dock. Iron sailing vessels were faced with the same loading and discharge facilities as wooden vessels. Where they may have benefited, however, was in the reduced amount of repair work generally required by iron vessels.[19] This, of course, meant a saving in both cost and time. Against this, it must be remembered that some repairs of a wooden vessel could be undertaken by the carpenter while she was on a passage or during loading and unloading in port. Repairs to iron vessels most often required docking.

One aspect of the upkeep of iron vessels, however, featured prominently in contemporary debates about their suitability. Iron hulls were highly susceptible to coatings of weeds and shells, particularly when travelling through tropical waters or when remaining in the same place for extended periods of time. Grantham believed that, 'both the effect and the ultimate consequences are greatly exaggerated'.[20] Not surprisingly, iron shipbuilders were quick to play down the consequences. Palmer believed that it only cost £100 annually to clean and repaint an iron hull, while Stephen put the figure at £70 to treat

a 900-ton vessel.[21] Peninsular & Oriental, on the other hand, claimed that it cost £70,000 to clean the hulls of their fleet.[22] The cost of marine fouling was not only to be measured in the time and cost of docking. One historian has estimated that moderate fouling can mean ten per cent more energy is required to drive a ship.[23] For a sailing ship, this implies a loss of speed of about 9 per cent. Lamport, speaking to the Institution of Naval Architects in 1864, was quick to draw attention to the extent and cost of this speed loss. He referred to a recent edition of the *Mercantile Shipping Gazette* and noted that of seven vessels overdue in Britain from China, six were built of iron. Rhetorically, he concluded, 'Will any gentleman tell me that an iron ship can be cheap, can be profitable, if she runs the risk of being from two to three months overdue?'[24]

One possible solution to the problem of marine fouling was to coat the iron hull with a paint which would prevent or at least mitigate the process. Many mixtures were tried and tested, particularly paints with a significant lead content. In 1863 W Hay, a chemist and lecturer at the Royal Naval College at Portsmouth, discussed his oxide of copper and explained how it would solve the problem.[25] T B Daft advocated a more flush arrangement of plates in order to reduce the water erosion on surfaces coated with antifouling paints.[26] Fouling, however, remained a problem for metal vessels well beyond the transition period. The problem was a comparatively manageable one and insufficient to challenge the clear superiority of iron in other respects. The expansion of docking facilities in many ports eased the problem of the treatment of fouling.

One of the ways in which marine fouling was overcome for wooden vessels was to fix a copper sheathing to the outside of the hull. However, it was soon established that this was not applicable to iron vessels because of the galvanic reaction between the two metals. One solution was to add timber planks around the metal frame, on top of which could be attached the copper sheathing. Thus, the timber would separate the two metals. In this idea lay one of the main justifications for the construction of composite vessels. In the Royal Navy the use of zinc sheathing was more common. There was no reaction between the two metals and, indeed, the iron stimulated the zinc to exfoliate more rapidly. Another proposal was to place a layer of bitumen between the iron hull and the copper sheathing, although scepticism centred around the risk of

18. A M Robb, 'Shipbuilding', in C Singer *et al*, *A History of Technology, Vol V. The Late Nineteenth Century, c1850-1900* (Oxford 1958), pp365-6.

19. C K Harley, 'The shift from sailing ships to steamships, 1850-90: a study in technological change and its diffusion', in D N McCloskey (ed), *Essays on a Mature Economy: Britain after 1840* (London 1970), pp226-7 claims that iron sailing vessels built in the United States in the 1880s required, 'almost no outlay for repairs during the first twelve years of their existence'.

20. J Grantham, *Iron Shipbuilding*, pp146-7.

21. J F Clarke, *op cit*, p43; D MacGregor, *op cit*, p144.

22. J F Clarke, *op cit*, p43.

23. F M Walker, *Song of the Clyde, A History of Clyde Shipbuilding* (Cambridge 1984), p42.

24. C Lamport, *op cit*, p314.

25. W J Hay, 'On the protection of iron ships from oxidation and fouling', *TINA* IV (1863), pp149-62.

26. T B Daft, 'The construction of iron ships and sheathing the same', *TINA* VI (1865), p146.

One advantage that wooden ships possessed over those with metal hulls was in the matter of protection against fouling. Wooden hulls could be covered with copper (or 'yellow metal' to be more precise), and between dockings this could be cleaned by the process of careening, by which the ship was hove down to expose one side of the underwater hull and then the other. This photo depicts a late occurrence of this operation, at Colon in 1921; the ship is the American barque C D Bryant, *a wooden ship built in 1878. (CMP)*

Initially, fears of the effects of the material on sensitive cargoes kept iron-hulled vessels out of some trades, but these had been largely overcome by 1875 when the Salamis *was built. The design of this extreme clipper was supposedly derived from the famous* Thermopylae, *and she was intended for a triangular trade, outward bound to Australia, then to China and home with a tea cargo.* (CMP)

such as sugar, might damage or corrode the iron plates. Periodic rinsing of the cargo decks combined with improved ventilation provided solutions to these problems.

The low quality of iron and poor construction of some early iron vessels was noted by contemporaries.[28] This 'boat' iron necessitated that only small plates be used. The iron passenger barge *Vulcan* was built in 1819 from plates only 24in wide. By the 1860s much larger plates in the region of 16ft width were being used, reflecting their improved quality and enabling substantial savings in labour and materials.[29] The Royal Commission on Unseaworthy Ships in 1873, however, still found evidence of poor construction methods and sub-standard iron.[30] The more general question emanating from this issue is that of comparative durability. Supporters of iron shipbuilding like Grantham were in no doubt that iron vessels would prove more durable by, 'a long period'.[31] While he was proved correct, his estimate of a thirteen-year lifespan for wooden vessels was probably an underestimate. In the Pacific grain trade iron and steel hulls proved twice as durable as wooden ones, being liable neither to dry rot nor to the risk of the working loose of their fastenings on this physically demanding route.[32] In fact an answer to this question could only really be known once a significant number of iron vessels had survived for twenty years or more and by this time the debate had already been won on other grounds.

27. C W Lancaster, 'On the preservation of the bottoms of iron ships', *TINA* III (1862), pp178-9.

28. For example, E J Reed, 'On certain cases of weaknesses in iron ships', *TINA* VIII (1867), p36, gave an example of a new 1200-ton ship that had forty-two leaking rivets after returning from India on its maiden voyage. Attempts to replace the rivets and improve the brackets failed and led to legal action against the repairers. H H West, 'On the quality of materials used in shipbuilding', *TINA* XXIII (1882), pp163-7, advocated systematic testing by iron manufacturers.

29. F M Walker, 'Precision construction: iron's contribution to modern shipbuilding', in J Lang (ed), *Metals and the Sea* (London 1990), p27.

30. 'Royal Commission on Unseaworthy Ships', Vol 1, British Parliamentary Papers XXXVI (1873) including questions 7927, 7929 and 9420.

31. J Grantham, *Iron Shipbuilding*, p102.

32. J G B Hutchins, *The American Maritime Industries and Public Policy, 1789-1914* (Cambridge, Mass 1941), pp421-3.

part of the bitumen breaking away during bad weather.[27]

The other shortcomings of iron vessels proved less intractable. The hammering and vibration experienced by a ship under construction was responsible for the development of a permanent and complex magnetic field. It took a series of shipping disasters to make clear the serious deviation to compass readings thereby caused. The Admiralty Compass Committee, Sir George Airy and Sir William Thomson (Lord Kelvin) between them found appropriate solutions. The effects were neutralised by placing soft iron spheres on either side of the compass and Flinders bars at its base. Another problem in iron ships was the effects of 'sweating' and bilge water effluvia upon cargoes such as coffee and tea. Conversely, it was feared that some cargoes,

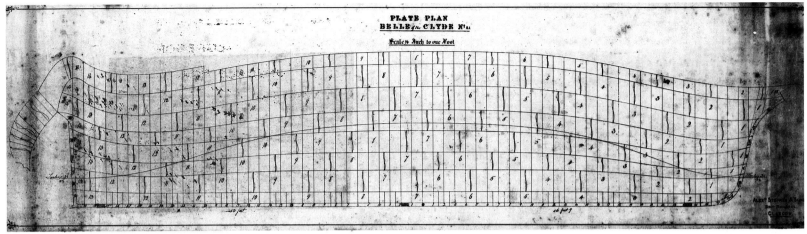

The plating expansion of the small brig Belle of the Clyde, *built by Alexander Stephen in 1865. Larger and better quality iron plates were available from the 1860s, producing labour and materials savings that made even comparatively small iron ships viable.* (By courtesy of David MacGregor)

It was mentioned above that composite vessels were viewed as a possible solution to the problem of marine fouling of iron vessels. There were a number of different types of composites built, not all of which were designed to address this particular problem. Composite construction had its advocates. G L Abegg, after visiting various shipbuilding centres, reported to the Institution of Naval Architects in 1864 that the com-

posite possessed a number of advantages over iron or wood vessels: it was as strong as iron, cheaper, nearly as light and required less docking. At the same time it was stronger, more durable and lighter than wood and required fewer repairs.[33] For others, though, it was, 'an unsatisfactory compromise' and 'the two materials were so widely different in character as to produce by their union a source of weakness of a most unsatisfactory descripton'.[34] The basic assumption behind the advocates of composites was that the superiority of iron over wood was only established in certain respects and not in others. However, by the 1870s it was clear that iron was

superior to wood in almost all respects, excepting the continued problem of marine fouling. To build vessels partly of both materials was in-

The internal profile and deck plan of the Belle of the Clyde, *200 tons net. This ship was built for the palm oil trade to the Gulf of Guinea, which required speed and the brig carried a lofty sail plan which included skysails.* (By courtesy of David MacGregor)

33. G L Abegg, 'On the combined system of wood and iron in shipbuilding', *TINA* V (1864), pp304-10.

34. Charles Palmer quoted in J F Clarke, *op cit*, p56; W Fairbairn, *op cit*, ppix-x.

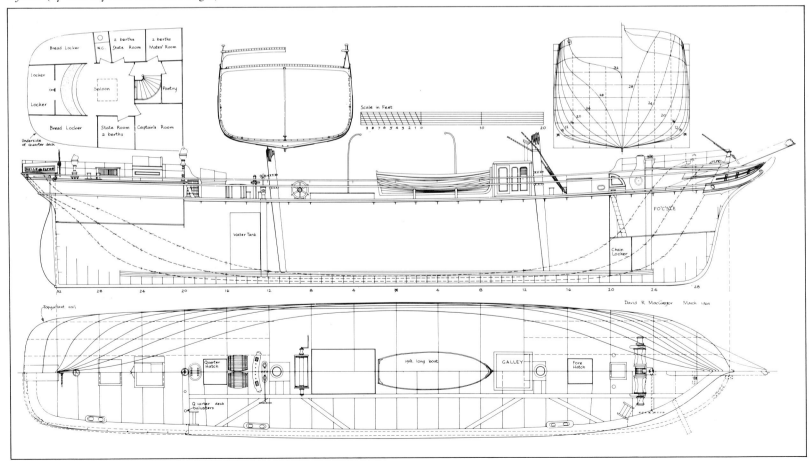

Steel possessed similar weight advantages over iron as the latter did over wood: it was calculated that an iron ships hull might take up nearly 50 per cent of its gross tonnage, whereas a steel vessel would be nearer 40 per cent. Added to its greater strength, this advantage encouraged ever larger steel ships. A typical end-of-century example of this development is the four-masted barque Brilliant, of 3609 net tons, built by Russell & Co, Port Glasgow, in 1901 for Anglo-American Oil for the case oil trade. (CMP)

deed an unsatisfactory compromise because it minimised the efficiency gains of the new material particularly in terms of carrying capacity, strength, durability, repair costs and design potential. Composites never formed a significant part of the mercantile marine and by the 1870s their day was clearly over.

Many of the features which accounted for the superiority of iron over wood also serve to explain the former's supersession by steel, particularly strength, lightness, stowage capacity and safety. In addition, since it could be worked on while cold this saved on fuel and furnace costs and avoided the risk of it becoming brittle from cooling too quickly.[35] With a carbon content in the region of 0.1 to 1.7 per cent, mild steel fell between wrought iron with virtually no carbon and cast iron with 3 to 4.5 per cent. The intention, therefore, was that it should possess the hardness of cast and the malleability of wrought iron. Its tensile and ductile characteristics are particularly noteworthy. Grantham observed that the tensile strength of best steel was 35–40 tons per square inch compared with 22–4 for iron.[36] The safety implications of steel's greater ductility were noted by Martell; steel vessels were more likely than iron to distort on collision or grounding rather than break up. The benefits for both owner and insurer from salvage and repair were clear.[37] Sailing qualities and safety en route might also be improved. The elasticity of the construction material mitigated the more violent impact with the sea and the consequent slowness to rise up on the waves.[38] The use of steel rivets also added local strength around the vessel.[39]

Martell also emphasised the lightness of steel ships. He gave an example of an iron sailing ship of 1700 gross registered tons which took about 840 tons of iron to build while the same vessel built of steel would require only about 680 tons. This weight saving of nearly 20 per cent was questioned by Reed, who noted that his experience suggested a saving more like 13 or 14 per cent.[40] Either figure suggests a substantial deadweight saving, providing more scope for heavier cargoes. Maywald's comparison of the average carrying capacity of wood and iron was extended to include steel: 2.2 deadweight tons per registered ton for iron compared with 2.7 for steel.[41]

The main argument used against steel in its

35. T A Rochussen, 'Treatment of steel plates in the shipbuilder's yard', *TINA* IX (1868), pp1-9.

36. J Grantham, *Iron Shipbuilding*, p243.

37. B Martell, 'A brief review of the progress of mild steel and the results of eight years' experience of its use for shipbuilding purposes', *TINA* XXVII (1886), pp60-1.

38. T A Rochussen, 'On the application of steel to the construction of ships', *TINA* VII (1866), pp57-8.

39. See the views of R Knight, *The Practical Boilermaker, Iron-Shipbuilder and Mast Maker* (London 1890).

40. B Martell, 'On steel for shipbuilding', *TINA* XIX (1878), pp9, 27. William Denny was of a similar sceptical view, *op cit*, p54.

41. Maywald, *op cit*, p47.

Figure 3/1: Sailing tonnage of national fleets, 1886

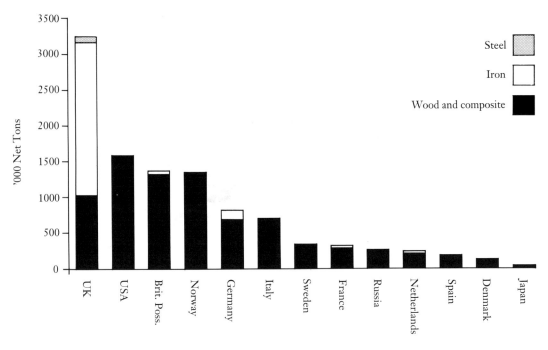

Source: Lloyd's Universal Register, *1886 (London 1886); Palmer, 'British shipping industry', p96.*

isting stock of tonnage and therefore it may be many years after the new material is dominant in the shipyard before the majority of the national fleet consists of metal vessels. Indeed, some shipowners deliberately pursued a policy of buying cheaply secondhand vessels of the obsolete technology. Figure 3/1 indicates that in 1886 the fleet of sailing vessels owned in the UK was double that of any other country. It also shows clearly that the vast majority of iron tonnage was owned in Britain, a natural result of British domination of shipbuilding in iron. Within about a year steel superseded iron as the principal building material for sailing vessels and yet only a small fraction of the existing British fleet was built of steel. Twenty-four years later with the rapid adoption of steam shipping in Britain her diminishing sailing fleet had been surpassed by that of the USA (Figure 3/2). Steel and iron ships dominated the British sailing fleet by this time but had made only a small impact upon American owners. The sailing fleets of France and Germany were predominantly built of steel whilst iron was of great importance in Norway and Italy.

Since we are concerned with the changing technology of the ship, however, it would be ap-

early years and delaying its widespread adoption was its inconsistent quality. The main problem concerned the use of steel made by the Bessemer process from the late 1850s, the carbon content and tensile strength of which were insufficiently specified. Barnaby, admittedly not among the supporters of metal in shipbuilding, exclaimed, 'the uncertainties and treacheries of Bessemer steel are such that it requires all the care which is bestowed upon it at L'Orient to avoid failure'.[42] The labour intensive methods used at the French naval dockyard were designed to avoid ruptures to the steel. The production of steel by the Bessemer process took little more than about 20 minutes. Thus, there was little or no opportunity for sample analysis and other forms of quality control in the process. The introduction of the longer Siemens-Martin process in the mid-1860s provided a solution to this problem and by the end of the following decade the basic process successfully reduced the level of impurities in the form of phosphorus.[43] Lloyds had become increasingly sceptical about Bessemer steel but it was not until 1900, shortly after its inventor's demise, that they eventually ended recognition of its use in shipbuilding.

Spatial diffusion of the metal sailing ship

In examining the spatial diffusion of the transition from wood to metal in sailing ships, there are two possible approaches. From the perspec-

tive of the shipbuilder, the transition occurs as vessels under construction are built of the new material. For the shipowner, however, the transition may occur at a much later stage. New builds constitute around five per cent of the ex-

42. N Barnaby, 'On iron and steel for shipbuilding', *TINA* XVI (1875), p135.

43. T Walton, *Steel Ships, Their Construction and Maintenance* (London 1950), p4.

Figure 3/2: Sailing tonnage of national fleets, 1910

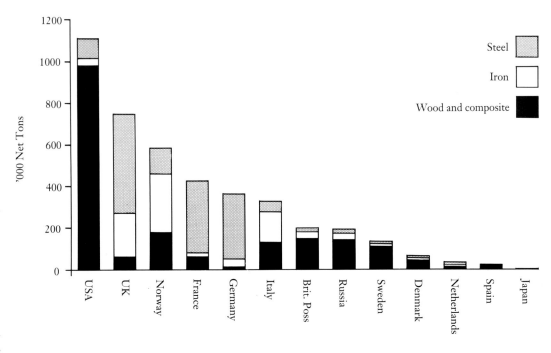

Source: Lloyd's Universal Register, *1910 (London 1910); Palmer, 'British shipping industry', p97.*

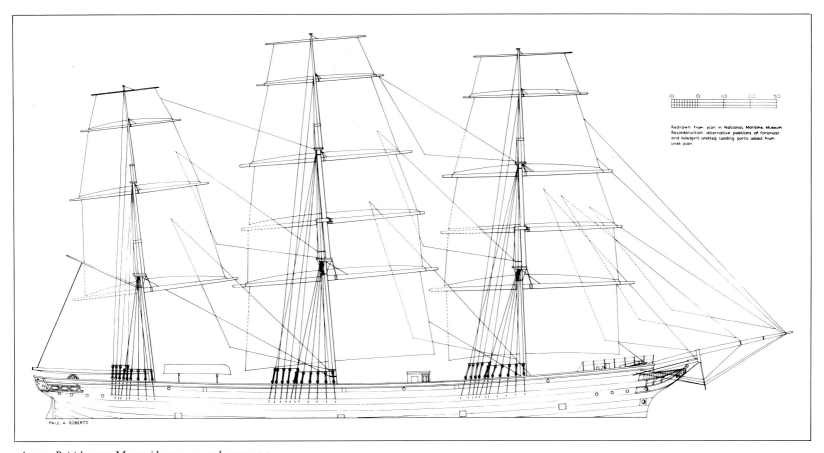

PAUL A ROBERTS

Among British ports Merseyside was an early convert to iron construction, and also experimented with composite building. This sail plan represents the Aphrodita, *a 1601-ton full rigged ship, built of iron in 1858 by Josiah Jones of Liverpool. The ship was long and full bodied, and in many ways foreshadowed the big iron and steel vessels for bulk trades built later in the century.* (By courtesy of David MacGregor)

propriate to concentrate upon the transition process in the shipyards, although noting that some of the pressure for change came from the offices of shipowners. While much contemporary data collection and historical comment has focused upon the transition from sail to steam, we do have good material on the wood to metal changeover in sail for several of the major shipbuilding countries. In particular, the discussion will centre upon Britain as the dominant shipbuilding country and the one that most clearly experienced a transitionary phase in sailing ship construction material.

Several builders began to produce iron vessels from the 1830s although by 1844 a total of only seven iron steamers and eleven sailing vessels had been launched.[44] By 1853 a Lloyds Register visitation committee was impressed by 'the rapidity with which the substitution of iron for wood in shipbuilding is progressing'.[45] Two years later Lloyds Register set out its first 'Rules for iron ships' although these amounted to little more than some general guidelines involving,

for example, the thickness of plates and the substance of frames.[46] It was also in this decade that larger iron sailing vessels began to be built and made their appearance in ocean trades including the tea trade, the East Indian spice trade and the carriage of wool from Australia.[47] Nonetheless, the number of large iron sailing vessels built in the 1850s was limited to little more than fifty.[48]

Composite construction was also a feature of the 1850s. *Excelsior*, built by John Jordan at Liverpool in 1850, is generally regarded as the first composite although several similar style vessels had been built in the previous two decades. Alexander Stephen Jr was active in promoting composites, particularly through his influence with Lloyds which led to them according such vessels high ratings and in 1867 issuing rules for the construction of composites.[49] The total output of composites was quite small, thus questioning the notion that they represented a separate stage in the transition process between wood and metal.[50] However, for a short period they represented a significant proportion of total output at several of the major centres of sailing ship construction. For example 26 per cent of sailing ship output on Clydeside in 1866 consisted of composite vessels. They were also of substantial importance for particular trades and vessel types; many tea clippers built in the 1860s were composites. In addition, the discussions cited in the first section of this paper, and the

fact that their main period of building occurred during the critical years for the supersession of wood by iron for British sailing vessels, suggests that, for a short period in the later 1860s, they were considered by some owners and builders a genuine alternative to wood.[51]

It was in the 1860s that the building of iron sailing vessels proceeded on a large scale with particular booms in 1864 and 1869. Figure 3/3

44. D F Clarke, *op cit*, p26.

45. D MacGregor, *op cit*, p144.

46. They were revised in 1857 and 1863. Lloyds first surveyed an iron vessel in 1836, the ketch *Goliath*. Early classifications were without a letter and, though this changed in 1844, A1 status was only granted for six years and depended upon an annual survey.

47. Although R V Jackson, 'The decline of the wool clippers', *Great Circle* 2 (1980), p91 indicates that the main transition to iron sail in the Sydney wool trade occurred in the 1870s.

48. See the list by MacGregor, *op cit*, pp146-7.

49. *Ibid*, pp156-60.

50. At their peak in 1866 composites represented 14 per cent of sailing ship output in Britain. B R Mitchell and P Deane, *Abstract of British Historical Statistics* (Cambridge 1988), pp223-4.

51. J F Clarke, *op cit*, p51 denies that composites were part of an intermediate phase in the transition from wood to iron, citing the fact that they were not built in large numbers until more than half of all new vessels were already built of iron. However, the comparison should be with new sailing vessels, not all new vessels, since the great majority of composites were sail.

Figure 3/3: UK sailing tonnage construction, 1850-1908

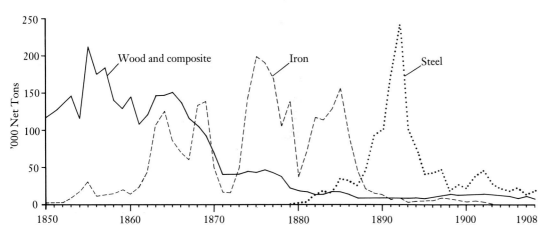

Note: Excludes foreign sales.
Source: B R Mitchell and P Deane, Abstract of British Historical Statistics (Cambridge 1988), pp223-4.

Figure 3/4: UK steam tonnage construction, 1850-1908

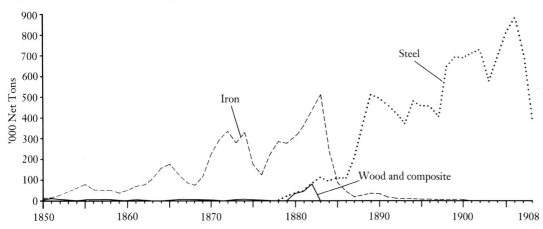

Note: Excludes foreign sales.
Source: B R Mitchell and P Deane, Abstract of British Historical Statistics (Cambridge 1988), pp223-4.

Table 3/1: Sailing tonnage construction at main UK ports, 1866-1913

Ports	Total sail output (All materials, in net tons)	Peak year	Main transition wood to iron	Main transition iron to steel
Clydeside	2,139,058	1892	pre-1866	1888
Sunderland	544,561	1869	1873	1888-1890
Liverpool	393,138	1869	pre-1866	1888-1891
London	230,369	1902	1866-1884	1893-1898
Southampton	147,246	1885	1876	1890
Belfast	146,692	1892	pre-1866	1882-1885
Stockton	136,847	1876	pre-1866	1891

Note: Final two columns exclude foreign sales before 1879.

Sources: 'Return of Number of Vessels Built at Each Port', *British Parliamentary Papers*, 1867-71; 'Annual Statement of Navigation and Shipping of UK', *British Parliamentary Papers*, 1872-1914.

shows that iron supersedes wood and composite building for British-built sailing ships by the early 1870s while the progression to steel occurs in the mid-1880s. Thus, the collapse of iron building is much more rapid than its original ascendancy. The sailing ship boom in the early 1890s mostly consisted of steel ships. Thereafter, sailing ship output declined rapidly with small volumes of tonnage being built of steel, wood and, least of all, iron. It was mainly for smaller river and coastal vessels that wood continued to be used as a shipbuilding material in the last couple of decades of the nineteenth century and, indeed, into the twentieth century.[52]

It is noteworthy to distinguish the transition process in construction material between sail and steam. The movement into iron vessels occurred much earlier in steam than sail. Relatively small volumes of wooden steamers were built because of the problems the material experienced in coping with heavy, vibrating engines (Figure 3/4). The advantages were less clear cut for sail or at least there was no major shortcoming in continuing to use wood and the transition process would be determined by comparative costs. By the time of the introduction of high quality steel, however, its benefits over iron had been established for both means of propulsion and therefore the transition occurred relatively simultaneously in the mid-1880s.

While J H Ritchie may have been of the opinion that, 'the port of Liverpool deserves the credit for having taken the lead in this great innovation', the earliest builders of iron vessels were to be found in a number of regions including the Lairds on Merseyside, Fairbairn on the Thames, Tod & MacGregor on Clydeside and Marshall in the northeast.[53] A comparatively comprehensive list of large iron sailing vessels built in the 1850s identifies Clydeside, Merseywide, Warrington, Newcastle and Hull as the main centres.[54] Even within the major building regions the picture varied somewhat between individual firms; on Clydeside Stephen 'settled to commence iron shipbuilding' in 1851 while Barclay, Curle continued mostly in wood until the following decade.[55]

Annual returns of trade and navigation submitted to Parliament each year on a port by port basis provide us with a more detailed picture of

52. B R Mitchell & P Deane, *op cit*, pp223-4 indicates the declining size of sailing vessels towards the end of the century.

53. J H Ritchie, 'Introduction to Lloyds revised rules', *TINA* IV (1863), p290. It is not easy to establish how many of these firms built sail as well as steam.

54. D MacGregor, *op cit*, pp146-7.

55. A M Robb, *op cit*, p350; D MacGregor, *Merchant Sailing Ships, 1850-75* (London 1984), p148.

One of the leading exponents of iron shipbuilding was John Laird whose Birkenhead shipyard built many of the earliest successful iron vessels. Engraving from the Illustrated London News *of 1861. (By courtesy of David MacGregor)*

the transition from the mid-1860s. Table 3/1 indicates the main centres of sailing ship construction in the UK between 1866 and the First World War. Clydeside, consisting of the shipbuilding centres of Glasgow, Port Glasgow and Greenock, was much the largest centre of shipbuilding. Table 3/1 and Figures 3/5–11 indicate that Clydeside, along with Liverpool, Belfast and Stockton, transferred comparatively early to iron construction. Sunderland followed suit by the early 1870s but the picture is somewhat more complex at Southampton and London. At London, iron supersedes wood gradually over the course of two decades to the mid-1880s. At Southampton a very sudden transition occurs in 1876 but by the mid-1890s wood is again the main building material. The figures for both London and Southampton, however, must be seen within the context of small, and in the latter case rapidly declining, volumes of output. Already in the mid-1860s the iron shipbuilding industry on the Thames was in trouble, with Samuda noting that many firms had collapsed.[56] The transition to steel at the main ports chiefly occurs between the mid-1880s and the early 1890s. Again, the transition in London is a little later, occurring in the mid-1890s. Significant

56. S Pollard, 'The decline of shipbuilding on the Thames', *Economic History Review* 2nd ser, 3 (1950), p84.

Figure 3/5: Clydeside sailing tonnage construction, 1866-1913

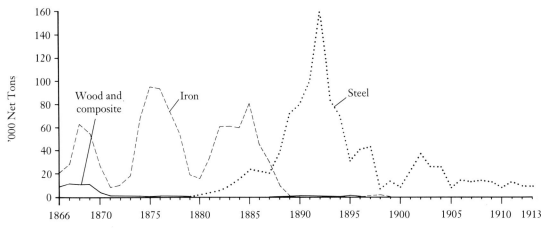

Note: Excludes foreign sales before 1879.
Source: See Table 3/1.

Figure 3/6: Sunderland sailing tonnage construction, 1866-1913

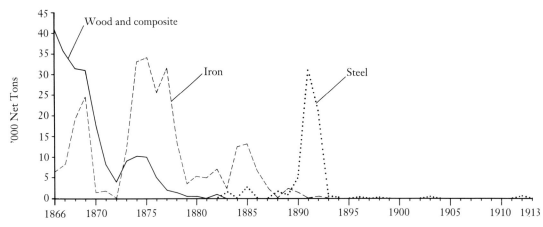

Note: Excludes foreign sales before 1879.
Source: See Table 3/1.

Figure 3/7: Liverpool sailing tonnage construction, 1866-1913

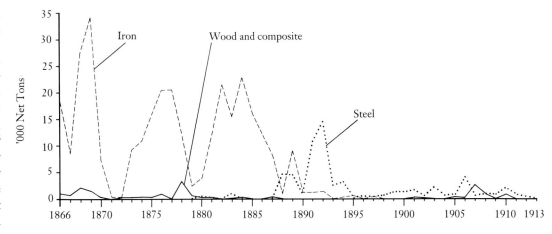

Note: Excludes foreign sales before 1879.
Source: See Table 3/1.

Figure 3/8: London sailing tonnage construction, 1866-1913

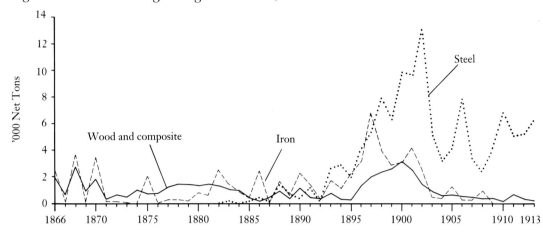

Note: Excludes foreign sales before 1879.
Source: See Table 3/1.

Figure 3/9: Southampton sailing tonnage construction, 1866-1913

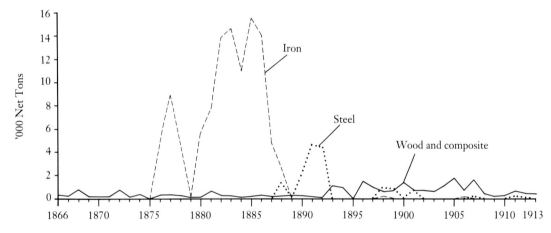

Note: Excludes foreign sales before 1879.
Source: See Table 3/1.

Figure 3/10: Belfast sailing tonnage construction, 1866-1913

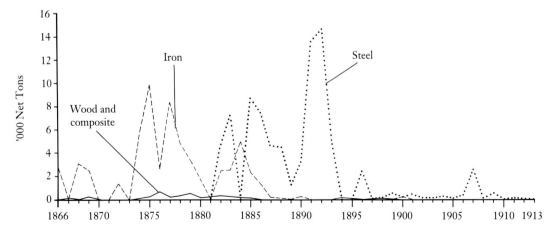

Note: Excludes foreign sales before 1879.
Source: See Table 3/1.

numbers of steel sailing ships were only produced at Southampton in the early 1890s. Clydeside was particularly dominant in the 1892 boom. Russell & Co of Port Glasgow was the main builder of large capacious steel sailing vessels, launching between twenty and thirty a year in the quinquennium from 1888.[57] Table 3/2 shows the geographical dispersion of composite building in Britain between 1866 and 1872. The picture is of the same ports dominating the building of composites and with the same order of rank. Bilbe & Perry of Rotherhithe built one of the earliest composites with the *Red Riding Hood* in 1857 but by the mid-1860s the northern yards dominated output.[58] Between 1862 and 1876 Stephens launched twenty-eight sailing vessels.[59]

In the United States a few metal sailing vessels were built in the 1870s and 1880s to be followed by greater numbers in the following two decades. Although almost as many metal as wooden sailing vessels were built in 1897 this was as close as the two sectors came and there was never a true transitionary phase in the declining years of US shipbuilding up to 1914. This was the peak year for metal sailing vessels but the 31,424 tons barely compares with the 1890s peak year for wooden sail of 144,079 in 1891. Many large wooden and steel barques in the range of 3000 tons were built for the Californian grain trade. When the opening of the Panama Canal in 1912 finally ended this trade it was soon to be followed by a reversion to the construction of wooden sailing ships during the First World War. Many wooden shipyards were reopened and others newly established.[60] In spite of a thriving industry in the construction of wooden sailing ships in mid nineteenth-century Canada there never developed an iron sailing ship industry. Abortive attempts were made to establish a steel shipbuilding industry at Quebec, Yarmouth, St John and Halifax but only one steel sailing vessel was ever built in Canada. Nor did Canadian shipowners move into the ownership of steel sailing vessels.[61]

Some of the earliest American iron vessels were built in Philadelphia while a series of small

57. B Lubbock, *The Last of the Windjammers* (2nd edn, Glasgow 1935), p18.

58. B Lubbock, *The Colonial Clippers* (Glasgow 1948), p124.

59. D MacGregor, *Merchant Sailing Ships, 1850-75* p132. The majority of composites were sailing vessels although Stephens also launched two steamers and three auxiliaries to composite design over the same period.

60. R W Kelly and F J Allen, *The Shipbuilding Industry* (Cambridge, Mass 1918), pp6-7.

61. R Ommer, 'The decline of the eastern Canadian shipping industry, 1880-95'. *Journal of Transport History*, 3rd ser, 5, 1 (1984), p40; F W Wallace, *Wooden Ships and Iron Men* (London 1924), p322.

iron sailing vessels and composites was built by E Woodall & Co of Baltimore in the 1870s for use on coastal surveys.[62] By the 1880s and 1890s, however, the construction of sailing ships had become concentrated mostly upon a handful of yards capable of handling large vessels in a few towns of New England and the Maritimes. These centres were particularly located at Bath, Thomaston, Rockport and Kennebunkport. Of particular note was the firm of E & A Sewall of Bath which built a series of large four-masted wooden vessels between 1889 and 1892. In 1894 the firm also built the *Roanoke* of English steel together with another eight steel sailing vessels, 1899–1901.[63]

In mainland Europe there was limited evidence of a transition from wood to metal in sailing ship construction: some saw their industry collapse in the face of the changing technology; others sought to establish an industry on the basis of the new developments. In Finland and the Scandinavian countries few iron sailing vessels were built. The shipbuilding industries of these countries were mostly in decline in the last quarter of the nineteenth century. A few larger yards survived in Norway by turning to the construction of iron sailing ships but most, especially the small yards in the south of the country, ceased building. In Sweden metal steamers were built by iron and engineering works such as Motala Verkstad although often this was only a temporary success. By 1890 the firm had collapsed. Keillers and Kockums, on the other hand, survived by diversifying out of shipbuilding as the prospects diminished. By 1897 only 4 per cent of sailing vessels under construction were of iron.[64] The German shipbuilding industry was of small proportions in the mid nineteenth century although the first iron sailing vessel, *Hoffnung*, was built in 1844 and a more substantial vessel, *Deutschland*, in 1858. The latter was built by the Hamburg shipyard Reiherstieg which produced another twenty or more such vessels up to 1875. Others changed to metal somewhat later. Joh C Tecklenborg Aktien-Gesellschaft built wooden sailing vessels until 1879 and then moved into iron sail and steam, including *Potosi*, a five-masted barque of 3854

Figure 3/11: Stockton sailing tonnage construction, 1866-1913

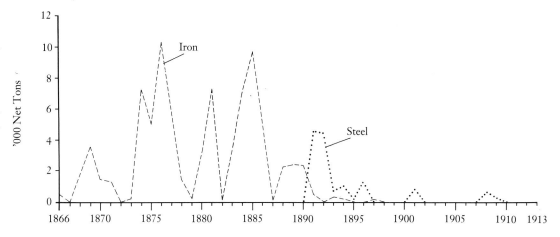

Note: Excludes foreign sales before 1879.
Source: See Table 3/1.

Figure 3/12: US sailing tonnage construction, 1880-1913

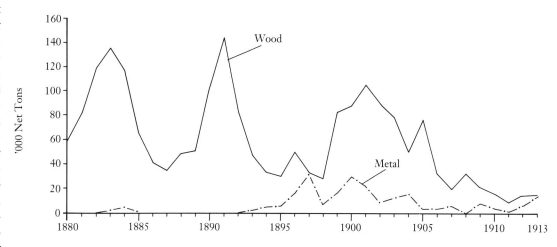

Sources: Smith and Brown, 'Shipyard Statistics' in Fassett (ed), Shipbuilding Business, p73; Historical Statistics of the United States, 1789-1945 (Washington DC 1949), p207.

Table 3/2 Composite sailing tonnage construction at main UK ports, 1866-1913

Ports	1866 Net Tons	1867 Net Tons	1868 Net Tons	1869 Net Tons	1870 Net Tons	1871 Net Tons	1872 Net Tons	Total 1866-1872 Net Tons
Clydeside	7657	8191	10,581	10,540	4131	176	28	41,304
Sunderland	6548	5572	3057	9137	3141	788	0	28,243
Liverpool	567	249	1117	0	0	0	160	2093
London	1747	299	643	692	824	0	0	4205
Southampton	0	82	0	0	0	31	0	113

Note: Excludes foreign sales.
Sources: See Table 3/1.

62. H Hall, *Report on the Shipbuilding Industry of the United States* (Washington DC 1884, reprinted London 1974), pp202, 2l4.

63. J G B Hutchins, *op cit*, pp378-9, 416-17.

64. M Fritz, 'Shipping in Sweden, 1850-1913', *Scandinavian Economic History Review* 28 (l980), p157; K Olsson, 'From warships to tankers, The Swedish shipbuilding industry, 1880-1939', in F Walker and A Slaven (eds), *European Shipbuilding* (London 1984), p64. On Norway see H Nordvik, 'The Norwegian shipbuilding industry: the transition from wood to steel, 1880-1980', in Walker and Slaven, *op cit*, pp194-204.

reason to suspect any strong prejudice against the new construction materials. This, however, must be distinguished from conservatism which is a rational act reflecting the varying levels of risk aversion amongst a cohort of entrepreneurs. Indeed, the early adoption of a new technology by a few when it remained inefficient and untried may be more of an irrational act. While Lairds may have been quicker than other Merseyside firms to build with iron, they were soon followed by their neighbours. The main pattern of diffusion was that iron and steel vessels were built first in those countries and ports where the cost advantages over the older technology was greatest. There was nothing irrational about

tons built in 1895. R C Rickmers made the transition yet later, not building its first iron vessel until 1890. Nonetheless, the ascendancy of the German shipbuilding industry in the last two or three decades of the century was based mainly upon steel steamers.[65] In France there was a slow drift to iron and steel sailing ships in a stagnant shipbuilding industry in the mid nineteenth century, a trend which was accelerated towards the end of the century. Some of the major Nantes yards, such as Gouin, Dubigeon and Jollet et Babin, were building iron and composite vessels from the 1870s.[66]

Explanations of the patterns of diffusion

In attempting to explain the pattern of diffusion of iron and steel in the construction of sailing ships, neither insufficient knowledge nor prejudice and inertia played a significant role.[67] The learning process was a remarkably short one: the current writer has demonstrated elsewhere that there were many vehicles for the international

transfer of new shipping technologies from Britain in the nineteenth century. These included direct observation of British ships in all the major ports of the world, overseas sales of new vessels, joint projects, visits to Britain including formal education, the assistance of consular officials and commercial agents and the activities of professional institutions including their publications.[68] If there was an absence of significant information asymmetries neither was there any

65. The information on Germany is taken from R Haack, 'The development of German shipbuilding', *Engineering Magazine* 17 (1899), pp729-42; D MacGregor, *Merchant Sailing Ships, 1850-75*, p11; D MacGregor, *Fast Sailing Ships*, p123.

66. D MacGregor, *Fast Sailing Ships*, p123.

67. Such a view is particularly associated with Joseph Schumpeter, see *The Theory of Economic Development*, (Cambridge, Mass 1934).

68. S Ville, 'Shipping industry technologies', in D J Jeremy (ed), *International Technology Transfer. Europe, Japan and the USA, 1700-1914* (Aldershot 1991), pp76-82.

One of very few steel four-masted barques built in the USA was the Arthur Sewall, *of 2919 tons gross, built by E & A Sewall of Bath, Maine, in 1899. The firm built its first steel vessel using plates imported from Britain in 1894, and the* Arthur Sewall *was one of eight steel sailing ships turned out by the yard in 1899-1901.* (CMP)

The German yard of R C Rickmers at Bremerhaven was a late convert to iron construction but graduated quickly to steel in the 1890s. One of the products of this period was the steel Mabel Rickmers *of 3250 dwt, built in 1898. She is seen here as the* Winterhude *off the Tyne some time before 1912. (By courtesy of David MacGregor)*

continuing to produce second best technology if this could still find a market and could be done more cheaply.

An alternative explanation of diffusion, consistent with this pattern, involves, 'a carefully specified model of competitive market behaviour'.[69] This sensibly takes account of both changing supply curves and the immobility of factors

69. C K Harley, 'On the persistence of old techniques: the case of North American wooden shipbuilding', *Journal of Economic History* 33 (1973), pp372-97.

One of the smallest of Alexander Stephens' iron sailing vessels was the barquentine Osburgha, *of 346 tons net, built in 1875. By this date metal fabrication so dominated Clydeside industry that it was already regarded as the norm for all but the smallest ships. (By courtesy of David MacGregor)*

"OSBURGHA" Nº 188

SCALE ¼ INCH TO A FOOT

Alexʳ Stephen & Sons.
ENGINEERS & SHIPBUILDERS
GLASGOW.
DRAWN Nº

of production and is couched largely in terms of the comparative costs of building sailing vessels by wood, iron and steel. If one distinguishes fixed from variable costs, it was probably the latter which proved more important. Opinions vary as to the costs of setting up a new iron shipyard or of converting from a wooden one. Iron shipyards tended to be both larger and require much more capital investment. Hall, in his report on American shipbuilding in 1884, suggested that many wooden sailing shipyards required less than $500 in fixed capital, helped by the fact that many workers provided their own hand tools. If the yard was steam-powered this figure might rise significantly to $15,000. However, an iron yard was likely to require a minimum of $60,000 of fixed capital.[70] The size of this investment was likely to affect the precise timing of their introduction and limit those with the capacity to build in iron. This may explain, as we saw earlier, why many of the early iron shipbuilders were already associated with the metal-

One of the final surge of British deep water sailing ships built in the 1890s, the four-masted barque Olivebank *was launched by Mackie & Thompson of Glasgow in 1892. This ship enjoyed a long career under a number of owners, finally coming to rest like so many others in the fleet of Gustaf Erikson. She was sunk by a mine in 1939. (CMP)*

lurgy industry where fixed capital ratios were high. Such a background may also have provided a pool of suitably qualified labour, although Hall regards this as less of a problem: 'a ship carpenter makes as good a man for the iron-ship yard as does the boilermaker, and with the aid of a very few machinists a wooden ship builder could transfer his whole work-force from wood to iron in six months.'[71]

The market had less impact upon the diffusion pattern. By the second half of the nineteenth century the market for ships had shifted away from its previously local base and had now become national and indeed international in scope. Thus owners from around the world were able to buy from ports where iron sailing vessels could be produced most cheaply. A modification from this general perspective, however, results from the impact of public policy in several countries which served to distort to some degree what was otherwise a free international market in ships.

With the development and expansion of the British iron and steel industry in the second half of the nineteenth century economies of scale and improved technology were responsible for a substantial secular decline in the cost of both materials for use in shipbuilding. Between 1856 and 1886 the price of iron ship plates in Britain

was declining at a rate of 3.7 per cent per annum which was reflected in declining vessel prices. At the same time, the scarcity of local supplies meant timber costs were probably rising as indeed they were in much of the USA and Canada.[72] The meeting point of the rising cost curve of timber and the falling one for iron appears to have occurred by about the 1860s in Britain. MacGregor believes that a price differential of 10–30s per ton in favour of iron vessels already existed by the late 1850s, while Hutchins suggests the discrepancy emerges during the 1860s, although Clarke's view is that there was little difference in price between the two materials by the end of the decade.[73] A complicating factor may have been the importation of cheaper Canadian, and after the repeal of the Navigation Laws in 1848, American, softwood vessels into Britain. In 1854 more than half of the vessels registered at Liverpool were Canadian-built. In spite of their supposed ephemerality many of these vessels proved reliable and profitable in the booming emigration trade to Australia in the

70. H Hall, *op cit*, p199.

71. *Ibid*, p198.

72. *Ibid*, pp377-381.

73. D MacGregor, *Fast Sailing Ships*, p143; J G B Hutchins, *op cit*, p401; J F Clarke, *op cit*, p49.

The advantages of iron and steel were not confined to the hull but also contributed to strengthening masts, yards and rigging. Masts and spars could be fabricated from tubular steel and many of the fittings were immeasurably stronger than their wood and hemp predecessors. This plate from a textbook of 1904 shows some of these fittings. (By courtesy of David MacGregor)

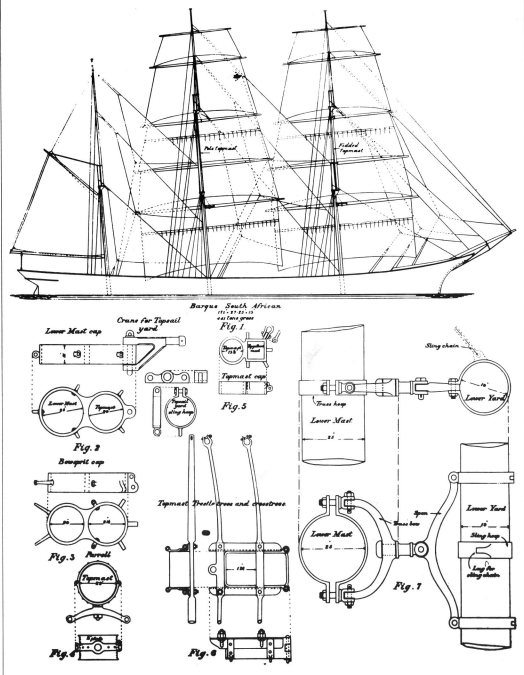

early 1850s and cost up to £10 per ton less than British vessels. The Black Ball Line bought a series of clippers from the yard of Donald McKay of Boston and relied heavily upon North American wooden sailing vessels before turning to iron ones built in Britain from the early 1860s.[74]

The evidence for the declining cost of steel in Britain is equally clear and quite dramatic: the price of ship steel in the early 1880s was only 20 per cent of its level in 1871. The ratio of the price of steel plates to those of iron declined in Scotland from 1.43 in 1880 to 1.06 in 1888–90.[75] The decision to build in steel, however, might be taken ahead of its price parity with iron because of the other perceived benefits for the owner. Martell gives an example in 1878 of an owner seeking a metal sailing ship of 1700 gross registered tons. In spite of the fact that the steel version would cost an extra £3000 (£25,000 total) he opted for this over iron, reckoning he would recoup the extra cost within two years.[76]

The spatial distribution of the adoption of iron in British shipbuilding is related closely to the existence of local iron and steel industries. Thus Clydeside and the northeast feature prominently. It is worth emphasising that it was the strength of the local iron and steel industries rather than simply indigenous supplies of metallic ores which was important. Although it was generally the initial existence of local ore supplies which led to the establishment of an iron and steel industry, these areas remained important centres of the heavy industries long after their ore supplies had become exhausted. In

74. M Stammers, *The Passage Makers* (Brighton 1978), pp1, 299–300, 361–4, 405.

75. J G B Hutchins, *op cit*, p404; McCloskey quoted in J F Clarke, 'The introduction of the use of mild steel into the shipbuilding and marine engineering industries', *Occasional Papers in the History of Science and Technology* 1 (1983), Newcastle-upon-Tyne Polytechnic, pp60–1. Also see K Maywald, *op cit*, p50.

76. B Martell, *op cit*, p9.

77. J Glover, 'On the decline of shipbuilding on the Thames', *Journal of the Statistical Society of London* 32 (1869), pp288–91 sees the difference in coal prices as the main advantage of the Clyde and Wear over the Thames.

78. In particular see S Ville (ed), *United Kingdom Shipbuilding in the Nineteenth Century. A Regional Perspective* (St John's, Newfoundland 1993).

79. J G B Hutchins, *op cit*, p414.

London the transition was delayed and involved only a small amount of tonnage because of the absence of a local iron and steel industry. The decision by Lloyds to tighten the rules on the quality of iron used in shipbuilding from 1855 reduced the permissible amount of scrap iron, thus exacerbating the problem for those areas lacking a local iron industry. The other major resource difference between the areas was their access to cheap coal, with London again at a disadvantage compared with Clydeside and the northeast.[77] Other factors, such as wages and land rents, play a role in explaining the significant changes in the regional location of British shipbuilding generally during the nineteenth

century and have been discussed in detail elsewhere.[78]

The belated and partial nature of the adoption of iron and steel in the construction of American sailing ships was attributed by one historian to the backwardness of iron builders, the high wage rates and the high cost of iron and steel.[79] Of these the third explanation probably possesses the greatest validity. If iron builders were backward this was no more than a reflection of the limited opportunity for the development of this form of production. Wage rates may have varied regionally but were presumably similar in iron and wooden yards. Wage rates were estimated at between 50 and 100 per cent higher than Britain

A typical British-built steel ship of the 1890s, the Dominion *of 2328 net tons, launched by Doxford & Sons at Sunderland in 1891 for W Thomas & Sons. Such vessels were the last deep water sailing ships built in any numbers in British yards before the steamship took over completely.* (CMP)

by 1900 and yet this did not prevent the production of either iron or wooden vessels because of protectionist policy in the United States.[80] In addition, American firms appear to have made effective use of labour-saving machinery. The cost differential between metal and wood in America was, however, significant. In 1884 Hall contrasted the cost of an iron vessel at $85–100 with that of a wooden one at $45–60.[81]

The high cost of iron and steel can be explained by a number of factors. The localisation of the iron and steel industry in Pittsburgh was unfavourable for the shipbuilding industry of the northeast coast of the country. The high price of steel was maintained by the steel trust operated by the dominant producer, US Steel Corporation. The lack of vertical integration between shipyards and steel producers put the trust in a powerful position. This extended to the Pittsburgh basing point system whereby shipbuilders

had to pay a phantom freight rate from Pittsburgh even when the steel was supplied by a seaboard mill. The power of the trust was reinforced by a protectionist policy which prevented yards from importing cheaper steel from Britain. Indeed, it was involved in 'dumping' practices so that foreign buyers could obtain American steel more cheaply than domestic shipyards. The tariff law of 1872 offered a slight concession in permitting some shipbuilding materials to be imported duty free. However, this had little practical effect because vessels built using such materials were not allowed to be deployed in coasting for more than two months per annum. This caused concern amongst potential customers who feared that their vessel might be inadvertently delayed on the coast. In 1894 the legislation was extended to all shipbuilding materials but with the same restriction. In 1909 the permissible time in coasting was extended to six months but by this time American steel was cheaper than British.[82]

Hutchins estimates that as early as the 1860s American wooden sailing vessels were becoming more expensive than British iron ships. The differential was significant by the late seventies and by 1900 he believes that American vessels cost

25 to 50 per cent more than British or German ones.[83] In a free international market, therefore, one would have expected the rapid decline of the American shipbuilding industry. The fact that America continued to build significant numbers of vessels owes much to a protectionist policy for ships as well as steel. This involved the restriction of American registry to domestically-built vessels and the exclusion of foreign operators from the American coastal trade.[84] This approach was part of an autarchist policy which perceived strategic benefits from the existence of a domestic shipbuilding industry. Not until 1914 was this policy mostly reversed, although restrictions on coasting extended beyond the First World War. The result, therefore, was to pro-

80. *Ibid*, p464.

81. H Hall, *op cit*, pp142-3.

82. This paragraph is taken largely from J G B Hutchins, *op cit*, pp464-7.

83. *Ibid*, pp401, 469; J G B Hutchins, 'History and development of shipbuilding, 1776-1944', in F G Fassett (ed), *The Shipbuilding Business in the United States of America* (New York 1948), p38.

84. Although an Act of 1852 admitted to the registry wrecked foreign vessels which had been repaired to the extent of three-quarters of their value.

vide a protected market for domestic shipbuilders. The benefit mainly went to wooden rather than iron sailing ship builders given the cost difference. However, some preferred metal because of its advantages over wood particularly in terms of its strength, durability and capaciousness. These were all key considerations in the demanding grain trade between the west coast of America and Europe via South America, which was the most important trade route for the country's sailing fleet by the later decades of the nineteenth century.

The geographical shift of shipbuilding within the United States meant that most metal sailing ships were built in New England. Within the protected American market regional cost differences mostly explain this movement. Most writers agree that it was variations in wage levels rather than material costs which were the main factor. Wage levels were reckoned to be higher in the expanding economies of New York and Boston. In contracting towns like Bath there were few alternative occupations and an unwill-

In France, government subsidy to French iron and steel shipbuilders and shipowners in the 1880s and 1890s stimulated the development of a fleet of large metal-hulled sailing ships, known as 'Bounty' ships. One of these, the four-masted barque Dunqerkue *of 5930 tonneaux, is shown here. She was built by Laporte & Co for A D Bordes, the leading owner of these ships. From* Le Yacht *of 26 December 1986.*
(By courtesy of David MacGregor)

ingness of an ageing shipyard workforce to move elsewhere for work. Although younger workers migrated, the remainder of the workforce was highly immobile. In other words, part of their wages had represented a quasi-rent which enabled firms to reduce their wage costs in the late nineteenth century.[85] In addition, New England was a low cost of living area, including land costs, and with little evidence of labour organisations which could have led to the unrest experienced in New York. The working day was also thought to be longer. Hutchins believes that wage costs in Maine were consequently 25 to 50 per cent lower than in other shipbuilding regions.[86] Unfortunately, historians have taken less time to estimate the relative cost of shipbuilding materials between the major shipbuilding regions. There is evidence to suggest that by the final decades of the nineteenth century dwindling timber supplies meant that New England was better supplied than further down the coast.[87] At the same time, the New England shipbuilding ports were furthest away from the centres of the American iron and steel industry. While regional variations in material costs were less significant to shipbuilding than wage discrepancies, it would appear that the locational shift in American shipbuilding took it into areas where the opportunity cost of metal shipbuilding was higher and thereby delayed its introduction on a large scale. By the time that these regional differences had been made insignificant by the falling price

of steel the American sailing ship industry was close to collapse.

One of the reasons for the reluctance of Americans to invest in new technology shipping was the movement of the country's economic orientation away from the Atlantic seaboard and overseas trade towards the expansion of domestic trade and industry. This was similarly the case for Canada, where investment in the late nineteenth century turned landwards into mining, manufacturing, insurance, banking, metallurgy and the railways.[88] Given the absence of protection for shipping and the high cost of iron and steel, 'it would have required an enormous effort and substantial subsidies to compete with British and European builders'.[89] Moreover, Canadian historians have correctly emphasised the important place of the wooden sailing ship within the economies of the Maritime Provinces. High input and output ratios with such industries as timber, sawmilling and merchanting made for low costs and help explain why, 'both the rise and the decline of shipping ... can be

85. In particular see C K Harley, *op cit*, pp383-4; J G B Hutchins, *op cit*, pp386-7.

86. J G B Hutchins, *op cit*, pp386-7.

87. *Ibid*, pp387-8.

88. R Ommer, *op cit*, p37.

89. E W Sager and L R Fischer, 'Atlantic Canada and the age of sail revisited', *Canadian Historical Review* 63 (1982), p148.

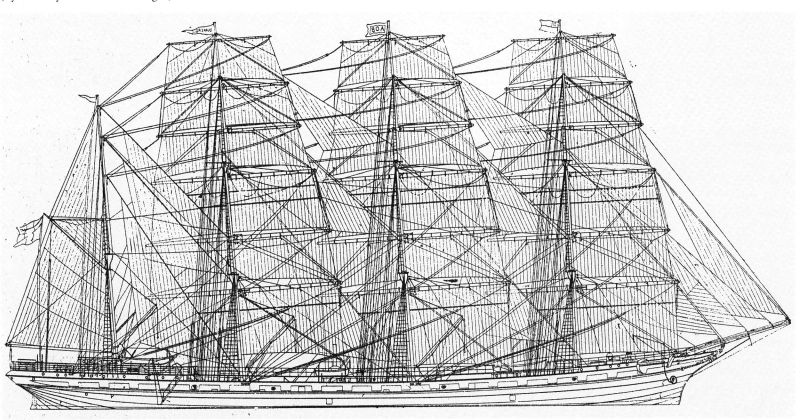

explained by the rise and relative decline of the staples.[90]

The failure of most European countries to build iron sailing ships in any significant numbers can be primarily attributed to their inability to compete with British overseas sales. In addition, the rapid technological change in British shipbuilding provided a large second market in comparatively cheap secondhand vessels. Ironically, it was generally those countries with the cheapest and most plentiful supplies of timber that also faced the highest iron and steel costs. This was particularly the case in Scandinavia. Norwegian and Finnish shipowners abandoned their local shipbuilding industry in the last two or three decades of the century and purchased new and secondhand vessels from Britain. For southern Norway, as for Canada, the vertical integration of wooden shipbuilding, forestry and saw milling hampered the adoption of iron. Shortages of finance for more capital intensive iron shipyards may also have been a factor in ru-

The five-masted barque France, *one of the subsidised 'bounty' ships of that country. She was built of steel by Hendersons of Glasgow in 1890 for the well-known firm of A D Bordes. She was not as large as other five-masters, being only 3784 tons; the men in the boat under her bowsprit give a sense of scale.* (CMP)

ral areas of Scandinavia though in the wealthier major cities such as Bergen, Stockholm and Gothenburg investment tended to flow into secondhand British steam tonnage rather than a domestic shipbuilding industry.[91] Sweden possessed plentiful supplies of mined iron ore although it was mostly exported and the growth of a domestic iron industry came only slowly.[92] Spain provides another example of a country with indigenous ore deposits which failed to develop a strong iron and steel industry before 1914.[93]

France possessed an iron and steel industry although it was located in the northeast away from many of the shipyards. Hutchins has also sought to explain the limited transition to metal by the backward state of shipbuilding, the small scale nature of many yards and the lack of suitable management experience.[94] These issues require further investigation before their validity can be fully interpreted. Public policy may also have played a role. From 1881 a subsidy of 60 francs per gross registered ton was to be paid to French builders of metal vessels. Its impact, however, was limited by a navigation subsidy to French shipowners of 1.5 francs per thousand sea miles which included a payment of half this rate for foreign-built vessels. In 1893 the shipbuilding

subsidy was increased to 65 francs and the navigation one to 1.7 francs but it was limited to French-built ships.[95] This time the stimulus to French metal sailing ship construction appears to have been greater although this has not been systematically measured.

The situation in Germany was quite different with the rapid development of a large and efficient iron and steel industry. As indicated above,

90. E W Sager and G Panting, 'Staple economies and the rise and decline of the shipping industry in Atlantic Canada, 1820-1914', in L R Fischer and G Panting (eds), *Change and Adaptation in Maritime History. The North Atlantic Fleets in the Nineteenth Century* (St Johns, Newfoundland 1985), p11. Also see their more recent full length study: E W Sager and G E Panting, *Maritime Capital: The Shipping Industry in Atlantic Canada, 1820-1914* (Montreal 1990).

91. M Fritz, *op cit*, pp155-60; Y Kaukiainen, 'The transition from sail to steam in Finnish shipping, 1850-1914', *Scandinavian Economic History Review* 28 (1980), p178.

92. A S Milward and S B Saul, *The Economic Development of Continental Europe, 1780-1870* (2nd ed, London 1979), pp495-6 provides some reasons for this.

93. A Gomez-Mendoza, 'Government and the development of modern shipbuilding in Spain, 1850-1935', *Journal of Transport History*, 3rd ser, 9, l (1988), p25.

94. J G B Hutchins, *American Maritime Industries*, p407.

95. This paragraph is largely taken from J G B Hutchins, *American Maritime Industries*, pp407-8.

A late product of the Rickmers yard was L'Avenir, *built in 1908 as a training ship for the Belgian government but acquired by Erikson in 1932. Although the long shelter deck was required for accommodation in her training role, it was a feature found in a number of the last generation of big sailing vessels, including the famous* Herzogin Cecilie. *(CMP)*

many of the new shipbuilding enterprises emerging from this progress immediately turned to the construction of steel steamers. Those that did build sail were in a position to sell competitively to local owners. The nitrate trade from South America provided suitable work for several large German sailing fleets. Ferdinand Laeisz deployed a fleet of sixteen steel sailing ships in this trade from Chile whilst D H Watjen & Co of Bremen operated a large fleet of forty-three sailing vessels.[96] German shipbuilding also benefited from vertical integration not only between

96. W Kresse, 'The shipping industry in Germany', in L R Fischer and G E Panting (eds), *Change and Adaptation*, p158; L Scholl, 'Shipping business in Germany in the nineteenth and twentieth centuries', in T Yui and K Nakagawa (eds), *Business History of Shipping* (Tokyo 1985), p195.

97. R Haack, *op cit*, p919.

metal and shipbuilding but also between the latter and shipowning. Rickmers, for example, built metal sailing ships for their own fleet deployed in the rice trade.[97]

Conclusion

This chapter has investigated the application of iron and steel to the construction of sailing vessels in the nineteenth century, focussing upon the benefits of the new technology and the nature of, and explanations for, its pattern of diffusion between ports and countries. A lively contemporary debate over the relative merits of wood and metal identified the benefits of the latter in terms of strength, safety, stowage capacity, speed, durability and repair costs. Its disadvantages were cited as magnetic deviation, inconsistent quality and hull fouling of which only the latter proved an enduring problem but one insufficient to offset its many advantages.

The adoption of the technology can best be explained in terms of construction costs and thus occurred earliest and most fully in Britain where rapidly developing heavy industries provided a good supply of metals whose quality was improving and price falling in a secular fashion.

The earliest producing regions were mostly those where the heavy industries were concentrated, and as the benefits of the localisation of shipbuilding in the northeast, Clydeside and Belfast became cumulative, output in other places declined. These adverse effects spread beyond Britain to other European countries whose builders were unable to meet the competition and the influx of secondhand vessels discarded by British owners. Germany, supported by powerful heavy industries, was an exception, as was France to some degree. In the United States a protectionist policy supported local builders against British tonnage although the transition to metal sailing ships was only partial given the high cost of steel in the New England states to which the industry had moved by the final decades of the century. Canadian owners were not protected and as a result their industry declined more rapidly and never made the technological transition.

Simon Ville

Acknowledgement

This chapter has benefited from the excellent research assistance of Helen Bridge, to whom the author is highly grateful.

4

The Iron and Steel Sailing Ship

WRITING in 1858, John Grantham the Merseyside shipbuilder recorded, 'Strange as it may appear our ship owners long resisted the conviction that iron could be advantageously applied for building *sailing* ships required for long voyages. Some, however, are now yielding to the opinions that we have so long urged and many large

Steel and iron sailing vessels gathered at Barry to load coal in the 1890s. The triple expansion engined steamer Margaret Jones, *built at South Shields in 1889, illustrates the kind of tonnage to which the sailing vessel was going to be able to offer competition for only a few more years, even in bulk trades.* (Basil Greenhill Collection)

and splendid specimens of naval architecture in the form of iron sailing ships are owned in every large port but especially at Liverpool'.[1]

There were in fact very good reasons for the relative slowness with which the merchant shipping industry adopted the iron sailing vessel, as opposed to the iron steamer. As has been explained in *The Advent of Steam*, wooden construction and steam propulsion were not in fact compatible. Iron construction was really essential if the steamer was to develop, doubly essential for the development of the screw steamship. Facilities for maintenance and repair of iron vessels in the 1830s and '40s were confined to a few ports within the steamer's necessarily restricted

sphere of operation, limited as she was by factors of design and the prodigious fuel consumption of her inefficient simple expansion engines to coastal and continental routes, except for the, latterly subsidised, Atlantic service.

The advantages and disadvantages of wooden sailing ships

The merchant sailing vessels' operations were by now worldwide and the facilities for the repair of wooden ships were, as David MacGregor has pointed out in the relevant chapter of this vol-

---

1. J Grantham, *Iron Shipbuilding* (London 1858), p15.

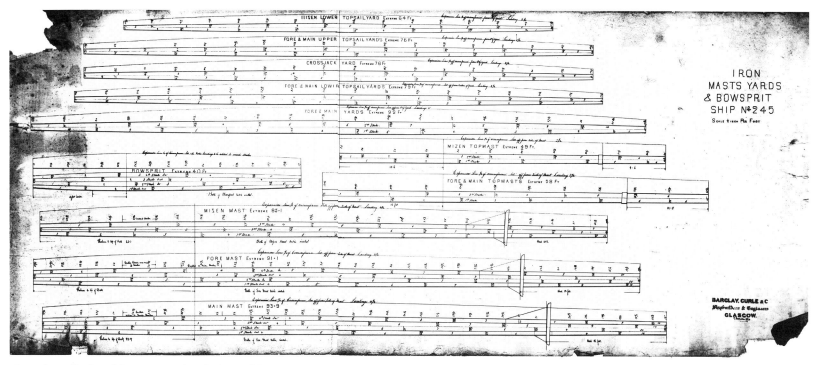

An early application of iron was to wire rigging and in due course to tubular masts and yards. This drawing shows the iron masts of the Thessalus *built by Barclay, Curle in 1874. A full rigged ship of 1781 tons net, Thessalus was one of a number of superb iron clippers built by this firm in the 1870s. (By courtesy of David MacGregor)*

ume, worldwide also. This factor alone was sufficient to ensure that the adoption of iron construction by merchant sailing vessel owners would be pursued with caution. In addition, of course, it had to be proved that the new technology would really work. The technology and the characteristics of the wooden ship were well tried and familiar. A vast body of knowledge had grown up over the centuries and especially since Captain James Cook had in the 1780s established that the small wooden merchant sailing vessel, properly manned, managed and commanded, could operate almost indefinitely in any of the world's oceans without the necessity of sophisticated shore support – in effect a self-supporting eco-system. With the slow adoption of improved navigation techniques which followed on Cook's pioneering work, the Industrial Revolution, the opening of the North American lumber trade, expanding world population, and many more short-lived factors, a pattern of world trade had developed of which the principal vehicle was the wooden sailing ship.

Her operation in the conditions of the early nineteenth century required skills of such a high order that they could only be acquired by prolonged total application from early youth. Some of the last exponents of these skills survived into the second half of the twentieth century and had

stories to tell of the re-rigging, even re-masting, of their vessels using entirely the skills of the crew and without shipyard support, either because it had to be done at sea or in a remote harbour without shore facilities, or simply because this was the cheapest and quickest way of doing the job. They spoke of the skills which had to be learned in handling vessels in port and loading and discharging cargo, and of the techniques of handling their vessels at sea, illustrating the all-pervading nature of a technology much of which was rendered obsolete by the introduction of iron hull construction and iron wire standing (and in due course partly running) rigging. Such skills, acquired at a high human cost, naturally resulted in a certain degree of conservatism towards innovation until it was proved beyond doubt to have overwhelming economic advantage.

But the wooden sailing vessel had grave disadvantages which, with the development of maintenance facilities for iron and steel vessels in many of the world's ports, ensured that she would be partly superseded by vessels of metal construction, particularly with the larger classes of tonnage. But only partly superseded, for, for all her disadvantages, the wooden sailing vessel, the barque of under 1000 tons, the schooner of all sizes from 100 tons or less to 3000 tons or more, the ketch of up to 150 tons, astonishingly survived the development of efficient marine steam-engines in the 1880s, even continued to develop, and were operated, as a later chapter shows, in some rather specialised trades until after the middle of the twentieth century.

The wooden sailing ship, for all her long his-

tory and for all the vast pattern of trading activities which had developed around her use by the 1850s, was a thoroughly unsatisfactory vehicle for sea transport in many ways. She was built up of hundreds, in a big vessel thousands, of separate pieces of timber of different kinds, fastened together with wooden trenails or iron or yellow metal bolts. In a big wooden vessel such was the flexibility that followed from this form of construction that the scarfs in bulwark rails could be seen to open and shut as the vessel worked in the swell. A result of this flexibility, among others, was that all wooden ships leaked to a greater or lesser degree, depending on the quality of their construction, their age, the usage to which they had been put and the care with which they had been maintained.

Wooden vessels had to be nursed carefully in port. Before the middle of the nineteenth century floating harbours were a rarity. Most vessels, in British ports at least, had to lie in tidal berths to load and discharge their cargo. A heavily laden wooden vessel lying in a foul berth or poorly berthed could be badly damaged when she took the ground if the main part of her weight was taken on a few of her frames forward or aft. She could indeed be twisted to a degree which meant her virtual ruin. The shape of a wooden vessel changed as she took the ground and floated off – indeed she groaned and creaked while these processes were taking place. A deep-laden vessel with a heavy cargo tended to pull in her topsides, compressing her beams and narrowing her width – though very slightly, still sufficiently to make the setting up of shrouds with the lanyards necessary as the rigging fell slack. Constant vigi-

Montrosa. *The iron barque* Montrosa *ex* Montrose, *built at Glasgow in 1863, one of the earlier iron sailing vessels, was employed by her first British owners in the Australian trade. In 1885 she was sold to German owners and in 1898 to owners in Lemland, Åland. From this small Baltic island she sailed all over the world for thirty years until she was broken up in 1929. She is shown here discharging timber from the Finnish port of Kotka at Strood on the Medway in 1924. (Ålands Sjöfartsmuseum)*

Early problems with iron ships

Despite these disadvantages of the wooden vessel there were in the 1830s and '40s a number of factors operating in addition to those already listed above against the introduction of iron construction in the merchant shipping industry. For a long time iron girders and plate were of uncontrolled and uneven quality and they were not readily available because of transport difficulties in many shipbuilding districts. The skills needed for iron working on the scale involved in building a vessel were not widely available. New techniques had to be developed in the light of experience. Indeed, it appears that some early iron ships were constructed shell first on wooden formers and the frames shaped to this shell and added as reinforcement – the type of construction used to build Viking ships and countless other small vessels and boats throughout history and across the world.

There were more technical problems to be solved. There was the problem of corrosion which occurred most in the area of the boot topping between wind and water and in the bow and stern which tended to be working in heavily aerated water. This problem could be met by the liberal use of white lead paint with pitch as a

lance and constant maintenance work was necessary. Moreover the wooden sailing vessel was built largely of what are now called bio-degradable materials (in the nineteenth century people simply said that they rotted) and frequent repair and replacement was necessary.

The life in first class service of a vessel sailed hard, in trades where, for instance the working of commodity markets placed a premium on early delivery of seasonal cargoes, could be short. Similarly the life of a wooden vessel which regularly carried heavy concentrated cargoes, especially in regions of frequent bad weather, such as copper ore cargoes from the west coast of South America round Cape Horn to the Bristol Channel ports, could be short also. Railway iron was another cargo which resulted in much damaged wooden tonnage and in some total losses.

Wooden vessels had another vice (which combined with their flexibility and liability to disintegrate into their constituent parts could be a formidable disadvantage), and that was their tendency to hog as they aged. Their sharp ends,

structurally the weakest part of the vessel, were, of course, less buoyant than their full amidships sections. Over the years they tended to drop at the ends and a concave curve developed, to greater or lesser degree, in the keel. To attempt to counteract this tendency some very big long narrow vessels were built with convex keels, curved to be a foot or so lower amidships that at the sternpost and stem. Thus over the years as hogging took place the keel straightened.

Otago, an iron barque of 346 tons built at Glasgow in 1869. She was commanded for some years by Joseph Conrad. Early iron ships required frequent docking if the gradual fouling of the underwater hull was to be checked. (The late Captain F C Poyser)

Thekla, ex Glenfarg, *an iron barque of 898 tons gross, built at Dundee in 1881. The damage to the paintwork in the area of the boot topping is very evident, caused by working in heavily aerated water, produced serious corroding in early iron vessels.* (Ålands Sjöfartsmuseum)

top coat. But the problem of antifouling proved much more intractable. Marine organisms of various kinds attached themselves to the underwater bodies of vessels' hulls and in due course their presence, many tons of them, could seriously impair a vessel's progress. The long-range trading vessel, operating for many months without facilities for docking, or even for drying out in a tidal harbour, could be faced with a formidable accretion which not only slowed her down but made her handling difficult.

Wooden vessels, as David MacGregor has explained in an earlier chapter, could be protected with yellow metal sheets laid over the underwater body on top of tar-soaked felt. The oxides of yellow metal were not adherent, so that as they washed off, so did the marine growth which had sought to establish itself. But 'coppering' as this process was loosely called could not be the solution with an iron structure since yellow metal and iron together in salt water constitute a primitive electric cell and disastrous electrolytic corrosion of the iron resulted. Much time and talent was spent on this problem, but it was to be many years before the development of effective antifouling paints solved it. A vivid example of the effects of fouling is provided by Corlett:

A Mr Lamport, in a paper for the Institution of Naval Architects in 1864, wrote, 'I took up the Shipping Gazette the other day and looked at all the ships overdue for China ... they were all over six months on a voyage, two to three months more than they ought to be. Out of the seven, six are of iron'.[2]

As David MacGregor has already explained, one solution to this problem was the development of the 'composite' vessel, usually wooden planked over iron frames and keel, stem and sternpost, but sometimes varied in construction. Composite construction was developed for a limited period in the 1860s and '70s. A composite vessel could be felted and yellow metalled but she retained some of the advantages of iron construction – lighter and smaller frames and she was probably cheaper to build than a wooden vessel of the same tonnage.

It would appear from contemporary accounts and correspondence that perhaps the most important problem in developing the iron ship was that of compass deviation. It was solved, at least

to the extent which made iron vessels on deep water an acceptable insurance risk, by a series of experiments initiated by William Laird & Sons of the Birkenhead Iron Works, who in the 1830s and '40s were engaged in a marketing drive to sell the idea of the iron ship both to the Royal Navy and to the merchant shipping industry. The result was that in 1838 Professor Airy, then the Astronomer Royal, developed a system of magnets and soft iron correctors placed within and around the binnacle. Modern research has shown that Airy's work had grave flaws and many losses of ships followed from the placing

of undue faith in his methods.[3] But the effect of his report as published in the *Transactions* of the Royal Society for 1839 was to lead to confidence that the problem of deviation was solved. This development in 1839 was perhaps the great breakthrough in making possible the widespread use of iron in shipbuilding for both steamers and sailing vessels.

2. Ewan Corlett, *The Iron Ship* (2nd ed, London 1990), p38.

3. A E Fanning, *Steady As She Goes* (London 1986), ppXXXII-XLII.

Joseph Conrad *ex* Georg Stage *(the first), an iron ship of 212 tons built at Copenhagen in 1882, but representative of the appearance of earlier square-riggers. Sailed round the world by Alan Villiers in 1934-37 she lies today preserved at Mystic Seaport, Connecticut.* (Basil Greenhill)

The birth of the iron sailing vessel

The development of iron hull construction was preceded by the general introduction of iron hanging and lodging knees – their early use can be seen today in the frigate *Unicorn* of 1828 preserved at Dundee – of iron beams, iron tubular lower masts and bowsprits, and iron chain cables. But the first iron vessel to make a sea voyage appears to have been the paddle steamer *Aaron Manby* of 1821 which was prefabricated at Tipton, near Birmingham, reassembled in the Surrey Docks in London and steamed across the Channel and up the River Seine to Paris. An account of the early development of the iron steamship is to be found in the relevant companion volume in this series. *Lloyd's Register* began to include iron ships as early as 1836 with an iron ketch called the *Goliath*, built at Liverpool, and a year later assigned a classification to the iron paddle steamer *Sirius* built on the Thames by Fairbairn.

By now the iron paddle steamer was fairly well established and the use of iron in the hull construction of merchant sailing vessels was about to begin with the *Ironside*. A contemporary, John Grantham, wrote of her as 'the first iron sailing vessel of any magnitude that was employed for sea voyages ... (she) fully realises all the advantages proposed in her construction'.[4] She was a little full rigged ship of 270 tons and just under 100ft long and she must have looked very like the small full rigged ship *Joseph Conrad*, ex *Georg Stage*, in which Alan Villiers circled the world in 1934-37 and which is now preserved at Mystic Seaport in Connecticut, USA.[5]

Larger iron sailing vessels were soon being built, three of them in 1840 alone, one on the Clyde and two at Aberdeen. One of the latter was the *John Garrow* of 711 tons. Every account of the development of the iron ship must inevitably dwell on her, not only because of her size but because she is the best documented of all these early vessels and the detailed information available gives us a picture of the problems met with at this early stage of iron construction. Her first voyage, to India, proved unduly protracted, partly because of the fouling with sea growths, inevitable with early iron vessels, to which refer-

ence has already been made, and partly because of poor design. The owners of the *John Garrow*, Anderson, Garrow & Co, who described the vessel as their 'experimental ship',[6] called in John Grantham, a well-known naval architect and engineer, to advise on what modifications might improve her performance and Grantham recorded the result in his monograph of 1842 referred to earlier. This describes the vessel's construction and form in detail and also the substantial alterations which were made to her

in 1843 to improve her sailing performance and to strengthen her. Grantham's report shows clearly how pioneer iron shipbuilders had to feel their way forward in the matter of construction techniques. The difficulties are admirably sum-

---

4. J Grantham, *Iron as a Material for Shipbuilding* (London 1842), p9.

5. See A Villiers, *The Cruise of the Conrad* (London 1937).

6. David MacGregor, *Merchant Sailing Ships 1815-1850* (London 1984), pp148-150.

marised in Ewan Corlett's *The Iron Ship* (Chapter 4), where he shows that even the caulking of the plates of these early vessels admitted of a number of solutions, some of them very crude. Grantham commented that the considerable alterations made to the *John Garrow* showed 'with what facility iron vessels may be altered and strengthened at pleasure ... Many of the plates and angle bars that were removed have been retained ... Not so with the woodwork: scarcely any of it could again be made use of'.[7]

Iron rigging

The *John Garrow* had iron wire rigging. This innovation was to be of great importance to the development of the sailing vessel of all kinds and sizes in the nineteenth century. The development of the use of iron in rigging appears to begin with chain and linked iron rods for standing and running rigging and patents were taken out as early as the first years of the century. The American historian Carl Cutler notes a very early example of the use of iron in rigging.

The next [large vessel] was built in 1827 in Matthews County, Virginia. This was the *Poca-*

A contemporary sheer and lines plan of the famous John Garrow, *taken from a book by John Grantham (*Iron as a Material for Ship-Building, *1842). Grantham modified the ship and wrote up his experiences in the above book. The drawing shows the ship's lines before and after his alteration. (By courtesy of David MacGregor)*

hontas, a tern measuring 380.45 tons, 122 feet × 29.3 feet. She had two decks and a figurehead. She was owned by Henry Mankin, a prominent ship owner and merchant of Baltimore, and is of special importance as the first sailing vessel noted in the American records fitted with iron rigging. The *Boston Gazette* for Nov 5, 1827, describes her as 'a schooner of three masts rigged fore and aft fashion. Her standing rigging is all iron served with rope yarn. The shrouds are continuous bars, and the cross pieces, usually termed ratlines, are strips of wood. The stays are composed of long links about a yard in length.'[8]

Another very early example of the use of iron in the rigging of American vessels is provided by the *Ferrata*. In the *American Daily Advertiser* of 1 November 1827, appeared the following:

There is now lying at Jackson's Wharf, Baltimore, a vessel which appears to use a novelty in naval architecture. She has three masts, rigged fore and aft fashion as it is called, or similarly to the ordinary schooner. Her standing rigging is all of iron served with rope yarn – the shrouds are continuous bars, and the cross pieces usually termed ratlines are strips of wood. The stays are composed of long links about a yard in length. The tonnage of this nondescript is 336 tons, custom house measure. She is expected to sail very fast and it is said works well, as was tested by her working out of Mile's River where she was built under

the direction of Captain Miles King, against wind and tide.[9]

It rather looks as though both these very early three-masted schooners were rigged by the same master rigger.

In 1835 one Andrew Smith patented in Britain a form of iron wire rope and also included a method of setting it up by means of a double screw thread. He and his agents vigorously marketed the idea and by mid-1841, according to a promotion pamphlet published in that year, eight steamers, the *John Garrow*, three barques, three schooners, two lightships and a yacht had been fitted with iron wire rigging of some kind.[10] MacGregor has shown that experiments with rigging screws were made as early as 1844 in the schooner *Foig a Ballagh* and the barque rigged steamer *Q.E.D.* and that they had been experimented with by the navy as early as 1831.[11] It seems that the navy's use of iron wire, at least in some parts of the rigging of paddle frigates, goes back also into the early 1840s. Thus in April/May 1847 the steam paddle frigate *Penelope* on the West African Station lay for two months in

7. J Grantham, *On Iron...*, pp46-47.

8. C Cutler, *Queens of the Western Ocean* (Annapolis 1961), p551.

9. *The American Neptune* I (October 1941), p399.

10. A Smith, *Observations on the Application of Wire and Hoop Iron ... for Cables, Standing Rigging, etc.* (London 1841).

11. David MacGregor, *op cit*, p151.

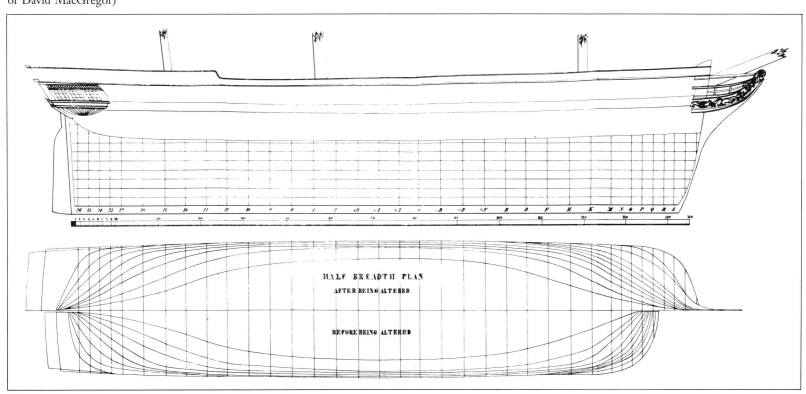

HALF BREADTH PLAN
AFTER BEING ALTERED

BEFORE BEING ALTERED

Ascension, 'changing wire rigging for rope, altering rig and upper works'.[12]

In these circumstances it is not surprising that the first modern ship, *The Great Britain*, with her six-masted schooner sail-assist, should have been initially equipped with iron wire standing rigging as was, almost certainly – though there is no positive evidence known at present – her sister ship the *Great Western* of 1838. The very sophisticated schooner rigs of these steamers could only have been developed by the use of iron wire. But it does appear that early iron wire proved unsatisfactory. The natural conservatism of the maritime community to which Grantham refers as, 'the opposition of seaman, who view innovation with an extraordinary degree of abhorrence' does not in itself explain the reversion to hemp on board the *Penelope* or the fact that *The Great Britain* was herself re-rigged with hemp, at least in part, as early as 1846.[13] Early iron wire was not a quality controlled product and may have presented serious problems. Nevertheless it had great advantages. Its use meant a reduction in the weight of the rigging because wire rope was lighter than hemp rope of the same strength. In due course it became more durable as production methods improved. Given the support of wire standing rigging, less bulky masts could be used, which further reduced the weight of a vessel's top hamper and also her cost. Wire rope was smaller in diameter than hemp rope of corresponding strength, which reduced the windage of the top hamper. It did not require so much maintenance as hemp, which had to be constantly tarred down.[14]

Given these advantages it is not surprising that progress was rapid, and by the early 1850s the use of iron rigging was becoming widespread in larger vessels. The thick hemp shrouds can still be seen in photographs of wooden schooners and ketches taken well into the twentieth century while the production problems of the rigging screw, plus the widespread belief that it lacked the elasticity of hemp lanyards and that this deficiency was most important in wooden vessels, ensured that deadeyes and lanyards remained the normal way of setting up shrouds until the 1870s and persisted in use for as long as vessels carried sails.

The commercial enterprise, the bold initiative investment, and the advanced and original thinking of Brunel become the more apparent when the facts of the early development of the iron ship are considered. With a few exceptions such as the *John Garrow*, early iron ships were small vessels; before 1850 most were of 250 tons or less. Against this background the 3000-ton *The Great Britain* seems all the more remarkable.

Iron shipbuilding 1840-1855

A number of builders, not surprisingly many of them based on engineering works with the skills and equipment necessary to handle the new machinery, began to specialise in iron vessel construction at the beginning of the 1840s, building iron paddle steamers and some sailing vessels, nearly all of them schooner rigged. Notable among these was John Laird of Birkenhead, who (as demonstrated in *Steam, Steel and Shellfire*)

was prominent in the promotion and vigorous marketing of the iron steamer, notably with his privateer of the First China War, the *Nemesis*. In 1841 Laird built the iron schooner *Proto*, 128 tons, for the Liverpool & London Shipping Company. In 1843 Coutts & Company of Newcastle built an iron schooner with iron rigging, the *Flash*, and three years later the schooner *Admiral Hood*. MacGregor gives an interesting example of collaboration between a shipbuilder and an engineering works to build an iron schooner.[15] The Blaikie Brothers of Aberdeen were the shipbuilders, while the engineering firm of John Duffus & Co provided the expertise in iron work. The result was the iron schooner *Mercury* of 1842, a vessel of 165 tons with a wooden keelson and beam shelves but with iron beams. Blaikie's went on to build other iron vessels, such as the brig *Centaur* of 1849. Another early iron vessel with timber in her hull construction was the sloop *Tinker* of 1839. Indeed a number of early iron vessels incorporated timber components in their construction. The fabricating of shaped iron members of sufficient size and strength was still a developing skill.

Other early iron vessels were built for special purposes. *The Vulcan*, schooner of 1841, 80 tons, was launched in Glasgow for service on the Forth and Clyde Canal. Other early iron vessels included the *John Laird*, a 270-ton iron barque of 1842 built, of course, at Birkenhead, the iron brig *Guide*, built for the East India Company, and the centreboard iron schooner *Annsbro*, built by William Denny at Dumbarton in 1846. The iron barque *Richard Cobden* was built in Liverpool in 1844 to the design of Thomas Guppy, who was one of the team that built *The Great Britain*.[16]

But the simple fact that iron construction was essentially associated with steam vessels, where

12. Captain's log of the *Penelope*, PRO Adm51/2956 & 2957.

13. Ewan Corlett, *op cit*, p105.

14. J C Martin, 'The Development of Wire Rope', *The International Journal of Maritime History* IV No 1 (June 1992), pp102-103 quoting *The US Nautical Magazine and Naval Journal* of October 1856, pp192-197.

15. David MacGregor, *op cit*, p154.

16. See *Lloyd's Register* and J Grantham, 'On the Richard Cobden Sailing Ship', *Transactions of the Institution of Naval Architects* XII (1871). Corlett, *op cit*, p23, has her as built in Bristol.

its advantages were overwhelming, is demonstrated by a report from the *North British and Railway and Shipping Journal* to the effect that of the thirty-seven vessels then under construction on the Clyde twenty-six were iron steamers and the rest were wooden vessels.[17] The iron ship was the product of the introduction of steam propulsion at sea and she was promoted, marketed and often built, by engineering firms rather than by traditional shipbuilders. Like the steam vessel herself, iron shipbuilding had a complex history of development. As Scott Russell put it,

> The kind of skill, required for the proper design of an iron ship, was new as well as rare, because of the total want of precedent for iron structure and sea-going ships. At first we naturally looked up to the wood shipbuilders, and to wooden ships, for the proper proportion of the iron parts of iron ships. ... The men who did know something of the qualities and properties of iron were quite another race, occupied in thinking of quite other things. The smith and the carpenter had little knowledge in common between them, and the smiths alone understood how to handle iron, and what they could make it do. There was also a race of iron boiler-makers, who were known to understand

Early iron sailing vessels built by Laird of Birkenhead: the pilot brig Guide (flying the East India Company's ensign), and the barque John Laird. (Indian Office Library)

how sheets of iron were to be cut and bent, and shaped and joined to one another. ... But as to general design, large mechanical principles and skill, enlightened by science, there was no race except the civil and mechanical engineer, who had already acquired great skill in using iron, by the extent to which he employed it in forming all parts of his machinery, where it had a very great deal of hard work to do, and had to be most skilfully proportioned to that work, in order to do it. Here was found a considerable amount of skill of the right sort, to be drawn upon whenever the necessities of iron shipbuilding required it ... It was from the mechanical engineers mainly, and not from the wood shipbuilders, that help ultimately came; and the new arts and science of iron shipbuilding had to be worked out mainly by mechanical engineers.[18]

Nevertheless, the advantages of iron vessels as vigorously promoted by engineering firms which had turned to shipbuilding were obvious. Grantham gave as a merchant vessel's most desirable characteristics 'strength combined with lightness; great capacity for stowage; safety; speed; durability; economy in repair; cost; draught of water'.[19] On all of these heads the iron vessel scored. By the late 1850s first cost of a new iron vessel was lower than that of a wooden vessel of comparable quality – 10-30 shillings (50p to £1.50p), in the values of the early 1990s perhaps £40-£120 a ton, less. Iron vessels were

already favoured by shippers for their greater safety, and their capacity was greater than that of wooden vessels of the same tonnage to the extent of being a fifth greater between vessels of comparable size and hull form. The following table shows this very clearly.[20] Iron ships were also longer-lived and markedly more economical in the matter of maintenance.

Table 4/1: Additional Capacities According to Materials (expressed as percentages)

Tonnage of ship	Excess of oak over fir	Excess of iron over oak	Excess of iron over fir
1000	7.54	14.0	21.46
500	6.8	16.0	22.8
200	10.0	18.6	28.6

By 1853 *Lloyd's Register* which, of course, is a somewhat incomplete record, lists sixty iron sailing vessels then in service. Thirty-two of these were schooners, from the 61 tons of the *Lioness* built at Shields in 1851 and registered in Leith

---

17. Reproduced in *The Times*, 7 July 1846, p7, col 1.
18. John Scott Russell, *The Modern System of Naval Architecture* (London 1865), Vol 1, p352.
19. J Grantham, *Iron Shipbuilding*, pp86-7.
20. *Ibid*, p96; G Moorsom, *A Brief Review and Analysis of the Laws for the Admeasurement of Tonnage* (London 1852), pp71ff.

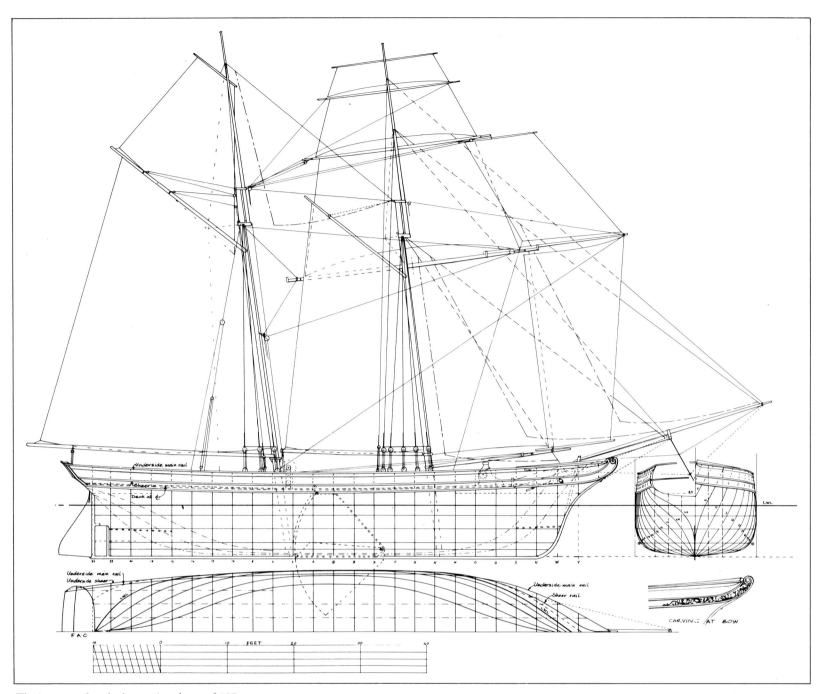

The iron centreboard schooner Annsboro *of 105 tons built by Denny in 1846. There is a propeller aperture but the engine cannot have been intended to be more than an auxiliary, given the amount of canvas, provision of a centreboard and sharp lines fore and aft, all suggesting that performance under sail was paramount.* (By courtesy of David MacGregor)

and then employed in the Australian trade, to the 271 tons of the *Q.E.D.* of 1844 – see above – now rigged as a schooner. Perhaps her very early rigging screws had proved unsatisfactory and had occasioned the change. There were eleven ships of from the 589 tons of the *Shandon*, built at Glasgow in 1851, to the 985 of the *Evangeline*, built at Liverpool in 1853 and in the New Orleans cotton trade, and the 965 of the Glasgow-

built *Typhoon* of 1852. There were ten barques also ranging in size from the *John Laird*, the tonnage of which was given as 264, to the 512 tons of the *Loharee*, built at South Shields in 1847 and bound for Calcutta in 1853. The remaining vessels comprise four brigs from the 184 tons of Glasgow-built *Haiti* of 1852 to the 232 tons of Blaikie's *Centaur* of 1849. There are two brigantines, the *Sally Gail* built at Newcastle in 1850 and the *Margaret*, 397 tons, built at Shields in 1848, and the Ipswich-built ketch *Vulcan*, built in 1846 and of 92 tons.

The same *Lloyd's Register* lists 135 iron steamers, 81 of which were screw propelled. The registration is at times quixotic: for example, the famous pioneer iron screw collier *John Bowes* of

1852, which had an exiguous three-masted schooner sail-assist rig, is listed as a sailing vessel.[21] But the list as a whole does give an idea of the relative rate of adoption of iron construction for steam vessels and for sailing vessels, and of the small number of iron vessels of all kinds at sea in 1853. The total of 195 iron vessels must be compared with the total of 9934 vessels listed in the register book. In other words, in 1853 as far as vessels in *Lloyd's Register* were concerned, almost exactly 2 per cent by numbers were built of iron of which 0.6 per cent were iron sailing vessels. Although the *Steam, Steel and Shellfire*

21. R Craig, *Steam Tramps and Cargo Liners* (London 1980), pp2, 6 and 7.

Star of Persia *in the Avon Gorge, Bristol. An iron ship of 1227 tons gross she was built at Belfast in 1868 and sold to German owners in 1893.* (The late Captain F C Poyser)

The iron clipper barque Derwent *of 599 tons net was built by Barclay, Curle in 1867. The acceptance of iron in the China tea trade, where doubts had been raised about possible deleterious effects on the tea cargo, marked the final victory for metal hulls in the most prestigious of all trades.* (Tracings by David MacGregor from builder's originals)

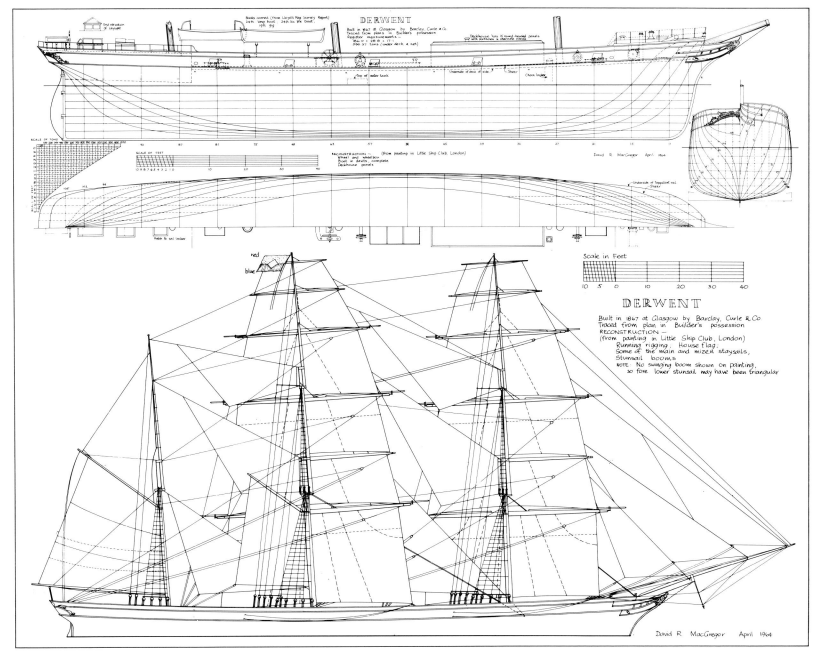

Coriolanus, an iron ship of 1046 tons gross built at Dumbarton in 1876. Employed in the Indian jute trade, she made a record 69-day passage to Calcutta on her maiden voyage. She survived to be broken up at Fall River, Massachusetts, in 1936. (CMP)

was accompanied by a great period of economic growth which affected shipping particularly. It was followed by bankruptcies and disasters and they in their turn by two decades of further expansion. This expansion was the consequence of the extension of currency and credit based upon the results of the Californian and Australian gold discoveries, the repeal of the Navigation Acts, which gave British shipowners the stimulus of much stronger foreign competition, the passing of the Companies Act of 1861, which enabled greater financial risks to be taken by entrepreneurs, the general development of banking, the spread of settlement in North America and the steadily developing industrialisation of the northeast of the United States and the development of railways on both sides of the Atlantic. United Kingdom registered sailing vessel tonnage increased by 23 per cent from 3,400,000 in 1850 to 4,200,000 in 1860. Steam tonnage, still confined to packet routes, towing duties, and subsidised deep sea routes, increased in the same decade from 170,000 net tons to 450,000 net tons.

During the same period United States sailing tonnage, virtually all of wood construction, in overseas, coastal and lakes trades, increased from 2,900,000 to 4,400,000. The American expansion, stimulated by industrialisation and the opening up of the West Coast, was largely in wooden square rigged vessels, many of them built in New England. At the same time the Canadian shipbuilding industry was steadily growing, but again the tonnage was entirely of wooden construction. It was at this time unusual for a wooden vessel built in Britain to exceed 1000 tons. Thus in terms of tonnage and size the largest British-built ordinary merchant sailing ships roughly doubled between 1820 and 1860 but Canadian-built vessels tended to be much larger, the largest of over 2000 tons and many of them of over 1500 tons. Thus for the real economies of scale in an expanding economy British shipowners had to turn to Canadian builders for large wooden ships.

The growing merchant fleets of a Europe slower to industrialise than Britain also showed the influence of the long period of expansion of

volume in this series has shown that the Royal Navy was by 1853 totally committed to the steam screw battlefleet, clearly in the merchant shipping industry the wooden sailing vessel was overwhelmingly predominant and she was to remain so until the development of the compound steam engine.

Nevertheless, the size of iron sailing vessels was steadily increasing. *Typhoon*, ship rigged, built at Glasgow in 1852, passed the 900-ton mark. She was rapidly followed by the *W S Lindsay*, built at Newcastle in the same year and by the *Ellen Bates* of 1853 built at Neath, which passed the 1000-ton mark. In the next seven years at least forty-two iron sailing vessels of over 900 tons were launched on the Clyde and the Mersey, the Tyne, the Humber and at Belfast.[22] The 2000-ton mark was passed by the ship *Bates Family* built at Hull in 1859.

This was still a period of transition and experiment when *Lloyd's Register* as a classification organisation was feeling its way towards a convenient method of categorising iron vessels. In the year 1853 the Visitation Committee reported that they were impressed with the rapidity with which the substitution of iron for wood in shipbuilding was progressing and of its great importance – particularly on the Clyde. They stressed the need to introduce rules 'by which, at least, the surveyors and the Committee might be ena-

bled to judge the fitness of the iron, from its size and quality, for the ribs, plates, beams and etc, of iron ships'.[23] Nevertheless, such were the complications of the problem that although a fairly comprehensive 'Form of Report Iron Ships' already appeared in the register book it was not until 1855 that a full set of rules appears in *Lloyd's Register*.[24] Even then there were difficulties with many builders who held widely diverging views on the methods to be used at various stages in the construction of an iron hull. As a result, many owners did not seek classification of their vessels by Lloyd's, with the result that this particular record material, although representative, is incomplete.

The brief heyday of iron and steel sailing vessels

Mid-century economics and the sailing ship

Such, then, was the birth of the iron sailing vessel. She had reached adolescence by the time of the War with Russia of 1854-56, latterly and misleadingly known as the Crimean War. This

22. See D MacGregor, *Fast Sailing Ships* (2nd ed, London 1988), p134.

23. *Lloyd's Register*, Visitor Committee Reports, 1853.

24. See, for instance, pp38-40 of the *Register* for 1853.

the 1850s and early '60s. Norway's merchant fleet grew from 300,000 to 560,000 tons, France's from 675,000 to 930,000; in both these cases also almost all of the increase was in wooden tonnage. In Scandinavia and Russia successive laws were passed reflecting a gradual change from the principles of mercantilism, state power based on absolute monarchy and the granting of shipping monopolies to the merchants of the towns. No longer was 'peasant sailing' by vessels not registered in the major ports strictly limited geographically as it had been in the eighteenth and early nineteenth centuries. The 'Sound dues', taxes levies by the Danish authorities on the cargoes of all vessels passing into or out of the Baltic through the Sound between Helsingør and Helsingborg, were withdrawn in 1857 after prolonged international negotiations in which the United States took the lead, paying compensation to the Danish authorities. There was something of an explosion of merchant shipping enterprise in northern Europe after this development, and vessels from the small Baltic ports, German, Polish, Swedish, Danish and Finnish, soon began to be met with all over the world.

But it was only in Britain that the construction of iron sailing vessels was rapidly expanding. In Britain this was a period of continuous Government legislation to improve the merchant shipping industry. Steady reforming pressure was applied. It was now seen as a function of Government to regulate the industry and from 1850 to 1906 scarcely a year passed in which a committee or a commission was not sitting or an Act of Parliament was not in course of preparation, or on its way through the House. Masters' and Mates' qualifications, food, the manning of vessels, the draught to which they could be loaded, and increasingly the very structure and maintenance of the vessels themselves, came under regulation. This process was to come to its climax later in the great Merchant Shipping Act of 1894, still the longest Act on the Statute Book.

All over the world charting improved, lighthouse services were established and other aids to navigation in restricted waters were introduced. But perhaps the greatest change of the period was that which followed the beginnings of the introduction of the International Electric Telegraph in the 1850s. The effect on merchant shipping was to be profound. No longer was the first news of a vessel's arrival overseas conveyed often by that same vessel on her return home.

No longer was the Master's limited information on the state of the freight market necessarily confined to the port in which he had arrived. When a vessel arrived in port, not only had arrangements been made to discharge her cargo, but her subsequent movements were likely to have been agreed, increasingly at least as far as the principal ports were concerned. In short, the Master received his 'orders' as soon as he berthed his vessel. This revolution greatly increased the proportion of the vessel's life which was spent in gainful employment. The whole technique of the world markets was changed and the commodity markets in the modern sense began to emerge. Sea-carrying power could now be mobilised and organised and the flow of international commerce enormously facilitated.

The consequence of this complex general economic and social revolution in Britain, Europe and North America was a demand for different types of merchant vessel. No longer were ships confined to a limited range of often seasonal trades; something like a world freight market began to emerge. Increasingly, time began to represent money. Higher standards began to be demanded for the proper combination of reasonable speed, good cargo capacity, and low operating costs for the overwhelming majority of the world's ordinary merchant ships, which were certainly not the much publicised 'clippers' which represented only a tiny minority of the world's tonnage.

In this expansive climate, as well as the construction of ever increasing numbers of iron vessels, many improvements were made on deck and in the rigging. In place of the simple windlass heaved round with hand spikes which had been in use since the sixteenth century at least, the 'Patent' windlass converting an up and down motion of levers into the rotary motion of the barrel was introduced and remained in large vessels until steam donkey engine power took over. Anchor cranes, brace and sheet winches, better cargo handling gear, improved pumps, iron lower masts and even lower yards, as well as the widespread use of iron wire for standing and for some running rigging developed as materials became commercially cheaply available. In the 1850s double topsails, sometimes only on the fore and main, began to appear in place of the huge, sometimes uncontrollable, single topsails, which had persisted since the late 1400s, and double topgallants were soon to follow. Better mast ironwork and steadily improving qualities of fabric readily and cheaply available for the sails themselves greatly increased sailing efficiency.

All these developments were reflected in the shipbuilding industry. In 1850, 120,000 tons of wooden shipping and 12,800 tons of iron ships were built in Britain. Ten years later the figures were 147,000 and 64,700. By 1870 the figures for wood and iron construction had at last been reversed as iron became better and cheaper and facilities for the repair and maintenance of iron vessels became almost worldwide. In that year a total of 161,000 tons of wooden shipping was built in Britain and 255,000 tons of iron ship-

The four-masted barque Bidston Hill, *at 2519 tons gross one of the larger iron sailing vessels; built at Liverpool in 1886 and lost off Cape Horn in the bad year of 1905.* (Basil Greenhill Collection)

Probably the finest photograph ever taken showing working conditions on board a big square rigged sailing vessel. Four hands securing a section of the fore sail which has come loose from the gaskets in heavy weather on board the iron barque Garthsnaid, *1614 tons, built at Greenock in 1882. (Commander Alexander Turner,* DSC, RNR)

The turning point for the sailing ship

The opening of the Suez Canal in 1869 has often been quoted as the turning point in the life of the sailing vessel, but this contention is not supported by the facts. The turning point had in fact already come four years before with Alfred Holt's successes. True, the opening of the canal in a situation rendered fraught for sailing ship-owners by the success of the compound engine gave a check for a year or two to the building of sailing vessels of either wood or iron in Britain. Before the compound engine the canal would not have mattered because even with a saving of 5000 miles on the route to the east the simple engine steamer using the canal could still not have been competitive with the sailing vessel going round the Cape. But the compound engine steam vessel could use the canal with great profit, and simple calculations showed that the

ping, including many first class sailing vessels. By 1870 the compound steam engine had been convincingly demonstrated by Alfred Holt of Liverpool – see Chapter 9 in *The Advent of*

South West India Dock, London, in the heyday of iron and steel sailing vessels, the late 1880s. (National Maritime Museum)

Steam in this series – and the construction of large sailing vessels had momentarily been much reduced. Ten years later the building of wooden sailing vessels in Britain was virtually confined to brigs, brigantines and small schooners, and of the half million gross tons of iron tonnage built only about one-fifth represented sailing tonnage.

A very small iron sailing ship, the schooner Naiad, *149 tons gross, built at Llanelly in 1867, shortening sail as she comes up to the entrance to Newlyn Harbour. St Michael's Mount is visible in the background. (The late H Oliver Hill)*

sailing vessel would not be able to compete in the bulk of contemporary Indian trades.

But in the crucial year of 1865 another event took place which in complex and different ways was to play a part in prolonging the life of the sailing vessel. In America the War between the States came to an end, leaving a triumphant industrial North and a shattered rural South. Four years later, in the same year as the opening of the Suez Canal, an event of even more importance in world history than the opening of the canal was the completion of the transcontinental railroad across North America. Now, with a great financial and industrial base in the northeast and a stable political situation, the continent could at last be opened up.

No society turns to the sea as a means of life if there is any acceptable alternative on land. To make a life on the sea one needs to be pushed by economic or social circumstances ashore. During the War between the States nearly half the American deep water merchant fleet had been destroyed, sold, or transferred to foreign flags. As Geoffrey Safford has shown, the contraction of the American merchant shipping industry had already begun well before the War between the States.[25] After that war it was obvious that the future of shipping lay with iron and steel and steam, but the high local cost of the former prohibited the building of a modern merchant fleet of steamships in North America and to some degree the same factor circumscribed the building of iron sailing vessels. A United States law effectively forbade the building up of a merchant fleet by the purchase of foreign-built tonnage. Rapid industrialisation and phenomenal population growth through massive immigration absorbed most American manufactured products, so there was relatively little export trade for American ships to carry. Money and men turned from the sea to industry, railroads, real estate, and the West. The West provided trades in which the big wooden square rigged sailing vessel lingered for another decade or so but the British merchant shipping industry lost its most serious competitor.

The world industrial expansion and the development of routes for compound engine steamers were based on coal as fuel and Britain was the world's largest exporter – the Persian Gulf of the period. So there was always an outward cargo for a British sailing vessel, a ballast on which freight was paid, and she took bulk products home. Increasingly it was to be an asset to a sailing vessel to be 'the cheapest warehouse in the world', to provide virtually free storage for cargoes which changed hands on the commodity market several times while she made a long passage. Hence, given an economy generally expanding over time, the sailing vessel was to continue to be a reasonable investment for British shipowners for at least a generation after the beginning of large scale building of compound engine steamships. British shipyards were to build many hundreds of big iron, and later steel, square rigged vessels until the final collapse of the market for new sailing tonnage in 1897.

That remarkable pioneer in merchant shipping historical studies (of the anecdotal kind fashionable in the 1920s) the late Basil Lubbock, published tables in the appendices of his great work *The Last of the Windjammers* which give some indication of the rate of increase in the construction of iron sailing vessels during the decades of the 1860s and '70s. Lubbock's lists of the vessels of the principal sailing fleets of the late nineteenth century, miscellaneous vessels and what he calls 'small fry', show 81 iron sailing vessels built in the 1860s, of which 76 are ships and only 5 are barques. They show 180 iron sailing vessels built in the 1870s, a total comprising 143 ships, 35 barques and, an innovation, 2 iron barquentines – the pioneer iron barquentine appears to have been the *Valetta*, built in 1854 on the Clyde. David MacGregor has already given an account of the history of the barquentine rig in an earlier chapter of this volume.

As to the economic structure which produced these vessels, C Knick Harley has demonstrated some of the factors involved.[26] Based on theoretical cost calculation and the actual composition of shipping on the relevant routes he presents sail and steam as competitive for bulk cargoes in the year 1870 in the North Atlantic grain trade and still, only one year after the opening of the

25. G Safford, 'The Decline of the American Merchant Marine 1850-1914: An Historiographical Appraisal', in L R Fischer and G E Panting (eds), *Change and Adaptation in Maritime History: The North Atlantic Fleets in the Nineteenth Century* (St Johns, Newfoundland 1985), pp51-87.

26. C Knick Harley, 'Aspects of the Economics of Shipping 1850-1913', in L R Fischer and G E Panting (eds), *op cit*, pp169-186.

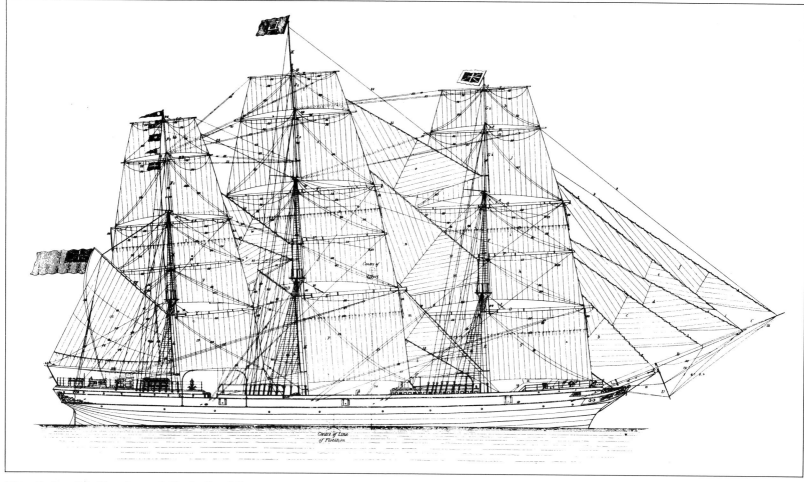

The sail plan of the Formby, *probably the first full rigged ship built of steel. Constructed by Jones, Quiggin & Co and launched in 1863,* Formby *was 1271 tons register. The ship featured in a number of plates in W J M Rankine's influential book* Shipbuilding, Theoretical and Practical *(1866). (By courtesy of David MacGregor)*

Suez Canal, in the Indian Ocean trade. In 1875 the cotton trade from the southern states of America, principally New Orleans, represented an important sailing vessel trade in competition with steam propelled vessels, as did five years later the bulk cargo trade (probably principally with coal out and jute home) round the Cape to Calcutta. Harley points out that in the period 1860-1890 the price of new sailing vessels in Britain fell by about one-third – a significant factor in encouraging continued investment in new sailing tonnage, even though throughout the period there was a steady decline of some 50 per cent in freight rates, and that the price decline was principally the product of technical improvements in iron shipbuilding and the falling price of iron (which declined by half between 1850 and the 1880s). These cost reductions were sufficient to offset the 50 per cent increase in shipbuilders' labour costs over this period. Thus, as Harley says,

The building of iron sailing ships in Britain had an enormous potential to expand at substantially unchanged costs. This ability to adjust output at constant cost determined the price of sailing ships in general. If the price of sailing ships were higher, output would expand almost immediately as iron shipbuilders shifted to sailers from building steamships, normally a larger part of their output than sailers. In the longer run, although shipbuilding was a large industry in Britain it was only a portion of a much larger metal working sector and would easily have been able to draw resources for expansion if the price of ships had been such as to generate greater profits in shipbuilding than elsewhere in British industry. Such expansion would have driven down ship prices and eliminated excess profits, and thus the price of ships internationally was dominated by British costs.

The price differential was big enough to ensure the competitiveness of the iron vessel with the product of the great Canadian wood shipbuilding industry. Here the indications are that to hold down prices to competitive levels North American shipbuilders had to maintain wages at their mid-century levels. Inevitably this led, in an expanding economy offering alternative em-

ployment for the skills of enterprising and mobile shipbuilding workers, to a drift from the industry and by the 1880s to its terminal decline.

The steel sailing ship

Lubbock's lists show very interesting developments in shipbuilding in the 1880s. He lists 275 vessels: of these 109 are iron ships, 16 are iron four-masted ships, 31 are iron barques, 15 are iron four-masted barques and there is one pioneer iron four-masted barquentine (the *Tacora*, built in 1888). But there is now a new element – steel construction. Lubbock lists 38 steel ships, 27 steel four-masted ships, 17 steel barques and 29 steel four-masted barques. Sarah Palmer, drawing her figures from *Lloyd's Universal Register* (London 1886), has shown that in that year 54.2 per cent of British merchant shipping by tonnage comprised iron and steel steamers, in addition to which there was a very small tonnage of wooden steamers.[27] The rest of the merchant tonnage comprised 13.2 per cent wooden sailing vessels, 1.2 per cent composite sailing vessels,

27. S Palmer, 'The British Shipbuilding Industry 1850-1914', in L R Fischer and G E Panting (eds), *op cit*, pp89-114.

29.8 per cent iron sailing vessels and only 1.1 per cent steel sailing vessels.

Nevertheless, as is explained by Simon Ville in the previous chapter, the steel sailing vessel had arrived, the period of transition was upon the industry, and in the eleven years which remained in which merchant sailing vessels were to be built in any numbers the steel vessel was going to become totally predominant. This was the beginning of the era in which the standard big British, and indeed German and to some extent French, merchant sailing vessel became the steel four-masted barque made familiar to those interested in the subject by the writings of Alan Villiers; by the television programmes incorporating the marvellous archival film material made by him and others on board such vessels in the 1920s and '30s, by the spectacular survival of one or two of these vessels, adapted as training ships, which are from time to time to be seen at

The steel four-masted barque Crown of Germany *2241 tons gross, launched at Belfast during the last British sailing vessel building boom of 1892, in drydock at Avonmouth. The long parallel section amidships is apparent.* (The late Captain F L Poyser)

'tall ships' rallies; and, most of all, for those who have been fortunate enough to see her, by the splendid *Pommern* lying in Mariehamn in the Åland islands of Finland, the only such vessel in the world to survive unchanged as she was working at sea. These last survivors are dealt with, with others, in the next chapter of this volume.

The transition from iron to steel in shipbuilding has been described earlier, but shipbuilders and shipowners clung to wrought iron construction far into the 1880s because it was readily available in the cheapest forms acceptable to Lloyd's and the other classification organisations. There was a world demand for steel for every conceivable industrial purpose, and particularly for railway development, and little incentive to the industry to produce cheap steel plates for shipbuilding. Once again, the fact that shipbuilding was one part of a very complex metal fabrication industry played its role in the history of the ship. It was not until 1885 that steel produced by the Bessemer and Siemens processes began to be used widely in shipbuilding. This new material, with its greater strength for weight, led to rapid augmentation of the size and carrying capacity of British merchant sailing ships and, though smaller vessels continued to be built into the 1890s, in the larger classes the 1500- or 2000-ton ship or barque became the 3000 tons or more four-masted vessel carrying 5000 tons or so.

In the 1870s something of a balance had been established between compound engine steamers and the sailing vessel. By the end of the decade the compound engine steamer seemed to have settled to near the limits of its possibilities, given the technology of the period. But at the beginning of the 1880s a further development established the steamship as the normal method of sea transport. With the exception of big wooden schooners in North American waters this development brought about the end of the building of new large sailing vessels within about fifteen years.

The second revolution had its preliminaries. By the end of the 1870s steel was already being used for boilers and furnace construction and this meant that steam pressures could be increased, with further consequent improvement to the efficiency of the compound engine – the fuel consumption was reduced by more than 60 per cent. And then on 7 April 1881 the steamship *Aberdeen* sailed from Plymouth towards Melbourne. She had an engine in which the steam, having done its work in the second cylinder of the compound engine, was admitted to a third cylinder, even larger than the second, and there completed its expansion. This process was made possible by the high steam pressures ob-

tained from steel boilers and improved furnaces. The development of this kind of marine engine represents one of the major landmarks in industrial history.

The *Aberdeen* completed her passage to Melbourne in 42 days with 4000 tons of cargo and only one coaling stop, working at a steam pressure of 125 psi (pounds per square inch). Within three years 150 psi was achieved in new steamships. In 1885 the two-cylinder compound engine almost ceased to be built and triple expansion engines working at 200 psi shortly followed. By the beginning of the 1890s a tramp steamer could operate at 9kts on a fuel consumption of half an ounce of coal per ton per mile steamed. Already by the mid-1880s the steam vessel was as economical as the new sailing vessels, bearing in mind that she could make three passages and thus carry three tons of cargo to the latter's one. It was the production and use of steel good enough and cheap enough to manufacture commercially practicable high pressure boilers which sealed the end of the sailing ship. The obsequies were merely hastened by improved port facilities, water ballast, better cargo gear, the introduction of self-trimming and the exploitation by steamship owners of the economies of scale.

It was this situation which led to the building in the 1880s of very large steel ships and steel four-masted ships and gradually more and more steel four-masted barques, until by the end of that decade the four-masted barque had become almost the world's standard big sailing vessel. Some modern writers have presented the four-masted barque almost as if she was the representative sailing ship of history. She was in fact anything but this and was built in numbers for only about twelve years at the very end of the long era in which it was possible for sail-propelled vessels to be operated profitably in the world's carrying trade. Four-masted barques were remarkable pieces of engineering. Often over 300ft long, with long square sections and full ends making up a burdensome but very strong and powerful hull capable of being sailed at consistently high average speeds if well-handled, they represented for a few years a class of sailing tonnage which, in some long range trades in years of prosperity, could still give a reasonable return on capital. They were equipped with steam donkey engines which, by ingeniously devised chain transmissions, drove winches which lifted the huge steel lower yards to set the sails and powered the windlass to raise the anchors. Other labour-saving devices were developed – brace winches, halyard winches, labour-saving modifications to the running rigging. On the whole these latter improvements were not widely adopted by British sailing shipowners, but

A few relatively small steel square rigged vessels continued to be built in Britain into the 1890s. This is the barque Favell, *1363 tons gross, launched at Bristol in 1895 and broken up in 1937.* (Basil Greenhill Collection)

they were taken up by German owners, some of whom for a short time in the early twentieth century ran perhaps the finest square rigged merchant sailing vessels ever to be at sea.

In consequence of these developments crews did not increase in size in step with the carrying capacity of these very large merchant sailing vessels. What happened is illustrated by the fact that the wooden full rigged ship *Ocean Queen* of Bristol, 630 tons, built in 1845, sailing to Quebec from the Bristol Channel in 1855 had a total crew of twenty: master, two mates, bosun, carpenter, steward, cook and thirteen seamen. A German four-masted barque of the 1890s carrying a cargo of 2,250,000 board feet of lumber from the west coast of North America to Europe had a crew of thirty-three. It was possible, though a somewhat stressful business, to handle these vessels with even fewer men. In the twentieth century a four-masted barque in the grain trade from Australia to western Europe carrying perhaps 4000 tons of cargo could be, and from

Figure 4/22: Metal ships, both steam and sail

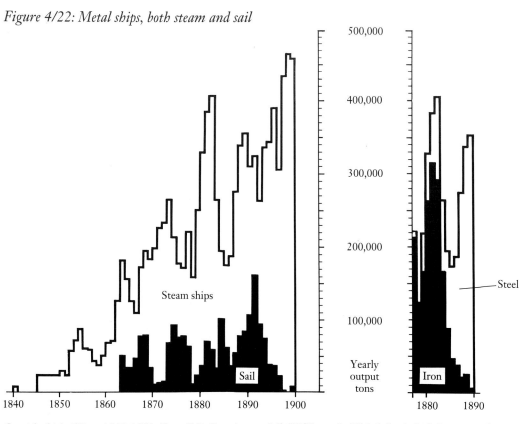

Scottish shipbuilding, 1840-1900 (from J B Cunnison and J Gilfillan, eds, Third Statistical Account of Scotland, *1958).*

The steel four-masted barque Archibald Russell, *2385 tons gross, built at Greenock in 1905.* (National Maritime Museum)

time to time was, handled by a crew of as few as twenty-five.

These last square rigged British merchant vessels were built in the second half of the 1880s and the early 1890s and especially during a shipping boom which lasted from 1888 to 1893. The graph reproduced here of Scottish shipbuilding from 1840-1900 shows clearly what happened.[28] From 1890 the building of steel sailing ships rapidly increased, reaching the highest peak in 1892 and then falling away rapidly until at the end of the century it was almost non-existent. The same graph shows the transition from iron to steel extremely well. Iron tonnage is absolutely in the ascendant until the early 1880s. It is then very rapidly replaced by steel. By 1890 iron shipbuilding has virtually ceased.

Sailing vessels in the 1890s

These last vessels of iron and steel were employed with surviving wooden vessels in carrying guano and nitrate from South America, canned salmon and lumber from British Columbia, coal from Britain to almost anywhere, grain from San Francisco to Liverpool, timber from Sweden to Australia and grain back to Europe, timber from Puget Sound to Britain, jute from Calcutta, and coal from Newcastle, New South Wales, to the west coast of South America. Together with the survivors of the 1870s and of the era of the wooden ship the steel vessels made up an enormous fleet of big merchant sailing vessels still in operation all over the world in the 1890s. They were not virtually self-supporting machines, as the old wooden ships had been. It was not possible for their crews to re-rig them after dismasting, replace their spars, repair their leaks and refit the vessels themselves. Steel masts and spars, steel hulls and fittings, required a shipyard for all major repairs. Masts and yards were no longer sent down in bad weather – the main yard of a four-masted barque, a tapering steel tube, could be over ninety feet long, two feet in diameter amidships, and weigh several tons. The ships depended on structural strength to see them through. Their crews were not called upon to be skilled in the ways the men of the 1840s had

28. Graph reproduced from Cunnison and Gilfillan (eds), *Third Statistical Account of Scotland* (Glasgow 1858), chapter on shipbuilding by Robb.

The watch taking in the main course on board Archibald Russell. (Captain Karl Kåhre)

Vimeira, *2233 tons gross, built at Glasgow in 1891, in 52° south on passage towards Brisbane.* (Basil Greenhill Collection)

been. The best portrait of the crew of a big vessel of this period is that drawn by Joseph Conrad in that sombre and powerful novel, written in a mood of nostalgia after he had left the sea, *The Nigger of the Narcissus*, which is also the best account of a passage in such a vessel ever written.

The new ships continued to be built in the 1890s because they could compete with steamships and offer reasonable return on investment in the few bulk cargo trades outlined above, and

in a few other trades, at a time of increasingly competitive freight rates and rising real costs of bunker coal. But in fact these vessels operated on the margins both of profits and of time and could not survive when a slight change in economic conditions took place. By 1897 this had happened and the recovery in the freight market for steamships accompanying the outbreak of the Spanish-American and Boer Wars finally and permanently shifted the balance in favour of the steam propelled vessel. In 1897 also a large and general increase in insurance costs at London for sail tonnage further weakened the position of sailing ship owners. Only a tiny trickle of big square rigged ships was launched after 1897 in Britain, some of them for German owners.

In 1900, at the very end of the period under review in this chapter and three years after the building of steel merchant sailing vessels in any significant numbers had ceased, there were still over 2,000,000 tons of sail propelled tonnage registered under the British Merchant Shipping Acts. Some general idea of the composition of this fleet can be gained by a study of *Lloyd's Register* for 1900 – always bearing in mind that the listing is somewhat arbitrary and by no means represents all British, much less all the world's, vessels. The list contains the names of over 13,000 sailing vessels. Despite all that has been written in this chapter they are, by numbers, overwhelmingly of wooden construction. There are rather fewer than 2200 iron and steel vessels, representing roughly 17 per cent, by numbers, of all vessels listed. But these iron and steel sailing vessels represented a disproportionately large percentage of the total sailing tonnage.

What had happened in the last forty years of the nineteenth century, of course, was that iron and steel vessels had increasingly replaced wood-

A fine example of German shipbuilding, the steel barque Penang, *1997 tons gross, built at Bremerhaven in 1905.* (The late Captain F C Poyser)

en ones at the upper end of the tonnage range. The majority of the vessels listed were iron barques from 500 to 1500 tons, but mostly around 1000 tons, or a little less, built in the '70s and early '80s, together with iron ships of the same period, and steel barques and ships of the late '80s and early '90s. Together with these there were smaller steel vessels, over 180 steel schooners, mostly three-masted, over 50 of them British, 28 or so German, 35 Dutch, together with 64 others, mainly Scandinavian and, perhaps surprisingly, South American, many of them British-built. Surprisingly also there were six iron brigs and ten iron ketches. These vessels were of much the same size as much of the wooden tonnage, which tended to be ageing. Although wooden merchant schooners continued to be built in Britain in north Devon and north Wales until the First World War, and in Scandinavia for very much longer, the building of large wooden vessels had almost ceased by the end of the century. Of course, very large wooden schooners and barquentines were still being launched in considerable numbers on both coasts of the North American continent for em-

Narcissus, *an iron ship of 1270 tons gross built on the Clyde in 1876. She was the original of the ship in Conrad's great sea narrative* The Nigger of the Narcissus. (The late Captain F C Poyser)

ployment in specialised trades and continued to be launched until the end of the first decade of the twentieth century.

The upper range of tonnage of the iron and steel vessels listed in *Lloyd's Register* for 1900 was represented by 218 four-masted barques, 160 or so of them British, 33 German, 23 French and over 40 British and German four-masted full rigged ships. The German and French listing is even less complete than the British, since many German vessels were classified by the Germanischer Lloyd Ship Classification and Survey Organisation and the French by the Bureau Veritas. Some of the German vessels were British-built.

By the 1890s German industrial development was beginning to be comparable with that of Britain but somewhat differently structured. German shipping was dominated to a great extent by the great city of Hamburg. The Hamburg sailing fleets grew in numbers and tonnage until 1912. Dr Jurgen Meyer has shown that at the turn of the century there were 106 sailing ships of over 1000 tons gross registered in the

Deck arrangement and bird's eye view of the Herzogin Cecilie, *a late example of the large steel sailing vessel, a four-masted barque of 4350 tons deadweight built by Rickmers of Bremerhaven in 1902. Originally designed as a cadet training ship as well as a cargo-carrier, the ship featured a long quarterdeck over the cadet's accommodation.* (Drawn by Edward Bowness)

port of Hamburg.[29] At the heart of German merchant shipping activity – though German vessels were employed in many trades – was a chemical industry presenting an insatiable demand for nitrates, obtained at the end of the nineteenth century from natural sources in Chile. Loading facilities in the nitrate ports were rudimentary –the vessels lay off in open roadsteads and loaded from lighters, bag by bag. In such a business a steel four-masted barque with her relatively low overheads had an advantage over steamers, even at the end of the nineteenth century, and the trade provided a hard core of more or less regular employment for four-masted barques. Many of these vessels were extremely well built, very well managed, heavily manned – with an element of subsidy for they provided potential recruits for the expanding German navy – and commanded and staffed by highly competent masters and mates whose appointments conferred social prestige in their communities. The later story of these German steel merchant sailing vessels is dealt with in the next chapter of this book.

The French situation was very different. In France, 212 big steel square rigged vessels were built or bought between 1897 and 1902 to take advantage of a government subsidy system so that they were not, strictly, commercial vessels. The larger the gross tonnage, the larger the subsidy. This meant that the French steel sailing vessels were built with large houses on deck, big

donkey engine rooms, long poops and long comfortable forecastles. All of these features brought up their gross tonnage and the subsidy on building them but also incidentally made them safer and infinitely more comfortable for their crews. As Alan Villers showed, the French sailing ships were paid a mileage as well as a building subsidy and this meant that they tended to take the longest sailing routes from port to port.[30] Their crews were strictly French and they tended to remain socially on the margins of the international world of the merchant sailing vessel of the late nineteenth century.

It was not until 1894 that the first steel sailing vessel was launched in America. She was built by Arthur Sewall & Co, shipbuilders and shipowners of Bath, Maine. She was a huge four-masted barque named *Dirigo* and, because of lack of American building experience of this class of tonnage, she was designed by J F Waddington of Liverpool who superintended her construction. All her steel plates and frames were manufactured at Motherwell near Glasgow and sent across to Maine by steamer. So the *Dirigo* was in fact very similar to a British four-masted barque of the same period. She was to be followed by a few more big steel sailing vessels, the four-mast-

29. J Meyer, *Hamburg's Segelschiffe 1795-1945* (Norderstedt 1971).

30. A Villiers and H Picard, *The Bounty Ships of France* (London 1972).

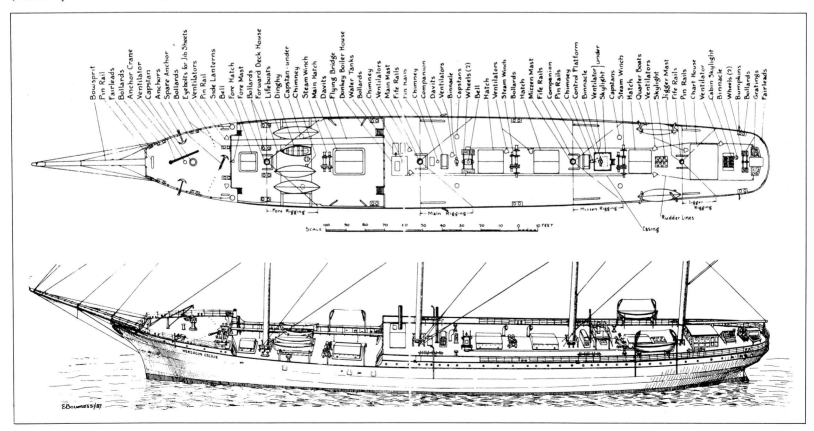

The accommodation under the poop in some of the steel four-masted barques was (relatively) luxurious. This photograph shows the saloon of an unidentified vessel of this rig – clearly, from the presence of the flowers, lying in port. (Basil Greenhill Collection)

ed barque *Erskine M Phelps* and three barques, the *Arthur Sewall*, the *Edward Sewall* and the *Kaiulani* which was built for a firm in San Francisco in 1899. Several more steel vessels were built by the Sewalls for the Standard Oil Company in the early years of the twentieth century.

Late nineteenth-century rigs

In the last years of the nineteenth century there were important experiments with new styles of rigging. The most important of these and the one which pointed the way to the future was the development of the big barquentine. As David MacGregor has already explained, the three-masted barquentine rig had been in use since the

1830s and was very successful in vessels of moderate tonnage in general trade. In the United States, and especially on the West Coast, bigger wooden barquentines became popular in the 1880s. They cost far less to build and sail than a ship or a barque and could run a schooner out of sight on an ocean passage.

The secret of the big barquentines, as of the big schooners, lay in keeping gaff sails reasonably small by increasing the number of masts as the vessel grew bigger. One of the most successful of the last American square rigged sailing ships was the six-masted barquentine *E R Sterling*. In Britain and Europe experiments made with big barquentines sometimes fell into the trap of too few masts for the size and consequently of gaff sails which were too big. The answer lay in multiplying the number of masts and in avoiding big gaff sails by the use of staysails. This was known in the 1880s when Captain R B Forbes, a distinguished American Master Mariner whose working life covered the rise of the

multi-masted schooner, wrote 'I have been trying for about twenty years to convince the builders and owners that my *staysail rig* is much safer and more manageable than the usual gaff rig. I speak now of the very large schooners with from three to five masts'.[31]

Captain Forbes' rig foresaw the use of staysails in place of gaff sails and something very close to his rig has been developed for the huge barquentines built in the late twentieth century for employment in the international passenger cruise trade.

The main builders of British barquentines, which on the whole were very successful commercially, were the Laird Brothers of Birkenhead (who appear to have pioneered the way with the iron four-masted barquentine *Cavan* of 1876), Russell & Company, and the Grangemouth Dockyard Company. The last built a

31. R B Forbes, *The Governor Ames: As She Was And As She Should Be* (apparently 1889, place not stated).

number of four-masted steel barquentines for owners in Nova Scotia as well as their most famous vessels, *Mozart* and *Beethoven*, built for German owners in 1904. *Mozart* made excellent passages in the Chilean nitrate trade and the transpacific trades, operating with a crew of only sixteen and twelve cadets. She was considerably bigger than most American five-masted schooners and her gaff sails must have been among the largest ever made. Sold in 1921 to Åland Finnish owners, she remained a profitable vessel. Indeed her owner under the Finnish flag, Hugo Lundquist, recorded of her 'she is an extremely handy vessel and can easily be navigated with a ship's company of fourteen all told' – as against the twenty-three or twenty-four required of a barque of the same cargo capacity. The cost of maintaining her sails, spars and rigging was markedly lower.

Though she was financially successful she was a sore trial for her small crews, who had endless work taking in and resetting her huge gaff sails to avoid expensive wear in adverse conditions of weather and sea. She would have been a far easier vessel to handle if her sail area had been spread over five masts – as was to be demonstrated by the six-master *E R Sterling*. This vessel was built at Belfast as an iron four-masted barque in 1883. She was dismasted in 1903, sold and re-rigged as a six-masted barquentine. The new rig saved eleven men before the mast; she was handled by seventeen instead of the minimum crew of twenty-eight she had needed in her original form. She was well known as one of the most comfortable merchant sailing ships ever at sea. She was wired from stem to stern for telephone, she had electric light and she was the first sailing vessel to be equipped with radio. She had a fast motorboat as a tender and was extremely comfortably fitted out, both in poop and forecastle. She was commercially highly successful and made a great deal of money for her owners before she was finally dismasted off Cape Horn in 1927.

Germany, the United States, and France were involved with long haul trades in which the sail-

ing vessel was still at an advantage competitively, even in the days of the fully developed triple expansion marine engine. This was because of delays in loading in these trades which made steamship operations uneconomic. In the first years of the twentieth century ship owners in each of these countries had built giant sailing vessels designed to exploit the economies of scale in these sheltered trades. This experiment produced the two largest sailing vessels ever constructed. As to which was the largest is a matter for (rather pointless) discussion. They were, in order of building:

1. The seven-masted steel schooner *Thomas W Lawson*, 5281 tons gross, measuring 395ft long by 50ft in the beam and with a depth of 32.2ft. She was built at Quincy, Massachusetts, in 1902 for the coal trade from Newport News to New England ports. She could carry the enormous cargo of 11,000 tons on a draught of 25ft but, with her two steam hoisting engines, required a crew of only sixteen. She was financially very successful but very difficult to handle under sail in anything but strong winds.

2. The steel five-masted full rigged ship *Preussen*, 5081 tons gross, measuring 407.8ft × 53.6ft × 27.1ft. The only five-masted ship ever built, she was launched at Tecklenborg, also in 1902,

The steel four-masted barquentine Mozart *was built at Greenock in 1904 as a cargo carrying training ship for Hamburg owners. She made excellent passages in the Chilean nitrate trade to Germany and in the trans-Pacific trades, operating with a crew of sixteen with twelve cadets. She was considerably bigger than most American five-masted schooners and her gaff sails, the cloths of which were sewn horizontally, instead of vertically as was the normal custom, must have been among the largest ever made. Like those of the big schooners they were set with the aid of a steam donkey engine.* (Ålands Sjöfartsmuseum)

for the trade with bagged nitrate from Chile to Hamburg. A very strong and powerful ship, extremely well managed and run, she also was very successful financially.

Two other very large vessels were the French twin-screw auxiliary steel five-masted barque *France II*, 5633 tons, built at Bordeaux and launched in 1911, and the German steam auxiliary five-masted barque *R C Rickmers*, launched at Tecklenborg in 1906.

Dr Basil Greenhill

The Motoketch. *This steel motor ketch, of 108 tons gross, shown here entering Cumberland Basin, Bristol, was built at Milwall in 1912 and was one of the relatively few iron or steel small sailing or sail-assisted vessels built in the United Kingdom.* (Bristol Museum)

Iron and Steel Sailing Ships: Typical Vessels 1840-1905

Name	Rig	Flag	Built	Completed	Hull	Tonnage (gross)	Dimensions (feet) (metres)	Remarks
JOHN GARROW	Ship	British	John Ronalds & Co, Aberdeen	1840	Iron	685	130.1 × 30.0 × 19.6 39.7 × 9.1 × 6.0	Largest iron vessel built to date
DOVE	Schooner	British	Laird, Birkenhead	1844	Iron	73 register		Early iron sailing vessel by Laird
RICHARD COBDEN	Barque	British	James Hodgson, Liverpool	1844	Iron	461 register		Early iron vessel in the Indian trade

Name	Rig	Flag	Built	Completed	Hull	Tonnage (gross)	Dimensions (feet) (metres)	Remarks
ANNSBRO'	Schooner	British	Denny, Dumbarton	1846	Iron	80 tons	71.75 × 18.0 × 8.75 21.9 × 5.5 × 2.7	Centreboard schooner in the West Indies trade
EVANGELINE	Ship	British	Jordane Getty, Liverpool	1853	Iron	985 register		These vessels demonstrate the rapid increase in size of iron construction in the early 1850s.
TYPHOON	Ship	British	A Stephen, Glasgow	1852	Iron	965 register		
ELLEN BATES	Ship	British	Neath Abbey Iron Co., Neath	1853	Iron	1098 register		First iron sailing vessel to pass the 1000-ton mark
NELSON	Ship	British	Hill & Co, Port Glasgow	1862	Iron	1333	214.4 × 36.2 × 22.9 65.3 × 11.0 × 7.0	Had three water-tight compartments and patent reefing single topsails
VALETTA	Barquentine	British	Tod & MacGregor, Glasgow	1854	Iron	464	186.2 × 29.9 × 14.1 56.8 × 9.1 × 4.3	A pioneer iron barquentine
CITY OF ATHENS	Ship	British	R Steele & Co, Greenock	1866	Iron	1144	222.9 × 34.2 × 22.8 67.9 × 10.4 × 6.9	In the Calcutta jute trade
NARCISSUS	Ship	British	R Duncan & Co, Port Glasgow	1876	Iron	1270	235.0 × 37.1 × 22.0 71.6 × 11.3 × 6.7	Original of Conrad's *Nigger of the Narcissus*
COUNTY OF PEEBLES	4-masted ship	British	Barclay, Curle, Glasgow	1875	Iron	1614	266.6 × 38.7 × 23.4 81.3 × 11.8 × 7.1	Still exists, laid up in Chilean waters
ROUTENBURN	4-masted barque	British	R Steele & Co, Greenock	1881	Iron	1997	289.0 × 42.2 × 23.9 88.1 × 12.9 × 7.3	Became famous in the 1920s as the Swedish training ship *Beatrice*
WANDERER	4-masted ship	British	C Connell & Co, Glasgow	1884	Iron	1982	292.7 × 42.0 × 23.8 89.2 × 12.8 × 7.3	There is a superb model of her in the National Maritime Museum
HALEWOOD	Ship	British	Oswald, Mordant & Co, Southampton	1885	Iron	2153	274.3× 40.1 × 24.4 83.6 × 12.2 × 7.4	Representative of the last generation of the three-master; bigger than some four-masters
PASS OF MELFORT	4-masted barque	British	Fairfield, Glasgow	1891	Steel	2346	298.8 × 44.0 × 24.5 91.1 × 13.4 × 7.5	Standard four-masted barque; others built to the same model
TACORA	4-masted barquentine	British	J Reid & Co, Port Glasgow	1888	Iron	911	204.7 × 35.6 × 18.3 62.4 × 10.9 × 5.6	Pioneer four-masted barquentine. Small enough for the rig and very successful
TITANIA	4-masted barquentine	British	Russell & Co, Port Glasgow	1895	Steel	1107	210.0 × 35.6 × 19.5 64.0 × 10.9 × 5.9	A very beautiful and successful vessel
OLIVEBANK	4-masted barque	British	Mackie & Thompson, Glasgow	1892	Steel	2824	326.0 × 43.1 × 24.5 99.4 × 13.1 × 7.5	Another standard four-masted barque; others built to the same model
LAWHILL	4-masted barque	British	Thompson, Dundee	1892	Steel	2942	317.4 × 45.0 × 25.1 96.7 × 13.7 × 7.7	No royals, very square yards. Very successful bulk carrier
PREUSSEN	5-masted ship	German	Tecklenberg, Geestemunde	1902	Steel	5081	407.8 × 53.6 × 27.1 124.3 × 16.3 × 8.3	Enormously strong, fast and of great cargo carrying capacity, the only five-masted ship ever built, set new standards of sailing vessel operation
THOMAS W LAWSON	7-masted schooner	American	Fore River Shipbuilding, Quincy, Mass	1902	Steel	5218	395.0 × 50.0 × 32.2 120.4 × 15.2 × 9.8	Third largest sailing vessel ever built. Very successful commercially but very difficult to handle under sail with her small crew

5

The Merchant Sailing Vessel in the Twentieth Century

AT THE end of the nineteenth century sail tonnage registered under the British Merchant Shipping Acts stood at over 2,000,000 tons. The building of large steel sailing vessels in any numbers had come to an end in 1897. A trickle of big square rigged vessels was launched between 1900 and 1906 from British yards. Some of this new construction was to the order of German owners. This short phase of building on a small scale ended with the launching of the four-masted steel barquentines *Mozart* and *Beethoven*, the four-masted barques *Moshulu* and *Archibald Russell* and the barques *Sunlight* and *Rendova*.

The new vessels built in the last boom of sailing vessel construction in the early 1890s had cost, say, £22,000 each to build, depending on the date of build, the building yard, the vessel's size and design and the quality of her construction. In the currency of the early 1990s this sum represents, very roughly, about £1.75 million. But, because these vessels were built to some extent on standard designs by a society fully familiar with the techniques involved and many of the fittings could be bought off the shelf, it would cost a great deal more to build a so-called replica of one of the steel four-masted barques of the 1890s a century or more later – quite apart from the fact that the navigational and safety equipment required by legislation and the features of construction necessary to meet the international safety standards of the end of the twentieth century would add greatly to the cost – and result in a vessel that differed in many ways very markedly from the original.

In the 1890s, then, the big four-masted barques cost about £8.50 per ton to their first owners. Ten years after the debacle of 1897 they were selling for less than half that sum, three years later for less than a quarter. The realisable return from freights to be made from these vessels in early twentieth-century conditions determined the capital value of the machine – the vessel – which returned the profits, such as they were. And even with such small capital investment as was now involved in large sailing tonnage the vessels had to be run very economically to make acceptable returns on the money invested in them. The consequence of the disposal of sailing tonnage which resulted in these low prices was that by 1910 British sail tonnage had been halved in ten years to just over 1,000,000 tons – with 10,500,000 tons of steam vessels. It is to be remembered that this figure of statutory registered British tonnage included the considerable numbers of vessels sailing from the Canadian Atlantic Provinces – the great majority of which were wooden schooners – and also Indian tonnage.

The owners of surviving big sailing vessels registered in United Kingdom ports had either invested relatively little in their vessels or had written down their book value to scrap prices. In either case there was little capital to depreciate and no idea of building up capital to replace the vessels. The result was that at least some of the vessels were managed on the bread-line by companies whose legal assets were limited to single ships. Many of them were run in thoroughly depressing conditions.

Alan Villiers in his book *The War With Cape Horn* gave an excellent and fully documented account of these big British sailing vessels of the era after new construction had ceased.[1] Taking Lloyd's weekly shipping index for 7 September 1905 as his source he finds

...well over 3500 large and medium sized sailing ships, including some large brigs. That day, 800 of them were British, 550 Norwegian, 215 French, 250 German, 350 Italian ... 150 Ameri-

1. A Villiers, *The War With Cape Horn* (London 1971).

Some of Gustaf Erikson's vessels, the last commercially operated deep water fleet, lying in the Western Harbour at Mariehamn in the 1930s. Nearest the camera is the steel full rigged ship Grace Harwar, *2950 tons gross, built at Port Glasgow in 1889 and broken up in 1935. (Sjöhistoriska Museet vid Åbo Akademi)*

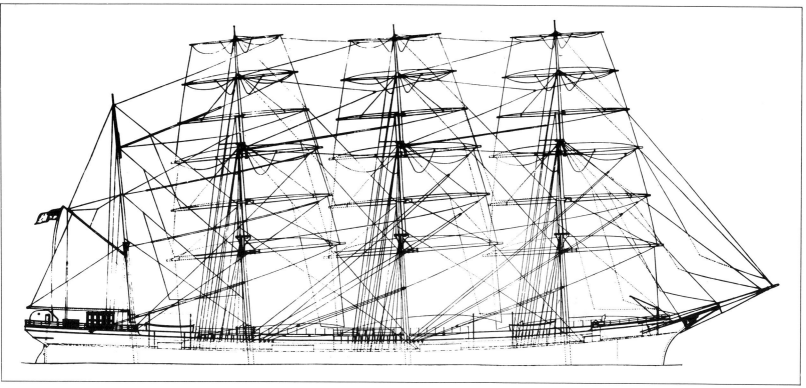

The sail plan of a typical big four-masted barque of the 1890s, the Mowhan *of 1892. From A C Holms'* Practical Shipbuilding, *published in 1904.* (By courtesy of David MacGregor)

can, and 52 Russian (Russian of this date meant almost entirely Finnish), as well as many Spanish, Portuguese, South American, Austro-Hungarian, Danish, Swedish, and some Belgian vessels. Almost all the British, French and German were large vessels well over 1200 tons, many over 2500.

Villiers continues:

the wind ships small and large were no longer viable. No matter how cheaply capitalised or carefully run, they were finished. Within five years from 1900, none was built in Britain or America and no large sailing ships were built anywhere (except the odd school-ship and three or four fine four-masted barques in Germany). A time of parsimony descended upon too many of the survivors, it seemed to me that the first sufferers were the masters. Through them, suffering descended to the officers, apprentices, and crews – fast – and stayed with them.

No longer properly paid and without hope of reasonable honest emolument these remnants in the condemned ships they were too old to leave were not to be blamed if they soon became embittered. The fruits of their bitterness were evident in many of these logs. Their good ships once so well and proudly run by owners interested in them became dispersed among the horde of one-ship companies run by those

hard-hearted skinflints, the owner/managers. In the true sense, nobody 'owned' or 'managed' those ships at all. The so-called managers were brokers for groups of shareholders who hoped for a reasonable dividend now and then and often had no other interest. The broker made a little on chartering, storing, insuring — indeed, on everything he could, in every possible way.

This gloomy picture painted by Alan Villiers was based on a detailed and thorough study of the evidence provided by the 'Articles of Agreement', the original contract between ships and crews. Villiers studied between five and six hundred sets of Articles of Agreement concerning the crews of big square rigged sailing ships filed in the years 1902-1908.

Schooners and ketches

Captain W J Lewis Parker has described elsewhere in this volume the history of the big wooden schooners on the east coast of the United States. These were to have a different later history to that of the last British steel sailing ships. The industrial boom which followed the Spanish-American war of 1898, with other factors, led to a great revival in their construction for the East Coast coal trade and other trades. It was the coal trade, despite their employment with many types of cargo and despite many crossings of the North Atlantic to European ports, which remained the backbone of the operation of these big schooners. In this trade one

of the big factors in favour of sailing vessels was the inadequacy of the facilities available at the coal loading ports in Virginia and the irregularity with which the coal supplies came down to the wharves from the pits.

The trade had really expanded too rapidly for rail and dock facilities to keep pace and it worked well enough so that the incentive to invest in improved and expanded facilities was small in a society in which the opportunities for profitable investment in other ways seemed almost limitless. In consequence vessels were frequently delayed for a week, sometimes much more, waiting for loads. Schooners with their low overheads could afford these delays, steamers could not. In this trade vessels were loaded in strict order of arrival at the ports and through pressure and through legal action the schooner owners succeeded in maintaining this practice until well into the twentieth century. So the schooner continued to prosper and to develop and took further steps forward, in competition with trains of towed barges, with the beginning of the building on the East Coast of five-masters as late as 1898 and of six-masters two years later. Thus the first six-master in the coal trade came fifty-six years after the world's first really big schooner rigged vessel, the SS *The Great Britain*, had been launched in Bristol, England.

However, in 1909 the Virginia Railway was opened for the sole purpose of transporting coal from new West Virginian fields to coal loading wharves at Norfolk for shipment. Norfolk's tidewater piers had the largest loading capacity in

The six-masted schooner Wyoming *built at Bath, Maine, in 1909 could carry over 6000 tons of coal. She made several transatlantic voyages and was financially highly successful and relatively easy to handle under sail. She is shown setting her driver with the aid of the steam hauler.* (Maine Maritime Museum)

the world and brought to an end the delays in loading which had precluded the employment of steamers in the New England trade. The effect was as decisive as the events of 1897 had been on the steel square rigged sailing vessels of Britain. In 1909 the launch of six four-masters and of the mighty *Wyoming*, the largest six-master and the second largest wooden merchant sailing vessel ever built, able to carry over 6000 tons of coal, marked the end of schooner building – at least for the time being.

Paul Morris has recorded no fewer than 521 four-masted schooners owned on the East Coast of the United States.[2] The four-masters formed the biggest element in the fleet of large schooners. In addition there were thirty-seven four-masters built in Canada, three American three-masters which were built in the United States, sold to Canadian owners and re-rigged as four-masters, and one four-master built in the Bahamas, making a grand total of 562 four-masted schooners, all but seven of them built of wood, operating on the East Coast of North America. As has already been noted, these vessels continued to be built through the first decade of the

twentieth century and, as we shall see, in a kind of resurrection during and after the First World War many more vessels were to be built into the early 1920s. Their last representatives were to survive working at sea just into the second half of the 1940s.

Among this great fleet of East Coast schooners were thirty-six four-masters which were built on the West Coast of the United States which, in most cases by way of Cape Horn, came round

to the Atlantic seaboard. The West Coast-built four-masted schooners were representatives of a great fleet which was built for the Pacific lumber and complementary trades. Drawing principally on the work of a great American merchant ship historian, the late John Lyman, James Gibbs has recorded some 138 four-masters, five five-masters and numerous three-masters built between the 1880s and 1908.[3]

West Coast-built schooners were mainly employed in the lumber trade down the coast to California, across the Pacific with lumber to Australia and back with coal or with copper or phosphate from the Pacific islands to the West Coast or Hawaii. Quite rapidly the schooners built on the West Coast began to develop away from the fashions of the East. They were built with full poops and raised topgallant forecastles, like British square rigged ships, although their crews were accommodated in deckhouse forecastles like those of the East Coast vessels. Many of these West Coast schooners were built without separate topmasts, so that each mast was one tall single pole, and many of them had a triangular sail on their aftermost mast instead of a gaff sail. Just as in Prince Edward Island, Canada, schooners and barquentines were built entirely

2. P Morris, *Four-Masted Schooners of the East Coast* (Orleans, Mass 1975), p5.

3. J Gibbs, *West Coast Windjammers* (New York 1968).

One of a small number of West Coast-built five-masted schooners, the Inca, *1014 tons gross, was built at Port Blakely, Washington State, in 1896; photographed here off Cape Flattery by G E Plummer. She was hulked at Sydney in 1920.* (Basil Greenhill Collection)

The three-masted schooner M A James *(125 tons gross, built at Porthmadog in 1900) photographed at Appledore in the early 1930s. She has been fitted with a semi-diesel auxiliary engine and her topsail and topgallant yards sent down. Under the managing ownership of Captain W J Slade and with his brother George as Master she was highly successful in the British home trade until the Second World War.* (The late H Oliver Hill)

of spruce and successfully employed on prolonged service in world trade; but spruce was not a favoured material for shipbuilding, so these West Coast vessels were built sometimes almost entirely of Douglas fir, sometimes called Oregon pine, a timber not regarded as ideal for shipbuilding purposes in Britain and on the East Coast of North America. Yet they gave many years of profitable service in the transpacific trade.

The building of sailing vessels on the West Coast of North America ceased, as did building on the East Coast, at the end of the first decade of the twentieth century. At the same time the building of schooners and ketches in Britain was at long last coming to an end. The demise of the small sailing vessel in Britain was to be a very slow process. Generally speaking, for reasons of draught, bigger crew requirements, initial capital investment, overheads and maintenance, very small steamers could not be built which could compete commercially with small wooden sailing vessels, and so the latter continued to be

built and operated as long as there were small cargoes to be loaded and discharged. Because of the general scale and pattern of industry and difficulties of land transport, this situation persisted

in many areas until the First World War. So in 1890 when the total of United Kingdom registered shipping came to about 8,000,000 tons (3,000,000 sail and around 5,000,000 steam), about 7½ per cent of the sailing vessel tonnage comprised wooden schooners and ketches. Between 1891 and 1913, thirty-three three-masted schooners were built at Porthmadog in Gwynedd for the salt fish trade from Newfoundland and the slate trade to Hamburg and other north German ports. In terms of quality and performance these were perhaps the finest schooners ever built in Britain. The last three-masters, the *P T Harris* and the *Gestiana*, were launched at Appledore, north Devon, and Porthmadog, respectively, as late as 1913.

During this very late period a new sailing vessel was developed in the Baltic. She appears to have been a product of the 1890s and to have been born on the southwest coast of Finland. This was the *slättoppare* as she was called in Swedish, the schooner with three or more masts of approximately the same height carrying not

Sail plan of the ketch Hobah *as she appeared about 1910. Originally built in 1879 at Mylor in Cornwall, she was one of the last surviving sailing coasters, making a living until the Second World War, although latterly with the aid of an auxiliary motor.* (Drawn by David MacGregor)

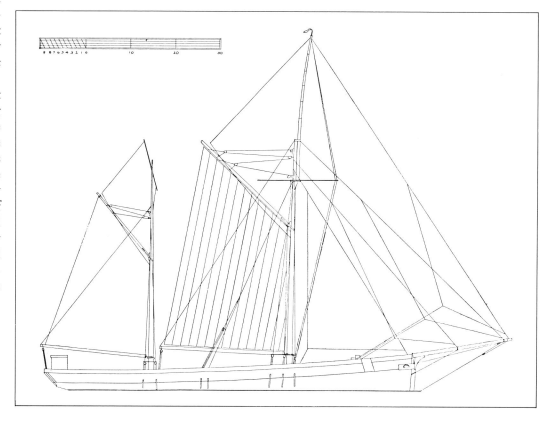

The three-masted schooner Fulton, *99.94 tons gross, built at Marstal, Denmark, in 1915 for the Newfoundland trade with dried and salted cod fish to Europe, photographed in Roskilde Fiord in 1991. A typical Danish* slettop skonnert *it will be noticed that she is hogged. She was due for extensive remedial work in the winter of 1991-92.* (Basil Greenhill)

more than one yard on her fore mast. It seems most likely that the *slättoppare* was an independent development from the characteristic two-masted schooner, locally known as a *galeas*, of the Finnish and Swedish archipelagoes and of the Åland islands. Indeed, early vessels of this type were often registered as three-masted *galeaser*. Vessels of this rig were launched in Finland in the early 1890s and in 1903 the type was taken up in Denmark, where it became much favoured and was built in large numbers. In Danish these vessels were known as *slettop skonnert*. But the building even of these vessels was much reduced after the end of the first decade of the twentieth century. The merchant sailing vessel of all kinds, sizes and nationalities, was now clearly mortally sick, it seemed, and would very soon be gone. But things are not always as they seem.

The First World War and its effects

There were three factors which were going to ensure the survival of the merchant sailing vessel until after the middle of the twentieth century. The first of these stemmed from the effects of the First World War; the second from the fact that, in some relatively under-developed societies where labour was cheap, opportunities for the alternative investment of capital were limited or non-existent, and the traditions of sailing ship seafaring had not been broken, it was still possible with good management to obtain a reasonable return on capital invested in sailing tonnage. The third factor, which applied only to smaller

vessels, was the development of compact reliable semi-diesel engines which could be installed in sailing vessels to give them greater safety, higher mobility and, in due course in some cases could become the principal means of propulsion with the sails remaining as 'sail-assist'.

To deal first with the effects of the First World War, for some months after its outbreak in August 1914 the world freight market was paralysed while industry and shipowners waited to see what the initial effect of hostilities would be. But before the end of the year freights began slowly to rise and by early 1915 they were going up very satisfactorily from the shipowners' point of view. Just before the outbreak of war a sailing vessel carrying lumber to a west European port from Canada might expect a freight of 42s 6d a standard; 42s 6d is £2.12½p and at early 1990s prices very approximately, say £85.00 a standard. By the end of 1915 freight had gone up to the equivalent of £292.00 a standard. By late 1916 freight was the equivalent of £700.00 per standard. By early 1917 pitch pine was being carried in sailing vessels from Pensacola on the Gulf of Florida to Liverpool at the equivalent in early 1990s money of £952.00 per standard. The 1914 freight for this particular cargo had been around the equivalent of £200.00 per standard.

Moreover these high freights were pre-paid and this was a tremendously important development for the merchant shipping industry. Instead of having to borrow money to outfit for the voyage and pay interest on the borrowed money, shipowners found shippers competing to pay them in advance, so that not only did they

not have to pay interest, but they could invest the surplus money at once and either gain interest on it themselves or invest in additional tonnage – if they could get it – and earn yet more big pre-paid freights.

It was no wonder in these circumstances that the world's old decrepit and obsolete sailing vessels could begin to earn handsome dividends. Indeed fortunes could be made with old tonnage. In 1916, for example, one thirty-three-year-old 800-ton barque with a deadweight capacity of 1500 tons earned 550 per cent of her 1913 market price. By then tonnage prices were increasing in step with freights and old sailing vessels laid up or working in a few marginal trades became very valuable assets. To give some examples, an 800-ton four-masted schooner was bought in the United States in 1901 for $18,000 and after earning clear profits of $44,000 in sixteen years she was sold in January 1917 for $38,000. An old 430 net tons wooden barque built by farmers on a Finnish island in 1881 which had already made her building cost many times over was sold for £300 in March 1914. She was caught by the outbreak of war in Rochester and laid up, but she was sold in May 1916 for £1600 and immediately fixed to load timber in Canada for Britain at 370 shillings a standard which gave her a freight for the one passage of between £4000 and £5000 – in terms of early 1990s currency at least £200,000, fifteen times her 1914 value. The great six-masted schooner *Wyoming*, 3730 tons gross and able to carry 6000 tons of coal, was launched in 1909 from the Percy and Small yard at Bath, Maine (now the site of the Maine Maritime Museum) and operated on her builders' account until 1916 when she was sold to the France and Canada Steamship Company for about $350,000. In the words of William A Baker, 'On 1 October 1919 it was reported that she had paid for herself more than twice over since 1916 and it would not be hard to do so again as she had just been chartered to carry coal from Norfolk to Genoa at $23.50 a ton.'[4]

In consequence of these great increases in freights and the price of tonnage, sailing vessels of all sizes were sought out from every backwa-

4. W A Baker, *A Maritime History of Bath* (Bath, Maine 1973), Vol 2, p769.

ter all over the world and fitted out for sea again. But more importantly, a large building programme was initiated on both sides of the Atlantic and it lasted until well after the end of the war. It was now that the schooner, after four centuries of slow development, in the form of the moderately sized four-master equipped with a diesel donkey engine, probably the most efficient merchant sailing ship which has ever existed, came into her own. Of the literally hundreds of new sailing vessels built, almost all were wooden schooners. The exceptions were two steel four-masted barques built in Germany, four barques built in Finland, a full-rigged ship built in Indonesia for Danish owners, and thirty or forty or so barquentines. Nearly all these vessels were of wooden construction, for this was a resurrection not only of the sailing vessel but also of wooden shipbuilding, and it took place largely in countries where suitable timber was still available and where sufficient elderly survivors of the ancient crafts could be assembled to

teach and supervise men not skilled in the necessary trades. Great Britain played no part in this resurrection of sail. The new tonnage very rapidly constructed in the United Kingdom was driven by triple expansion marine steam engines and it was built of steel.

The scale of sailing ship building between 1916 and 1921 was vast. It is best expressed in simple figures. On the West Coast of North America ninety-nine very big five-masters, fifty-six four-masters and three six-masted schooners were launched, and in addition to these eight big three-masters and sixteen four- and five-masted barquentines. This total of five-masters was more than twice as many as were launched on the East Coast throughout the history of the big schooners and the five-master might be considered to be a typical West Coast vessel. But in fact, of the ninety-nine five-masters, most of them fitted with auxiliary engines of one kind or another, steam or diesel, which were built during the war boom, no fewer than forty-five were

built for the French government, together with nine of the four-masters. Four of the five-masters and nineteen of the four-masters were launched for Norwegian owners. Built in some cases roughly and not always of high quality materials, many of them were short-lived vessels. Nevertheless some of them, like the *Valborg*, the *Odine* and the *Gunn*, worked successfully for years in the Baltic timber trade to western Europe.

The French vessels were ordered as a result of a mission to the United States by André Tardieu, a prominent politician of the era, who was sent there in 1917 in the role of 'High Commissioner For War'. He asked for authority to negotiate two hundred wooden transport schooners of about 3000 tons each fitted with auxiliary motors. In fact many of this great fleet which was duly constructed were laid up soon after the end of the war on the beach at Portstren, beyond the commercial port to the east of Brest, and there they stayed while the local children played around them (and dubbed them 'Tardieu's fleet') until they were broken up for firewood, some as late as the Second World War. A few were sold to American owners and one lasted, laid up in Brooklyn, until at least 1938. One or two were sold to British owners. The *Astri 1* built at Astoria, Oregon, in 1917 for Norwegian owners, already by 1921 was a fishmeal plant hulk at Brightlingsea in Essex under the name of *Gloria*. Another of these vessels (or perhaps she was the *Gloria*) still lay moored in the Thames as a great blackened hulk in 1946. A few years later she was abandoned in a Kentish creek and the author remembers sailing round her many times in his first boat, the *Puffin*.

In the eastern United States, 133 four-masters, ten five-masters, many big three-masters and a dozen or more very big barquentines were launched. In eastern Canada at least 323 schooners were built, the great majority of them terns, but with a dozen or more four-masters amongst them and at least two barquentines.

These Canadian tern schooners developed into a class of their own. Like the Finnish Swedish *slättoppare* they were three-masters with the masts all the same height and the topmasts, fore and main gaffs and booms, and much of the rigging often interchangeable between the masts. The name 'tern' was taken from a poker term meaning 'three of a kind'. These vessels were built in Prince Edward Island, New Brunswick,

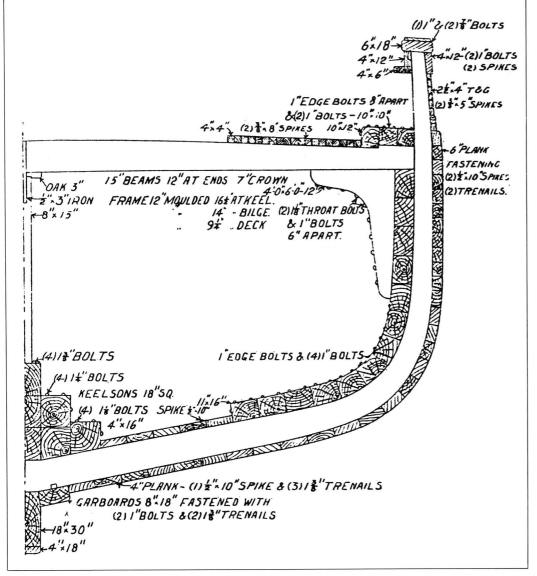

A structural section of a typical Pacific coast wooden schooner, the four-master J W Clise, *built by the Globe Navigation Co at Ballard, Washington, in 1904. From* The Marine Review *of April 1909. (By courtesy of David MacGregor)*

The five-masted schooner Rebecca Palmer *(2556 tons gross, built at Rockland, Maine, in 1901) photographed by Fred Kitto lying in Fowey, Cornwall, waiting to load china clay for New York City. She was the first five-masted American schooner to cross the Atlantic.* (Basil Greenhill Collection)

and in Newfoundland, but especially in Nova Scotia where the great majority of them were launched. They were employed in international trade to and from the United States and the West Indies and many of them in the salt fish trade from the Atlantic provinces, the Gulf of St Lawrence, and especially from Newfoundland and Labrador to European ports. Altogether over 800 of these vessels were built. Some of the later ones, like the *Nelly T Walters* built at Shellburn, Nova Scotia, in 1920, were among the finest and most efficient sailing ships of their size ever launched. Over the years 1922-27, taking passages both ways and including a passage of thirty-one days in 1926, the *Nelly T Walters'* average transatlantic passage was twenty-two days. One of her runs was from Marystown, Newfoundland, to Oporto in only fourteen days, a passage to equal the best passages of schooners in this trade.

Here is the description of one of these Nova Scotian three-masted schooners written by the British maritime historian Sir Alan Moore.[5]

> A few days later we left Gibraltar in the afternoon and when clear of the harbour took a monitor in tow. While we were so doing one of the most beautiful vessels I have ever seen sailed into the Bay, rounded-to in her own length almost, and began to shorten sail. She was a Nova Scotiaman, a three-masted fore and aft schooner, *Frances Louise*. She had a low, graceful hull painted black, a yacht-like counter, and a rounded cut-away stem. Her masts raked slightly and the mizzen mast was the tallest. Her spanker or mizzen was really her mainsail, in that it was the largest of the three. All three sails and the fore staysail were laced to booms.
>
> Her bowsprit was horizontal, and she set a single jib. All her canvas was beautifully cut. She seemed the last word in sail and contrasted strongly with the Spanish brig which we saw a few minutes later.[5]

5. Sir A Moore, *The Last Days of Mast and Sail* (Oxford 1925), p203.

The Canadian tern schooners Daniel Getson, *295 tons gross, built at Bridgewater, Nova Scotia, in 1917 and* E C Adams, *330 tons gross, also built at Bridgewater in 1919 at anchor in the La Have River, Nova Scotia.* (Basil Greenhill Collection)

The Finnish four-masted schooner Svenborg, *380 tons gross, built at Odense, Denmark, in 1921. Lost in the North Sea in 1957, she may have been the last cargo-carrying four-master.* (Sjöhistoriska Museet vid Åbo Akademi)

The *Frances Louise*'s bowsprit was, in fact, steeved and what the author meant by a single jib is not clear, but all the essentials are here. The *Frances Louise* was built at Lunenberg, Nova Scotia, in 1917 and she and her sisters with the rounded stem and cut-away forefoot represented the last distinctive individual type of merchant sailing ship ever to be developed. They were the products of the twentieth century and before it was a generation old they were obsolete.

The large schooners of the United States and Canada were not the only sailing vessels. Working on the coasts of Florida, of the Carolinas and in Chesapeake Bay, on the West Coast, and above all perhaps on the coasts of New England, Nova Scotia and Newfoundland there were literally tens of thousands of small schooners carrying cargoes between the minor ports, and these vessels persisted in steadily diminishing numbers into the 1940s. Those of New England have been very well recorded in John Leavitt's *Wake of the Coasters* (Mystic, Connecticut 1970).

Danish shipbuilders and shipowners made a remarkable contribution to the resurrection of sailing vessels during the First World War and immediately afterwards. Holm Petersen[6] has shown that between 1913 and 1923 at least fifty-three small four-masted schooners were built in Denmark, a dozen or more of them of steel. The first of the steel schooners was the *Morten Jensen* of 1913 and the longest-lived was the *Caroline*, sold to Portuguese owners in 1934 for the Newfoundland and Greenland dory fishery – of which more later in this chapter – and not lost until 1968. Nearly all these vessels were built with auxiliary engines but fully rigged with tall fidded topmasts, and many of them with square topsails on the fore topmast. One, the *Gertrude Rask*, built for the Greenland trade in 1923, was equipped with a steam auxiliary engine. She had a bridge amidships and a tall funnel and was a very handsome vessel. Besides these four-masters an unknown number of two- and three-masted schooners and ketches were built in Denmark over these years.

In Finland at least twenty-four three- and four-masted schooners were launched during the wartime boom, besides four wooden barques. In Germany two steel four-masted barques were built during the First World War and after the war a number of steel three-, four- and five-masted schooners were launched and another four-masted barque, the *Padua*, as late as 1926. A degree of subsidy was indicated perhaps by the fact that she cost more to build than a motor vessel of the same cargo capacity. Today she is well known as the Estonian training ship *Kruzenstern*. In Holland big steel four-masted schooners were still being launched in the mid-1920s. In Greece, Italy and Spain considerable numbers of schooners, barquentines and ketches were built during the wartime boom. So between 1916 and the early '20s more than a thousand big sailing vessels and an unknown number of smaller ones were launched. The seas were full of sailing ships again and to some people in such places as the small ports of Nova Scotia and Denmark it seemed as if the great days had come back.

In 1920 the *Norske Veritas Register Over Scandinaviske Skibe* listed some 558 sailing vessels and 312 auxiliary motor vessels as owned in Sweden, Denmark and Norway. Of the sailing vessels fifty-two were full rigged ships, nineteen were four-masted barques and no fewer than 141 were barques, most of them wooden and old. There were fifteen brigantines and six brigs. There were fourteen four-masted schooners, two five-masters and seventy-seven barquentines. The rest of the vessels were schooners and ketches. Although many of the schooners listed were to survive until the Second World War – indeed some of them right through until the 1950s – the square rigged elements of this great fleet, especially the small wooden barques, were to vanish in the next year or two as sculptures made from snow vanish in a thaw. Increasingly from now on the sailing vessel became associated with what are now called under-developed countries, societies without sufficient capital to invest in steam vessels, with a sufficiently low standard of living to make employment in sailing vessels still attractive and with low enough labour costs to make them economical.

As far as big British square rigged sailing vessels were concerned, when a vessel incurred damage – by minor collision, by grazing a dock wall, by a small fire, or by stress of weather – she was sold for the scrap value at which she had probably been bought by her last owners. If she was totally lost the shareholders might do quite well out of the situation. Vessels were sold to owners in Germany, Norway, Sweden and Denmark, to South American owners, to Spanish, Portuguese, Greek and Italian owners and, for operation under Russian registration, to Finnish owners. A number of the very few remaining British big square rigged sailing vessels were sold to Finland after that country gained her independence from Russia at the end of the First World War. The last big square rigged sailing vessel to be registered at a home port in the United Kingdom, the fully rigged ship *William Mitchell*, was broken up in 1927.

But because of the great wartime and postwar building boom, the big merchant sailing vessel did not vanish in the second decade of this century, as had seemed inevitable, but lingered on

6. Holm Petersen, *Danske firmastskonnerter* (Marstal 1989).

The steel full rigged ship William Mitchell, *2035 tons gross, built at Londonderry in 1892. Broken up in 1927 she was the last big steel square rigged merchant vessel to be registered at a home port in Britain.* (The late Captain Malcolm Bruce Glasier)

ish archipelago in the mouth of the Gulf of Bothnia, the big merchant sailing vessel, steel barques, wooden barques and wooden schooners both large and small, survived in numbers until the 1930s, in the contemporaneously famous Australian grain and Baltic timber trade fleets.

In the Åland Islands a merchant shipping industry had begun to develop only after the end of the so-called Crimean War of 1854-56 between Britain and France on the one hand and Russia on the other. Finland at this time was a grand duchy of Russia and although the Czars imposed little of Russian law on Finland, they had imposed trading restrictions of which the grand duchy was progressively relieved after the end of the war. Capital generation was necessarily slow and it was not until 1927 that one of the leading local shipowning families, the Lundqvists, began continuous investment in steam tonnage. The names of Gustaf Erikson of Mariehamn and Hugo and Arthur Lundqvist of Mariehamn and Wårdö go down in history as the last great owners of big sailing vessels in Europe. The descendants of the sailing ship men in Åland today own a very efficient modern fleet which comprises about a third of the merchant shipping tonnage of Finland, and which is still prospering at the time of writing, even in the world recession of 1992. But the last sailing voyages were made, very unprofitably, as late as 1949 by the four-masted barques *Pamir* and *Passat* in the trade with bagged wheat from South Australia to Britain. Today the British-built steel four-masted barque *Pommern* lies in Mariehamn alongside the Ålands Sjöfartsmuseum just as she

into the fifth. After the collapse of the postwar boom a substantial number of three-, four- and five-masted schooners remained in commission under the United States and Canadian flags. They did well out of the brief Miami boom of the mid-1920s. But slowly the fleet dwindled, with increasing rapidity during the years of the great depression, the early 1930s, so that by 1941 only a few were left. The last of the big three-masters was the *Frederick P Elkin*, built in Nova Scotia and last owned in Barbados. She made her last passage with cargo (coal from Newport News to Barbados) in 1947. There is a splendid account of one of these late Canadian tern schooners in Charles H Turnbull's *The Last Voyage of the Jean F Anderson*, published by Mystic Seaport in 1990. It is the story of a passage in

a Canadian tern schooner from Nova Scotia to New York and on to Jacksonville, Florida, in the summer of 1941.

These schooners comprised one of the last two fleets of large merchant sailing vessels in the western world. The other fleet was in Europe. Here, in the extraordinary economic and social circumstances of the Åland Islands in the Finn-

The steel four-masted barque Pommern, *2376 tons gross, built at Glasgow in 1903 for German owners. She was owned from 1922 to 1953 by Gustaf Erikson and, after Gustaf's death in 1947, by his son Edgar and daughter Eva. Today she lies in the Western Harbour of Mariehamn in the Åland Islands, the only big steel square rigged sailing vessel which survives unchanged from her working days.* (Basil Greenhill)

The steel three-masted schooner Kalmarsund V, *585 tons deadweight with a diesel of 287kW, built at Kalmar in 1944. One of a standard type built at Kalmar in the 1940s, she represents the final development of the motor schooner in Europe. In 1953 she was converted to be a fully powered motorship.* (Basil Greenhill)

came in from the sea in 1939, the only unchanged big steel square rigged merchant sailing ship in the world and the world's finest preserved merchant ship.

No small powered vessel could be built to profit from the centuries-old trade with salt cod across the north Atlantic from Newfoundland to Europe. In the last century over the years hundreds of British schooners sailed in this trade. But after the 1914-18 war it became the preserve of Nova Scotian and Danish schooners, most of them built during the wartime boom or just after it. In the middle of 1928 there were over forty of these ships on their way across the Atlantic together. It was not until the end of the Second World War that the work of small schooners on the north Atlantic came to an end and, indeed, as late as 1950 the Danish schooner *Start*, which had delivered a timber cargo in Bristol, was fixed to sail to Black Tickle, Labrador, to bring back to Europe a cargo of salted cod.

Motor-sailers

In short sea trades small vessels using sails were to persist even longer. This was because of the third reason for the survival of sail in the twentieth century, a development not foreseen in

Helsinki's classical waterfront by Carl Ludwig Engel seen through the rigging of the galeas Astrid *built in the 1960s for the aggregate trade from the Gulf of Finland to Helsinki and later working as a cruise vessel.* (Basil Greenhill)

After the Second World War under the terms of the peace treaty with the Soviet Union Finland was required to build 581 vessels totalling 365,155 tons gross by way of reparations. This incredible feat was accomplished between 1945 and 1952. A substantial number of these vessels were wooden three-masted schooners and barquentines of which the vessel here shown is a typical example. (Basil Greenhill)

1914. By then there were already a number of small vessels which had been equipped with auxiliary oil motors of various kinds, mostly semi-diesels of the hot bulb variety. The effects of the auxiliary engine were complex. Where the investment in an old vessel was low, or where there were cargoes to be carried between islands or on coasts with particularly bad land communications, or where manning legislation particularly favoured the vessel equipped with sails, as it did for some years in Sweden, the auxiliary schooner and ketch with a very hard-working master, who was a shareholder and had no shore overheads to carry, remained profitable even to a degree which made the construction of new tonnage commercially worthwhile. Thus as late as the second half of the 1940s a series of three-masted steel motor schooners, some of them with jib-headed sails, with deadweight tonnages running up to 600 and diesels of about 300 horsepower, were built in Sweden, notably at Kalmar Varv. In the rapidly changing conditions after the Second World War these vessels comprised useful tonnage for a number of years but in the 1950s most of them were converted to be fully-powered motorships. As late as the 1960s wooden motor ketches – *galeaser* – were built for the aggregate trade along Finland's south coast. Under the terms of the peace treaty with Russia after the Second World War Finland built dozens of three-masted wooden motor schooners as reparations. These vessels were used by the Soviets for transport, for fishing and for 'research'. As to the older vessels, as they wore out, as land communications were improved, as the men to whom this was a way of life died and as protective legislation was amended, so the schooners and ketches dropped out of use.

The last British square rigged ship to operate commercially carrying cargoes was the wooden barquentine *Waterwitch* of Fowey in Cornwall, owned by Edward Stephens of that port. She made her last passage with cargo as a British-registered vessel in 1936, was sold to Estonian owners and operated in the Baltic timber trade and finally sank in a storm off Kaunus, Latvia, in 1942. It was appropriate that the last British square rigged merchant ship was a small wooden vessel, the *Waterwitch*, built as a brig in 1871. She was far more representative of the sailing ships of history than the great steel barques of the late nineteenth century. At the outbreak of the Second World War there were still one hundred schooners and ketches fitted with auxiliary motors, even three schooners without mo-

The Waterwitch *was built as a collier brig at Poole, Dorset, in 1871. Converted to the handier and more economical barquentine rig in 1884, she survived to become the last working square rigged merchant sailing ship to be registered at a home port in the United Kingdom.* (Amos & Amos)

Looking aft on board the three-masted schooner Kathleen & May, *139 tons gross, built at Connah's Quay, Clwyd, in 1900, under sail and power off the Welsh coast in 1959.* Kathleen & May *was the last schooner working in the British home trade. (Basil Greenhill)*

tors, trading on the coasts of Britain, but by 1960 the last of them had ceased to carry cargoes at sea. One survives, the *Kathleen & May*, a three-masted schooner, built at Connah's Quay, Clwyd, in 1900. At the end of the twentieth century she lies in a dock in Southwark, London, adjacent to St Giles Cathedral, saved by the Maritime Trust from decay, laid up in some westcountry creek.

On the coasts of Newfoundland, of Italy and of Spain, among the Greek islands and on the coasts of the Levant, also in the West Indies, auxiliary sailing vessels, and even a few without engines, were still to be found in the 1950s. In 1954 the author came across a whole fleet of pole-masted two-masted schooners heavily rigged with jib-headed sails at the Island of Ruad off the coast of Syria. They were regular traders between Ruad and Egypt. A fleet of ketches and schooners equipped with roller-reefing square topsails continued to carry pitprops and onions from ports in Brittany to south Wales until the Second World War. Often these vessels had re-

tailers on board equipped with bicycles with strings of onions hanging from the handlebars. These men cycled around the villages of Wales and the westcountry, even to London, selling their onions, and returned to the schooner for the passage back to Brittany. Today the vegetables from the fertile and climatically favoured area around Roscoff still come – on almost every tide in season – in ten-wheeled lorries which use the Roscoff-Plymouth ferry service and which distribute the product direct in huge quantities all over Britain.

Wooden three-masted schooners and ketches continued to be built in Denmark until the end of the 1940s. In 1950 there were still six hundred Danish schooners and ketches in commission, some of them in transatlantic trade and all equipped with auxiliary engines. Not until the early 1960s did this great fleet finally succumb to the rising costs of labour, of sails and rigging, to the effects of the building of bridges between the Danish islands, and the establishment of scheduled roll-on roll-off ferries, together with chang-

ing practices in packaging, marketing and distribution.

In the deep sea fishing industry of the north Atlantic, vessels equipped with sails persisted well into the second half of the twentieth century, though the French barquentines and schooners from St Malo and other Brittany ports appear to have ended their activities with the fishing voyages of the *Lt René Guillon*, a heavily motorised former barquentine, in the early 1950s. Portuguese three- and four-masted schooners, some of them very heavily rigged, persisted in the Newfoundland Banks and Greenland dory fishery into the 1970s. As late as the 1950s there were still over thirty of these vessels, fourteen of them four-masted schooners, some of them built as late as 1948, in the dory

A Terre-Neuvier, *a French barquentine from St Malo employed in the dory fishery on the Newfoundland and Greenland banks, setting sail while under tow. The vessel appears to be somewhat hogged.* (Basil Greenhill Collection)

fishery. There was even a wooden barquentine in the fleet. In the great dory fishery of the east coast of North America, for which the ports of Gloucester in Massachusetts and Lunenburg in Nova Scotia became world famous, very handsome two-masted schooners continued to be built also to the end of the 1940s. These vessels were pole-masted and usually equipped with 300hp engines, but they maintained their sailing ability. It had been the practice to rig down topmasts for the winter fishery even before the auxiliary engines were introduced in the early 1920s, and the vessels were designed to perform very well under lower gaff sails and headsails only. The very end of this fishery came in the spring of 1963 when the *Theresa E Connor* returned to Lunenburg harbour, fully equipped for a season's fishing but unable to fish, her eight dories snug and untouched nested inside one another on deck. She had returned to harbour because men no longer could be found willing to stake life, limb and livelihood fishing hand trawls from dories off the coasts of Newfoundland and Greenland. Visiting the small ports of Newfoundland where she had normally recruited her crews, no men had come forward for the job so vividly and accurately portrayed in the classic Spencer Tracy and Freddie Bartholomew movie, *Captains Courageous*, of 1936.

Sherman Zwicker, a typical 142ft Lunenburg 320hp motor schooner built there in 1942 for the Atlantic dory fishery. She is shown as she is now, based at Bath, Maine, as a museum and cruise vessel. As a working schooner she set a gaff sail on the fore, a jib-headed sail on the main and two headsails. (Basil Greenhill Collection)

Late twentieth-century renaissance

So much for the commercial sailing vessel in the twentieth century, her resurrection during and after the First World War, and her subsequent very long goodbye. But she was to be subject to another, small, resurrection in the 1980s. This was the cruise business carrying not cargoes but paying passengers whose fares provided a reasonable return on capital invested in the vessels. The roots of this industry go back a long way. The decline of the fleet of small schooners serving the ports of New England was a very slow business. Indeed a new two-master without an engine, the *Endeavour*, was built for the trade as late as 1938 and successfully operated. But three years earlier Captain Frank Swift conceived the idea of organising 'windjammer cruises' using old coasting schooners equipped with plain but comfortable accommodation, taking out summer tourists on weekly trips in the beautiful, island-studded Penobscot Bay region. The idea caught on and, with an interval during the Second World War, the industry has persisted down to the present day when new schooners are built specially for the business, vessels which externally very closely resemble their coaster forebears but which are fitted out to a degree of luxury on board which has gradually developed with the changes in demand and passengers' expectations over the years.

By the last decade of the twentieth century the sail cruise business has become worldwide and very many vessels have been adapted, refitted or specially built for the business. For example, in 1992 a large tern schooner of the type built in Finland during and after the First World War, very much on the lines of the Canadian tern schooners, was launched at Mariehamn in the Åland Islands as a business venture for passenger carrying. She is the *Linden*, externally to all intents and purposes a tern of the 1920s. On

The crew of a Lunenburg motor schooner of the 1940s. Note the dories stowed on deck, nested inside one another. The vessel is under sail in company with another similar schooner. (Basil Greenhill Collection)

board she is fitted out with every luxury. She is fully powered – even equipped with bow thrusters – and has every modern device for navigation and safety.

But, following on the success of a pioneer, the four-masted barque *Sea Cloud* built as a yacht at Kiel in 1931 and adapted for cruising in the 1970s, much larger vessels have been built for this business. These are four- and five-masted staysail schooners, bigger than most merchant sailing vessels, cruising in the Mediterranean and in the West Indies. These are extremely sophisticated vessels, motor-sailers with automated computer-controlled running rigging so that apart from maintenance and repair work there is no sail handling to be done aloft or on deck. Designed after careful market research to attract a defined segment of the cruising public, they have been most successful and their success has led to one of the most spectacular developments, perhaps, ever to take place in the history of the merchant sailing vessel. This was the building of the White Star barquentines, 194-passenger vessels which were genuine sailing vessels rather than motor-sailers. There are two of them, launched in 1991 and 1992. Over 300ft long, built to the highest standards, those of *Lloyd's Register* and the United States Coastguard, they are rigged with four steel masts from which are set staysails in a sail plan reminiscent of that recommended by Captain Forbes for the big American schooners way back in the 1880s (see Chapter 4). The square sails are furled into hollow aluminium alloy yards using a system powered by geared hydraulic motors in the yardarms. This means that the yards must be long enough overall to accommodate the full width of the foot of each of the square sails; this makes the rig of the fore mast very square. The braces are controlled by a developed version of the Jarvis brace winch of the early years of the twentieth century (see Chapter 4). The total sail area is 3300 square metres. The vessels are equipped with auxiliary engines but are operated in the Mediterranean and the Caribbean as sailing ships, the engines being used only in emergency or in circumstances when a cargo-carrying vessel would have taken the assistance of a tug.

The cruise schooner Heritage, *launched at Rockland, Maine, in 1982 and photographed off Damariscove Island in 1989 is, in hull form and rig, a close reconstruction of a small Maine coaster of the nineteenth century.* (Basil Greenhill)

The steel four-masted barque Sea Cloud *was the successful pioneer in initiating the cruising business in large auxiliary and sail-assisted vessels. Photographed in Stockholm in 1980 she was built as a yacht at Kiel in 1931.* (Basil Greenhill)

So in the last decade of the twentieth century there are still large commercial sailing vessels at sea. There is also all over the world a great fleet of 'sail training ships' of every conceivable kind. Underhill in his great work *Sail Training and Cadet Ships* lists over 240 of them as sailing before 1956. They vary between vessels barely distinguishable from small cruise ships to naval and state-supported vessels which combine showing the flag with training and social experience for future professional seafarers. There are so many of them that it is possible to name only a few of the best. The finest of the big vessels and perhaps the nearest in her design and sail plan to a four-masted barque of the 1890s is the Japanese *Nippon Maru*, a new vessel of the 1980s. The Estonian/Russian *Krusenstern*, already mentioned, is one of the spectacular survivals of the commercial era. The Danish *Georg Stage*, a small full rigged ship, is one of the most handsome of the training ships and one of the best run. Seeing her at sea is to get some impression of the appearance of an average merchant ship of the middle of the last century, if allowance is made for her double topsails. The Chilean four-masted schooner *Esmeralda*, although built of steel, gives some impression of the appearance of the big North American schooners. The Danish *Fulton*, again an extremely well managed vessel, is, above decks, virtually an unchanged *slettop skonnert* of the early years of the twentieth century. The two French naval training schooners *L'Étoile* and *La Belle Poule*, with their roller-reefing topsails, give some impression of the appearance of the French Grand Banks fishing schooners and coastal traders of the early years of the twentieth century.

Besides these vessels there are replicas built, often to a very high standard, as national or civic symbols. One of the most impressive of these is the Canadian schooner *Bluenose II*, a reproduction of a classic Lunenburg fishing schooner of the 1920s which became so much a national symbol that she appears on the Canadian ten cent piece. *Bluenose II* operates out of Halifax,

The steel auxiliary four-masted barque Nippon Maru *(2284 tons gross, built at Kobe in 1930) photographed off the coast of Japan. A very successful state training vessel, she has recently been replaced in service by an almost identical four-masted barque. She herself has been preserved as a national monument.* (Basil Greenhill)

The Danish steel full rigged ship Georg Stage *(203 tons gross) built at Copenhagen in 1935 and still at sea in the 1990s is one of the most handsome and best run of sail training vessels. Trainees casting off the gaskets to set sail.* (Basil Greenhill)

The Danish full rigged sail training ship Danmark *photographed from the training schooner* Fulton *in the Baltic.* (Basil Greenhill)

Nova Scotia, and serves a multiplicity of social and educational purposes. Some vessels adapted on motorship hulls to be available for charter to film and television companies have been very well fitted out and rigged so as to resemble quite closely recognisable vessel types of the nineteenth century. Some of these have been chartered from time to time for training, cruising, or representational purposes and it is difficult, sometimes, to draw the line in defining a vessel's functions.

In addition, perhaps the most important are the preserved ships. Again there are very many of these in the world today and it will perhaps be permissible to refer only to one or two of the most important. Outstanding is the wooden barque *Sigyn* lying in the harbour at Turku

The Finnish wooden barque Sigyn *of Wårdö, Åland, 359 tons gross, built at Goteborg in 1887. She now lies in Turku (Åbo) in southwest Finland, the property of the Swedish language university, the Åbo Akademi. She is the last ordinary wooden barque, the standard merchant vessel of previous centuries.* (Basil Greenhill)

The beautiful iron full rigged ship Jarramas, *350 tons displacement, built in 1900 and formerly a Swedish naval training ship as she lies today preserved at Karlskrona in southern Sweden.* (Basil Greenhill)

sage to the fishing banks. The ketch rigged river Tamar sailing barge *Shamrock* lies, beautifully and expertly maintained, at the National Trust's Cotehele Quay in east Cornwall. These are only a few of the best of the preserved vessels which lie in harbours around the world, many of which are worthy of what will be a rewarding visit.

The last commercial square-riggers

Back in 1924 Sir Alan Moore, in that brilliant and most valuable book *The Last Days of Mast and Sail* (Oxford 1925) wrote – he was perhaps something of a romantic as well as a meticulous and knowledgeable observer and recorder of the rigging of sailing vessels – 'Here and there in little lonely havens and about the coasts of a few primitive lands the white sea wings will linger awhile, but not for long'. Sir Alan Moore spoke more truly than he knew. In one area big square rigged sailing vessels of traditional form remained commercially profitable in significant numbers until after the middle of the twentieth century. A fleet of wooden barques, brigs, brigantines and full rigged ships of from about 200 to 700 tons operated on the coasts of India, in the Arabian sea and in the Bay of Bengal through the 1920s and '30s and survived into the 1950s, if not the next decade – indeed a number of them were built during the Second World War. They worked on the coast of Sri Lanka, to Tuticorin, to Malabar, to Thailand, and on the coast of Madras. Some of them came from the Maldive Islands. Their big annual cargo was a yearly rice lift from Burma to Sri Lanka and India. It is not possible to determine how many there were, but there were very many of them. K B Vaidya's study *The Sailing Vessel Traffic on the West Coast of India and its Future*, published in Bombay in 1945, indicates their existence in considerable numbers at that time. As to when the last of them sailed, in 1959 the author saw a brigantine, partly rigged down, laid up among the smaller vessels during the southwest monsoon in Chittagong.

In many ways it was appropriate that these vessels should have been truly the last group of square rigged merchant ships without engines operating in history, for down to the end they carried single topsails, studding sails and skysails, the rig of the new ships of the 1850s, which they also resembled in hull form. They had natural fibre standing rigging, and some of them were without ratlines on the shrouds. In ballast or bad

(Åbo) in southern Finland. Built in Sweden in 1887 she is the last wooden three-masted square rigged merchant sailing ship in the world and as such represents the ordinary merchant ship of the period before the development of the triple expansion marine steam engine. The only representative of the great steel sailing ships of the late nineteenth century which survives unaltered since her working days as a merchant vessel is the *Pommern*, already mentioned, lying preserved by the city in the western harbour of Mariehamn in the Åland Islands of Finland.

Two other wooden barques which have been most successfully preserved are the steam auxiliary *Discovery* lying in Dundee, built as an exploration ship very closely on the lines of a whaler of the late nineteenth century, and the *Charles W Morgan*, a whaler of the 1840s which is to be seen at Mystic Seaport in Connecticut along with a number of other vessels and boats of great historical interest. The Lunenburg fishing schooner *Theresa E Connor*, referred to earlier in this chapter, is to be seen as a museum ship at Lunenburg, equipped as she was for her last pas-

The Indian wooden barquentine
Paruathararthaniamma, *built in 1937, photographed in the Bay of Bengal by the late Frank Lisle Taylor. Note the deep single fore topsail.* (Basil Greenhill Collection)

weather they sent down upper yards, topgallant masts and topmasts in the manner of the early nineteenth century. The crew slept on deck, the master and mate under the low poop. The social system on board was very communal. John Seymour gives a good account of a short passage in one of these vessels in his book *Round About India* (London 1953). Captain G V Clark in several well illustrated articles in the old PSNC house magazine *Sea Breezes* in the 1930s first drew attention to these vessels.

Like the Baltic sailing timber ships of the 1920s and '30s, freights were often high enough to give them a good living with two or three passages a year. What may have been the world's last traditional square rigged merchant sailing vessel to earn her living from freights was one of these – a beautiful brigantine which in every respect resembled a British vessel of the 1840s and which was still sailing without an engine in the 1950s. Her name was *Mina* and she was registered in Minikoi, an island geographically between the southernmost of the Laccadive Islands and the northernmost of the Maldive Islands. She was sailed by Maldivi crews between Minikoi and Tuticorin almost on the southernmost tip of the Indian sub-continent. These men were professional seamen, Lascars, who

were on their way to or from Calcutta (by rail from Tuticorin), where they joined the crews of large deep sea powered vessels, British and other. In Tuticorin stores were purchased for Minikoi and shipped over in the *Mina*. Sometimes on inward voyages from the islands she called at Colombo to offload copra. In 1957 she made a long voyage to Calcutta, which, with many calls, took her several months.

It was on one of her calls at Colombo that the author saw her in the 1950s, looking like a ghost ship, something dredged up from another age. She had a deep single topsail of a shape and col-

our that put her back 150 years or more. Her round bows and massive stem, with carved trailboards and figurehead, were of the eighteenth century, and above them was a short bowsprit and a great downward-curving jibboom, nearly half as long as the ship herself, from which two white jibs curved and arched, most inefficiently but very beautifully, over a sea that was nearly royal blue. As she came in through the harbour mouth and close under our stern it could be seen

Three wooden barques and two brigantines seasonally laid up in Puttalam Lagoon off Karaitivu, Sri Lanka, photographed on 18 May 1935. (Ian Merry)

The wood brigantine Mina of Minikoi *sailing on the starboard tack into Colombo Harbour, Sri Lanka, in September 1952.* (Basil Greenhill)

that she had a short poop and a galley on deck in the classic pattern of small sailing vessels of the mid-nineteenth century. One man was at her great open wheel, five others about her decks and rigging, and their seamanship was most impressive. These heirs to a thousand years of sail-ing history knew what they were about very well. She ran in through the harbour mouth, hauled up on the starboard tack to beat halfway down the harbour, taking in her topgallant sail as she did so, went about the bows of a Blue Funnel liner, beat across the fairway on the port tack, went about again, and then once more right in among the little group of lateen rigged sailing craft from the Maldive Islands that lay at the head of the harbour, and she came up to an anchor among them without fault. The shiphan-dling could not have been better in the days when the world was full of such vessels.[7]

Dr Basil Greenhill

7. The author is indebted to Captain John M Gray, formerly of the Brocklebank Line, for details of the *Mina's* occupation. The final identification of the vessel remained something of a mystery for a number of years.

The Merchant Sailing Ship in the Twentieth Century: Typical Vessels

Name	Rig	Flag	Built	Completed	Hull	Tonnage (gross)	Dimensions (feet) (metres)	Remarks
ARCHIBALD RUSSELL	4-masted barque	British	Scott & Co, Greenock	1905	Steel	2354	291.3 × 42.9 × 24.0 88.8 × 13.1 × 7.3	Sold to Gustaf Erikson of Åland, 1924; broken up 1949
MOZART	4-masted barquentine	German	Grangemouth Dockyard, Greenock	1904	Steel	2003	277.4 × 42.9 × 21.4 84.6 × 13.1 × 6.5	Sold to Hugo Lundqvist of Åland, 1922; broken up 1935
VALBORG	4-masted schooner, auxiliary	Canadian	Victoria, British Columbia	1919	Wood	964	197.5 × 40.0 × 16.5 60.2 × 12.2 × 5.0	Sold to Hugo Lundqvist, then Gustaf Erikson, then Norwegian owners
M A JAMES	3-masted schooner, auxiliary	British	David Williams, Porthmadog	1900	Wood	125	89.6 × 22.7 × 10.6 27.3 × 6.9 × 3.2	A fine example of the last British merchant schooners; broken up 1952
HALDON	3-masted schooner, auxiliary	British	Hawke Bros, Plymouth	1893	Wood	113	88.0 × 21.6 × 9.9 26.8 × 6.6 × 3.0	Launched as a ketch, she became one of the most successful motor schooners
PROGRESS	Ketch, auxiliary	British	W Date, Kingsbridge	1884	Wood	76 net	80.2 × 19.2 × 9.2 24.4 × 5.9 × 2.8	Employed for 19 years in Newfoundland trade. Broken up early 1970s after years laid up.

Name	Rig	Flag	Built	Completed	Hull	Tonnage (gross)	Dimensions (feet) (metres)	Remarks
ST. CLAIR THEVIAULT	3-masted schooner	Canadian	Siffroy Deveau, Belliveau Cave, NS	1919	Wood	284 net	135.5 × 31.6 × 11.3 41.3 × 9.6 × 3.4	An excellent example of the Canadian tern schooner; abandoned at sea and burned, 1939
MARGOT	4-masted schooner, auxiliary	Danish	Skibsvaerft, Svendborg	1919	Steel	387	139.3 × 29.7 × 11.0 42.5 × 9.1 × 3.4	Typical Danish steel four-masted schooner; broken up in 1957 when owned in Chile
FULTON	3-masted schooner	Danish	C L Johanson, Marstal	1915	Wood	99.9	86.8 × 22.9 × 8.5 26.5 × 7.0 × 2.6	Typical Danish *slettop skonnert* built for Newfoundland trade; 1992 very active as training vessel
LILLA B BOUTILIER	2-masted motor schooner	Canadian	Smith & Rhuland, Lunenburg, NS	1938	Wood	185	129.6 × 27.1 × 10.4 39.5 × 8.3 × 3.2	Fine example of last-stage dory fisherman. Lost at Carboneau, Newfoundland, 1971
INGRID	3-masted schooner	Finnish	E Söderström, Greta, Åland	1907	Wood	305	132.0 × 27.0 × 13.0 40.2 × 8.2 × 4.0	Typical Åland Finnish *Skonert-skepp*; sold to British owners 1919. Renamed *Rigdin*. Broken up 1939
TJALFE	Brig	Danish	P Brandt, Svendborg	1853	Wood	222	92.7 × 25.5 × 13.4 28.3 × 7.8 × 4.1	North Europe's last surviving brig; broken up 1950
HELEN BARNET GRING	4-masted schooner	American	R L Bean, Camden, Maine	1919	Wood	1226	202.0 × 40.4 × 20.8 61.6 × 12.3 × 6.3	Typical US World War One built vessel. Wrecked on Cuba, 1940
WATERWITCH	Barquentine	British	T Meadus, Poole	1872	Wood	207	112.0 × 25.8 × 12.8 34.1 × 7.9 × 3.9	Last square rigged merchant vessel sailing from home port in Britain; lost in Baltic, 1942
STATSRAAD ERICHSEN	Brig	Norwegian	Norwegian Naval yard, Carljohs-vearn	1858	Wood	119	115.7 × 23.4 × 11.1 35.3 × 7.1 × 3.4	Early sail training vessel (1901-38). Very beautiful brig with single topsails in her early days. Formerly a naval vessel
ALBATROS	4-masted motor schooner	Swedish	Boström, Göteborg	1942	Steel	1052	221.3 × 37.7 × 23.2 67.5 × 11.5 × 7.1	Mid twentieth-century staysail and jib-headed cargo carrying sail training vessel; converted to motor ship
HERZOGIN CECILIE	4-masted barque	German	Rickmers, Bremerhaven	1902	Steel	3111	314.8 × 46.3 × 24.2 96.0 × 14.1 × 7.4	Early twentieth-century cargo carrying and flag showing sail training vessel. Sold to Gustaf Eriksen, 1922
NIPPON MARU	4-masted barque, auxiliary	Japanese	Kawasaki Dockyard, Kobe	1930	Steel	2284	260.0 × 42.5 × 25.7 79.2 × 13.0 × 7.8	Built as national training vessel. Recently replaced by identical new vessel and preserved as a national monument
ALICE C WENTWORTH	Schooner	American	South Norwalk, Conn; rebuilt 1905, Arthur Stephens, Well, Maine	1868	Wood	68	73.2 × 23.7 × 6.1 22.3 × 7.2 × 1.9	Typical local New England coaster. Rebuilt 1905; became cruise schooner on Maine Coast, 1946
HYASTAN	Barquentine	Indian	A C Martin & Co, Rangoon	1919	Wood	750	200.0 × 38.0 × 18.6 61.0 × 11.6 × 5.7	Built for Indian Ocean trade
STAR FLYER	4-masted barquentine, auxiliary	Belgian	Belgian Shipbuilders, Langerbrugge	1991	Steel	2298	315.2 × 49.2 × 29.5 96.1 × 15.0 × 9.0	Built as the first of a fleet of three for commercial cruising under sail

6

The Schooner in America

DURING the half century between the close of the American Civil War, in 1865, and the nation's involvement in the First World War, the United States underwent a drastic decline in its stature as a maritime country. In the 1850s, the era of the Californian and Australian gold rushes, the American clipper ships had made a serious challenge to British shipping supremacy, but this challenge was

Two handsome three-masters, the Margaret H Ford *(right) built at Vinalhaven, Maine, and the* F H Odiorne *built at Newburyport, Massachusetts, lying off Brown's Head, Fox Island Thrufare, Penobscot Bay, Maine. They were bound from Stonington, Maine, to the westward with granite and the photographer has caught them just drifting with the tide.* (Edward Strong Clark via W J Lewis Parker)

short-lived. The Civil War, because of the depredations of Confederate commerce raiders and even more from the fear which they instilled, resulted in the destruction, sale or transfer to foreign flags of nearly half of the American deep-water merchant fleet.[1] After the war, when, as Britain demonstrated so effectively, the future in shipping lay with iron or steel and steam, the high cost of metal precluded the building of a modern merchant fleet in American yards, and the stringency of American registry laws barred the purchase of foreign-built tonnage.

Needless to say, a modest revival of American seagoing shipping did occur after the Civil War. The magnificent 'Down Easters' then built in New England yards were as large as the largest of the clippers, superior to them in strength and

carrying capacity, and not greatly inferior to them in passage-making ability. For a time, such full-riggers competed ably on the long voyages around the Capes, but British iron and steel sailing ships and steam tramps proved their nemesis, and they ceased to be built in significant numbers after the mid 1880s.

The closing decades of the nineteenth century were, nevertheless, a period of intense internal development, of rapid industrialisation, and of phenomenal population growth. The domestic market proved large enough to absorb most of

1. Winthrop L Marvin, *The American Merchant Marine* (New York 1902), p338; George W Dalzell, *The Flight from the Flag: The Continuing Effect of the Civil War on the American Carrying Trade* (Chapel Hill 1940), p247.

The four-master Charles A Dean *was built at Camden, Maine, in 1919. She is shown here loading plaster at a wharf at Walton in the Minas Basin, Nova Scotia. Twice a day on the ebb of the Minas Basin's great tides the* Charles A Dean *grounded on the hard red mud, so that her keel, some of her frames amidships, and the wharf, took the huge weight of the vessel and her cargo. The vessel was lost on Frying Pan Shoals, North Carolina, in December 1926. (W J Lewis Parker Collection)*

America's tariff protected manufactures, so that there was not the same incentive to fight for export markets which were so essential to European industrialised nations. Within such a context, a foreign going merchant marine was by no means so vitally important as it was, for example, to England. Thus, a certain apathy prevailed towards shipping, and the prewar Boston and New York shipping fortunes were transferred into more lucrative investments in manufacturing, railroads and real estate.

The industrial expansion which absorbed so much of America's energy to the detriment of its overseas shipping proved a boon, nevertheless, to its coastwise fleet. From as long ago as 1817, not only has an Act of Congress absolutely prohibited foreign flag vessels from trading between American ports, but it has also barred foreign-built American flag craft from coastwise service.[2] Under such protection, the coasting trade enjoyed a long prosperity which was shared by American shipbuilders. From 1838, until the Second World War reversed the relative proportions, a greater tonnage was 'enrolled' in the coastwise trade than was 'registered' for foreign trade.[3] The transport of bulk cargoes to sustain the new industrial society brought, in addition, an altogether new impetus to coastwise shipping, and the vessel almost universally favoured was the wooden, multi-masted schooner.

The coasting schooners on the Atlantic seaboard profited greatly from the phenomenal growth of the coal trade to New England. This increase was due in large measure to the almost complete exhaustion of sites where water power could be employed. This necessitated the building of the new factories in locations where only steam power was viable. The fuel requirements of the railroads, the growing popularity of coal for domestic heating, the wider use of coal gas for lighting, and, in the 1890s, the sudden development of electric power, all swelled New England's need for coal. In 1871 Boston alone received 931,821 tons of coal, virtually all by water, from Philadelphia, Baltimore, New York, Georgetown, DC and the Virginia ports of Alexandria and Richmond. By 1879 this traffic had more than doubled, and Boston required 'some

four thousand cargoes of nearly 500 tons each, or eleven cargoes every day in the year.'[4] By 1900, the water-borne coal landed at Boston was 4,064,100 tons, more than a fourfold increase in thirty years.[5] Commencing in the early 1880s, the traffic was much augmented by West Virginia bituminous coal brought by newly-built railroads to the Hampton Roads ports of Norfolk and Newport News for shipment by water to New England markets. Not only Boston, but other New England ports such as Providence, Portsmouth and Portland shared a proportionate increase in coal receipts.

The small schooners of 1870 were quite inadequate to cope with such an upsurge of traffic and their successors grew marvellously in size. The largest schooner built in 1870 was the 518-ton three-master, *Mattie A Franklin*, although the average of the thirty-four three-masters built in that year was closer to 350 tons. Four-masters appeared in 1879, the first five-master in 1888, and in 1900 the first two six-masters were launched. The larger of these, the *Eleanor A Percy*, measured 3401 gross tons, with a length of 323.5ft, a beam of 50ft, and a depth of 24.8ft. This giant, one of the five or six largest wooden sailing vessels ever built, was capable of carrying

about 5500 tons of coal. To keep a proper perspective, though, it should be said that one of the sixteen four-masters built on the Atlantic coast in 1900, with an average of 1250 tons, was a much more typical coaster than the *Percy*.

Maine and the schooner

To a remarkable degree, during this period, wooden shipbuilding on the Atlantic coast became concentrated in the State of Maine. Between 1870 and 1899, inclusive, there were 702 ships, barques and barquentines built on the East Coast, Maine's share being 493 or 70 per cent. A full three-quarters of these square-riggers were constructed in the 1870s, 20 per cent in the 1880s, and only 5 per cent in the 1890s.

2. American Navigation Act of 1 March 1817. Presently incorporated in 46 USC 883.

3. *Report of the Commissioner of Navigation, 1904* (Washington 1904), p360.

4. W J Lewis Parker, *The Great Coal Schooners of New England, 1870-1909* (Mystic 1948), Chapter 1; *New York Maritime Register* (29 October 1879).

5. *Fifteenth Annual Report of the Boston Chamber of Commerce in the Year Ending December 31, 1900* (Boston 1901), p226.

The four-masters J Holmes Birdsall and Mary Manning under construction at the yard of Holly M Bean at Camden, Maine, in 1894. The Mary Manning was to be abandoned at sea in 1906 and the Birdsall was wrecked on Puerto Rico in 1916. (W J Lewis Parker Collection)

This tradition persisted after the Civil War. This was chiefly because, as the centre of population of the country moved westward, Maine's lack of raw materials for large scale manufacturing and its growing remoteness from potential markets proved formidable handicaps to its participation in the industrial expansion which swept the other shipping states.

Maine's shipping prominence was also due in no small measure to the decay of the old shipping interests in New York and Boston. The excellent New York shipyards, whence came the famous transatlantic packets and a goodly share of the clippers, succumbed to high labour costs and high real estate values after the Civil War; Boston was beset somewhat less seriously by similar problems. The shrunken shipbuilding inheritance of these ports passed to Maine largely by default. In these cities and in Philadelphia and Baltimore, where the charter markets were still controlled, the high proportion of ship-brokerage firms with strong 'Down East' connections explains much of the strength of Maine shipping. These brokers, often successful shipmasters who had 'swallowed the anchor', ably represented the vessels from their home towns.

Among the obstacles which Maine yards had to overcome was a lack of suitable timber. Its oak was as scarce as its white pine by 1870, and it was necessary to procure white oak frames in Virginia or Maryland. The hard pine used for keels, keelsons, planking and ceiling came from Georgia. Much of the hackmatack used for knees came from Canada. Far offsetting this disadvantage, however, was an abundance of skilled shipyard labour and the low wages for which they gave an honest ten hours of work per day. In 1880 the daily wages paid to ship carpenters in Bath, the largest shipbuilding centre in the state, were only $1.50 to $2.00 in accordance with their skill.[7] There was, however, always a serious attrition of skilled labour during the prolonged depressions which beset the industry. Young men tended to seek pursuits which offered steadier employment, and one prominent

Maine's dominance in the building of big schooners was equally impressive. From 1870 until the end of the First World War there were 1758 three-masters built in the Atlantic states, and of these almost exactly a half came from Maine shipyards. Of the 459 East Coast four-masters launched after the advent of the rig in 1879, Maine accounted for no fewer than 326. She also produced all but three of the fifty-six Atlantic five-masters and all but one of the ten giant six-masters. The rest of the building was divided among all eighteen of the other Atlantic states, the most productive of which was New Jersey, whose total of 243 schooners stood far below Maine's output in average size as well as in numbers.[6]

What was there about Maine which led this northeasternmost corner of the united States to such ascendancy in American shipping during the waning years of sail? Maine is a state the

equal of Ireland in area, a country of great forests and a long coastline of rugged beauty. During Colonial times it was a sparsely populated eastern frontier of Massachusetts, of which it remained a district until it gained statehood in 1820. Its seemingly inexhaustible stands of splendid white pine, which before the Revolution served as a source of mast timber for the Royal Navy, vanished in a transient prosperity of large scale lumbering between 1820 and 1865. There remained, however, ample forest of less valuable timber for less intensive exploitation.

Under the impetus of lumbering, Maine grew to be one of the major shipbuilding centres of the country, although the prestige of its vessels was inferior to that of the thoroughbreds from New York and Boston yards. In a score of towns and villages in coastal Maine, shipbuilding, ship-owning and seafaring became a way of life to which there were very few local alternatives.

6. Francis E Bowker, *Three-Masted Schooners: a Compilation of Three-Masted Schooners Built on the American East Coast* (Mystic 1991; John Lyman, *Log Chips* (Washington 1948-1959).

7. Henry Hall, 'Report on the Shipbuilding of the United States' in *Report of the Tenth Census*, VIII (Washington 1884), p103.

The four-master Agnes Manning *is an example of an East Coast schooner not built north of Long Island Sound. She was launched at Camden, New Jersey, in 1892 as the* George Tarline *and renamed* Agnes Manning *after stranding a year later. She crossed the Atlantic in 1916 and was sold to British owners after having been laid up at Appledore, North Devon. (W J Lewis Parker Collection)*

Bath builder was heard to complain that he was running an 'old men's home' at his yard.[8] Nonetheless, during the busy years labour deficiencies were made up by an influx of able ship carpenters from Nova Scotia and New Brunswick, many of whom settled permanently.

Despite these advantages, Maine shipbuilding would have been doomed in the 1880s if the demand for large coasting schooners had not increased markedly while construction of square-riggers virtually ceased. It would also have been doomed had it not been possible to improve the efficiency as well as the size of the schooner. The simplicity of rig, with its minimum of necessity to go aloft, made the schooner naturally economical of manpower, but by 1879 the back-breaking work of handling the sails and gear of a three-masted 'hand puller' of 700 or 800 tons had reached a limit. The solution was found in that year by the introduction of the steam donkey engine for running the windlass, hoisting sail and working the pumps. This innovation made possible the manning of four-masted schooners of 1500 tons with a crew of ten or eleven men, and ultimately of five- and six-masters with twelve to fifteen hands.[9] Few vessels, sail or steam, were ever so efficient in the number of tons of cargo per crew member as the largest of the schooners before the advent of automation and the monstrous bulk carriers of our own time.

Shipping has always been marked by violent fluctuations in building activity which reflect and lag a year or so behind the peaks and depressions of the economy. One of the greatest booms occurred in 1872-1874 when 211 three-masted schooners were launched, the climax be-

ing reached in 1874, the year the bleak depression of the 1870s commenced. Two years later, production had fallen to fourteen three-masters. A revival in the early '80s reached its high point in 1883, with 136 three-masters and three four-masters. In 1886 only thirteen three-masters and five four-masters were added to the fleet. A

smart revival in 1889 was followed by the good years of 1890 and 1891, during the latter of which seventy-five three-masters and thirty-seven four-masters where turned out. The extreme depression of the 1890s brought near-extinction to the industry in 1897, when only five schooners (three three-masters and two four-masters)

8. C V Minot, Jr to Capt Wylie R Dickinson (Phippsburg, Maine 10 October 1907). Author's collection.

9. *Report of the Commissioner of Navigation, 1904*, pp127-128.

The long open main deck of the four-master Helen Barnet Gring, *built at Camden, Maine in 1919, on a passage to Bermuda with coal. Note the open rail with turned stanchions typical of many of these vessels and the use of rigging screws in place of deadeyes and lanyards which would have been extremely difficult to set up with these huge lower masts. (W A Funderburk via Francis E Bowker)*

The Gring *off Haiti. She was one of the last two big East Coast schooners to cross the Atlantic, discharging a cargo at Liverpool in 1937. She was lost by stranding off Cuba three years later. (Francis E Bowker)*

erly weather would cause a large fleet of loaded schooners to accumulate inside Cape Henry. When the weather finally broke, they would all get away together and some spirited races ensued. The leaders were often able to charter and get away for another load before the market became glutted and the discharging berths were overtaxed by the later arrivals. Rates varied all the way from $2.00 or more per ton to 45 or 50 cents, with an average of 75 cents being fairly profitable.

The lack of co-ordination in the bituminous coal trade, where mines, railroads, shippers and vessels were separately controlled, resulted in much detention of the vessels in loading and discharging, and this in turn caused frequent claims for demurrage. Many a suit resulted because schooners were denied their turn in loading due to some alleged 'custom of the port'.[11] In 1885, the Vessel Owners' and Captains' National Association was formed to combat such grievances and to attempt to establish minimum freight rates. The president was Charles Lawrence of

were built. The result of these spurts of building in times of prosperity and high freights was a surplus of tonnage in the poor years which served further to depress freights to a very unremunerative level. The inevitable attrition of the fleet from marine disasters in the lean years produced, in turn, a shortage of tonnage and artificially high freights in the good years.

Schooner trades

The big schooners carried a great variety of cargoes. Space will not permit a thorough analysis of all of the trades in which they were engaged, but brief mention must be made of some of the important ones. The largest of the schooners were built to carry coal to New England and, unless lured away for a time by unusually high freights in some other trade, they seldom deviated from a monotonous monthly round from the bituminous ports of Philadelphia, Baltimore, Norfolk, and Newport News to Providence, Fall River, New Bedford, Boston, Salem, Portsmouth and Portland, the return passage being made without ballast. The 1200-ton four-master *George M Grant*, for example, did nothing else in her early years. In May 1896 she was reported to be carrying her ninetieth cargo of coal for the Pomeroy Coal Company, of Providence. She had been under charter to that firm continuously since she was built in 1889, and all but two of her cargoes had been loaded at Norfolk. She had averaged nearly fourteen round trips and sailed

The six-master George W Wells *built at Camden, Maine, in 1900 was the first of her kind. She was among the largest wooden vessels ever built and was able to load 5000 tons of coal. (Basil Greenhill Collection)*

nearly 10,000 miles per year. As she carried over 2000 tons, she had landed nearly 180,000 tons of coal at Providence during that time.[10]

The *Grant* was obviously time-chartered by the year. More often charters were made for a specified number of trips, perhaps three to six, and it was even more common to charter for a single voyage. When a vessel sailed unchartered for a coal port, she was said to be 'going seeking'. Many factors caused quite violent fluctuations in coal freights. A prolonged spell of east-

10. *New York Maritime Register* (6 May 1896).

11. W J Lewis Parker, *op cit*, pp95-100.

Shore riggers from the Perth Amboy Drydock Company, New Jersey, bending a jib on board the four-master Herbert L Rawding *in November 1941 after the vessel had been equipped with a new fore mast. Note the huge size of the wooden bowsprit and jibboom. The* Rawding *was built at Stockton Springs, Maine, in 1919 and sank on passage from Cadiz towards Newfoundland in June 1947. She had then been converted to be a motor schooner. (G I Johnson via Francis E Bowker)*

Philadelphia, but as a majority of the committee and membership were New Englanders, the meetings were held in Boston. Within six months the Association claimed to have enrolled eighty per cent of the coal schooners. They adopted a bill of lading which gained the grudging acceptance of the shippers and published minimum coal freights on a basis of 95 cents from Norfolk to Boston. As business conditions improved in the late 1880s, the Association grew in membership and apparent influence, but it failed to weather the severe test to which it was put in the depression of the 1890s. On 31 January 1894, Captain J P Tripp of the big four-master *Marguerite*, wrote to his agent from Hampton Roads, Virginia, where he had been waiting a month for a charter:

I don't know how this thing is going to end but if it is as the coal men claim that they are getting all the coal they want and most of it carried by the vessels that don't belong to the Association, it don't look to me a very bright thing to keep the rates where they are and help out the party that don't belong to the Association. I would put the rates down to fifty cents and let them kill themselves out.

This sort of warfare was ruinous to captains with crews of healthy appetite signed for a round voyage. Lack of solidarity developed among the owners and well-founded rumours were rife of Association vessels undercutting the rates by 5 cents. Captain Tripp pointed out what was to become a major problem. 'It is the barges,' he wrote, 'that are knocking us out. There has been ten barges and two steamers went out of here the first of the week and now there is seven more waiting to go out.'[12]

There was a close interrelation between the coal and the ice trades due to the fact that the principal markets for Maine ice – Philadelphia, Baltimore, Washington and New York – all provided return cargoes of coal to eastern New England, and many three-masters found regular summer employment 'ice and coaling'. Throughout the 1880s and '90s, the annual Maine ice crop averaged over a million tons. During a rela-

tively good year, upwards of 2500 cargoes were shipped, most of it from the huge ice houses on the Kennebec River. At rare intervals a warm winter would ruin the substantial local ice harvests in New York's Hudson Valley and Philadelphia's rivers and ponds. Such a year was 1890, when Maine, in a frenzy of speculation, cut a record crop of three million tons to cover the shortage. As a result, ice freights of $1.00 to $1.50 proved a bonanza to the 'ice and coalers'.[13]

After the hurricane season was past in September or October, many of the three-masters which had been plying to the eastward from the coal ports went south of Cape Hatteras, sometimes with coal or ice, sometimes in ballast, to the hard pine ports in the Carolinas, Georgia, Florida or the Gulf states. From Savannah, Brunswick, Jacksonville and Pensacola, they returned north with this excellent lumber which was so widely used for the frames of brick-faced factories, houses and bridge trestles which today's fire codes require to be of steel or concrete. Great quantities of hard pine were also used in the Maine shipyards for planking, keelsons and ceiling, and still more was hewn into railroad ties or sleepers.

The tempo of the lumber voyages was more relaxed than that of the coal trade. It was rare to

spend less than two weeks each loading and discharging a cargo of 500,000 board feet. The distances involved also lengthened out the voyages, it being, for instance, 1000 miles from Jacksonville to Boston, or 1900 miles from Pensacola to Portland. Consequently, it was seldom that a round trip was completed in less than six weeks to a South Atlantic port or two months to a Gulf port. Freights were based on Georgia ports to New York, with $5.00 per thousand board feet being about average. There is no doubt that lumber stood second to coal in the bulk coasting trades.[14]

The carriage of phosphate rock developed as another major trade, especially after the abundant deposits in central Florida were opened for shipment through Port Tampa in the 1890s.

12. Capt J P Tripp to William B Church (Hampton Roads, Virginia, 31 January 1894). In Cross Schooner Collection, Harvard Business School Library.

13. Henry Hall, 'Report on the Ice Industry of the United States', in *Report of the Tenth Census*, XXII (Washington 1888), pp21-30; L C Ballard, 'Maine Ice Industry', Maine Bureau of Industrial and Labor Statistics, *Annual Report for 1891* (Augusta), p165.

14. Frederick Kaiser, *Built on Honor, Sailed with Skill* (Ann Arbor 1989), pp3-24; Robert H Burgess, *Coasting Schooner: the Four-Masted Albert F Paul* (Charlottesville 1978), Chapter IV.

A shore rigger setting up the rigging on the new fore mast of the Herbert L Rawding *in November 1941. Francis Bowker, who was a member of the vessel's crew, comments, 'As soon as the crew comes aboard, they will go aloft to do a more seamanlike job than a yard rigger ... After all, he won't be aboard to worry about it when the going is rough.' (G I Johnson via Francis E Bowker)*

brokers, ship chandlers, shipbuilders or sailmakers. Several quite sizeable fleets under a common management developed a strong identity with such outward symbols of unity as a houseflag. Ordinarily the agent received about two per cent of the gross earnings for his services. If he was also a broker he, of course, received commissions on charters.

The several owners were divided into two groups: those within the shipping community whose investment entitled them to provide services to the vessel and the 'dry owners' who bought vessel property solely as an investment. The former group was generally the larger, and the resulting intricate relationships led to an odd sort of inbreeding within the industry which helped to sustain it in defiance of its sometimes questionable economic merits. Long, hard passages with resulting heavy stores and chandlery bills were not unprofitable to certain of the owners, even if meagre dividends proved disappointing to the 'dry owners'.

It was common the for the builder, even of contract-built schooners, to 'take a piece' of the vessel. Thus, H M Bean owned one-eighth of the *Malcolm Baxter, Jr*. The builders, in turn, pressured the master builder and master workmen to take shares. Among the owners of Percy & Small's big Bath-built four-master, *William H Clifford*, in 1895, may be noted the designer, blacksmith, rigger, fastener and joiner.[18] The New York firm of Cooney, Eckstein & Company, from whom the southern hard pine was purchased, owned one sixty-fourth of the *Clifford*. The well established New York house of James W Elwell & Company, whose senior partner came originally from Bath, bought two shares for the ship brokerage interest, and the Bath sailmaker, William H Clifford, secured his business and the privilege of naming the vessel

Most of the rock vessels took coal out to Galveston or Vera Cruz, Mexico, and came north with phosphate to the fertilizer factories in Baltimore. The fertilizer industry also provided many southbound cargoes of evil-smelling fish scrap from the menhaden rendering plants in New England.[15]

The West Indies sugar and molasses trades were yet other mainstays upon which the schooners depended, the outward cargoes to the islands being lumber, coal, ice and general cargo. At times much spruce lumber was shipped by three- and four-masted schooners from Portland, Boston and Nova Scotia to the River Plate.[16] The Argentine boom in 1889 drew so many big schooners from the coasting trades as to be a major factor in the revival of shipbuilding in Maine yards the following year. Although generally considered, with some reason, to be an undesirable rig for offshore trades, considerable numbers of schooners made transatlantic voyages with lumber, barrelled or case oil, tobacco or guano to Europe, returning with Welsh coal to the West Indies, Cadiz salt for the New England fisheries, or Sicilian fruit to New York or Boston. On rarer occasions, three- and four-masters made successful voyages to Australia and the Far East.

Financing and operating schooners

It will perhaps be worthwhile to take a close look at the mechanics of financing and operation of the big American East Coast schooners. With a few exceptions, all of which occurred after 1900, these vessels were run individually as a simple corporate enterprise. They were financed by the sale of shares of one sixty-fourth or some multiple or fraction of this ancient unit. It was by no means uncommon to have thirty or forty individual owners. Always, there was an 'agent' or managing owner who took the initiative in 'getting up a vessel', as the saying went. His share in the vessel was usually quite modest, often less than an eighth. He signed the building contract on behalf of the owners and assessed them for their shares as construction proceeded. The provisions of the contracts varied, but that between Captain George Bailey and the Camden, Maine builder, H M Bean, for the $60,000 four-master *Malcolm Baxter, Jr*, a vessel of 1732 gross tons built in 1899, was typical. Payments of one-fifth were made when the keel was laid, when the frame was up, when the ceiling was finished, when the vessel was planked, and when she was launched ready for the sea.[17]

After the vessel entered service the agent took a more or less active part in the direction of her business, received remittances of freight money from the captain, distributed the dividends to the owners, and levied assessments (known as 'Irish dividends') on them if the vessel became heavily indebted. The agent might be an individual, often a retired shipmaster or even the active captain. Among the latter was Captain Andrew Adams who sailed the four-master which bore his own name. More frequently the managerial function was performed by firms of ship

15. Frederick Kaiser, *op cit*, pp34-45.

16. W J Lewis Parker, 'To "The River", an Offshore Schooner Trade', *The American Neptune* XXXV (1/1975), pp5-19.

17. Contract for building schooner *Malcolm Baxter, Jr* between H M Bean, Camden, Maine and Captain George Bailey, Manasquan, New Jersey (8 March 1899). Author's collection.

18. Percy & Small *Day Book*. In library of Maine Maritime Museum, Bath, Maine.

Taking in the gaff topsails on board a four-master in a squall. (From a pen and ink drawing in the possession of W J Lewis Parker)

ered by rail or steamer from the lofts in Bath or Thomaston.

Perhaps the most important of all owners was the captain. Until the late 1890s, when the rapid increase in size and cost of schooners led to substitution of wages of $40 or $50 per month and primage of five per cent of gross earnings, the captains had sailed their vessels on 'shares' or 'square halves'. They were commonly required to own a one-eighth interest and to find owners for another eighth among their fellow shipmasters and the brokers and chandlers with whom they dealt in Boston, New York or other large ports. There was a moral obligation to return the favour when their friends were 'getting up' a vessel. For example, no fewer than seven of Captain Jonathan Strong's seafaring neighbours in the Maine village of St George took shares in his three-master *Louisa Bliss* when she was built in nearby Thomaston in 1869.[20]

Under the 'square halves' system, the port charges – pilotage, towage, stevedoring, brokerage commission. etc – were deducted from the gross earnings. The money remaining was divided equally between the vessel and the captain. From the vessel's part were paid all capital expenditures such as sails, chandlery and repairs. Even a towage bill to or from dry-dock came in this category. Whatever was left of the vessel's

with a three sixty-fourth interest. Percy & Small, who were managing owners as well as builders, owned the unusually large interest of 24½/64th when the schooner was ready for sea in this depression year of 1895, but as opportunity availed, they reduced their holding to more normal proportions. The chandlery interest in the *Clifford* was divided between a Bath owner and the Philadelphia house of Jonathan May & Sons.

The inefficiency of being required to buy from a chandler in a port hundreds of miles from where a vessel happened to be located seems incredible. When Captain Frank Magune, of the four-master *Edgar W Murdock*, was negotiating with Amos Carver, a shrewd Maine-born partner in the New York chandlery firm of Baker, Carver & Morrell, the latter set forth a hard bargain in return for buying the vessel. 'He will take 1/64,' reported Captain Magune to his owners, 'to have New York and all ports south but to take 1/32 he would want from Boston to all south, Boston included...'[19] Without competition, the chandlers were in a position to milk their vessels by supplying them 'in wholesale amounts at retail prices'. There were few complaints, however, and the bonds of friendship be-

tween captains and chandlers were often very strong. It was perhaps in situations where the chandler was also managing owner that the 'milking' was most common and most unobtrusive.

The sailmaking interest was also of continuing value. Schooners were seldom in port less than a week, even in the coal trade with its relatively quick turn-around. A vessel passing Vineyard Haven the day before her arrival in Boston would send messages to her agent and sailmaker via the steamer *Susie D*, ordering such sails as she might require. Before she was ready for sea again the great bundles of sails would be deliv-

19. Frank A Magune to Carleton, Norwood & Company (Perth Amboy, New Jersey 16 December 1902). Peabody & Essex Museum, Salem, Mass.

20. Schooner *Lousia Bliss*. Abstract of register, Thomaston, Maine 12 November 1869. Author's collection.

The after accommodation on board the four-master James C Hamlen *built in 1920 at South Portland, Maine. Even at this late date the master and mates were very well housed. The vessel became the Estonian* Jaan *in the Baltic timber trade to Denmark from the Gulf of Bothnia and was broken up at Kiel in 1947.* (Basil Greenhill Collection)

The five-master Cora F Cressy *was built at Bath, Maine, in 1902 by Percy & Small on a site now occupied by the Maine Maritime Museum. She looks particularly handsome, deep laden and sailing hard on the port tack.* (W J Lewis Parker Collection)

part was paid out as a dividend to the owners by the agent at the end of each voyage. From the captain's half came the crew's wages and subsistence. No funds were retained to cover depreciation.[21]

A captain sailing on shares had a remarkably free hand in determining what business his vessel accepted. Although he generally sought the advice of his agent, the captain was always empowered to use his best judgment in closing a charter which was binding on vessel and owners. A great deal of his time in port was spent in seeking new business, either by making a round of the shippers' offices, or more often by waiting for rumours in the comfort of a broker's office or a chandlery. Here, one would find a large coal stove in the front section of the store, surrounded by 'captains' chairs' and spittoons, and here every day captains whose ships were in port would gather and reminisce amid a pleasant haze of cigar smoke.

A measure of the trust which they had in their captains is revealed in the incoming correspondence of Dunn & Elliott of Thomaston, Maine, managers of a score of schooners in the 1880s. With astonishing frequency, their captains fairly pleaded for a word of approval or advice.[22] That such a light rein was not unusual may be inferred from the story of Captain Fred Crowell of the Bath schooner *Edwin R Hunt*, who fell into

the sin of letting his mate take the vessel when she was ready for sea, while he spent a few more days at home on Cape Cod. He was always careful to be in the next port just ahead of the *Hunt*, and this fraud went undetected by his owners for several years, until on one voyage the vessel was posted overdue and finally fetched up in the West Indies, short of sails and provisions after having been blown off the coast.[23]

'Dry owners' provided perhaps a quarter of the capital for these schooners. A good ship broker often had shoreside friends with money to invest and during the good years there was no dearth of capital lured by prospective dividends of 20 per cent. Percy & Small obtained many a dry owner through the efforts of a travelling salesman or 'drummer' named Ocea Cahill. In addition to his principal line which he sold to dry goods stores in upstate New York, Cahill peddled shares in Captain Percy's schooners to people in the inland towns who had never seen a vessel. His salesmanship was the basic reason for Governor Brooks' investment in the five-master which bore his name, as well as in the mighty six-master, the *Wyoming*, which was named in honour of his state. Cahill received a commission of 2½ per cent on his sales and he was also an owner in his own right. Two governors of New England states also owned much vessel property. One was Oliver Ames of Massachusetts, who gave his name to the first five-master, the *Gov. Ames*, in 1888. Ames' fortune was made in the manufacture of ploughs and shovels. An ardent Methodist, he and his family attended the camp meeting on Martha's Vineyard over many

summers, and here they met and became close friends of the Davis family which 'got up' and sailed the *Ames* and several other fine schooners. The other gubernatorial 'dry owner' was Henry Lippitt, chief executive of Rhode Island in 1875-76. Both a three- and a four-masted schooner were named for this textile magnate and avid yachtsman.

It seems likely that a romantic fascination with the sea was important in enticing such very practical and successful men to invest in vessel property. This attraction was certainly evinced by the affluent Philadelphians who summered at Camden, Maine. Here they were able to watch with fascination as the big four- and five-masters took shape in Holly Bean's shipyard. They thrilled to the carnival spirit of launching day, and the ownership of a small interest in these vessels must have given them a sense of belonging in a community where the natives viewed them with a certain aloofness. It became the fashionable thing to take a large enough interest to have the privilege of naming a big schooner for a wife, son or daughter. There seems a touch of irony that one of these wooden schooners, the *Henry W Cramp*, was named for a member of the Philadelphia family which controlled the largest steel shipbuilding yard in the country.

21. A good example is Captain C A Davis' account with Schooner *Wm P Hood* and Owners, 1880-1888. Author's collection.

22. Such complaints are fairly common in Dunn & Elliot's incoming letters in writer's possession.

23. Statement of Carroll A Deering to writer.

24. Percy & Small *Day Book, loc cit.*

The profitability of schooners

It would be interesting to reach some conclusions as to the profitability of this class of tonnage. This is no easy task, because, while much scattered evidence of earnings exists, we rarely find data covering the complete life of a vessel. Too often, when the dividend record is complete, there is no evidence of the vessel's cost. To say the very least, they were a speculative investment. Their average life was not overly long. For example, the average usefulness of the seventy-three three-masters built in 1881 was just under fourteen years; of the 181 four-masters built before 1900, the average was slightly over sixteen years. No fewer than twenty-three of these four-masters were lost when less than four years old. There is sufficient evidence to suggest that schooners depreciated in value about 6 per cent annually.[25] Insurance, if carried, took another 7 per cent on a new vessel and as much as 12 per cent on the depreciated value of an old vessel. Thus dividends at a rate of some 20 per cent were necessary to ensure a 5 or 6 per cent yield on the investment. Indeed, this was quite possible if a vessel stayed clear of casualties. Even the best of the big schooners could be accident-prone, however, and a dismasting such as the *Gov. Ames* sustained on her maiden voyage could result in a large assessment and shut off dividends for many months.[26]

A few large four-masters for which substantial data exist must serve, for the time being, as representatives of the returns paid by vessel property. The earliest was the *Augustus Hunt*, 1200 gross ton schooner, built in Bath in 1882 by B W & H F Morse for their own management. She cost $58,983.13, and paid in dividends the sum of $186,015.92 before she was lost in 1904. This was an annual return of almost 16 per cent, and it was reported that the owners were never called upon for an assessment.[27] Another fortunate vessel was the *Charles P Notman*, Bath-built in 1894 by Percy & Small and, like the *Hunt*, managed by her builders. Shares in her cost $1007.77 per sixty-fourth, making $69,497.55 for the whole. She paid for herself in just five years, and her loss immediately afterwards in collision with a steamer resulted in a settlement which brought her total earnings to 190 per cent of her cost, thus yielding her lucky owners an annual return of 36 per cent![28] Another four-master for which complete records of earnings have survived was the 1247-ton *Malcolm B Seavey*. Built in 1901 at Bath by Gardiner

The Cora F Cressy *still exists as a hulk at Bremen, Maine. Note the high flaring bows and powerful hull.* (Basil Greenhill)

G Deering, she cost $63,918.44. During the ten years before she foundered in a hurricane off the South Carolina coast, she paid $117,618.56 in dividends, an annual return of almost 18½ per cent.[29] On the other hand, it is possible to cite the occasional example like that of the *Millie G Bowne*, a splendid big four-master which was dismasted and abandoned before she ever delivered a cargo.[30]

The First World War building boom

By 1910 the building of big schooners had all but ceased due to increasingly stiff competition from steamers and barges, and it was widely felt that coastal sail would soon wither away. The First World War was destined, however, to bring a frenzied reprieve. A very large part of American overseas commerce had been carried in steamships belonging to the belligerent powers. In the opening weeks of the conflict German merchant ships were swept from the high seas by the dominance of British sea power, and by the summer of 1915 British tonnage was being increasingly redeployed to provide more direct support to the war effort. In response to the consequent scarcity of tonnage, freights from American Atlantic ports rose sharply, and by the summer of 1915 schooners were avidly sought for service in waters far removed from the milieu of their accustomed employment. Prepaid freights became the rule so that it mattered not whether a voyage was completed. Many owners sold their schooners for as much or more than they had cost to build a decade earlier.[31] The most spectacular of such transactions involved the sale, in 1917, of the two dozen vessels managed by J S Winslow & Company of Portland, Maine, to opportunistic New Yorkers. Comprised of five enormous six-masters, nine five-masters, and ten large four-masters, the

Winslow fleet was rightly considered the finest of its kind.

Unfortunately, we do not know the price for which this entire fleet was sold, but such records do exist for Winslow's newest and largest vessel, the six-master *Edward B Winslow*, and they provide a fascinating contrast between her very satisfactory peacetime operation and the soaring profits of offshore trade commencing in 1915.[32] Completed late in 1908 by Percy & Small at Bath, the *Winslow* measured 3424 gross tons with the following impressive dimensions: length 418.4ft; breadth 50ft; depth 23.7ft. Her cost was $172,800. In a little more than five years she averaged twelve trips per annum with cargoes of about 5600 tons of coal, chiefly from Hampton Roads to Portland and Boston, the rates being a trifle over 70 cents per ton. By March 1915 her net earnings in this prosaic trade amounted to nearly 90 per cent of her cost. She then forsook coastal water to accept a pre-

25. A R Reed to Dunn & Elliot (Waldoborough, Maine 18 August 1908). Auction sales of vessel shares reported in Maine newspapers.

26. Captain C A Davis' record book of his account with Schooner *Gov. Ames* and owners, 1889-1899. Davis family collection.

27. Undated newspaper clipping from *Bath Daily Times*.

28. Percy & Small *Day Book, loc cit.*

29. Schooner *Malcolm B Seavey*. Construction account (Bath, Maine 30 March 1901), and thirty-five dividend statements, 1901-1909. Author's collection.

30. *New York Maritime Register* (8 January 1890).

31. The five-master *Gardiner G Deering* was a typical example. She was 1928 gross tons and carried 3200 tons of coal. Her construction account, dated Bath, Maine 15 April 1903, gives her cost as $84,894.72. The reported price of her sale in the *New York Maritime Register* (18 July 1917) was $140,000.

32. The cost and earnings of the *Edward B Winslow* are from the building contract and a complete file of her statements issued by J S Winslow & Company at the end of each voyage.

The Jessie G Noyes *under construction at Thomaston, Maine, in 1917.* (W J Lewis Parker Collection)

paid charter of $7.50 per ton on coal from Norfolk to Rio de Janeiro, whence she returned to Baltimore with manganese ore at $3.25 per ton. A similar round to Rio de Janeiro ensued, the rates being increased to $8.25 on coal and $6.00 on ore homeward. In August 1916 she sailed once again for Rio de Janeiro with coal at $16.50, and early the next year she took coal from Norfolk to Barcelona at a rate of $15.00 on a 4978-ton cargo. The dividends paid from the receipts from these offshore voyages under Winslow's management amounted to $225,280.

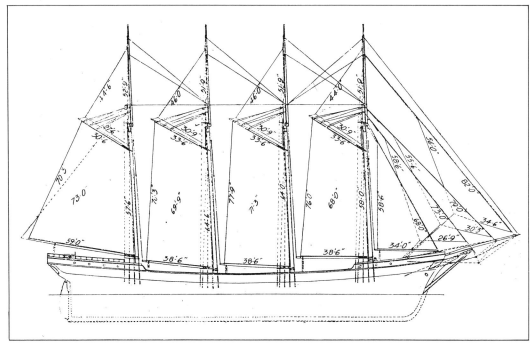

The sail plan of a typical four-master, the J W Clise, *built on the Pacific coast by Globe Navigation of Ballard, Washington, in 1904. The sail area here depicted amounted to 15,145sq ft.* (By courtesy of David MacGregor)

Four two-masters, two three-masters and three four-masters lying in Bangor, Maine. The four-masters are the Wesley M Oler, *built at Bath, Maine, in 1891, the* Jennie S Butler, *also built at Bath in 1891, and the* King Phillip, *built at Camden, Maine. She sank in November 1898 off Cape Cod, so this photograph was taken before that date. (W J Lewis Parker Collection)*

Upon her return from Barcelona, her owners were doubtless overjoyed when she was sold for $325,000. Altogether, she had disbursed $712,969 in dividends, a sum more than four times her cost!

It was inevitable that such extraordinary profits would lead to a frenzied boom in the building of new tonnage. No doubt steel steamships would have been preferred, but the probability of American involvement in the war had led to the creation of the United States Shipping Board in 1916, and the pre-emption of steel shipbuilding facilities for construction of government-owned steamers. As a result, private ownership was forced to turn to wooden sailing craft.

The outcome of the owner's collective activities was impressive. Of four-masted schooners – the most popular rig of the war-inspired fleet – no fewer than 138 were completed within the six-year span 1915–1921, and this amounted to a full 30 per cent of all East Coast four-masters constructed during the entire forty-one years since the rig was introduced in 1879. Within these six years there were also built ten five-masters, some fifty three-masters of moderate size, and twenty-one barquentines.[33] This accomplishment is the more noteworthy when it is realized how few yards remained in business in 1915 which were capable of building *large* wooden vessels. Bath's Percy & Small, G G Deering, and Kelley, Spear & Company, and Rockland's Cobb, Butler & Company were the only firms left in Maine with such a tradition.[34] Thomaston yards had been idle since 1905 and Camden's since 1909, although their plants were essentially intact. Other once-active centres of the industry such as the Down East villages of

Stockton Springs and Harrington had built nothing for a generation. In these places, and in a dozen more Maine localities, shipbuilding was revived with enthusiasm.

The not untypical record of the 1162-ton four-master *Nancy Hanks* goes far to explain this enthusiasm. Launched in June 1917, she was built at Thomaston on speculation by George Gilchrist at a cost of $110,000. He sold her while she was still on the ways for $150,000, whereupon her fortunate buyers chartered her at $225,000 for a voyage to South Africa with general cargo and back with palm oil from West Africa.[35]

Perhaps the greatest difficulty encountered by the builders was the scarcity of experienced labour. There were few able young journeymen to be found in the yards. Since about 1905, the obvious decline of the industry had made it less and less appealing to young men of ambition. On the other hand, there were not enough of the wonderfully skilled old-timers to make up even a small fraction of the manpower required by the new yards. Every octogenarian still capable of wielding and adze or broad axe was recalled from retirement to set the pace for the greenhorns, whose employment in the yards could be speedily terminated by a call to military service.

Although rather more than half of the building which occurred during these rousing times took place in Maine, it is startling to note how large a contribution was made by yards located in southern states, all the way from North Carolina to Texas. From cities such as Savannah and Brunswick, Georgia, and from numerous Gulf Coast sawmill towns with fanciful names like Bagdad, Shellbank and Chickasaw, there came a

full quarter of the East Coast four-masters of the war years. The number of southern schooners built before 1915 was so negligible that the industry could hardly be said to have existed.[36] In worse plight than northern yards for labour, those few builders who were able to secure a good Down East Yankee master builder were most fortunate. With few exceptions, the southern craft lacked the graceful model and fine finish which were the hallmarks of Maine builders.

Along the entire Atlantic seaboard about three-quarters of the wartime building was concentrated in the three years 1917-1919. The four- and five-masters launched in the third year, forty-two in number, were mostly ordered before the Armistice. The following year production was nearly halved, and the end came in 1921 with four stragglers from Maine yards. Building costs, which rose to double or more prewar prices, greatly diminished the chances that the later vessels would prove profitable when freights returned to normal. There was, however, the greatest reluctance to believe that the bonanza must come to an end, and freight rates continued to support this optimism until midsummer of 1920. By then the flood of government steamships, laid down for the eventuality of a longer war, was in full spate. The requirements of world shipping were grossly oversupplied, and freights fell disastrously. No class of vessel was more adversely affected than the relatively inefficient schooner. The chilling effect of this debacle on one fine craft, the *Edna Hoyt*, the last of all the five-masters, was all too common. She was launched from Dunn & Elliott's yard at Thomaston, Maine, on 11 Decem-

33. The five-masted barquentines were built in Texas and Mississippi. They were ungainly craft of about 2400 gross tons. They were undercanvassed, and most of them were fitted with auxiliary oil engines which made them prone to early destruction by fire.

34. Kelley, Spear & Company had built its last schooner in 1912, but the firm remained very active in building barges throughout the war years. Two other builders of excellent repute, I L Snow & Company, of Rockland, Maine, and Frank S Bowker, of Phippsburg, Maine, were still active. They are omitted because their prewar building was largely confined to moderate sized three-masters.

35. *New York Maritime Register* (26 June 1917).

36. Between 1900 and 1915, only four schooners of more than 400 tons were built in the south. No two of the four were built in the same place.

ber 1920. As managing owners, they sold shares in the vessel at the rate of $200,000. She paid only one dividend, $2400, in 1922 and, early in 1924, she was sold for $23,000.[37]

The final years of the trading schooner

In the 1920s and '30s, schooners were increasingly restricted to a marginal existence in nearby waters. They were almost completely forced by steamers and barges from the coal and phosphate rock trades in which they had once been dominant. They fared somewhat better in the lumber trades, especially in the transport of hard pine and railroad ties from Brunswick and Jacksonville to New York and Boston. Occasionally, they found employment in carrying gypsum

The four-master Jessie A Bishop, *building in 1908 at Rockland, Maine, with two other schooners under construction at the Cobb, Butler & Co yard. (W J Lewis Parker Collection)*

from Nova Scotia to New York, or rough jetty stone which went from Maine's quarries for use in harbour improvements in southern ports. Two or three times a year they were able to secure a coal cargo from Hampton Roads ports to Bermuda, where it was stockpiled for bunkering steamers. There was also a limited amount of business for them in the Caribbean. The French islands still imported a modest amount of coal, and there were sometimes homeward cargoes to be had of logwood from Haiti, goat manure from Venezuela or salt from Turks Island.

Inexorably the fleet dwindled throughout the 1920s. There were losses from marine casualties, there were longer and longer periods of idleness awaiting charters, and mounting indebtedness all too frequently led to the ignominy of libels and forced sales by United States Marshals. The collapse of the Boston firm of Crowell & Thurlow relegated the largest and finest remaining fleet to lay-up berths in Down East coves at

Boothbay Harbour and Eastport during the great depression of the 1930s, and only three of them were destined for a brief reprive under American ownership. By 1940 it would have been hard to muster more than a half-dozen four-masters and perhaps as many three-masters which were still trading on the Atlantic coast. At the close of the Second World War only one vessel, the four-master *Herbert L Rawding*, remained seaworthy, and she was very soon sold for a brief career under Newfoundland ownership.[38]

W J Lewis Parker, USCG (ret)

37. From the Dunn & Elliot *Ship Book* which records costs, earnings and operations of the firm's vessels. It should be noted that the *Edna Hoyt* cost $30,000 more than the *Edward B Winslow* did in 1908. Her coal capacity was 2300 tons, compared with the *Winslow's* 5600 tons. Author's collection.

38. Francis E Bowker, *Atlantic Four-Master: The Story of the Schooner Herbert L Rawding* (Mystic 1986).

Vessels under repair at the South Marine Railway, Rockland, Maine. The two three-masters are the Annie Ainslie *(centre) built at Camden, New Jersey, in 1883 and the* Adelia T Carleton, *built at Rockport, Maine, in 1892.* (W J Lewis Parker Collection)

American Schooners: Typical Vessels 1865–1920

Name	Built	Launched	Tonnage	Dimensions (Feet) (Metres)	Remarks
Three-masted					
LOUISA BLISS	Walker, Dunn & Co, Thomaston, Me	1869	429	136.0 × 31.0 × 15.0 41.5 × 9.4 × 4.6	In sugar and molasses trade from Cuba, as well as 'ice and coaling'. Wrecked 1885
B R WOODSIDE	Adams & Hitchcock, Bath, Me	1883	535	158.0 × 33.5 × 12.0 48.2 × 10.2 × 3.7	Carried coal, ice and lumber. Lost 1902
BRADFORD C FRENCH	David Clark, Kennebunkport, Me	1884	920	184.3 × 37.5 × 19.2 56.2 × 11.4 × 5.9	Largest of all the three-masters; for coal trade. Like many big schooners of the 1870s and '80s, she was fitted with a centreboard. Foundered 5 July 1916
CHARLES W CHURCH	New England SB Co, Bath, Me	1884	802	179.3 × 37.9 × 15.5 54.7 × 11.6 × 4.7	Chiefly engaged in coal trade; another centre-boarder. Foundered 31 October 1914
SADIE C SUMNER	Dunn & Elliot, Thomaston, Me	1890	639	154.4 × 37.5 × 14.1 47.1 × 11.4 × 4.3	Versatile vessel. Frequently used in lumber trade from southern and Gulf of Mexico ports
Four-masted					
WILLIAM L WHITE	Goss, Sawyer & Packard, Bath, Me	1880	996	189.9 × 39.9 × 17.4 57.9 × 12.2 × 5.3	The first four-masted schooner designed and built as such; fitted with centreboard

Name	Built	Launched	Tonnage (gross)	Dimensions (feet) (metres)	Remarks
AUGUSTUS HUNT	B W & H F Morse, Bath, Me	1882	1141	208.0 × 40.7 × 20.6 63.4 × 12.4 × 6.3	Another centreboarder, used mostly in ice and coal trades. Lost 1904
MARGUERITE	New England Co, Bath, Me	1889	1553	234.6 × 46.1 × 20.8 71.5 × 14.1 × 6.3	Designed primarily for coal trade to New England. Sunk by U-boat, 4 April 1917
EDWIN R HUNT	G G Deering Co, Bath, Me	1892	1132	196.6 × 38.9 × 19.4 59.9 × 11.9 × 5.9	Sunk by U-boat, 7 April 1917
WILLIAM H CLIFFORD	Percy & Small, Bath, Me	1895	1594	221.6 × 43.5 × 19.6 67.5 × 13.3 × 6.0	Sunk by U-boat, 8 September 1917
HENRY W CRAMP	H M Bean, Camden, Me	1896	1629	231.8 × 44.2 × 19.7 70.7 × 13.5 × 6.0	Built primarily for coal trade to New England. Went missing in 1919 with crew of ten
L HERBERT TAFT	Dunn & Elliot, Thomaston, Me	1901	1492	221.0 × 44.7 × 20.0 67.4 × 13.6 × 6.1	Coal to New England during summer months; the rest of year took coal and steel rails south, returning with phosphate rock and railroad ties. Wrecked 19 December 1912
EDGAR W MURDOCK	Carleton, Norwood & Co, Rockport, Me	1902	1451	217.3 × 42.7 × 19.6 66.2 × 13.0 × 6.0	Made five round voyages to River Plate with lumber and back with hides or quebracho wood. Coasting with coal and phosphate rock. Wrecked 1917
HERBERT D MAXWELL	New England Co, Bath, Me	1905	772	185.9 × 38.4 × 14.0 56.7 × 11.7 × 4.3	Typical of many single-deck four-masters of moderate tonnage designed for hard pine lumber trade from southern ports; fitted with bow ports for loading long sticks
ROSALIE HULL	Georgia SB Co, Savannah, Ga	1918	827	179.3 × 38.8 × 16.3 54.7 × 11.8 × 5.0	One of four near-sisters built in Savannah, Georgia, from a design prepared by Percy & Small, Bath, Maine
COMMACK	Naul SB Co, Wilmington, NC	1918	1446	228.0 × 40.0 × 19.0 69.5 × 12.2 × 5.8	Typical large and awkward-looking product of southern shipyards during First World War
HERBERT L RAWDING	Stockton Yard Inc, Stockton Springs, Me	1919	1219	201.7 × 38.5 × 21.9 61.5 × 11.7 × 6.7	Typical of the splendid fleet of some thirty-one four-masters built for the Boston firm of Crowell & Thurlow during the First World War. Sold in 1945 to Newfoundland owners

Five-masted

Name	Built	Launched	Tonnage (gross)	Dimensions (feet) (metres)	Remarks
GOV. AMES	Levitt Storer, Waldoboro, Me	1888	1778	245.6 × 49.6 × 21.2 74.9 × 15.1 × 6.5	Generally considered to have been the first real five-master, and, without doubt, the first vessel so rigged on the Atlantic coast. Largest centreboard schooner
HARWOOD PALMER	George L Welt, Waldoboro, Me	1904	2885	301.7 × 46.3 × 27.8 92.0 × 14.1 × 8.5	One of thirteen big five-masters and two four-masters of the Palmer fleet, all built between 1900 and 1908. All were painted white
GOVERNOR BROOKS	Percy & Small, Bath, Me	1907	2628	280.7 × 45.8 × 26.5 85.6 × 14.0 × 8.1	Named for governor of Wyoming. Foundered 23 March 1921 off Montevideo, Uruguay
EDNA HOYT	Dunn & Elliot Co, Inc, Thomaston, Me	1920	1512	224.0 × 41.1 × 20.8 68.3 × 12.5 × 6.3	Last of the fifty-six five-masters built on the Atlantic coast and the last in active service. Hulked at Lisbon, Portugal, in 1937

Six-masted

Name	Built	Launched	Tonnage (gross)	Dimensions (feet) (metres)	Remarks
GEORGE W WELLS	H M Bean, Camden, Me	1900	2970	319.3 × 48.5 × 23.0 97.3 × 14.8 × 7.0	First of the ten six-masters, all built between 1900 and 1908. Employed chiefly in coal trade to New England
EDWARD B WINSLOW	Percy & Small, Bath, Me	1908	3350	320.2 × 50.0 × 23.9 97.6 × 15.2 × 7.3	Considered by many to have been the best of the six-masters. Burned 10 July 1917 off St Nazaire, France
WYOMING	Percy & Small, Bath, Me	1909	3730	329.5 × 50.1 × 30.4 100.4 × 15.3 × 9.3	Probably the largest wooden merchant sailing vessel ever built. Built for New England coal trade, but made long offshore voyages during First World War. Foundered 12 March 1924 off Chatham, Mass

7

Schooner Development in Britain

SAILING vessels of various sizes and shapes may be described as schooners. Common to each is the rig. While ships, barques, snows and brigs are mainly propelled by square sails attached to yards, the schooner is driven chiefly by fore-and-aft sails set from gaffs and booms. She has at least two masts, each of which generally comprises a short topmast fitted to a much larger lower mast. If equipped with two masts, the schooner's principal canvas is not set from her fore mast – in which case she would be a ketch – but from her second or main mast.[1] Such vessels have been put to multifarious uses, some being deployed as naval patrol craft, others as fishing vessels and still more as yachts. Yet during the nineteenth century the schooner was essentially a merchantman, carrying cargoes along the coasts and across the oceans, particularly on the short- and medium-distance routes. Indeed, in mid-Victorian Britain the schooner was the archetypal small merchant sailing ship.

Pictorial evidence indicates that a form of schooner rig was applied to Dutch *jaghts* in the early seventeenth century. It was also found in small river craft and fishing shallops on both sides of the Atlantic long before 1700.[2] Yet it was not until the eighteenth century that the rig was widely used in larger commercial vessels. Precisely when this occurred is uncertain, though legend has it that the term 'schooner' was coined in 1713, when an excited onlooker remarked 'see how she scoons' as a vessel was launched at Gloucester, Massachusetts. Flattered that the movement of his vessel should be likened to a stone 'scooning', or skimming, across the water, Andrew Robinson, her builder, responded: 'let her a scooner be!' While the veracity of this tale is open to question,[3] its location in the early part of the century is telling, for the schooner was well established by the 1740s when at least twenty-two were fitted out as private men-of-war.[4] Moreover, its situation in colonial America is equally significant, for it was here

that the schooner was first deployed to any great extent as a seagoing vessel, chiefly in the coastal and inter-colonial trades.[5]

Over time, of course, the 'scooner' developed in various ways. While the design and efficiency of her rig tended to improve, the size and capacity of her hull increased and she was therefore employed in a growing number of trades. Development was also evident in a spatial sense, with schooners being produced in more and more regions of the North Atlantic basin as the eighteenth century progressed. In Britain, the rig was occasionally deployed in new-built vessels from the 1760s, though it remained an oddity until the early nineteenth century. Thereafter the schooner was widely adopted by British shipowners and shipbuilders, so much so that by the 1860s the schooner was the most common form of rig deployed in the British mercantile marine. The construction of these fore-and-aft vessels tended to decline thereafter, though many remained in service until the First World War and beyond. This chapter examines the development of the British schooner. In particular, it focuses on the changing extent and regional distribution of the 'schooner fleet', the main trends apparent

in vessel size and design, and the factors which conditioned the diffusion and deployment of the rig. By so doing, it is hoped that some light will be shed on the significance of the small sailing ship in Britain during the nineteenth century.

Britain's schooner fleet

Estimates as to the number and regional distribution of the schooner rigged vessels registered in Britain can be gleaned from *Lloyd's Registers* and the *Mercantile Navy Lists*. While both sources provide a wealth of information on merchant

1. B Greenhill, *Schooners* (London 1980), pp7-17.

2. On the origins of the schooner, see E P Morris, *The Fore-and-Aft Rig in America* (Yale 1927); B Greenhill, *The Merchant Schooners* (4th ed, London 1988), pp6-8; D R MacGregor, *Schooners in Four Centuries* (Hemel Hempstead 1982), pp13-5.

3. D R MacGregor, *op cit*, p16; H M Hahn, *The Colonial Schooner 1763-1775* (London 1981), pp14-5.

4. C E Swanson, *Predators and Prizes: American Privateering and Imperial Warfare 1739-1748* (Columbia, South Carolina 1991), pp56-8.

5. D R MacGregor, *op cit*, pp19-21; H I Chapelle, *The History of the American Sailing Ship* (New York 1935), pp31-43.

A painting by Simon de Vlieger who lived from 1600 to 1653, showing a Dutch jaght *with an early form of schooner rig.* (National Maritime Museum)

This drawing, believed to be by Ashley Bowen of Marblehead, Massachusetts, is titled, 'This shows the Schooner Baltic coming out of St Eustatia y. 16 of Nov. 1765'. It shows a North American schooner of mid eighteenth century type. (Peabody Museum of Salem)

to question due to the changing nature of the business they reflect. On the other hand, *Mercantile Navy Lists* comprise a comprehensive catalogue of British-registered vessels, but the series does not commence until the mid-1850s and does not distinguish rigs until the early 1870s. Despite such problems, and the fact that the vast volume of the data available renders a selective approach inevitable, these sources can be used to provide a broad overview of the development of Britain's schooner fleet between the 1770s and 1900.

Extent

Incidental evidence suggests that a number of schooners were operating out of British ports during the third quarter of the eighteenth century. For instance the *Cybella* schooner owned Benjamin Vaughan of London and declared to be 50 tons burden, sailed with a letter of marque in 1758,[6] while the *Hawk* and the *Ann*, both of which left Dartmouth for Newfoundland in the

---

6. PRO (Public Record Office), HCA 26/9, Letter of Marque Declaration, 3 May 1758.

shipping, some reservations should be made concerning their scope and utility. For instance, neither source offers much information about the occupations of the vessels listed, so that the 'schooner fleet' inevitably contains vessels which were deployed in fishing, river work and yachting as well as those engaged in trading. At the same time, the schooner rigs commonly used in sail-assist steamships in the mid-nineteenth century are excluded from the fleet. Moreover, contemporary definitions of rigs varied over time and between districts, while methods of tonnage measurement were also subject to change in the long term. For such reasons, the enumeration of vessel types based on *Lloyd's Registers* and the *Mercantile Navy Lists* largely assume the form of rather crude 'head counts'.

It should also be borne in mind that *Lloyd's Register* and the *Mercantile Navy List* were pro-

duced for different purposes, and are therefore not strictly compatible. Thus, vessels built and owned by foreigners were classified and listed by Lloyd's, while the *Registers* obviously take no account of vessels which were not insured by the society, and their consistency over time is open

A number of foreign-built schooners were bought by British owners and run in the British home trade and on deep water, usually successfully. This steel vessel was built at Hammelwarden, Germany, by Carl Luhring as the Weser *and under the British flag was re-named S F Pearce. The photograph shows her at a late stage of setting sail - the flying jib is still being hauled up, the mizzen sheet has not been properly cleared, the fore lower topsail has not been properly sheeted home. The port anchor is just breaking water - she has evidently set sail from anchor - and, of course, the running bobstay has not yet been hauled tight on the windlass. (Amos & Amos)*

The schooner largely replaced the brig as the preferred British small merchant vessel as the nineteenth century progressed (see Table 7/1). This brig, the Pelican, *is shown moored bow and stern off Hastings beach in the 1860s awaiting the ebb when her coal cargo will be discharged into carts.* (The late Michael Bouquet)

early 1770s, were schooner rigged.[7] Moreover, a number of schooners registered in the late 1780s had been built in Britain. For instance, the *Good Intent*, registered at Exeter in 1787, had been constructed at Lympstone in 1766,[8] the year in which the *Mercer* had been launched into the Mersey according to her Liverpool registration.[9] Yet these were isolated examples. In 1776, schooners represented just 0.4 per cent of the British-built vessels listed in *Lloyd's Register*, the proportion shrinking to 0.1 per cent in terms of tonnage. Square rigged vessels dominated Britain's shipping stock at this time, with brigs accounting for 1633 (47.1 per cent), and fully rigged ships for 886 (25.6 per cent), of the 3464 home-built vessels classified by Lloyd's.[10]

This pattern changed significantly over the next hundred or so years. In particular, the balance between brigs and schooners – rigs deployed in roughly the same tonnage range – shifted substantially in favour of the fore-and-after during the first sixty years of the nineteenth century. Whereas 'the absence of schooners [had been] the most striking feature of the English shipbuilding industry before 1776',[11] schooner construction was a notable and growing facet of shipyard output from the 1790s. Thus, as Table 7/1 shows, the number of schooners classified in *Lloyd's Register* increased from 164 to 2837 between 1791 and 1831, the rate of growth apparently slackening thereafter so that almost 3000 schooners were listed in 1861. In contrast, the brig population declined from the early nineteenth century, the rate of contraction being most marked after 1831. As a consequence, the

relative significance of the schooner increased steadily during the 1791-1861 period, while the brig's prominence diminished. By the early 1860s, over twice as many schooners as brigs were listed in *Lloyd's Register*, the former now accounting for more than a quarter of the total number of vessels classified.

An examination of the schooner fleet by place of build presents a slightly modified outline of the prevalence of the rig in Britain. As Table 7/2 indicates, the majority of schooners cited in *Lloyd's Register* in the late eighteenth century were of foreign or colonial build, the proportion of British-built vessels rising to 56 per cent in

1821 and 92 per cent in 1861. More significantly – for this shifting balance might simply reflect a change in the orientation of Lloyd's' business – the absolute number of listed schooners which had been constructed in Britain increased substantially between 1781 and 1861. Starting from a low base, the rate of schooner building appears to have intensified during the 1780s, quickening still further between 1791 and 1821 when the number of British-built schooners in the *Register* increased from 66 to 758, a rise of 1150 per cent. During the next four decades the rate of accretion eased, but there were still some 2753 home-built schooners classified by Lloyd's in 1861, a 350 per cent increase on the 1821 figure.

It would appear that schooner building reached its height in Britain during the 1860s. Analysis of the 1890 *Mercantile Navy List* reveals that 2357 home-produced schooners were registered in the British Isles, 396 fewer than the equivalent aggregate drawn from the *Lloyd's Register* of 1860. As the latter source offers a large sample, while the former provides a thorough

---

Table 7/1: Brigs and schooners listed in Lloyd's Register *in selected years, 1791-1861*

	Total Number of Vessels	Schooners No	Schooners %	Brigs No	Brigs %
1791	7843	164	2.1	3369	43
1811	14,716	777	5.3	5176	35.2
1831	17,902	2837	15.8	4796	26.8
1861*	11,242	2993	26.6	1433	12.7

* 1861 is used in tables and text to denote the period from 1 July 1860 to 30 June 1861 covered by *Lloyd's Register* of 1860.

Source: Lloyd's Register, 1791, 1811, 1831, 1860.

Table 7/2: Schooners listed in Lloyd's Register *by area of build in selected years, 1781-1861*

	1781	1791	1821	1861
Britain	14	66	758	2753
British North America	12	42	92	159
United States	72	39	130	9
Europe	71	16	350	60
Not known	0	1	23	12
	169	164	1353	2993
% built in British Isles	8.3	40.2	56.0	92.0

Source: Lloyd's Registers, 1781, 1791, 1821, 1860.

---

7. PRO BT 98/4-5, Dartmouth Muster Rolls.

8. DRO (Devon Record Office), Exeter Ship Registers.

9. R Craig and R Jarvis (eds), *Liverpool Registry of Merchant Ships* (Manchester 1967), p87.

10. J A Goldenberg, 'An Analysis of Shipbuilding Sites in *Lloyd's Register* of 1776', *The Mariner's Mirror* 59 (1973), pp419-35.

11. *Ibid*, p419.

census, the decline was undoubtedly greater than the figures suggest. That the 1860s, rather than the 1870s or 1880s, witnessed the peak in schooner construction is borne out by the breakdown of the 1890 fleet by decade of build, as presented in Table 7/3. While only 10.7 per cent of the schooner rigged vessels afloat in 1890 had been launched in the previous ten years, and 28 per cent had been built in the 1870s, almost one-third of the total had been produced in the 1860s. Moreover, on the assumption that longevity decreased the chances of survival, it is highly probable that Table 7/3 understates the significance of schooner building in the 1860s.

Table 7/3: British-built schooners registered in 1890 by decade of build

	Number	*Tonnage*	*Average Tons*	*% of Tonnage*
1770-1819	31	1833	59.1	0.9
1820-9	36	2688	74.7	1.2
1830-9	95	7482	78.8	3.5
1840-9	194	14,283	73.6	6.6
1850-9	453	36,665	80.9	17.1
1860-9	773	68,786	89.0	32.0
1870-9	592	60,001	101.4	28.0
1880-9	183	22,927	125.3	10.7
	2357	214,665	91.1	

Source: Mercantile Navy List, 1890.

Thus, from a very low base in the eighteenth century, the number of schooners owned and built in Britain increased appreciably down to the 1860s. Thereafter, the rate of new building slackened so that by 1890 the schooner population was both diminishing and ageing. Nevertheless, as Table 7/4 shows, the schooner remained the most common form of rig in the British sailing fleet in 1890. By this date, some 2533 (17.4 per cent) of the vessels registered in the British Isles were described as schooner rigged, while just 759 (5.2 per cent) were listed as brigs or brigantines, a reversal of the imbalance which had pertained a century earlier. With over 2000 ketches also in existence in

1890, the supremacy of fore-and-aft over square sails at the lower end of the tonnage spectrum was even more pronounced. At the same time,

Table 7/4: Sailing vessels registered in the British Isles by rig, 1890

Rig	*Number*	*%*
Barque	1004	6.9
Ship	907	6.2
Barquentine	150	1.0
Schooner	2533	17.4
Ketch	2071	14.2
Brigantine	578	4.0
Brig	181	1.2
Snow	43	0.3
Dandy	1284	8.8
Cutter	1005	6.9
Smack	922	6.3
Sloop	590	4.1
Yawl	391	2.7
Lugger	288	2.0
Wherry	30	0.2
Spritsail	1749	12.0
Flat	512	3.5
Barge	179	1.2
Trow	66	0.5
Keel	19	0.1
Others	63	0.4
	14,565	

Others = 10 hookers, 11 jiggers, 6 square, 10 jury, 4 boomsail, 9 lighters, 7 galliots, 3 hermaphrodites, 2 gaffsails, 1 polacre.

Source: Mercantile Navy List, 1890.

the emergence of these ketches – fewer than 100 had been classified by Lloyd's in 1861 – was closely related to the contraction of schooner building apparent since the 1860s.

Regional distribution

Schooner rigged vessels were built in virtually every maritime district in the British Isles during the 1775-1900 period. While some areas were always more committed than others to schooner building, there were also long-run shifts in the locational focus of the activity, both between and within regions.

In the late eighteenth century, northwest England was the leading producer of schooners in Britain. For instance, in 1776 the northwest accounted for eight of the fourteen British-built schooners listed in *Lloyd's Register*.[12] In 1791, as Table 7/5 shows, the region remained the principal building area, producing twenty-eight (42.4 per cent) of the sixty-six home-constructed schooners listed, twice as many as the next most important region, southwest England. During the next thirty years, the rapid expansion of schooner building was associated with a marked change in the distribution of this output. While less than 10 per cent of the British-built schooners listed in 1821 had been launched in the northwest, the contribution of southwest England had risen to over 40 per cent, Westcountry shipyards having built nearly four times as many schooners as those of any other region. Significant increases were also evident in the districts bordering the North Sea – East Anglia, northeast England and east Scotland – and schooners

12. *Ibid*, p424.

A considerable number of small British owned merchant sailing vessels were built in Canada, as analysed in Table 7/2. This brigantine is the Jean Anderson *built at Mount Stewart, Prince Edward Island, in 1877. She is on the starboard tack in a light breeze.*
(Peabody Museum of Salem)

Table 7/5: British-built schooners listed in Lloyd's Register *by region of build, 1781-1861*

Region*	1781		1791		1821		1861	
	No	%	No	%	No	%	No	%
England								
Southwest	–	–	14	21.2	306	40.4	669	24.3
Northwest	3	21.4	28	42.4	69	9.1	149	5.4
Northeast	–	–	1	1.5	90	11.9	339	12.3
East Anglia	–	–	1	1.5	63	8.3	200	7.3
South East	1	7.1	9	13.6	51	6.7	160	5.8
Wales	–	–	–	–	28	3.7	620	22.5
Scotland†	2	14.3	–	–	12	1.6	–	–
West	–	–	3	4.5	17	2.2	90	3.3
East	–	–	1	1.5	90	11.9	361	13.1
Ireland	5	35.7	3	4.5	27	3.6	62	2.2
Other British	3	21.4	6	9.1	5	0.7	103	3.7
Total	14		66		758		2655	

* Regions – Southwest = Poole–Gloucester; Northwest = Chester–Carlisle; Northeast = Berwick–Boston; East Anglia = Lynn–Harwich; Southeast = London–Lymington; Wales = Chepstow–Connah's Quay; West Scotland = Dumfries–Durness; East Scotland = Thurso–Dunbar, including Orkney & Shetland; Other British = Channel Islands, Isle of Man, unknown ports.
† Vessels listed as built in Scotland, no port of build specified.
Source: Lloyd's Registers, 1781, 1791, 1821, 1860.

constructed in Wales featured in the *Register* for the first time.

In ensuing decades, schooner building spread more widely. Accordingly, in 1861, the number of listed schooners launched in the southwest stood at 669, more than double the 1821 figure, but this represented just 24.3 per cent of the British-built total. Such a marked relative decline reflected the expansion of schooner building in regions such as northeast England, east Scotland, and most notably in Wales, where 620 (22.5 per cent) of the 1861 stock had been constructed. The regional distribution which emerges from the *Mercantile Navy List* of 1890, as shown in Table 7/6, implies that these trends continued during the final quarter of the nineteenth century. While the southwest was still the most important source of schooners at this time, the region's share of British-built tonnage had fallen to 20.3 per cent as a consequence of the increased contributions of other districts, most notably west Scotland and the resurgent northwest.

Within these regional settings, the production of schooners was concentrated at different times in certain ports or districts. According to the 1791 *Lloyd's Register*, for instance, Liverpool shipyards had launched nineteen of the twenty-eight schooners built in the northwest, with four of the remainder emanating from Lancaster and three from Chester. In southwest England, Bristol, with five vessels, was the leading centre of schooner production, while a further seven had been built in Dorset and South Devon. The other schooner rigged vessels had been constructed in ports as diverse as Dungarvan and Yarmouth, Dundee and Cowes, though only London, with four, and Aberdeen, with two, built more than a single vessel.

By 1821 a number of ports had emerged as significant schooner building centres. In southwest England, the most productive region of the day, the ports of South Devon were the main foci of this activity. Indeed, Dartmouth, Plymouth and Brixham, with fifty-three, forty-nine and forty-five vessels respectively, were not only the leading producers in the Westcountry, but also in the nation as a whole. That a further eighteen schooners had been built at Topsham, and some twenty-five had been constructed at

Salcombe, Shaldon, Teignmouth, Torquay and Totnes, meant that South Devon supplied 25.1 per cent of the British-built schooners classified in the *Register*. Elsewhere, Yarmouth, with thirty-six vessels, dominated schooner building in East Anglia, while the northeast's contribution was focused on Berwick and Hull, and east Scotland's output was drawn from seventeen different sites, with Aberdeen, Dundee and Peterhead the most prominent. Having constructed twelve listed schooners, Liverpool remained the leading port in the northwest, but in a national context the Mersey was no longer an important source of schooners.

The pattern evident in 1821 had altered slightly by 1861. South Devon remained an important schooner building area, while Yarmouth, Hull, Dundee and Aberdeen continued to contribute significantly to east coast production. Nevertheless, shipbuilders in a variety of

Table 7/6: Schooners registered in the British Isles by region of build, 1890

Region*	Number	Tonnage	% British Tonnage	Average Tonnage
England				
Southwest	450	43,572	20.3	96.8
Northwest	257	23,339	10.9	90.8
Northeast	192	17,566	8.2	91.5
East Anglia	79	7237	3.4	91.6
Southeast	270	21,324	9.9	79.0
Wales	411	36,505	17.0	88.8
Scotland				
West	201	19,318	9.0	95.7
East	290	30,601	14.3	105.5
Ireland	93	7079	3.3	76.1
Other British	114	8124	3.8	71.3
Total British	2357	214,665		91.1
British North America	120	10,410		86.8
Foreign	56	5271		94.1
Total	2533	230,346		90.9

*For definition of regions see Table 7/5.

Source: Mercantile Navy List, 1890.

The Susan Vittery, *shown here at Falmouth loading china clay, was built as a two-masted schooner at Dartmouth, Devon, in 1859, the shareholders including members of the Vittery family of Brixham. She spent years in the Azores orange trade and other deep water trades and was subsequently employed principally in the Newfoundland trade. This photograph was taken after 1903 when she was rerigged as a more handy and economical three-masted schooner, a change which meant less wear and tear on her gear, and probably a man less in the crew. It may in fact have been taken during her conversion. Note that the planking up to a strake down below the clearly visible loadline has been sheathed over with an extra layer to lessen leaks and help to keep her together despite rotting frames - a sure sign of an old vessel. Yet the* Susan Vittery *lasted until 1953 when she was lost at sea, still working at least 30 years after this photograph was taken. (From an old postcard)*

Of these, twenty-three had been built on the Mersey, one had been constructed at nearby Parkgate and the remainder originated in Folkestone, Hull, Massachusetts or Newfoundland.[13] Likewise, the construction and ownership of schooners were closely allied in the ports of South Devon during the mid nineteenth century. Here, over 75 per cent of the 500 or so schooners registered at the Customs Ports of Dartmouth, Exeter and Plymouth between 1825 and 1864 had been built in the locality.[14] *Lloyd's Register* of 1861, and the 1890 *Mercantile Navy List*, both of which include port of registry as well as place of build, tend to confirm this pattern, at least for newly constructed schooners. Naturally, the picture is more obscure for older vessels, for the chances of transfer to another registry increased with age. Even so, as most transfers were either within regions or between ports with established fleets, a strong relationship is still evident between patterns of schooner construction and ownership.

However, there were exceptions to this general rule. There are signs that certain ports were more concerned with owning than building schooners. Thus, in 1860, over one hundred schooners were listed by Lloyds as registered in Liverpool, though only twenty-nine had been constructed in the port, an imbalance apparent also at ports as diverse as London, Montrose, and Penzance. Similarly, individual shipowners occasionally developed business links with shipbuilders in other regions; for instance, James Fisher & Co of Barrow, owners of perhaps the largest schooner fleet in the country during the late nineteenth century, purchased twelve three-

places had evidently commenced schooner building in the mid nineteenth century. Thus, ports such as Yarmouth and Ipswich, Aberystwyth and Porthmadog, and, most notably, Sunderland featured prominently in *Lloyd's Register* of 1860. Further developments in the regional distribution of activity took place as schooner building declined over the next thirty years. According to the 1890 *Mercantile Navy List*, the ports of the Bristol Channel, notably Padstow, Bideford, Barnstaple and Bridgwater, accounted for most of the southwest's schooners from the 1870s as South Devon's output diminished. Meanwhile, the Furness ports of Barrow and Ulverston, the shipyards of Mid and North Wales,

notably Portmadog, Amlwch and Connah's Quay, the yachting bases of Cowes and Lymington, and the harbours of the Scottish highland and island districts, especially those in Elgin, Banff and Moray, emerged as the focal points of schooner building in their respective regions.

Though evidence relating to the ownership of schooners is less accessible, it would seem that a strong correlation existed between the place of build and the port of registration. Such a connection can be discerned throughout the period. In 1786-1788, for example, under the terms of the new registry act, twenty-eight schooner rigged vessels were registered at Liverpool, then the chief schooner building port in the country.

---

13. R Craig and R Jarvis, *op cit.*

14. See DRO, Dartmouth, Exeter and Plymouth Ship Registers.

This photograph shows a classic fruit schooner, the Queen of the West, *in her old age lying at anchor off Liverpool. She was built at Salcombe in Devon in 1849 and employed in the trade to Britain with ripening oranges from the Azores. The sheer is flat. Unlike the big American schooners and the wooden barques, a vessel of this size will not have hogged - sagged at the ends - much, even in 75 years of active life. An early painting shows that the* Queen of the West *was, like many of her contemporaries, very flat-sheered even when she was new. The curved, raking, stem and the sharp waterlines forward (which made her very wet in a sea) are all characteristic of the fruit schooners, which were built to get their small, light, cargoes home to Britain as quickly as possible. When she was in the fruit trade she carried an extra yard and square sail, but otherwise was rigged much as she is seen in this photograph taken in the 1920s. (Basil Greenhill Collection)*

masters from the yard of Paul Rodgers at Carrickfergus.[15] Imports of schooners represented a further deviation from the general trend, the colonies of British North America supplying a large number of schooners and other vessels to the British market in the mid nineteenth century.[16] Schooners were also bought from other foreign owners, fifty-six of the vessels listed in 1890, for example, having been constructed outside the British Empire, many in France, Denmark and Germany.

Nevertheless, the great majority of Britain's schooners were purchased from local shipbuilders. The distribution of these fore-and-afters – in terms of ownership as well as construction – changed dramatically between 1775 and 1900. Centered initially on Merseyside, and then much more emphatically in the southwest, particularly in South Devon, the schooner spread to most maritime districts of the British Isles between the 1820s and the 1860s. Thereafter the production and operation of this archetypal small sailing vessel contracted steadily, so that on the eve of the First World War the schooner was a feature of the shipbuilding and shipping industries of just a few of Britain's smaller, largely peripheral, ports.

The hull form of one of the later Porthmadog schooners is shown very well in this photograph of the David Morris, *built in 1897 and wrecked in November 1924. She is lying at low tide on a bank of the river Parret, the Bridgwater river, in Somerset. (W A Sharman)*

Size and design

A great range was evident in the tonnage of Britain's nineteenth-century schooners. In 1890, for instance, the Clyde-built *Earl of Aberdeen*, of 2084 register tons, was the largest schooner rigged sailing vessel recorded in the *Mercantile Navy List*. At the same time, numerous schooners of less than 40 tons were registered in Britain. Within this broad spectrum, two clear traits can be discerned. In the first place, the vast majority of schooners measured between 50 and 200 tons by the late nineteenth century, most falling within the 75/150-ton range. As Table 7/6 indicates, an average of 91.1 tons applied to the

15. T Latham, *The Ashburner Schooners: The Story of the First Shipbuilders of Barrow-in-Furness* (Manchester 1991), p90.

16. DRO, Barnstaple, Bideford and Plymouth Ship Registers.

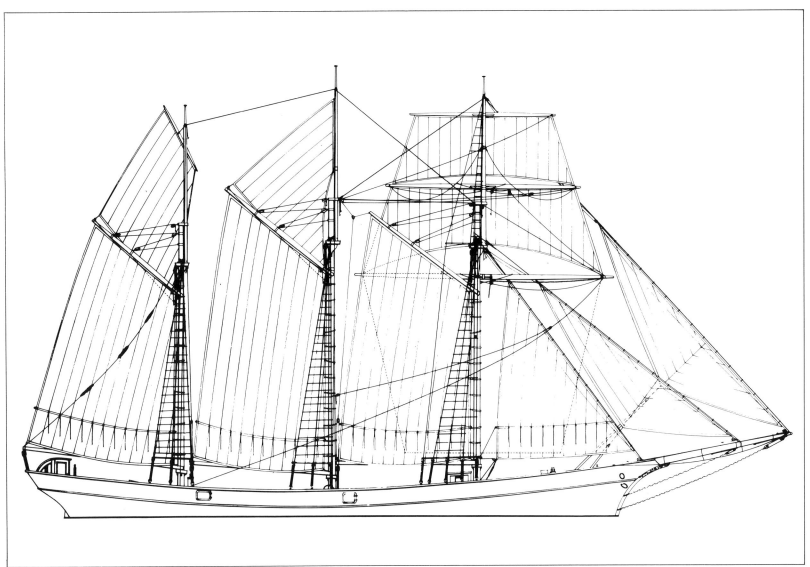

One of very few British-built steel schooners, the 98-ton (net) Result *built at Carrickfergus, Northern Ireland in 1892 by Paul Rodgers. She was built for the well-known shipowners, the Ashburners of Barrow, to the design of Richard Ashburner. (By courtesy of David MacGregor)*

British-built schooners afloat in 1890, with most regions conforming more or less to this mean. Secondly, as Table 7/3 shows, the typical schooner increased in size during the course of the 1775-1890 period; thus, a mean of 59.1 tons was exhibited by the vessels built before 1820, as against the averages of 78.8 and 125.3 tons apparent in those launched in the 1830s and 1880s respectively. Analyses of Customs House Ship Registers support this contention. The tonnage of Fowey's schooners, for example, increased consistently during the mid nineteenth century, the average rising from 79 tons in the 1840s to

The Rhoda Mary, *a fast-sailing Westcountry schooner of 129 tons gross, built in 1868. She was originally two-masted. (By courtesy of David MacGregor)*

Lines and sail plan (reconstructed by David MacGregor and Ralph Bird) of the Millom Castle *of 91 tons gross built by William White at Ulverston in Cumbria in 1870. This vessel has an 'Irish Sea stern', which was rounded, although the bulwarks flared out above the sternpost. (By courtesy of David MacGregor)*

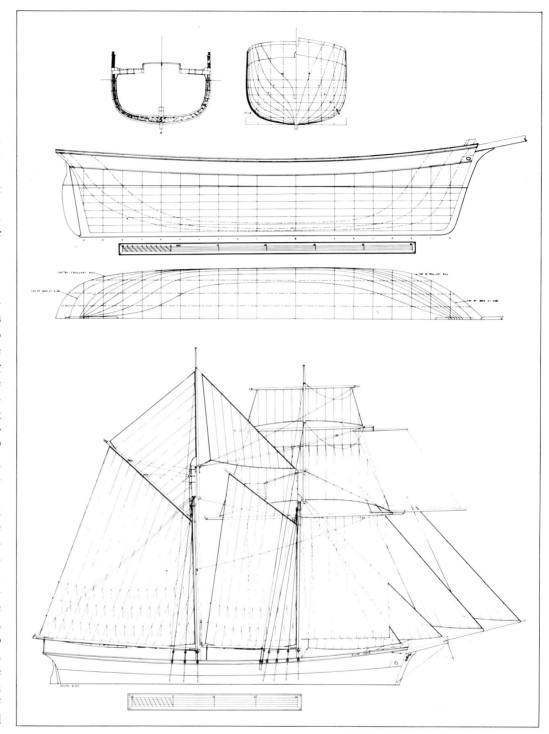

92 tons in the 1860s and 116 tons in the 1870s.[17] A similar pattern was evident in Brixham, where the average schooner measured 128 tons in the 1840s and 149 tons in the 1860s, though Bideford's typical schooner remained unchanged at 82 tons over the same period.[18]

The hull of the British schooner was generally constructed in wood, even in the final third of the century when iron, and then steel, emerged as the principal building material in Britain's shipyard output. Though a number of iron schooners – most built on the Clyde – were classified by Lloyd's in 1861, the shipbuilding firms which possessed the necessary capital goods to build such hulls general concentrated on the production of steamers and much larger sailing vessels. For similar reasons, steel schooners were rarely built in Britain, though a few were constructed during the 1890s and early 1900s, Frank and James Cock, for instance, launching four steel three-masters between 1906 and 1909.[20] These were exceptional, however, for the British schooner was essentially a product of the wooden shipbuilding industry.

Over time, the dimensions of the typical hull changed, a development closely related to the increase evident in average tonnage. In particular, the length of the schooner tended to increase as the nineteenth century progressed. Again, this trend is clearly evident in the Customs House Ship Registers of various ports. The maximum length of Brixham-built schooners, for example, increased from 71ft in the 1820s to 95ft in the late 1850s and still further to 105ft in the late 1860s,[21] while at Fowey the average length of the port's schooners increased from 62ft to 87ft between the 1840s and the 1870s.[22] At the same time, the draught of the typical schooner became progressively shallower, largely because she was obliged to compete ever harder for cargoes as the nineteenth century wore on, and this entailed entering small harbours and tidal havens as often and for as long as possible.[23] Despite these long-term changes, the shape of the schooner remained fairly constant, normally assuming one of two forms throughout the nineteenth century. The first was used for fast sailers and was commonly found in the products of Westcountry shipyards. It 'consisted of a long convex entrance with almost vertical bow section, together with a long and concave run'. A second form was designed to maximise

cargo-carrying capacity, and offered the vessel 'more balanced ends, possibly even with hollows in the fore-body but certainly hollow aft'.[24]

The sail arrangement deployed in British-built schooners varied greatly in detail, both between districts and over time. Yet, in general, the rig was characterised by two main features during the nineteenth century. First, the British schooner was essentially a topsail schooner, for she was almost invariably equipped with square sails on her fore topmast, which were sometimes being supplemented by topgallants, especially in the larger vessels of the late nineteenth century.

17. C H Ward-Jackson, *Ships and Shipbuilders of a Westcountry Seaport: Fowey 1786-1939* (Truro 1986), p35.

18. DRO, Bideford, Brixham and Dartmouth Ship Registers.

19. D R MacGregor, *Schooners*, p72.

20. *Ibid*, p85; G Farr, *Shipbuilding in North Devon* (Greenwich 1976), p16.

21. DRO, Brixham and Dartmouth Ship Registers.

22. C H Ward-Jackson, *op cit*, p35.

23. B Greenhill, *Merchant Schooners*, pp44-5. This trend was much less pronounced in the ports between the Humber and the Thames where flat-bottomed vessels had always been produced.

24. D R MacGregor, *Schooners*, p72.

The lines and deck plan of a small schooner of about 50 tons built at Bristol by J M Hilhouse in 1803. (By courtesy of David MacGregor)

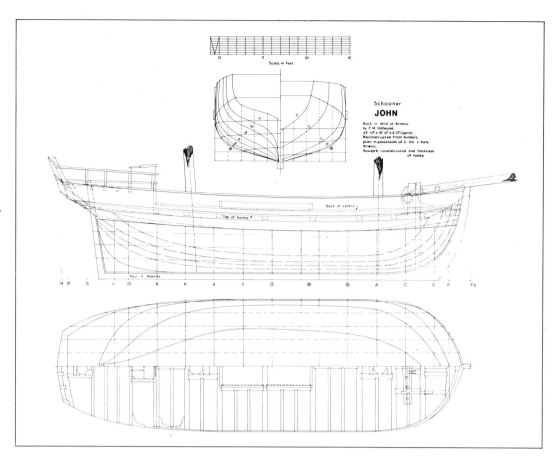

Second, only a handful of British schooners, all built in the 1890s, were fitted with more than three masts.[25] In the first half of the nineteenth century the two-master was predominant, though a number of three-masted schooners were in service, perhaps the earliest being the *Jenny*, built in Bristol before 1791, and the *Curlew*, launched in Teignmouth in 1794.[26] From the 1850s, however, a growing number of schooners were fitted with an extra mast, some being new built while others were lengthened and provided with a reduced main boom to allow the insertion of a mizzen. While there were countless minor changes in her sail plan, most reflecting general improvements in the quality of sailcloth, ropes, blocks and other materials, the addition of the third mast was essentially the most important development in the rig of the British schooner during the nineteenth century.

Relative to the change which transformed other classes of vessel, the improvements in the size and design of Britain's schooners were modest. Ships and barques, for instance, increased dramatically in tonnage from the 1840s, largely as a consequence of the widespread use of iron in hull construction. Moreover, comparison with schooner development elsewhere, especially in North America, further indicates that the British variant of the rig experienced relatively little long-term change. Not only did the American schooner exhibit different design traits – she carried no square sails and was usually fitted with a centreboard as well as deckhouses – but in terms of tonnage and rigging she developed substantially as the nineteenth century progressed. Thus, during the 1880s and 1890s, four- and five-masted schooners of over 1000 tons became a prominent feature of the United States' mercantile marine, the genre reaching a climax with the construction of ten six-masters and one seven-master, the *Thomas W Lawson*, in the shipyards of Maine and Massachusetts in the early 1900s, and then reviving again during the building boom of the First World War.[27]

In contrast, the British schooner remained a small sailing ship. This was due, in part, to the concentration of Britain's shipbuilding and shipping energies into the production and operation of ships, barques and ultimately steamers. More significantly, it reflected the existence of niches in the tonnage market which relatively diminutive sailing vessels could still profitably exploit, even in the early twentieth century. This basic market force essentially conditioned the diffusion and deployment of the British schooner.

Diffusion and deployment

British shipbuilders and shipowners played little part in the early development of the schooner rig. It would appear that only a handful of schooners were registered in Britain before the American Revolution, and few of these were home-produced. In contrast, the schooner 'was probably the most numerous of all classes of carrier' in American waters,[28] a 'local' pre-eminence that was to extend to the transoceanic routes by the Anglo-American War of 1812-1814 when the 'Baltimore clipper', a specialist form of schooner, conveyed approximately 90 per cent of the foreign trade of the United States.[29] Even in a European context, Britain appears to have been relatively slow to adopt the fore-and-after. Thus, in *Lloyd's Register* of 1781, 71 of the 169 schooners listed had been built in continental Europe, while a mere 14 had been constructed in Britain (see Table 7/2). No fewer than 59 of the European vessels had been produced in Portugal. Moreover, at a mean of 96.8 tons, with some dating back to the 1750s at least, these Portuguese schooners were larger and from an older tradition than their British counterparts, which averaged 58.6 tons and had all been launched since 1766.

It is conceivable that the marked growth in Britain's schooner population apparent between the 1790s and the 1820s (see Tables 7/1 and 7/2)

was unrelated to the relative proliferation of the rig in other areas. However, the weight of available evidence suggests that the British schooner was not an indigenous product but a modified version of a vessel type developed elsewhere, a technological transfer rather than an innovation. It also indicates that the principal source of the transfer was North America. Of course, the seemingly well-established Portuguese interest in schooners may well have influenced British vessel design. Yet data to substantiate this possibility are lacking. Indeed, the classification for insurance purposes of so many Portuguese-built schooners in 1781 probably reflects the high risks of wartime trade, for most were surveyed at Cork, one of the principal convoy collection centres, and most were bound for Lisbon, Oporto or St Ubes at a time when the trade war in the Western Approaches and the Bay of Biscay was at its height.[30] Significantly, these vessels were owned as well as built in Portugal and

25. *Ibid*, pp83-5.

26. D R MacGregor, *Merchant Sailing Ships 1775-1815: Sovereignty of Sail* (London 1980), p157.

27. D R MacGregor, *Schooners*, pp109-17; B Greenhill, *Schooners*, pp108-17, 132.

28. H I Chapelle, *op cit*, p41.

29. B Greenhill, *Merchant Schooners*, p9.

30. D J Starkey, *British Privateering Enterprise in the Eighteenth Century* (Exeter 1990), pp224-6.

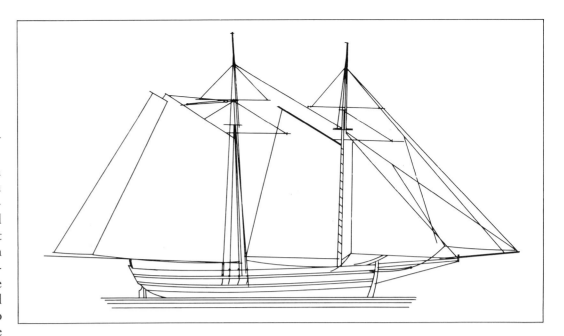

The sail plan of an early British schooner traced from a drawing in the Brocklebank collection in the Liverpool County Museum. It is unidentified but may represent the Experiment *of 1802. The two positions of the jib and topsail yards without sails set are exactly as the original.* (By courtesy of David MacGregor)

there is no indication that any were subsequently registered in Britain.[31]

On the other hand, various means by which the American schooner was translated into a British setting can be perceived. In general, given the extent and character of intra-imperial trade and defence, British naval and merchant seafarers, and their employers, must have been familiar with the development of the fore-and-aft rig across the Atlantic. Equally, it must have become apparent to these observers that this sail plan was not only better to windward but also handier in shallow and estuarine waters than the square rig. From an economic point of view, the schooner possessed advantages over the brig, in that she was cheaper to build and rig, while smaller crews were needed to manage her fore-and-aft sails.[32] When these attributes of speed, manoeuvrability and economy were more widely appreciated, and when, during the final quarter of the eighteenth century, the rig was successfully applied in larger vessels, it would seem that the American schooner was procured, copied or, occasionally, seized by British shipping interests.

Within this broad transatlantic framework, three points of contact were particularly important. In the first place, the Royal Navy, in an effort to improve the efficiency of its coastal patrols in North American waters, purchased a number of fast-sailing 'Marblehead' schooners in the late 1760s.[33] Though somewhat remote from the centres of the shipping industry, these purchases nevertheless suggest that British naval architects were beginning to accept the fore-and-aft rig. Secondly, the American Revolutionary War expedited the diffusion of the schooner. In the conflict at sea, the sailing qualities of the American schooner were often highlighted when she was in pursuit of, or in flight from, the generally larger, less nimble, British square rigged warship or merchantman, a demonstration effect that was perhaps even more pronounced in the 1812-1814 war.[34] Emulation was one response, with at least eleven privateer schooners fitted out in British ports in 1781.[35] At the same time, the

seizure and condemnation of vessels such as the *Jenny* and the *Polly* provided another, more direct, means of adding the American schooner to Britain's shipping stock.[36] And, of course, the chief political consequence of the Revolution, American independence, had a vital bearing on trade and shipping, for erstwhile colonial vessels were re-defined as foreign properties and therefore excluded from the British market. With the American supply now denied to British shipowners, some impetus was given to the domestic construction of schooners, a stimulus apparent

31. Only six Portuguese-built vessels were listed in *Lloyd's Register* of 1791, a peacetime year.

32. B Greenhill, *Merchant Schooners*, pp8-9; D R MacGregor, *Schooners*, p68.

33. H M Hahn, *op cit*; D R MacGregor *Schooners*, p21; H I Chapelle, *op cit*, pp33-41.

34. H I Chapelle, *The Search for Speed under Sail* (London 1968), pp210-54; T C Gillmer, *Pride of Baltimore: The Story of the Baltimore Clippers* (Camden, Maine 1992).

35. *Lloyd's Register*, 1781.

36. The *Jenny* was seized in the Caribbean in 1781, PRO, HCA 42/130. The *Polly* was condemned in 1782 and registered in Exeter in 1787, DRO, Exeter Ship Registers.

By the middle of the nineteenth century British schooners carried a loftier rig. This is the Victoria *of 1838, built in East Looe by Joseph Alinock. She has the full and deep hull form of Cornish schooners, before the shallower form became popular in the 1840s.* (By courtesy of David MacGregor)

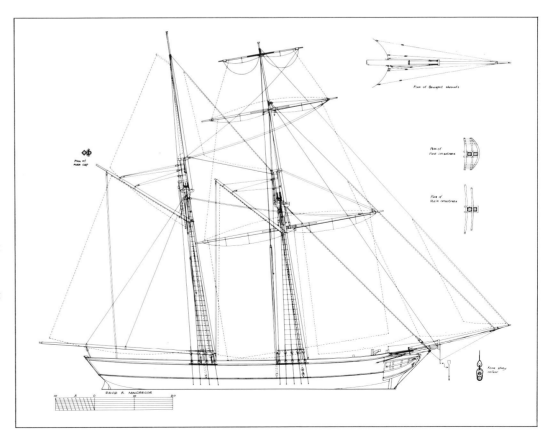

The ketch partly replaced the schooner towards the end of the century. This photograph shows the ketch Alpha, *built at Sunny Corner, Truro, in 1871, as a schooner without square topsails for the Newfoundland trade, discharging coal from Ellesmere Port in Boscastle, Cornwall, in 1902. She is moored 'on fours' with her own ropes. To hold her in this harbour should a ground sea come up the starboard bow rope is six inches in diameter. Additional mooring ropes are coiled ready on the rails. The shute for discharging into carts is seen hanging on the rail amidships. (The late Captain W J Slade)*

in the fact that all but four of the twenty-eight schooners registered in Liverpool during 1786-1788 had been produced in Britain since 1783.[37]

The third, and most significant, avenue by which the schooner rig was transferred across the Atlantic was the Anglo-American trade in staple commodities. In particular, Liverpool's comparatively early adoption of the schooner was probably related to the port's pre-eminence in the African and Caribbean trades. Thus, of the twenty-eight schooners registered in Liverpool in 1786-1788, at least six were subsequently lost or sold off the African coast, while a further eight were sold in the Caribbean.[38] In *Lloyd's Register* of 1791, moreover, twelve of the nineteen schooners described as Liverpool-built were destined for Africa, and another two were bound for the West Indies. It may be surmised that the sailing qualities of the schooner rig, to which Liverpool's seafarers and shipowners were exposed in the West Indies and elsewhere, rendered it especially well-suited to the relatively confined environment of the Caribbean and the treacherous waters off West Africa.

While Liverpool's interest in schooners was somewhat marginal and short-lived, the West-country adopted and applied the rig to a much greater degree. This was essentially a function of the region's pivotal position in the fishery, trade and settlement of Newfoundland. An ancient business, which had developed an extraordinary migratory character, the Newfoundland trade was largely centred on Dartmouth, Teignmouth and Poole by the late eighteenth century. The ship registers of the port of Exeter, which included Teignmouth, point to the significance of the trade in the diffusion of the schooner. Whereas before 1810 only a handful of schooners were registered in Bideford, Chepstow and Fowey[39] – ports no longer engaged in the Newfoundland trade – no fewer than fifty-seven were registered at Exeter, most belonging to investors

37. R Craig and R Jarvis, *op cit.*

38. *Ibid.*

39. DRO, Bideford Ship Registers; G Farr, *Chepstow Ships* (Chepstow 1954); C H Ward-Jackson, *op cit.*

resident in Teignmouth. That sixteen of these schooners had been built and registered in Newfoundland and subsequently transferred to Exeter registry – a precursor of the links which developed between Prince Edward Isle and North Devon in the mid nineteenth century[40] – underlines the importance of the island in the transmission of the rig. Moreover, as these Newfoundland-built schooners were nearly all transferred in the 1790s, when they dominated Exeter's supply of fore-and-afters, the initial diffusion of the rig was marked by the acquisition of overseas products, a contention supported by the fact that prizes represented the main source of the port's schooners in the early 1800s.[41] In other words, it would seem that Westcountry shipyards did not begin to produce the bulk of the region's schooners until the second decade of the nineteenth century.

The Newfoundland trade was significant to this process in other ways. During the late eighteenth century, the basic character of the trade changed fundamentally as the island's population at last began to grow and the migratory fishery collapsed. With the fishing operation now largely prosecuted by the islanders, the southwest's Newfoundland merchants concentrated on the carrying facet of the trade, a branch which they had long since cultivated.[42] At base, this business entailed the conveyance of supplies out to the fishery, the shipment of dried fish to the markets of southern Europe, and the carriage of wine, fruit and specie back to Britain. In the years after the Napoleonic War, it was the third leg of this triangular commodity flow which experienced the most dynamic growth. Indeed, this expansion was so pronounced that a specialist fruit trade emerged, with schooners built and owned in the Westcountry, especially in Brixham, Dartmouth, Salcombe and Plymouth, employed in the carriage of oranges from Spain and the Azores, currants from the Aegean, and pineapples from the West Indies to the burgeoning urban markets served by the ports of London and Liverpool. While such highly perishable cargoes required a relatively swift passage, the small, difficult creeks and harbours in which they were loaded rendered handiness of the essence. The schooner, with her speed and manoeuvrability, proved to be the optimum vessel of the day for such a business. Accordingly, as the fruit trade developed, so the shipyards of South Devon increasingly turned to the construction of sharp, fine-lined 'fruit' schooners.[43]

In different contexts, with suitably modified designs, schooners became increasingly prevalent in other British regions from the 1820s. This diffusion was perhaps accomplished by observation and personal contact. For instance, the growing deployment of the schooner clearly enabled more shipowners to witness the rig's advantages over the square rigged brig. South Devon's schooners were visible in ports throughout the country, delivering fruit to the Thames and the Mersey during the autumn, but employed in a range of coastal and short sea carrying trades during the rest of the year. Likewise, shipbuilders such as Daniel Bishop Davy of Topsham, who 'composed' several fast-sailing schooners 'well calculated for the Newfoundland trade and general purposes', visited numerous shipyards throughout the country making assiduous notes on the practices and designs current elsewhere. Though hardly engaged in 'spreading the gospel' of the schooner, it is likely that Davy left behind some of the ideas and principles which informed the shape and propulsion of his vessels.[44]

At a broader level, the dissemination of the schooner rig was a function of general economic development. Industrialisation was proceeding apace in the mid nineteenth century, and this led to the emergence of new seaborne trades. For example, during the Victorian era, the production of increasing quantities of slate in Mid and North Wales, the exploitation of iron ore reserves in the Furness district of Lancashire, and the riverine shipment of an ever-growing volume of coal and manufactured produce from South Yorkshire and the East Midlands increased the local demand for shipping. While the tonnage registered in these regions increased accordingly, variations of the schooner rigged vessel evolved to meet the particular requirements of the local topography and cargo. As a consequence, there emerged Welsh schooners, Barrow 'flats', Yorkshire 'billy-boys' and various other sub-species to dilute the pre-eminence that the Westcountry had evinced in the production of schooners from the 1810s.[45]

While the industrialisation process impacted on more and more regions, it also entailed improvements in the efficiency of transportation. In essence, this trait had underpinned the growing prevalence of the British schooner, for she was generally faster and cheaper to operate than a brig or a snow and therefore tended to supplant the square rigged vessel in a range of trades, particularly those like the fruit trade and the coastal packet service which required swift

40. See B Greenhill and A Giffard, *Westcountrymen in Prince Edward Island: A Fragment of the Great Migration* (Toronto 1967).

41. DRO, Exeter Ship Registers.

42. See K Matthews, 'A History of the West of England-Newfoundland Fishery' (unpublished DPhil thesis, University of Oxford 1968); D J Starkey, 'Devonians and the Newfoundland Trade', in M Duffy *et al* (eds), *The New Maritime History of Devon* (London 1992), Vol 1, pp163-71.

43. B Greenhill, *Merchant Schooners*, pp14-17; D R MacGregor, *Schooners*, pp66-8.

44. C N Ponsford, *Shipbuilding on the Exe: The Memoranda Book of Daniel Bishop Davy, 1799-1874, of Topsham, Devon* (Exeter 1988).

45. B Greenhill, *Merchant Schooners*, provides a comprehensive coverage of the various types of schooner and their trades.

A typical auxiliary motor ketch of the end of the sailing era. The ketch Ketch, *with reduced pole-masted rig, motoring up the Torridge off Appledore, North Devon, in the 1930s.* (Basil Greenhill Collection)

passages.[46] Over time, of course, it was this inexorable drive to enhance the speed and efficiency of communication that led to the decline in schooner building and deployment. This gradual, uneven demise was conditioned by transport improvements on both sea and land. The growing efficiency of the steamship was the paramount influence on the oceans, serving to restrict the schooner's ability to compete to an ever diminishing range of trades from the third quarter of the nineteenth century. Ousted first from the coastal packet services, and then in the 1860s from the fruit and other short sea carrying trades, the schooner retreated to the Newfoundland trade – which had contributed so much to her development – and to general purpose employments in home waters.[47] In the transatlantic fish trade, most notably in the shape of the

three-masted 'Western Ocean Yachts' of Porthmadog,[48] the schooner was able to fend off steamship competition until the early twentieth century. But in the home trade she was largely eclipsed by the ketch, a smaller type of fore-and-after which proved more economical and was deployed in growing numbers from the 1870s.[49] On land, the railways impinged on the schooner's business by accounting for an increasing volume of the nation's internal commerce, a tendency reflected in the shift in schooner construction to districts like the north coasts of Devon and Cornwall, northeast Scotland and North Wales – a 'Celtic fringe' remote from the rail network – apparent in the 1870s and 1880s. It took several more decades, and the introduction of the motor lorry, before the small sailing vessels (and by now these were mostly ketch rigged and equipped with an auxiliary engine) ceased to serve these areas.

The dotage of the British schooner was therefore as lengthy as her youth. Adapted from the North American fore-and-after via a number of channels in the late eighteenth century, she became the archetypal small sailing vessel of mid-Victorian Britain before declining in numbers

The sails of the Pet, *built in Scotland in 1876, are old and patched but well cut and set, though the gaff topsail with its tiny jackyard is too small to be of much use and has the look of having been made for another vessel. Notice that she is the first vessel so far illustrated to have four shrouds to her main mast, necessary because she was a big-built heavy vessel and liable to be laboursome and hard on her gear in a big sea. She made many deep water voyages, but was eventually wrecked near Wick in the winter of 1931. (Amos & Amos)*

and significance down to the First World War. Unlike her American sister, the British schooner did not change substantially in size or shape during this time, while she generally remained a wooden-hulled vessel. Nevertheless, she represented an important shipyard product, a significant means of communication and a valuable source of earnings, particularly in the many small ports which witnessed little of the shipping and shipbuilding 'revolutions' of the nineteenth century. As such, the schooner formed an important part of Britain's mercantile marine during the last century of merchant sail.

Dr David J Starkey

46. D R MacGregor, *Schooners*, 44-51.

47. See C H Ward-Jackson, *Stephens of Fowey: A Portrait of a Cornish Merchant Fleet 1867-1939* (Greenwich 1980).

48. See A Eames, *Ventures in Sail* (Gwynedd 1987).

49. See W J Slade and B Greenhill, *Westcountry Coasting Ketches* (Greenwich 1974).

British Schooners: Typical Vessels

Name	Rig[1]	Built	Registered	Launched	Hull	Tonnage	Dimensions (feet-inches) (metres)	Fate	Remarks
SULTANA	2-masted	B Hallowell, Boston, Mass	– [Navy]	1772	Wood	52	38-5$\frac{1}{8}$ × 16-0$\frac{3}{4}$ × 8-4 11.7 × 4.9 × 2.5	Condemned 1772	One of the first naval schooners
CRESCENT	2-masted	Liverpool	Liverpool	1786	Wood	64	51-5 × 17-9 × 9-1 15.7 × 5.4 × 2.8	Sold in West Indies	Early British-built merchant schooner
HARVEY	2-masted	Trepassey, Newfoundland	Exeter	1788	Wood	88	61-7 × 19-1 × 10-10 18.8 × 5.8 × 3.3	Lost, date unknown	Transferred from St Johns, Newfoundland
ELIZA	2-masted	? [prize; foreign-built]	Exeter	?	Wood	84	58-3 × 19-2$\frac{1}{2}$ × 9-2 17.8 × 5.9 × 2.8	Lost 1809	Condemned in High Court of Admiralty, 16 April 1806
ELIZA	2-masted	William Follett, Dartmouth	Dartmouth	1831	Wood	124 (om)	67-0 × 20-8$\frac{1}{2}$ × 12-1$\frac{1}{2}$ 20.4 × 6.3 × 3.7 Remeasured 1836: 113 64-0 × 18-9 × 12-0 19.5 × 5.7 × 3.7 Lengthened 1851: 151 77-7 × 21-0 × 12-2 23.7 × 6.4 × 3.7	Unknown	Lengthened and third mast added 1851
ISABELLA	2-masted	Gibbs, Galmpton	Dartmouth	1864	Wood	60	75-10 × 18-9 × 9-5 23.1 × 5.7 × 2.9	Lost 1813, at St Johns, Newfoundland	Fruit schooner, later in Newfoundland trade
LIZZIE TRENBERTH	2-masted	Samuel Moss, Par, Cornwall	Fowey	1867	Wood	124	96-7 × 22-2 × 11-5 29.4 × 6.8 × 3.5	Missing at sea, October 1923	Azores and West Indies fruit trade to London and Bristol, 1868 to at least 1876
RHODA MAY	2-masted (later 3)	J Stephens, Point, Cornwall	Falmouth	1868	Wood	130	101-2 × 21-10 × 11-6 30.8 × 6.7 × 3.5	Converted to a yacht; fell to pieces, Medway, in 1950s	One of the most famous and fastest British schooners employed in Baltic and Mediterranean trades
MILLOM CASTLE	2-masted[2]	William White, Ulverston	Barrow	1870	Wood	78	81-2 × 20-7 × 9-6 24.7 × 6.3 × 2.9	Hulked, later abandoned, Lyner River, 1930s	A Barrow 'flat'; highly successful and profitable vessel
ULELIA	2-masted[3]	Charles Dyer, Sunny Corner, nr Truro	Truro	1877	Wood	58	75-5 × 19-10 × 9-5 23.0 × 6.1 × 2.9	Lost with all hands off Ireland, 1930	Newfoundland trade, then sold to Appledore owners and converted to ketch for home trade
CHARLES AND ELLEN	2-masted	D Noble & Co, Barrow	Barrow	1878	Iron	145	106-2 × 22-7 × 10-6 32.4 × 6.9 × 3.2	Unknown	Iron schooner
SNOWFLAKE	2-masted	Brundritt, Runcorn	Runcorn	1880	Wood	109	88-2 × 21-9 × 9-8 26.9 × 6.6 × 3.0	Sold to Yugoslavian owners, became a motor schooner	Originally employed in Newfoundland trade; last heard of in 1970s trading in the Mediterranean
JAMES POSTLE-THWAITE	3-masted[4]	William Ashburner, Barrow	Barrow	1881	Wood	134	99-9 × 23-0 × 10-1 30.4 × 7.0 × 3.1	Unknown	Typical product of a leading schooner builder
RESULT	3-masted[5]	Paul Rodgers, Carrickfergus	Barrow	1893	Steel	122	102-2 × 21-9 × 9-1 31.1 × 6.6 × 2.8	Preserved by the Ulster Folk Museum, Belfast	Steel-hulled three-master
WILLIAM MORTON	3-masted	David Jones, Porthmadog	Caernarfon	1905	Wood	143	104-3 × 23-9 × 11-9 31.8 × 7.2 × 3.6	Abandoned at sea, 1919	'Western Ocean Yacht' in the Newfoundland trade

[1] All British schooners were rigged with square topsails on the fore unless otherwise stated.
[2] Later a ketch, then 3-masted schooner with motor and no square topsails.
[3] No square topsails; later a ketch.
[4] Later with motor and no square topsails.
[5] Later with motor and no square topsails; finally limited sail-assist only.

8

The Sailing Ship in the Baltic: from Skuta to Galeas

O N THE Åland Islands, midway between Sweden and Finland, all the bigger cargo carriers until the beginning of the nineteenth century were called '*Skutor*'. This is an old name and was common to all Scandinavian countries. In the Icelandic sagas '*skutor*' were mentioned as being especially swift vessels. Later, in medieval times, the name covered small coasters and cargo carriers. In the sixteenth century, and later on, the word appeared in various circumstances; finally the term '*skuta*' covered ships of every description.

Early evidence for the *skuta*

From early times the Ålanders needed roomy vessels. The transport of firewood from Åland to the city of Stockholm, which continued from the Middle Ages until the 1970s, required burdensome hulls. Another bulk cargo was lime, which was carried from Åland in considerable quanti-

Two skutor *with square sails entering Stockholm harbour in the 1640s. A detail of a copper engraving by Sigismund von Vogel.* (Stockholms stadsmuseum)

A three-masted skuta *manoeuvring in the crowded inner harbour, called Stockholm Strom, with Dutch-type yachts. This is a detail of a typical copper engraving by the talented Erik Dahlberg - Count and Field Marshal - collected in a book called the* Svecia Antiqua et Hodierna *from the late nineteenth century.* (All illustrations by courtesy of the author)

ties from the sixteenth century. From this epoch onwards we are in possession of figures covering quantities actually loaded. With a knowledge of the carrying capacities of vessels it is possible to extrapolate their basic dimensions, was well as being able to make comparisons with ships of later epochs.

The larger *skutor* belonged to the inhabitants of the Åland mainland, because the firewood and lime cargoes were produced there. The islanders of the archipelagoes, carrying commodities for domestic consumption, used smaller undecked craft called *Kajut-båtar*, more specifically *storbåtar*. Such was the situation until the middle of

the nineteenth century, when the islanders built or acquired ships suitable for the carrying of bigger cargoes.

The earliest source documented for the export of lime from the Åland isles dates from 1506. In October that year Jon from Jomala loaded 20½ lasts of lime for Stockholm; the

A section of Stockholm harbour with timbered sheds on modern jetties from the 1760s, depicted by Johan Svenbom. The artist demonstrates (left) a stor-båt (great-boat), (right) a two-masted skuta, carrying the rig typical to the Åland vessels of the seventeenth and eighteenth centuries: square sails only. Observe the entrance to the cabin, the flat roof of which constitutes a 'deck' for the helmsman. Painting in oil in the town museum of Stockholm by Johan Svenbom.

same Jon carried 17 lasts in the following month. We know that another Ålander carried 27 lasts on his first outward voyage. In the mid sixteenth century around 4000 barrels of burned lime were exported annually from the islands.

A total of thirty-nine *skutor*, registered in the parishes of Jomala, Lemland, Eckerö, Hammarland and Geta carried 1500 fathoms of firewood during a single year to Stockholm. The average cargo carried per vessel was around 15-20 fathoms. Frequently the same skipper-farmer carried numerous cargoes within the same year, as for instance Erik Björnson in Gottby, Jomala, who delivered a total of eight cargoes within a year.

From the seventeenth century we are in possession of additional information as to the actual quantities of lime and firewood carried. Compared with the sixteenth century the *skutor* now employed were bigger. This is apparent in connection with the loading of firewood. In the autumn of 1682 Per Ersson from Kungsö in Jomala lost his ship when trading to Stockholm. In the ensuing court case the following year the owner stated that the ship had served him only two and a half years and that she carried forty lasts. The farmer Matts Jakobsson, from the parish of Jomala, in 1682 authorised the skipper Clemet from Övernäs to load 29 lasts of lime for carriage to Stockholm. In 1663 a *skuta* from Hammarland was lost with 44 fathoms of firewood; in 1681 a *skuta* from Geta was wrecked with 55 fathoms of pine timber and other cargo, including livestock.

What are the modern equivalents to the lasts and the fathoms of the sixteenth and seventeenth centuries? During a law suit in the parish of Finström a statement was registered to the effect that the respective weights of one 'last' of lime and one fathom of firewood were equal. Burnt lime was shipped in barrels whereof twelve made a last. The capacity of such a barrel was 50 litres, and considering the specific weight of burnt lime the weight must have been around 130 kilos. Accordingly one last of lime roughly corresponds to 1.5 tons. The weight of one fathom of mixed firewood, half-seasoned, was about the same. Consequently we find the cargo capacity of the biggest ships called *skutor* of the six-

teenth century to be around 30 tons, the equivalent of a *jakt* or a bigger *sump* – single-masted trading sailing vessels – of the early twentieth century.

The capacity of the *skutor* of the seventeenth century was actually doubled; so the ship from Hammarland, which was lost in 1681 with 55 fathoms of pine timber, loaded around 80 tons, equivalent to the capacity of a medium-sized *galeas* of the early twentieth century.

Thus we are in a position to estimate the carrying capacities of the *skutor* of the sixteenth and seventeenth centuries. Our knowledge of the appearance of these vessels is limited. Probably the Ålanders used boats and craft fairly similar to those of their closest neighbours on the Swedish side. From later centuries we find *skutor* in Åland ownership purchased from Swedish owners.

Copper engravings and other representations of the waters of the Swedish capital in the sixteenth and seventeenth centuries show these peasant craft rigged with one or two masts. The small ships carried a single square sail while the

bigger *skutor*, carrying firewood, sported a main and a fore mast, both with a single square sail. On the main a small topsail was frequently carried. This type of rig was common also in the Åland isles. From inventories preserved, the oldest being from 1706, we know something of the equipment of the *skutor*: sails were of a homespun cloth, and a fore sail is mentioned – this was not a staysail, but the square sail carried on the fore mast. Of the old ships mentioned in inventories many had been trading since the seventeenth century.

In a partition of inheritance between brothers on an estate in Klemetsby, parish of Lumparland, executed in 1706, a *skuta* is mentioned which was equipped with a main and fore sail, a dinghy, various hawsers and a compass. A further 10 yards of homespun cloth are mentioned, apparently belonging to the ship's stores. The farmer Per Jacobsson in Västanträsk, parish of Finström, in 1707, was the owner of a third-part of a *skuta*, as well as of clinker-built boats, one of which was used as an 'iceboat' (propelled over the frozen waters in winter). In an inventory from 1727, covering the properties of the deceased farmer Erik Persson in Ytternäs, we find one-fourth of a *skuta*, framed up in 1723 and rigged with homespun sails and a fore sail.

The ships mentioned were valuable assets, as the inventories show. A well-to-do farmer in the parish of Hammarland owned a new as well as an old *skuta*. The former, with sails and equipment, was valued at 600 Daler, while the old craft, inclusive of tar, hemp and iron for future upkeep, was valued at only 150 Daler. In comparison, the buildings and the land of the homestead amounted to 162 Daler only, so it can be seen that considerable sums were invested in these vessels.

In 1715 the Swedish government ordered a general inventory of ships, great and small, within the province of Stockholm. The nation was at war and the army in need of transports. In the lists we find numerous ships from Åland; the islands were emptied in those years as the inhabitants fled before the ravaging Russians, carrying their moveable properties with them. From available documents it is evident that the ships from Åland loaded almost double the cargo of craft from the Swedish archipelagoes. Only the town of Öregrund possessed some ships with greater carrying capacity. Of eighteen *skutor* know to be owned by Ålanders, sixteen were said to carry 80 lasts. In addition it was found that one last and one fathom of firewood were of equal weight, about 1.5 tons, similar to conditions in the seventeenth century. One detail regarding the rigging of the *skutor* of Åland origin is worth noting: two *skutor* from Åland, abandoned by refugees in Vaxholm, were observed as peculiar in being rigged 'in the manner in vogue in the Åland isles'. The exact meaning of this is unclear, but we may assume that the rigging of the Åland vessels differed slightly from that of Swedish craft, probably because the Ålanders were conservative in their rigging styles.

From the minutes of a law case of 1746 regarding the loss of a *skuta* on the sea of Åland, causing the loss of 50 fathoms of firewood, we note interesting details as to the equipment and the appearance of the *skutor*. The juror Erik Ersson from Lemböte summoned his brother Mats Ersson from Knutsboda to law for overloading their jointly owned *skuta*, this being the cause for the loss of the craft.

According to the minutes the craft set sail

A three-masted Finnish skuta *for the firewood trade, measured and drawn by F H Chapman for his collection of ship drawings in copper engravings, the* Architectura Navalis Mercatoria, *published in 1768. The length of the hull is 19.5m; the beam 7.8m.*

The typical stor-båt, *also called* Kajut-båt *(cabin-boat) manoeuvring past the old town of Stockholm. This type of handy undecked craft was common in the waters of eastern Åland, while the peasants of the mainland of Åland relied on roomier types with better carrying capacity. Part of an engraving by J F Martin from the 1790s, in the town museum of Stockholm.*

from the Nätö Klippa in light airs. In open water the ship encountered heavy weather, springing the topsail yard, whereupon the hull was filled with water and capsized. In the master's opinion the reason was not excess of cargo, but the breaking of the topsail yard, 'eliminating the easing effect of that sail on the craft in high seas'. This should possibly be understood to mean that the topsail when set gave the vessel a heel, raising the windward bulwark enough to keep off breaking waves. As long as the topsail was set, the minute continues, all went well and the craft proceeded safely despite high seas. A witness who had observed the ship before departure from Nätö reported that the cargo was so immense that a man, standing on the roof of the stern cabin, was unable to look over the cargo to

see the stem head. Hasselberg, a boatswain of the crew, reported that the firewood around the mast was levelled to such effect that all entrusted to keep the helm of the ship, when mounting the roof, were able to perform the task, as well as to look forward. From the minutes it is clear that the *skuta* here mentioned carried a main, a topsail and a fore sail.

From this we may conclude that in the mid eighteenth century the craft of Åland carried square sails on both masts as well as a topsail on the main, and this is confirmed by numerous contemporary inventories. A peculiar detail is the fact that the helmsman steered from the cabin roof. The undecked hulls incorporated a stern cabin, the roof of which constituted a poop or stern deck, crossed by the long tiller where stood the helmsman. Such craft, two- as well as three-masted, are seen in paintings by Johan Sevenbom from the 1760s and 1770s, depicting the waters surrounding Stockholm.

The sizes of the *skutor* seem unaltered from the seventeenth century to mid eighteenth century; also the number of such craft seems fairly constant from the mid eighteenth century until the early nineteenth century. Samuel Ehrenmalm, a member of the Court of Appeal, reported in 1759 on the maritime trading of the Ålanders: with around eighty *skutor* carrying between 40-50 fathoms, of clinker (lap strake) construction, to which should be added numerous smaller *kajut-båtar*, the main trade of these farmers was with Stockholm, but they also accepted charter to carry firewood or sawn wood from the town of Björneborg or from the skerries of the coast of Nyland.

Later *skutor*

When coming closer to modern times we are better informed about the actual appearance of *skutor*. From the second half of the eighteenth

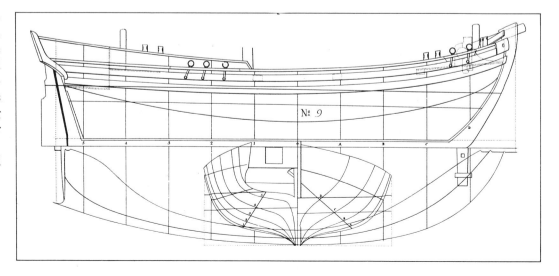

Ålanders used the so-called stor-bat *(great-boat) for minor transport tasks, and every household in the archipelago had a* stor-bat *to take goods to the cities. These vessels were originally rigged with a square sail, but the fore-and-aft rig became widespread in the second half of the nineteenth century. There has been a revival of this boat type in recent times and several new boats have been built.* (Jerker Örjans).

century we are in possession of certificates of measurement, of the official register kept by the district bailiff, as well as of detailed descriptions of contemporary *skutor*, built in various parishes of the province of Åboland (Finnish Turku). Of the greatest value in the reconstruction of a *skuta* from the eighteenth century are some draughts published in the famous *Architectura Navalis Mercatoria* by the Swedish naval architect Fredrik Henrik af Chapman. In his work, first published in 1768, we find plans of a *skuta* of Finnish origin for the carriage of firewood. By using such pictorial sources, combined with underwater observations and fragments, we are today able to reconstruct, with a certain degree of accuracy, the appearance of a square rigged *skuta* from the end of the eighteenth century.

In an inventory from 1760 covering the properties of Lisa Matsdotter from Söderby parish of Lemland, we find a list of equipment belonging to *skutor*. All the proper names given to sails, and their dimensions, are of special interest. This *skuta* carried a main, a topsail and a fore sail; from dimensions given all must be square sails. The height of the main sail was 9m (29.5ft), of the fore sail 7m (23ft), and of the topsail 3.5m (11.5ft). Various items of running rigging are listed: bowlines to a fore sail and to a topsail, 'penter-hooks', 'carvat tackles', halliards, iron work for deadeyes etc, etc. The purpose of the bowlines and the hooks mentioned was to tighten the windward leech of square sails when tacking; the carvat tackle was a purchase attached to the braces of the yards. The local name for a halliard was '*dragrep*', the ancient name for the combined backstay and halliard of Viking ship rigging.

We have a detailed description from the 1730s of two hay barges in Stockholm, originally purchased from the parish of Korpo in the province of Åbo. They were both ancient *skutor*, rebuilt for their new purpose in Stockholm. They were very similar in form and dimensions, clinker-built of pine timber with a length of about 21m (70ft) and a beam of 6m (20ft). The hulls were undecked but fitted with a cabin aft, with two windows above the flat stern, a fixed bunk, a locker with doors, and a small detachable table. The cabin had a door on hinges, which could be locked. We have reasons to assume that these hay barges come very close to the Finnish *skuta* from the 1760s, represented by Chapman.

These ships from Korpo were three-masted, probably similar to those three-masted *skutor* found in certificates of measurement from the late eighteenth century. A single square sail was carried on the fore mast. On the main, which had a separate topmast, was carried a main sail and a topsail. The mizzen carried a gaff sail, in contrast to the square rig of the other masts.

From description of the ships from Korpo we note further details of the interior of the cabins, relevant to these years. The ships were crowded by numerous passengers, all requiring bed space. In the minutes of a law case of 1647 we find a description of the crowded conditions on board a *skuta* from the islands of Kökar, where three men and two women shared a single bedplace. The minute reports the sufferings of one Wallborg Grellsdotter who was sleeping above and

across the people mentioned. Conditions were just as crowded and uncomfortable as on board a *skuta* from Finström in 1652, in which a mother and her daughters occupied a single bed, while three persons slept in the other bed of the cabin; the master and his crew lived in the forward cabin.

The Finnish *skuta* for the transport of firewood, represented in *Architectura Navalis Mercatoria* by Chapman, is a three-masted craft. Most probably Chapman measured such a vessel when discharging firewood in Stockholm. The hull represented has the same dimensions as the three-masted Åland hulls from the late eighteenth century, entered in the registers of ships measured. Also when comparing the beam and the draught the dimensions correspond. The general shape of the hull is reminiscent of *storbåtar* preserved today from the early twentieth century, in being of low freeboard but full in the

The artist K E Janssons' initial sketch to an 1871 painting called 'Ace of Clubs', which was to show peasants at cards in the cabin of an Åland skuta. Observe the brick oven, common to these ships. (Åland Museum of Arts)

bow and the stern sections. A difference is apparent in the fact that the *skuta* has more draught than ordinary workboats of later times. Like the above-mentioned ships from Korpo the hull is undecked, with the exception of a short deck in the bows and the crowded cabin aft. Two square windows in the stern light the cabin. Amidships two heavy beams are laid athwartships to stiffen the hull, allowing loose boards to be laid to form a working deck.

Chapman's *skuta* has considerably more beam in comparison with her length when compared with the *jakts* and the *galeases* of later times: a length of 19.5m (64ft) and a beam of 7.8m (25.5ft), a 2.5:1 ratio apparently common to *skutor* and workboats of the older type. This is obvious when studying the registers of the official measurers. The undecked *jakt* called the *Nord* from Kumlinge was measured in Stockholm in

A two-masted undecked skuta *of the eighteenth century. The reconstruction, by Berti Bonns, is based on facts collected from inventories, minutes from law sessions, and certificates of ship measurements. These square-riggers were heavily worked, requiring many hands, this being the reason for the introduction and speedy growth of the galeas rig in the early nineteenth century.*

1831: her length was 12.5m (41ft), her beam a full 5m (16.4ft).

From the year 1782 the 'bailiff' of the province of Åland annually registered and marked by a crown the craft owned by farmers: these ships were ships officially measured and holders of a certificate. The 'crowning' was effected by a representative of the administration who branded the bow timber with an iron. The earliest ship registers only contain names and part-owners, but from the mid-1780s the cargo capacity is added. From these documents we note that the biggest vessels belong to the mainland of Åland, and were mostly employed in carrying firewood to Stockholm.

In the year 1785 a total of eighty-seven *skutor* were registered in regular trade with firewood to Stockholm – actually the same number as in 1759. More than half of them belonged to the parishes of Lemland, Jomala and Finström. Their capacities were roughly unaltered from the seventeenth century; the biggest carried 40-60 fathoms of firewood.

The importance of the bailiff's registers is increased still further by the fact that we are able to compare these with contemporary certificates of measurement. In the customs archives at Blockhusudden, at the entrance to Stockholm's harbour, we find series of copies of ships' certificates from the years 1798-1815. The ledger, covering undecked craft, shows entries for the year 1799 for around thirty vessels apparently built in the Åland isles, in addition to which we find numerous smaller *jakts* from the outer archipelagoes. The certificates – or letters – of

measurements contain the vessel's name, building place, length between bow and stern timbers, breadth taken from the inside of inner planking or cargo battens, depth of the hold from inner planking to the deck, and the number of lasts. The master's name is given but not the actual home port.

The number of *skutor* owned in Åland amounted to eighty in 1799. In the ledgers in Stockholm thirty-two vessels are mentioned: fifteen three-masted clinker-built *skutor*, ten undecked *skuta* with *galeas* rig, one undecked clinker-built *skuta* built of pine, and two undecked *jakts*. The first-mentioned showed lengths about 18m and 22m (59ft – 72ft) and capacities between 20 and 40 heavy lasts (50-100 tons). The *skutor* rigged as *galeases* were of the same lengths, but their carrying capacities were smaller, between 14-25 lasts (34-60 tons). The reason for this difference may be the greater draught, evident from the certificates of measurement. The *Dockan*, a *galeas* rigged *skuta*, with a length of 19m (66.3ft) had only 1m (3.3ft) between the deck and the inner planking of the hold, while the three-masted *Stora Dockan*, of 18m (59ft) length showed a deeper hold, of 1.8m (5.9ft) height. The capacity of the latter vessel was thus double, or 33 lasts, in comparison to 14.5 lasts for the first-mentioned with *galeas* rig.

The *galeas* of the nineteenth century

The customs officers at Blockhusudden (Stockholm) described the various vessels by type of rig. New types thus appeared with the change of rig. From the registers of measurements we may follow the birth and the acceptance of the name *galeas* in the early nineteenth century. In the earliest books from 1798 we find 'two-masted *skutor* rigged as *galeases*'. Some years later they are called '*galeas-skuta*', and still some years later 'undecked *galeases*'. The three-masted vessels diminished in these years until, in the registers of the 1820s, such vessels disappear. All bigger vessels are called *jakts* and *galeases*. In the 1870s three-masted vessels are again found in the ledgers, but now these are regular schooners fully developed, and much bigger than the old *skutor*. These ships we know very well from painted ship portraits. The modern *galeas* rig was easier to handle compared with the square rig, this being the reason for its popularity in the Åland Islands, but ships with the new rig sailed better, especially when reaching and tacking. Tacking with the old square rigged vessels was probably not common, masters preferring to wait for a change of wind; alternatively oars were used. A minute from 1807 concerning a *galeas* called the *Maja Stina* reports 'Lofnering' (tacking against the wind), as the vessel had encountered contrary winds for some days when departing from Stockholm.

To discover the appearance of the undecked *galeses* of the first half of the nineteenth century, it is possible to study maritime declarations containing details of interest. From these we note that the *galeas* rig of the twentieth century was already fully developed in the 1830s; we have details of *galeases* rigged with triangular fore sails, topsails, gaff main sails and gaff mizzens. The cabin was still located in the stern under the deck, and fitted with two windows above the transom. A maritime declaration from 1832 attributes the loss of a *galeas* called *Seraplin* partly to water entering through these windows in high seas.

The *galeas* developed her present hull shape only in the middle of the nineteenth century, when the ancient lapped strake clinker technique was abandoned in favour of carvel (edge-to-edge) construction. Around this time the ancient restriction requiring country craft to be undecked was finally abandoned. By the end of the Crimean War (1854–55) almost all Åland vessels of some size were fully decked. The introduction of the carvel technique and of complete weather decks caused radical changes in hull forms. In general, draught was increased; the full rounded bows, typical of smaller workboats, were now replaced by the modern raked clipper bow. The cabin was moved up to the weather deck, and the tiller was replaced by the steering wheel.

Per-Ove Högnäs
Translated by Professor Christoffer Ericsson

Ketches were still being constructed on Åland in the 1930s. They were built and owned by farmers and were used primarily for transporting firewood to Stockholm. (Ålands Museum)

9

The Changing Problems of Shiphandling in the Nineteenth Century

D URING this period two fundamental changes occurred in the maritime world, one having an impact on the established methods of shiphandling, the other resulting in a totally new approach being required. Firstly, the introduction of iron and later steel in the construction of hull and rig allowed much larger vessels to be built than had been possible with wood and there was a general shift in favour of more fore-and-aft canvas. But perhaps more importantly, steam power, already well established ashore, was adopted and developed as a more practical and economic way of moving a vessel than wind and sail.

Since the beginnings of seafaring, the mariner had been forced to use a fickle and ever-changing source of energy, or indeed, his own muscle power, to supply the motive force. In areas of higher latitude this wind power was mostly unpredictable for more than a day or two, unlike other parts of the world, where, depending on the season, the 'Trade Winds' or 'Monsoons' blew with some regularity. Furthermore certain parts of the oceans are subjected to calms and light variable breezes which could not be avoided, making it difficult to predict the length of a voyage. There could also be a delay of days or even weeks at the outset, waiting for the wind to change to a more favourable direction.

Sailing ships primarily depended on the wind for their movement, but when engaged on deep water voyages advantage could be taken of the ocean currents. In a similar way the tidal ebb

A brigantine under way in calm conditions, being towed by three men in a coble. The small boat trailing astern shows that she is moving slowly ahead. The main boom is topped up and the gaskets off ready for hoisting the sail. The port anchor is on board but there appears to be a smaller one hanging just clear of the water from the hawse pipe ready to let go in an instant if needed. The small boat appears to be a Holmsbupram from the Oslo Fiord area and the brigantine looks from her hull form as if she might be Danish. A hand is aloft casting off the gaskets on the fore course. Note the bentinck boom. (Basil Greenhill Collection)

This photograph shows the smack Volunteer, *built at Padstow in 1860 being hobbled, or towed, seaward out of Porth Gaverne, North Cornwall. Two boats are used, each with a three-man crew who are pulling away, each with a single oar in preference to rowing with two. (See Eric McKee,* Working Boats of Britain, *London, 1983, p135.) There is little wind in the vicinity of the vessel, perhaps because she is in the lee of the high land from which the photograph was taken. The topsail is being hoisted aloft and once set may catch a slight breeze as indicated by the flat at the topmast truck. She may well be rolling what little drive there is out of the sails as the backwash from the rocks indicate a moderate ground sea. (Gillis Collection)*

and flow around the shores were of great assistance, especially to those with local knowledge such as the coasting seaman, bargee and waterman. Although the direction changes approximately every six hours, the adverse set can often be 'cheated' while full use is made of the fair tide. Compared with the wind, the tides have an important advantage in that they are at least predictable.

Sometimes the only option for larger vessels having to be moved within the confines of a small harbour was kedging or warping. The first case involved running out a light anchor to the desired spot and heaving on a line attached to it. Instead of an anchor, buoys were often laid in strategic positions for the sole purpose of shifting vessels. If close enough, a long rope could be taken ashore and used to warp the vessels alongside or into a dock. In calm conditions and slack water it was possible to tow a vessel using one or two large open boats with a dozen or so men in each pulling away at the oars. By the end of the century, steam tugs were common in all of the large ports frequented by the big steel barques.

At the beginning of the nineteenth century, wind, tide and muscle power were still the only means of moving a vessel, but during the next one hundred years all this was to change. The paddle wheel and, later, the propeller, allowed the seaman to move and control his vessel, the steam engine providing him with the power; but he could never ignore the wind and tide completely, particularly in the early stages of development when vessels still carried sail. The twice-daily rise and fall which governed the depth of water was to be considered and related to the vessel's draught in shoal water and both the strength and direction of the stream and wind were of vital importance when manoeuvring in a close quarter situation.

Thus the term 'shiphandling' took on an entirely new meaning, and in this respect the nineteenth century is the most interesting era in all our maritime history. It covers the transition from sail to steam; engines being installed in

rigged ships in the first stage, then, as the propulsion units became more reliable and economic, the gradual reduction of canvas, until finally, in the last decades of the century, steel vessels were being built with no sails at all. Even so, large sailing ships continued to be built in the 1880s and '90s and the early part of the twentieth century, the Second World War marking the virtual end of deep water commercial sail. Alongside the development of mechanical propulsion, and to some extent because of it, the pure sailing ship underwent its last great period of improvement.

This chapter will concentrate on 'shiphandling' as it affects the pure sailing ship and therefore this term is defined as: 'the art of manoeuvring a vessel by control of her sails and rudder using wind and tide to advantage, the working of anchors, both for maintaining position and regulating her movement, and the getting on and off a buoy or berth by warping'. In practice it is seldom an exercise on its own but linked to 'sailhandling' and, when close to land or shoals, to 'pilotage'. However, there is only space enough to examine the basic principles of this vast subject, which did not fundamentally change with the introduction of larger vessels and different types of rig. Certain aspects became more difficult while others required a different approach. It is the purpose of this chapter to examine them against this background.

The increase in size and introduction of alternative rigs

It must be self evident that the larger a vessel, the more room she requires in which to manoeuvre, and the slower she will be to respond. The nineteenth century saw a gradual increase in the size of deep water sailing ships, especially

in the last two decades. The competition from steam powered vessels resulted in an ever increasing search for economies. By the 1890s high carrying capacity and low running costs were the order of the day. Some of these huge ships still retained the three-masted rig when the increased size dictated four, and their hulls were often of poor hydrodynamic shape – nothing more than floating steel warehouses. The three-masted fully rigged ship had developed from a wooden vessel just over 100ft in length in 1800 and around 190 gross tons to, taking a typical example in 1895, 260ft long, 1800 gross tons, loading over 3000 tons. The largest built in Great Britain was the *Ditton* of 2901 gross tons, over 310ft in length. At this size a fourth mast would have made her more manageable. The earlier smaller ship with her tall narrow sail plan and large crew would be capable of working in and out of harbour; the latter, with her relatively squat rig of great width (lower yards over 90ft long), was at a disadvantage in the same circumstances and required a tug.

Changes came about to the rig and sail plan as hulls increased in size. Individual sails could not become larger in proportion as there is a limit to what can be handled by an ever decreasing number of crew, hence the need for an extra mast and the introduction of the four-masted ship, or more commonly the four-masted barque (fuller descriptions of rig type are given in the Introduction). In relation to the waterline length these rigs were less tall with greater width, the yards longer due to the proportionally longer hulls and greater mast spacing. In comparison the much smaller wooden ship could have a length to beam ratio of not much more than 3:1 and a lofty narrow sail plan, the height of the main truck above the deck equalling the waterline length.

The Åland Finnish four-masted barque Viking *getting under way off Penarth Head with the help of two tugs, one aft, and bound for Sharpness under tow in 1937. Her starboard anchor has not been hove clear of the water. The Finnish ensign flying from her gaff and smoke from the tug would indicate a moderate breeze off the land. While at anchor she may well have laid head to wind, almost opposite to that required for the first part of her passage to Sharpness. The second tug aft would be there to help pull her stern round against the wind and thus accomplish the manoeuvre in a relatively small area required due to her loaded draught and the proximity of shoal water. A single tug would do the job if there was plenty of sea room to leeward in which to get the tow under control, that is, moving through the water in the right direction with sufficient way on to assist with her rudder. (Welsh Industrial and Maritime Museum)*

While this general trend to larger vessels on deep water routes increased after the middle of the century, the smaller wooden sailing ship continued to cross the oceans of the world, the only significant changes being the introduction of more economic rigs and improved hull shape. Just as the advent of much larger vessels did not drive the smaller ones off the world's trade routes, these 'new' rigs such as the topsail schooner, brigantine and barquentine did not at first replace the brig and full rigged ship, which continued to flourish. Of all rigs the barque was popular in all sizes right up to the end of commercial sail.

There was, however, a distinct tendency to make more use of fore-and-aft canvas in the smaller and medium sized vessels, which enabled fewer crew to be carried. In terms of 'handiness' it is often thought that these 'new' rigs were better than the brig, but from the evidence of the North Sea colliers, required to trade up and down the East Coast both summer and winter and work their way up the Thames, a very crowded waterway in those days, this is open to doubt. These would carry more crew per ton of cargo and cost more to maintain with the extra spars and sails, and hence it was economic factors that saw a decline in their numbers.

'Tacking' or putting a vessel about is one of the most important manoeuvres for the sailing ship and there are slight differences in how this is performed between the purely fore-and-aft rigged craft and those setting some square sails on the fore mast. The former relies mostly on carrying enough way so as to swing head to wind by the action of the rudder. Hardening in the aftermast sail will help, as will easing up on the headsail sheets. Once close to the eye of the wind these headsails should be 'aback', thus helping the bows round on to the new heading. However, if way is lost before this point, the rudder is of no more use unless she gathers sternway and she will probably fall off on to her original heading. However, the topsail schooner, for example, would have her yards braced sharp up on the fore mast and the action taken the

The beautiful brigantine Polly, *built at Brixham in 1864, illustrates the older style of rig with deep single topsail with two rows of reef points and a narrow sail plan on the fore mast. As she is close to land in this photograph she may well be standing in to a port or anchorage, still carrying full sail in the light conditions. The crew are about the decks, perhaps waiting for the order to take in sail, the anchor is hanging clear ready to let go, the boat swung out and pilot ladder rigged on the port quarter.* (Bristol Museum)

same as on the purely fore and aft rigged craft; that is, harden in the aftermast sail, ease up the headsail sheets after putting the helm down and she will start to come up into the wind. Very soon after the square sails on the fore mast will be 'aback' and their action will be to assist the swing while slowing her down. Even if she is not quite head to wind and has no way on, the leverage of these sails will put the vessel about.

During this period the windward performance of sailing vessels generally improved with the introduction of rigs having more fore-and-aft canvas and better shaped hulls, but attention was also given to improving vessels that carried predominantly square sails, *ie* the full rigged ship, barque and brig. One of the factors has always been the limitation on how far the yards can be braced round imposed by the standing rigging and the long weather leech of the earlier single topsail. The first was improved by carrying the lower yard farther ahead of the mast using a metal bracket or truss, the weight being supported by a chain sling. This allowed the spar to be trimmed much farther round before it touched

the forward shroud on the lee side, and hence the head of the sail was held closer to the fore and aft line.

The single deep topsail with its many rows of reef points and long leech was split into two, reducing the area to roughly half for each sail, now termed upper and lower topsail. This was inevitable as vessels grew in size, and the topgallant was soon to follow suit. The resulting sails were proportionately shorter on the leech and better able to stand on the wind. In the final development only the upper topsail and course retained reef points, and usually only a single row on each sail. Furthermore, flexible steel wire boltropes were introduced on these later big steel ships which could have a greater tension applied without stretching the foot or leech. They were used as much as possible instead of hemp, which made a big difference with the long lengths leading from the upper sails to the deck.

The use of iron wire for standing rigging was a great improvement. Introduced in the late 1830s it soon superseded hemp, which required almost full-time work in maintaining the correct

The Åland Finnish barquentine Frideborg *which is virtually head to wind is going about on to the port tack. The square sails on the fore mast are aback, as are the three headsails as the sheets have not been let go. The main staysails also appear to be aback. All these sails which are ahead of the balance point of the vessel are assisting her through the eye of the wind which is almost calm. She is lightly loaded or in ballast with little of the rudder immersed, and in these conditions it is of little use in the manoeuvre. However, under the influence of the sails alone she will fall off onto her new heading. With very little way on due to a lack of wind and perhaps being near shoals or in a narrow channel the port anchor is hanging ready to let go. The* Frideborg *was built at Sunderland in 1866. In her youth as a barque she was in the China tea trade. When this photograph was taken in the Baltic in the 1930s she was the last tea clipper at sea; she was wrecked in 1937. She has a suit of secondhand sails. (Basil Greenhill Collection)*

tension. Chain, at first viewed with great suspicion, was adopted instead of the huge hemp cables and, along with the improvements made to the windlass, fewer men were required to work the anchor, perhaps the heaviest job on board if only muscle power was available.

Stability

The ability of a sailing vessel to stand up to her canvas in strong winds is of vital importance in terms of her safety, and has a direct influence on her handling. If, through lack of stability, she had to reduce sail area, and hence speed, every time the breeze picked up, lest she be blown over, the vessel was termed 'crank'. This condi-

tion could be due to her hull shape, the stowage of cargo, insufficient ballast or to a combination of these factors. At the other extreme was the vessel that carried a great deal of sail without lying over much on her side; she would be termed 'stiff'.

Very few vessels could sail around entirely empty; some, still afloat, fell over against the quay when the discharge of the cargo was completed. Most barges, and some coasting craft, could make passages in sheltered waters without ballast, but the majority of seagoing vessels needed some if a very light cargo was carried, or if there was no cargo at all. Depending on the nature of the voyage, the amount of ballast taken on board would be assessed. If, for example, the vessel was to be moved to a different part of the same port on completion of discharge of her cargo, only a small amount would be taken. Outward bound around Cape Horn on a winter passage would require a great deal more, well secured against shifting.

Ballast could be of iron, stones, gravel or sand, or even part cargo remaining on board if on a regular run with a bulk commodity and short passages. Earth was sometimes used, but should the vessel leak badly this would form slurry with dire consequences. It was vital to keep the pump wells clear of any blockage. Either way, only the minimum consistent with safety would be carried, not only for stability, but to immerse the hull sufficiently to give adequate 'grip' on the water, so as to reduce leeway when going to windward.

A vessel's stability, or lack of it, was due in

A steel mast and steel yards, the lowest of which, from which the course is set, is shown in this photograph taken on board the four-masted barque Passat *held well ahead by the truss and supported by a chain sling. This allowed the yard to be braced round farther than had been possible with the old system of jeer blocks and parrel, and thus much improved the weatherliness of square rigged sailing vessels. The truss also allowed the yard to be cockbilled, that is, rotated in the vertical plane, pivoting about the outboard end of the truss hinge. This was required in port to clear cranes and obstructions ashore as well as sailing barges that might work cargo alongside when the vessel was moored out in the stream. Cockbilling also had the advantage of shedding water more readily in this position, an important consideration if the yards were made of wood. Cockbilled yards were less likely to develop rot because any rainwater that entered the folds of the sail would run off. The barque is the* Warma, *built at Uusakaupunki in Finland in 1922. She is shown laid up in Göteborg in 1932. (Basil Greenhill/Ålands Sjöfartsmuseum)*

some part to the shape of her hull. During the nineteenth century there was a gradual change from short deep hulls with barrel shaped bows and heavy quarters to proportionally longer leaner vessels with a shallower depth as size increased. The midship section and how far it is carried forward and aft has an important bearing on initial stability, that is, without ballast or cargo. Comparing two floating planks, one 4in × 1in in section and the other 2in × 2in, both with the same cross-sectional area, it is obvious which one is the more stable. Therefore the beam-to-depth ratio related to length was one consideration, the other was the actual shape. A hull with almost a flat bottom with a sharp corner to the sides, or in other words having little rise of floor and a hard turn of bilge, was better in terms of stability than a more V-shaped section, having a considerable rise of floor and soft turn of bilge. The former could stow more cargo, but the latter was potentially the faster hull, all other considerations being equal.

To a large extent the vessel's use dictated the shape of hull. Coasting craft that frequented drying harbours tended to have little rise of floor so as to remain nearly upright when the tide was out. This shape was also required to give adequate support to the weight of vessel and cargo. A clipper ship, on the other hand, was built for speed and to stay afloat all the time unless for a specific purpose. In comparison to the coaster her length-to-beam ratio could be 5:1 as against 4:1 or even 3:1 in the earlier vessels, with a sharper entrance forward leading gently to her maximum hull section and then almost immediately forming into a long run aft. She would probably have a good rise of floor, resulting in an easily driven hull. These fast ships were but a small, well publicised, proportion of the total tonnage. Most vessels had carrying capacity as the foremost consideration and thus tended to have a midship section that was more box shaped, this section carried well forward and aft, giving a good internal volume.

Stability, therefore, depended on the hull shape in relation to the height of the rig and sail plan in the first instance, and on the amount of ballast or cargo in the second. However, a full cargo of hay might need some ballast, while it would need only a fraction of the capacity of the hold space for a cargo of copper ore. In the latter case the stability could be too high if the ore was loading in the bottom, resulting in a short sharp roll at sea, putting great strain on the masts, rigging and hull. It was not unknown for damage aloft to occur due to this violent motion, even to the extent of losing the masts. To overcome this problem of the vessel being too 'stiff', a strong platform with substantial sides was often built into the vessel so as to raise the centre of gravity when carrying cargoes of ore. This type of load would also be kept out of the ends of the vessel, as in heavy weather it was often only the middle of the ship that was supported by a large wave, leaving the ends virtually in mid-air. Excessive weight at either end would strain the vessel badly, and make her very wet, putting her bows under frequently in a head sea, especially if she were fine lined.

The handling characteristics of a vessel when light or loaded differed considerably, therefore draught had its effect on shiphandling. Legislation in the Merchant Shipping Act of 1876 resulted in vessels having the depth to which they could load marked on the ships' sides. Even before this, Underwriters Associations in the major ports had their own tables specifying the amount of freeboard, or portion of the hull to be above water when loaded. Surveyors checked that vessels complied with their rulings; for example, the Liverpool Underwriters' Association scale of 1867 specified:

> This scale is intended for first class vessels only; subject in all cases to the judgement of the surveyor which is influenced by the vessel's age and class, her form (rise of floor, amount of sheer, general proportions, closed-in spaces on deck, as poop, spar deck etc), the intended voy-

Ketch Charlotte *discharging at St Ives. Her full bodied hull has little rise of floor amidships with a hard turn of bilge and this section is carried well forward and aft as can be seen from the bilge rubbing strake. She therefore has a good cargo capacity and will sit nearly upright when dried out. There had been recent rain and the headsails on the bowsprit have had the gaskets slacked off to allow the water to run out. The main boom, gaff and sail are lashed out of the way and the mainsheet is partly unrove. The cargo gaff guy has fouled the main topping lift. The staysail halyard and block have been made fast temporarily on the after end of the (staysail) boom as the sail has been covered over. Her port anchor is possibly farther up the beach and she has picked up a heavy rope aft leading from the starboard side. The more normal four-inch circumference mooring lines can be seen leading from the starboard bow. (Gillis Collection)*

age, season, nature of cargo, and such other circumstances favourable or otherwise, as may come under his notice.

It is worth mentioning that athwartship stability is not the only consideration. If a deep loaded vessel is fine lined forward with hollow waterlines and 'V' sections, has a long bowsprit and jibboom and a tall square rigged mast placed only a little way aft, the combined lack of buoyancy and inertia created by this weight and press of sail in the fore part of the vessel will be sufficient to drive her under when running before a gale in a heavy sea. If she does not lift quickly the result is another tragic loss. It was to avoid this situation that the square rigged mast of *The Great Britain* was made the main, rather than the fore.

Sail balance

The distribution of sail area forward and aft of the vessel's point of balance, and the control of each individual sail and her rudder, forms the basis of shiphandling. For the most part such canvas that is carried will be set to provide maximum drive, but, when manoeuvring, individual

If the conditions were right large sailing vessels could manage without tugs when clearing or entering a harbour. Here the barquentine Mozart is sailing from Mariehamn's Western Harbour under fore upper and lower topsails, main staysails, gaff main and mizzen. She is in ballast with a light draught and moving slowly in a slight breeze, which although fair, is causing her to make considerable leeway as indicated by the 'smooth' on her weather quarter. In these circumstances the rudder is not very effective and every effort would be made to set and trim sail about her point of balance so as to maintain the required heading without use of the helm. (Sjöfartsmuseet vid Åbo Akademi)

sails can be trimmed to provide a greater or lesser turning moment as required, or in the case of the square sail when 'aback', to provide sternway as well.

It follows that the placing of masts in a vessel and the amount of sail each is designed to carry is of fundamental importance, and will directly affect her handling characteristics. If we take for example the typical three-masted fully rigged ship of the 1850s, R H Dana states in *The Seaman's Manual*:

For a full-built ship, take the extreme length and divide into sevenths. Place the fore mast one-seventh of its length from the stem; the main mast three-sevenths from the fore mast, and the mizzen mast two-sevenths from the main mast. If a vessel is sharp-built and her

stem and stern post rake, her fore mast should be further aft, and her mizzen further forward than the rule of sevenths would give.

Just as important to overall balance is the length of bowsprit and the number and area of the headsails as a proportion of the sail plan as a whole. Because they are set so far forward, area for area they will have a greater effect on the steering than canvas set near the centre of the vessel. This also applies to the sail which is farthest aft – in the case of the full rigged ship this will be the gaff sail set from the mizzen, the spanker.

Under full sail, provided all the canvas is drawing well it should be possible in many cases to keep the vessel on a desired heading relative to the wind without the use of the rudder. Fluctuations in the strength and direction of the wind will result in the heading changing, and in consequence her progress will be somewhat erratic.

It is usual, therefore, to have the sails set so that there is a slightly higher rotational effect aft of the balance point, which will result in the vessel having a tendency to turn into the wind. This is counteracted by the rudder being held over at a small angle to the fore and aft line by the helm being pulled up to windward. She is then said to

Alastar, an iron barque of 860 tons gross built at Sunderland in 1875, is seen approaching a roadstead on a fine evening. Sail is being taken in and her starboard bower anchor is ready to let go. (Basil Greenhill collection)

be carrying 'weather helm', albeit slight, and there is now 'feel' in the steering.

Heavy 'weather helm' was to be avoided as it slowed the vessel down and was hard work for the crew. This could be due to poor sail balance or the ship heeling over due to an increase in the wind's strength. It was often the case, especially in vessels that were fine lined, that, in addition to laying over, the bows were depressed by the sail pressure forward, which moved the balance point towards the bows. Thus the sails set aft had an increased lever arm and the rudder being less deeply immersed, was not so effective, and with the ship heeled over the water pressure on the lee bow was increased. In a fierce squall, the combination of these factors could well result in the vessel flying up into the wind with the rudder hard over. If this was to be avoided then sail pressure aft would have to be reduced quickly, usually by easing off the sheets or taking in sail aloft so as to reduce the amount of heel.

If the wind draws well aft the sails in the fore part of the vessel will be partly blanketed and hence lose some of their drive; the overall balance thus being changed will affect the steering. It is usual in this situation to reduce the amount of canvas set aft, which will help to provide a clean flow of air through to the sails in the fore part of the vessel. This is especially important in bad weather with the ship running before a gale in heavy seas. The rudder is often working in broken water as the wave crest passes underneath and may not be effective in these extreme conditions, so the majority of the reduced sail area would be set well forward to prevent her 'broaching' – that is, swinging beam-on to the sea.

When manoeuvring, or endeavouring to establish a good balance, the rotational effect of individual sails may be more important than their prime function of driving the vessel forward. For example, when tacking it is advantageous to increase sail pressure aft of the balance point and reduce it forward. This will help to swing the ship up into the wind independently of the rudder. In the case of the full rigged ship the aftermost sail or spanker can have its rotational effect increased by hauling the boom to weather (the windward wide of the fore and aft line). In addition, the jib sheets can be eased up so as to reduce sail pressure ahead of the balance point. As the vessel approaches the eye of the wind these sails will start to flog or shake, tend-

ing to reduce the momentum. Therefore in light winds it may be advisable to drop them temporarily down their stays, especially in a slow moving and unhandy vessel. However, it is more usual to keep them set, as once she is head to wind, provided the sheets have not been let go, these sails will be 'aback'. They will now assist in swinging the bows on to the other tack, being retrimmed on the new leeward side once there is no chance of her reverting to the original heading. As mentioned, any square sails set on the fore mast will be aback before the headsails, reducing the vessel's speed but at the same time pushing her head round.

On the other hand, should the vessel be required to 'bear away', that is, alter heading away from the wind, the helm would be put 'up' and sail pressure aft of the balance point reduced. Provided the wind was forward of the beam, the aftermost fore and aft sail, or the spanker in the case of the full rigged ship, would be eased off so as to spill the wind. If the apparent wind was blowing from any direction aft of the beam, the spanker would have to be brailed in, it being impossible to lose drive or, more importantly, the rotational effect, just by slackening up the sheet or scandalising the sail.

In a similar way the square sail sheets can be let go or the yard lowered as the case may be with the same results. However the flogging sail and slack gear banging about aloft is likely to cause damage so it is usual to clew up the sail to the yard. If only a temporary loss of 'drive' or rotational effect is required without furling the sail, the yard can be braced round so as to point

at the apparent wind, possible only if it is blowing from approximately 45 degrees on the bow round to 45 degrees on the quarter. Usually all the square sails on one mast were 'shivered' together.

One advantage of the square sail is that it can be braced round so as to have the wind strike the forward face, providing the wind is anywhere between right ahead to some way aft of the beam. If the vessel is heading close to the eye of the wind the yards can be braced at right angles to it, thus providing maximum stopping power, with the sails 'aback' or if required greatest rotational effect by being trimmed at the most effective angle to it. Thus the full rigged ship can be slowed down or stopped without taking in all her sails by 'backing' those on the main mast to counteract the forward drive of the fore and mizzen.

Sometimes, due to an accident or severe weather, the rig is badly damaged and the sail balance cannot be maintained. For example, the loss of the fore mast and bowsprit due to a collision will leave the full rigged ship with canvas only aft of the pivot point, thus making her unmanageable. Usually some form of jury rig or temporary repairs could be effected – a difficult task at sea with the constant motion – and once the vessel was again under sufficient command she would head for a port where a proper restoration of the mast and spars could be effected. The smaller wooden vessels with their simpler technology and comparatively lighter gear were more easily repaired by the crew than the big steel square riggers, where, depending on the

With a light wind almost directly aft, the four-masted barque Clan Graham *has no fore-and-aft canvas set; of the courses, only the fore is needed since the others would tend to blanket one another. (CMP)*

and trimmed down by the head (bows deeper in the water) will have its pivot point well ahead of the centre of the vessel. Trimmed down by the stern and moving backwards she will have the pivot point well aft. Therefore much depends on the vessel's trim and hence her loading, and distribution of cargo or ballast is of great importance. When the vessel is heeled over due to the wind the balance point will shift and therefore cannot be considered as static.

If she has neither headway or sternway this balance point will be close to her centre of lateral resistance (CLR), or in other words the geometric centre of the vessel's underwater profile, and is thus dependent on the immersed shape of the hull. Drifting downwind with no sail set the vessel will lie, subject to her draught, trim and rig, at a certain aspect to the wind. If the wind forces acting on the exposed hull, masts, spars and rigging are equal each side of the CLR, she will move bodily downwind at right angles to it. Most sailing vessels in normal trim have a greater windage forward of this point and hence tend to drift with their bows turned downwind to some degree. If this is the case, depending on the strength of the wind she will probably start to forge ahead and hence establish a flow past the rudder. Once she has steerage way it is

damage, they were sometimes faced with an impossible task and in extreme circumstances the vessel would have to be abandoned, the last act being to scuttle her so as not to be a danger to other shipping. Even if a safe haven were reached, these later large steel sailing ships required specialised equipment and skilled personnel to effect the repairs, and in out of the way places would find such facilities lacking and therefore sail no farther. This accounts for the large number of derelict vessels in the Falkland Islands, which, being downwind from Cape Horn, could be reached by ships damaged in attempting to round the Cape but could not provide repair facilities.

General principles – pivot or balance point

To quote again from Dana's *The Seaman's Manual*: 'The centre of rotation is not necessarily at the centre of the ship. On the contrary, as vessels are now built, it may not be much abaft that part of the deck to which the main tack is boarded'. He is referring to the three-masted fully rigged ship sailing with the wind forward of the beam when the main course has the tack led forward on the weather side. As well as rotating about this point the turning vessel will move bodily sideways, still having a tendency to carry on in the original direction.

Hauling round the head yards on the big barque Parma. *With the small crews of late nineteenth- and early twentieth-century sailing ships various mechanical aids were employed, including the brace winches shown here. (By courtesy of David MacGregor)*

With reference to her centre of gravity, this balance or pivot point is slightly ahead when the vessel is moving ahead, but should she have sternway then it will move aft of it. This fact is of great importance when manouvering square-riggers. If for some reason weight is added in the fore part of a vessel so that she no longer floats on her correct waterline, her centre of gravity will move towards the bow and so will her pivot point. The opposite occurs when weight is added near the stern. Thus a vessel moving forward

The paddle tug United Service *towing a brigantine named the* Anna *into Yarmouth in heavy weather. She is at the critical point coming through a narrow entrance in a confused sea with a strong following wind. The tow line is hanging slack over the tug's port quarter because her prime function is to help the brigantine with her steering and to prevent the tow yawing off to one side or the other. It is probable also that the brigantine is tending to overtake the tug even under bare poles. The situation is very tense and a group of people have gathered on the pier to watch.* (The late Captain F C Poyser)

possible to bring the vessel under some sort of control and either angle her across the wind or run off before it under 'bare poles'. How she will react in the circumstances is vital knowledge when shiphandling, as is her rate of drift in ballast and loaded and how far she will continue or 'carry her way' when all sail is taken off her. Each vessel had her own characteristics and these were known to her master, especially her point of balance.

The use of tides as the prime motive force

This chapter on shiphandling has so far concentrated on wind and sail with reference to the fully rigged ship. However, should a vessel be required to proceed inland to the upper reaches of a harbour or even further up river, the state of the tide, which not only governs the depth of water but its direction of flow, may provide the only means of moving her. The very nature of the twists and turns deny the mariner a steady fair breeze, his heading constantly changing in relation to the true wind, and any steep sided hills on either bank will further distort the air flow. Furthermore, as the river narrows there is less room to manoeuvre, making 'tacking' impossible.

At this stage, should the tide be running in his favour, this alone can be utilised to carry the vessel towards her destination; the mariner can now drop the sails and providing the stream is swift enough it will overcome a slight headwind. The vessel thus drifting at virtually the same speed as the tide is not under control (unless the adverse breeze can be used to provide steerage way under bare poles), but providing there are no obstacles in her path she is in no danger. In smaller craft and barges some steerage can be established with the use of sweeps (long oars) or long poles used to keep her off the shoals or banks. She may even be towed from ahead using the ship's boat, but a safer method on larger vessels was often resorted to. This was called 'dredging', the anchor being lowered to the river bed sufficient to retard the vessel's progress but not stop

her. Now she was no longer just drifting with the current but swung round to stem the stream and travelling stern first. For example, if the tide is running at 4kts, and she has now slowed down, moving at only 2kts over the ground, a flow of 2kts is established past the rudder; she will now react as if she has a slight amount of headway and can be sheered from one side of the river to the other as desired by the action of the rudder. As the river deepens or shallows constant attention is required as to the amount of cable paid out – too much will stop her, and in the deep patches the anchor could be off the bottom, the vessel once more drifting freely with the current at the same speed and no longer under command.

Great care is needed not to run aground as the rudder will strike first with the whole weight of the vessel behind it; and, should the wind become fair the vessel is facing the wrong way. However, it is basically a safe way of travelling on a rising tide, local knowledge being vital, and thus was only used by regular traders or vessels with a pilot on board. The stronger the flow the more positive the control, and therefore this method was well suited to areas with a large tidal range such as the upper reaches of the Bristol Channel and River Severn, where the bottom is mainly mud. 'Dredging' was commonly used by the smaller vessels in the early part of the century, both coasters and deep sea ships, but once steam tugs became available the larger iron and steel square riggers made use of them.

In port

Any vessel is most at risk when entering or leaving a port, for no longer can she give a wide berth to rocks or shoals as she did on passage. The very nature of the task requires passing close to the shore and over banks with little clearance under the keel, or to negotiate a narrow entrance. For the pure sailing vessel dependent on the wind for her movement and at times subjected to strong tides during this period, the dangers are obvious and more acute than for the power driven vessel. Added to the chance of running ashore or aground is the risk of collision in a busy port where close-quarter situations are unavoidable with vessels passing one another in a narrow channel. She could only be considered 'safe' when made fast alongside a quay in a floating dock.

During the nineteenth century every large port developed its system of docks where ships remained afloat after 'locking in' and were thus free of the problems associated with tidal berths. Even some of the smaller ports had a floating dock which was not only more secure but made loading and discharging of cargo easier.

Many places traded to and from by the smaller coastal craft, by comparison with the larger ports, were far from 'safe'. A shift of wind to an unfavourable quarter and strengthening to gale force could result in serious damage or loss of the vessel, not only by the sheer power of the wind causing the anchor to drag and lines to part, but also due to the state of the swell and surge created by the increasing height and ferocity of the sea. It must be remembered that many of these locations were no more than small coves, sometimes given added protection by a pier or breakwater or even an open beach. The dangers being well known, as little time as possible was spent there, perhaps the loading or discharging being accomplished between two tides

Both the smack in the foreground and the ketch have rigged coir bow and stern lines supplied by the port. They are shown set up with considerable tension, even at low water - see text - and chafing gear in the form of old canvas strips can be seen where the ropes come inboard. The smack has a section of bulwark removed in way of the bitts aft to facilitate belaying these large diameter ropes. The tillers of both vessels have been lashed so as to prevent rudder movement. The vessels are in Porth Gaverne, Cornwall, a little creek in the rocks now in the care of the National Trust where coal was discharged and slate from the great Delabole quarries loaded. The waiting carts are laden with big slates. Coal is being discharged from the smack which is probably the Electric *built at Porth Gaverne in 1863. Porth Gaverne was considered a relatively safe place, usually free of ground sea. Nevertheless great precautions have been taken to secure the vessels on the beach, even on what is apparently a nice summer's day in the middle 1860s.* (Basil Greenhill Collection)

as more often than not vessels took the ground towards low water. Vital to the safe outcome was the prediction of weather and sea conditions by the master, on whose judgement alone success or failure depended.

If, due to rapidly worsening conditions, the vessel could not get clear and find shelter elsewhere, or perhaps the loading or discharging had not been completed or for whatever reason she was forced to stay, efforts were made to minimise the damage that could ensue. In many of these locations the foreshore, harbour or quay dried out at low water, a vessel therefore having to take the ground on each tide, and herein lay the real danger. Even if not dried out completely she could contact the bottom near low water. In these circumstances a heavy swell running in due to the sea outside, or indeed a 'groundsea' as it is called, sometimes with little wind, would cause the vessel to pound the bottom on each tide in that critical period when it was neither fully afloat nor hard aground. Added to this vertical movement was a surge back and fore which would develop once the vessel was sufficiently waterborne to allow it; the keel thus sawed its way to and fro with considerable weight bearing down on it. Both actions could damage the vessel severely. In places subjected to these conditions extra heavy mooring lines were available, the object being to reduce as far as possible the vertical movement and to damp down the surge back and forth. Shore labour was usually on hand to help rig these coir ropes, 10in or 12in in circumference, which were led from either bollards ashore or ground chains and set up as taut as possible on board the vessel. Coir was chosen in preference to manila as it was less likely to rot and had more 'spring', the vessels that traded regularly to these places being modified and strengthened where required to handle these much bigger lines, the normal size being 4in-6in.

Sometimes it was better to lighten the vessel or re-trim her so as to get farther up the foreshore, or extra anchors were laid to maintain position. The rudder and sternpost were particularly vulnerable as in most cases the vessel would be pointing bows in towards the shore and it was likely therefore that the stern would lift first on the flood, with the consequence of heavy pounding in this area. The rudder blade itself would be restricted in its movement, the object being to prevent it swinging from side to side as the vessel surged back and forth.

Even when made fast to a quay there was the additional hazard of the side or bulwarks being stove in despite the fenders, and it was not unknown in extreme conditions for the bollards ashore to be ripped out along with the stonework, let alone the cleats, bitts or sampson posts on the vessel.

Peter Allington

Bibliography

Edited by Robert Gardiner from information supplied by the contributors

GENERAL

As a subject for publication the last hundred years of the commercial sailing ship has inspired an enormous outpouring of books, papers and articles. Much of the first generation of such writing, being produced as the sailing ship disappeared from the world's oceans, was amateur, antiquarian and frankly nostalgic. Nevertheless, whatever their shortcomings in terms of method, many of these pioneering authors had the advantage of contact with those who had made their livings at sea and often had first-hand experience themselves. Basil Lubbock is the archetypal example of this approach, and although his many works now seem unscholarly and even a little naive, they are still the basic introduction to the subject for many readers. Besides those quoted below in relation to specific chapters, he also produced: *The China Clippers* (1914) on British fast-sailing ships of the 1860s; *The Western Ocean Packets* (1925), a study of North Atlantic passenger and mail services; *The Opium Clippers* (1933) on small fast smuggling vessels; *Coolie Ships and Oil Sailors* (1935) about the case-oil carriers which returned with indentured labourers from the East; and *The Arctic Whalers* (1937). All were published in Glasgow and have been reprinted a number of times since.

Of the new generation of more technically minded writers Howard I Chapelle stands out, not only because he was the first, but because his works have been so influential. The most important are listed under particular chapters below, but *The National Watercraft Collection* (Washington, 1960; 2nd ed 1976), a superb catalogue of the Smithsonian ship model collection, is also valuable. Chapelle's first major work, *The Baltimore Clipper* (Salem, Mass 1930; reprinted New York 1969), is largely concerned with an earlier period but does give a view of the American schooner around 1830.

A number of books of interest which have not found a specific place under the various chapter divisions below are listed here.

R G ALBION, *Square-Riggers on Schedule: The New York Sailing Packets to England, France and the Cotton Ports* (Princeton, NJ 1938; reprinted 1965).
Includes substantial tabular data on all vessels covered.

GEORGE F CAMPBELL, *China Tea Clippers* (London 1974).
Not a narrative history but an analysis of detail differences in hull form, construction, fittings etc; covers American and British ships.

A H CLARKE, *The Clipper Ship Era, 1843–1869* (New York 1910; reprinted 1969).
Lists famous American and British vessels, with their owners, builders, commanders, etc.

CARL C CUTLER, *Queens of the Western Ocean: The Story of America's Mail and Passenger Sailing Lines* (Annapolis, Md 1961).
Covers small coastal packets as well as trans-oceanic carriers; lists thousands of vessels and their masters.

W A FAIRBURN *et al*, *Merchant Sail*, 6 vols (... 1945–55).
An incredible compilation, largely the work of one man who was closely involved with American shipbuilding, listing over 13,000 vessels. Apart from Vol 1, which covers the pre-1812 period, it is all relevant to the last century of sail; difficult to find since the whole print run was distributed to chosen libraries.

OCTAVIUS T HOWE and FREDERICK C MATTHEWS, *American Clipper Ships, 1833–1858*, 2 vols (Salem, Mass 1926 and 1927).
A substantial alphabetical listing.

C NEPEAN LONGRIDGE, *The Cutty Sark*, 2 vols (London 1949).
Very detailed monograph, with the modelmaker in mind, on the famous preserved composite tea clipper.

DAVID MACGREGOR, *The Tea Clippers: Their History and Development, 1833–1875* (London 1952, 1972 and expanded edition 1983).
The best single volume on British clippers; a classic work, gradually expanded over thirty years. Well illustrated with plans, photographs and paintings.

FREDERICK C MATTHEWS, *American Merchant Ships, 1850–1900*, 2 vols (Salem, Mass 1930 and 1931; reprinted 1969).
Good for later American sailing vessels.

E P MORRIS, *The Fore-and-Aft Rig in America* (New Haven, Conn 1927; reprinted New York 1970).
An important early survey, much relevant to the post-1830 period.

ALEXANDER STARBUCK, *A History of the American Whale Fishery* (New York 1876; reprinted 1964).
Lists virtually every American whaler and their voyages down to 1876; continued to 1928 by R B Hegarty as *Returns of Whaling Vessels sailing from American Ports* (Dartmouth, Mass 1959).

Because of the way this volume is organised, many titles relate to more than one chapter, so some have been repeated under different headings to make each section complete.

INTRODUCTION

Most of the topics dealt with in the Introduction are covered by the reading lists for later chapters, but among the very numerous academic papers, reports, and so forth on maritime historical subjects published in the last twenty years I would recommend especially the six volumes published by the Memorial University of Newfoundland (at St John) between 1977 and 1984. They are as follows:

K MATTHEWS and G E PANTING (eds), *Ships and Shipbuilding in the North Atlantic Region* (1978).

D ALEXANDER and R OMMER (eds), *Volumes Not Values* (1979).

L R FISCHER and E R SAGER (eds), *The Enterprising Canadians (1979)*.

R OMMER and G E PANTING (eds), *Working Men Who Got Wet* (1980).

L R FISCHER and E R SAGER (eds), *Merchant Shipping and Economic Development in Atlantic Canada* (1982).

L R FISCHER and G E PANTING (eds), *Change and Adaptation in Maritime History* (1984).

Despite their inevitable Canadian bias these volumes are of great importance and essential reading to those concerned with merchant shipping history. Also essential is the *International Journal of Maritime History* published twice a year, also at the Memorial University of Newfoundland and now the world's leading journal in its field.

CAPTAIN W J SLADE, *Westcountry Coasting Ketches* (London 1974).
Some idea of the contribution to the understanding of ships and shiphandling which could be made by men who spent their lives in the heart of the old sailing tradition can be gained from this book.

THE WOODEN SAILING SHIP: OVER 300 TONS

HOWARD I CHAPELLE, *The Search for Speed under Sail, 1700–1855* (New York 1967).
Written by a naval architect using plans and mathematical analysis to describe and compare the ships. He judges a ship's potential from her hull plans; he includes few sail plans of the larger ships. Unrivalled for this type of material.

CARL CUTLER, *Greyhounds of the Sea: the Story of the American Clipper Ship* (Annapolis, Md 1961; reprint of 1930 ed with similar pagination).

The best book on American clipper ships together with accounts of earlier fast ships. Many quotations from log-books; very detailed lists in Appendices of 443 clippers, 100 transatlantic packets, and others; also passage times in the California and China trades.

BASIL LUBBOCK, *The Down Easters: American Deep Water Sailing Ships, 1869–1929* (Glasgow 1929; reprinted frequently).
Concentrates on ship-by-ship descriptions, arranged chronologically according to date of build, of these large vessels, with informative text and numerous personal reminiscences collected by the author. Well illustrated.

——, *The Blackwall Frigates* (Glasgow 1922; reprinted frequently).
This is about successors to the East Indiamen and continues the story up to 1875, although no wooden ones were built after 1866. An informative description of the ships, the captains and their voyages. Lubbock's *Last of the Windjammers* concentrates on iron and steel ships for vessels over 300 tons, and he wrote no general one on wooden ships.

DAVID R MACGREGOR, *Merchant Sailing Ships 1815–1850: Supremacy of Sail* (London 1984).
Section of vessels of over 300 tons are arranged according to the shipyard, and the products of the chosen yards are discussed in depth. The influence of textbooks and the plans they contain are appraised. The best source for illustrating the types of merchant ships in existence during the period 1815–1850.

——, *Merchant Sailing Ships 1850–1875: Heyday of Sail* (London 1984).
The plans of ships form an important part of this work and the other illustrations augment this. There is much information in the text on the ships and their builders. Appendices contain shipyard lists with some prices, and a specification.

——, *Fast Sailing Ships: their Design and Construction, 1775–1875* (London 1988).
Enlarged and revised from 1973 edition. Concentrates on ships built for speed, mostly British, some American and a few North European. Useful information on shipbuilding illustrated with plans and photographs; informative diagrams to show between what points a ship's length was measured.

ANDREW SHEWAN, *The Great Days of Sail* (London 1927; reprinted 1973).
An entertaining account of British tea clippers by a man who once commanded the *Norman Court*. Valuable comparisons of ships and captains.

FREDERICK WILLIAM WALLACE, *Wooden Ships and Iron Men* (Belleville, Ontario 1976).
This reprint of the 1924 edition is useful as it contains an index which the other lacks; it also has more illustrations. There was also a 1937 edition published in Boston. A generally discursive account of Canadian ships with quite a lot on the shipbuilders.

THE WOODEN SAILING SHIP: UNDER 300 TONS

HOWARD I CHAPELLE, *The History of American Sailing Ships* (New York 1935; many later reprints).
A valuable study of American ships of all types, using plans as the major source of illustrations, from c1760 to c1930.

ROGER FINCH, *Sailing Craft of the British Isles* (London 1976).
Traditional craft described and illustrated with halftones and sail plans; useful for reference.

BASIL GREENHILL, *The Merchant Schooners*, 2 vols (London 1951 and 1957).
The standard work on trading craft in Great Britain, well illustrated and well researched, also covering construction and rigging. Subsequent editions extensively revised with new illustrations; latest edition is in only one volume (1988).

JOHN LEATHER, *Gaff Rig* (London 1970).
Explains numerous ways of setting gaff sails and explores the rigs which employ them; covers merchant ships, yachts, fishing boats, pilots etc. Sail plans and halftones, but no plans of hulls.

JOHN F LEAVITT, *Wake of the Coasters* (Middletown, Conn 1970).
Drawn from personal experience, there are many stories about the two-and three-masted schooners, as well as much informative material. Apart from the numerous halftones, the author's own pen-and-ink drawings supply a wealth of information.

JOHN LYMAN (ed), *Log Chips*, 4 vols (Washington 1948–59).
Excellent reference material on shipbuilders in Europe and North America, with 'thumbnail' histories of many vessels. Not illustrated; type-written format.

DAVID R MACGREGOR, *Schooners in Four Centuries* (London 1982).
With the exception of Chapters 2 to 5 and 16 to 17, the remainder covers schooners in the nineteenth century in Great Britain, Europe, North America and elsewhere; good illustrations and captions.

——, *Merchant Sailing Ships 1815–1850: Supremacy of Sail* (London 1984).
Although this work covers all sizes of vessels, there is much on craft of under 300 tons. The plans, many of which are drawn by the author, form an important part of this well-illustrated book, and he has taken trouble to search for examples of smaller craft as well as the larger ships.

——, *Merchant Sailing Ships 1850–1875: Heyday of Sail* (London 1984).
Like the earlier volume, a large number of plans of vessels under 300 tons covering Europe and North America as well as Great Britain. The illustrations complement the text, which concentrates on design and construction rather than on voyage descriptions. Schooners have received much written comment in other works, but here brigs, small barques and ketches are compared with other classes of ships.

HANS SZYMANSKI, *Deutsche Segelschiffe* (Hamburg 1972).
This is a reprint of the work first published in 1934, and although the text is in German, there are numerous plans and photographs of German and North European craft. It is sub-divided by types of vessels.

THE TRANSITION TO IRON AND STEEL CONSTRUCTION

There is no single study which deals solely with the theme of the transition from wood to metal in sailing ships. Most work on shipping technology in the nineteenth century has emphasised the change from sail to steam. Where the change in construction materials is investigated there is rarely a distinction between sail and steam. However, a number of works include some information on particular aspects of the topic. Brief introductions include chapters by G Naish and A M Robb in *A History of Technology*. The leading study of British shipbuilding in this period is by S Pollard and P Robertson. The development of the

sailing ship in its various forms through the nineteenth century is looked at in a series of studies by David MacGregor listed in the earlier sections. Similarly helpful information can be found in the works of Basil Greenhill, especially those quoted below. Earlier works by Basil Lubbock provide interesting detail but are more antiquarian in approach.

While MacGregor and Greenhill give emphasis to the British experience, that of America is covered in J G B Hutchins' outstanding work, which includes a considered explanation of the limited nature of the transition process in North America and also draws comparisons with the experience of European countries. Statistics and organisational aspects of American shipbuilding can be found in F G Fassett. The failure of Canada to build steel sailing vessels is covered in a number of effective studies of the decline of the Canadian maritime sector, particularly those listed below.

The European shipping industries are less well covered, although there is useful information in the volumes edited by F Walker and A Slaven, and L R Fischer and G Panting, the latter including a good paper on Britain by S Palmer. There is also a special edition of *Scandinavian Economic History Review* 20 (1980). Several regional studies contain worthwhile detail, particularly those by F M Walker and that edited by S Ville, which offers detailed coverage of the main regions.

Plenty of technical detail of the transition process can be found in J F Clarke's paper, although it is backed up with little analysis. Also see S Ville's paper in the same series. Contemporary discussion of the relative merits of wood and metal can be found in the pages of the *Transaction of the Institution of Naval Architects* from 1860. Among contemporary publications one of the most noteworthy is J Grantham, *Iron Shipbuilding* (London, 5th ed 1868).

On the issue of the transfer and diffusion of shipping technologies in the nineteenth century, the article by N Rosenberg offers a general perspective; S Ville's 'Shipping industry technologies' provides an international comparative approach; C K Harley addresses a particular example, while K Maywald yields valuable information on a vital aspect of the transition.

Further relevant works can be found amongst the footnotes of the chapter.

J F CLARKE, 'The Changeover from Wood to Iron Shipbuilding', *Occasional Papers in the History of Science and Technology* 3 (1986), Newcastle-upon-Tyne Polytechnic.

F G FASSETT (ed), *The Shipbuilding Business of the United States of America*, Vol 1 (New York 1948).

L R FISCHER and G PANTING (eds), *Change and Adaptation in Maritime History: The North Atlantic Fleets in the Nineteenth Century* (St John, Newfoundland 1985).

A GOMEZ-MENDOZA, 'Government and the Development of Modern Shipbuilding in Spain', *Journal of Transport History* third series 9/1 (1988).

BASIL GREENHILL, *The Life and Death of the Merchant Sailing Ship, 1815–65* (London 1980).

C K HARLEY, 'On the Persistence of Old Techniques: The Case of North American Wooden Shipbuilding', *Journal of Economic History* 33 (1973).

J G B HUTCHINS, *The American Maritime Industries and Public Policy, 1789–1914* (Cambridge, Mass 1941).

BASIL LUBBOCK, *The Last of the Windjammers*, 2 vols (Glasgow 1927; many later reprints).

——, *The Colonial Clippers* (Glasgow 1921; many later reprints).

K MAYWALD, 'The Construction Cost and the Value of the British Merchant Fleet, 1850–1938', *Scottish Journal of Political Economy* 3 (1956).

G NAISH, 'Shipbuilding', in C Singer *et al* (eds), *A History of Technology, Vol IV: The Industrial Revolution, c1750–c1780* (Oxford 1958).

R OMMER, 'The Decline of the Eastern Canadian Shipping Industry, 1880–95', *Journal of Transport History* third series 5/1 (1984).

S PALMER, 'The British Shipping Industry, 1850–1914', in FISCHER and PANTING listed above.

S POLLARD and P ROBERTSON, *The British Shipbuilding Industry, 1870–1914* (Cambridge, Mass 1979).

A M ROBB, 'Shipbuilding', in C Singer *et al* (eds), *A History of Technology', Vol V: The Late Nineteenth Century 1850–1900* (Oxford 1958).

N ROSENBERG, 'Factors Affecting the Diffusion of Technology', *Explorations in Economic History* 10 (1972–3).

E W SAGER and G E PANTING, *Maritime Capital: the Shipping Industry in Atlantic Canada, 1820–1914* (Montreal 1990).

E W SAGER and L R FISCHER, 'Atlantic Canada and the Age of Sail Revisited', *Canadian Historical Review* 63 (1982).

S VILLE (ed), *Regional Fluctuations in United Kingdom Shipbuilding in the Nineteenth Century* (Liverpool 1993, forthcoming).

——, 'The Introduction of the Use of Mild Steel into the Shipbuilding and Marine Engineering Industries', *Occasional Papers in the History of Science and Technology* 1 (1983), Newcastle-upon-Tyne Polytechnic.

——, 'Shipping Industry Technologies', in D J JEREMY (ed), *International Technology Transfer: Europe, Japan and the USA, 1700–1914*, (Aldershot 1991).

F WALKER and A SLAVEN (eds), *European Shipbuilding* (London 1984).

F WALKER, *Song of the Clyde: A History of Clydeside Shipbuilding* (Cambridge 1984).

THE IRON AND STEEL SAILING SHIP

The literature of iron and steel sailing vessels and their operations is extensive. For all its faults as they appear to the modern reader – lack of sources quoted, anecdotal approach, failure to analyse the economics of the business or to examine the social structures associated with it – the work of Basil Lubbock remains invaluable, if not always totally reliable as to detail.

BASIL LUBBOCK, *The Last of the Windjammers*, 2 vols (Glasgow 1929; many later reprints).

——, *The Nitrate Clippers* (Glasgow 1932; many later reprints).

DAVID R MACGREGOR, *Merchant Sailing Ships 1850–1875* (London 1984).

——, *Fast Sailing Ships* (revised ed, London 1988).
Both MacGregor titles contain much valuable material, although neither goes beyond 1875.

HAROLD UNDERHILL, *Deep Water Sail* (Glasgow 1963).
Much valuable and reliable information on iron and steel vessels, together with plans.

——, *Masting and Rigging: The Clipper Ship and Ocean Ship and Ocean Carrier* (Glasgow 1946).
Now unlikely ever to be surpassed as a source of information on the masting and rigging of the large iron and steel vessels. Both these Underhill books can scarcely be too strongly recommended to any reader who wishes to acquire the solid grounding in technology and terminology which must precede any serious study of maritime aspects of history.

ALAN VILLIERS, *The Way of a Ship* (New York 1953; many later editions).
Best summed up in its rather eighteenth-century-style subtitle: 'Being some account of the ultimate development of the ocean going square rigged sailing vessel, and the manner of her handling, her voyage making, her personnel, her economics, her performance and her end'. Written by a professional seaman with immense experience of sail propelled vessels who was also a highly competent writer, this book is invaluable.

—— and HENRI PICARD, *The Bounty Ships of France* (London 1972).
Very useful for the French iron and steel sailing vessels.

Besides these general studies, there is a number of publications dealing with the history of individual iron and steel vessels. These include:

T J AARNIALA, *Favell* (Jyväskylä 1985).

V DARROCH, *Barque Polly Woodside* (Kilmore, Victoria, Australia 1978).

J MACMULLEN, *Star of India: The Log of an Iron Ship* (Berkeley, Cal 1973).

Of the many contemporary technical treatises on shipbuilding, the following are the most accessible to the layman:

D POLLOCK, *Modern Shipbuilding and the Men Engaged in It* (London 1884).
Useful general work.

EDWARD REED, *Shipbuilding in Iron and Steel* (London 1869).
A more comprehensive work of somewhat earlier date than Thearle. This book is particularly well illustrated with diagrams and detailed drawings.

J THEARLE, *The Modern Practice of Shipbuilding in Iron and Steel* (Glasgow 1891).
A very useful elementary work published when the building of big steel sailing vessels was at its height.

THE MERCHANT SAILING VESSEL IN THE TWENTIETH CENTURY

There is a vast literature of the merchant sailing vessel in the twentieth century. Some of these books are mentioned in footnotes and in the text. There are, for instance, at least thirty-three books in English on the subject of the vessels sailing from the Åland Islands of Finland in the 1920s and '30s alone, besides George and Karl Kåhre's masterly and comprehensive *Den Aländska Segelsjöfartens historia* (Mariehamn 1988). Of these perhaps the best are:

BASIL GREENHILL and JOHN HACKMAN, *Herzogin Cecilie* (London 1991).
Written from company records, correspondence and the vessel's logs, this book represents a factual and unromantic view of the history of Gustaf Erikson's business, centred round the career of the famous four-masted barque.

W M HUTTON, *Cape Horn Passage* (London 1934).
Account of a passage from Port Victoria to Falmouth in the four-masted barque *Viking*. Considered by some Åland 'Cape Horners' to be the best and truest of its kind.

GEORGE KÅHRE, *The Last Tall Ships* (London 1990).
The official account of the history of Gustaf Erikson's sailing fleet by the brother of one of Erikson's managers. Informative and reliable, but, of necessity, takes a generous view of what was (of necessity also) a hard-headed, highly successful, commercial enterprise.

ELIS KARLSSON, *Mother Sea* (Oxford 1964).
Despite its title, and some fictional elements, this is an admirable account of a childhood in Wårdö in Åland and subsequent service in various Åland vessels. Exceptionally well-written by the author straight into English. Recommended also is the same author's *Pulley Haul* (Oxford 1966), but beware of his accounts of the loss of the *Herzogin Cecilie*.

BJÖRN SVENSSON, *Pommern* (Mariehamn 1988).
A very good account of the history of the only unspoiled survivor of the four-masted barques.

ALAN VILLIERS, *Falmouth for Orders* (London 1929, and numerous later editions).
Classic narrative of a passage in 1929 from Port Lincoln to Falmouth and on to Cardiff in the four-masted barque *Herzogin Cecilie*. The book which first brought the Åland sailing fleet to popular attention.

Besides the vessels of the Åland Islands, the last years of deep water commercial sail under other flags are covered by the following:

H C P ROHRBACH, J H PIENING and F SCHMIDT, *A Century and a Quarter of Reederei F Laeisz* (Flagstaff, Ar 1957).
A very useful study of some of the best of the later German sailing vessels.

ALAN VILLIERS, *The Way of a Ship* (New York 1953; many later editions).
Part one is good on the later square-riggers.

——, *At War with Cape Horn* (London 1971).
Valuable material on the later German sailing vessels in addition to its account of selected British vessels.

—— and HENRI PICARD, *The Bounty Ships of France* (London 1972).
Excellent coverage of the subsidised French merchant fleet.

North American sail in the twentieth century has an extensive literature. Some titles relating to the larger schooners are listed in the next section of this bibliography, but the following are of wider reference.

M V BREWINGTON, *Chesapeake Bay Bugeyes* (Newport News, VA 1941).
A model study of an American local sailing craft which has survived in to the last years of the twentieth century.

HAAKON CHEVALIER, *The Last Voyage of the Schooner Rosamund* (London 1970).
An account of a round-the-world voyage in a West Coast-built four-master in 1920–21; the vessel was laid up at its conclusion and never went to sea again.

JIM GIBBS, *West Coast Windjammers* (New York 1968).
Based largely on the work of Dr John Lyman, this book, despite its title, is a comprehensive and valuable study of the history of West Coast shipbuilding in both the USA and Canada.

JOHN F LEAVITT, *Wake of the Coasters* (Middletown, Conn 1970).
The best study of the two-masted and smaller three-masted schooners of New England in this century.

JOHN PARKER, *Sails of the Maritimes* (privately published by the author, North Sydney, NS 1960).
The standard work on Canadian tern schooners and four-masters.

GILES M TOD, *The Last Sail Down East* (Barre, Mass 1965).
A useful source of reference on the later survivors of all types on the East Coast.

ALAN VILLIERS, *In the Quest of the Schooner Argus* (London 1951).
A first-class professional seaman's record of the Portuguese Atlantic fishing industry under sail just after the war.

A unique book describing local craft of the Mediterranean in the early years of the twentieth century is:

SIR ALAN MOORE, *The Last Days of Mast and Sail* (Oxford 1925; reprinted Newton Abbott 1970).
Described as an essay in nautical comparative anatomy, it analyses British, Mediterranean and Near Eastern practice regarding rigs and rigging.

For first-hand accounts of the last years of operation of small British merchant sailing vessels see:

HERVEY BENHAM, *Last Stronghold of Sail* (London 1948).
The story of Essex sailing smacks, coasters and barges.

EDMUND EGLINTON, *The Mary Fletcher* (Exeter 1990).
Gives a minute-by-minute account of the handling of a Devon coasting ketch for one week of her life.

W J SLADE, *Out of Appledore* (London 1980).
A classic personal study of the operations of a schooner-owning family in the first half of the twentieth century.

There are very interesting accounts of the cruise business in sail-assisted and sailing vessels in:

JOSEPH NOVITSKI, *Windstar* (New York 1987).

PETER H SPECTRE, *A Passage in Time: Along the Coast of Maine by Schooner* (New York 1991).

HAROLD UNDERHILL, *Sail Training and Cadet Ships* (Glasgow 1956).
Despite its age, by far the best study of the subject.

Two classic restorations of small vessels are described in professional detail in:

WILLITS ANSEL, *Restoration of the Smack Emma C Berry* (Mystic, Conn 1973).

ALAN J VINER, *The Restoration of the Ketch Rigged Tamar Sailing Barge Shamrock* (London 1983).

THE SCHOONER IN AMERICA

CAPTAIN FRANCIS E BOWKER, *Blue Water Coaster* (Camden, Me 1972).
This is a well-told account of life before the mast in the last days of the big schooners.

——, *Atlantic Four-Master: The Story of the Schooner Herbert L Rawding* (Mystic, Conn 1986).
This is another of Bowker's wonderful first-hand accounts of time in the former Crowell & Thurlow schooner *Herbert L Rawding.*

ROBERT H BURGESS (ed), *Coasting Captain: Journals of Captain Leonard S Tawes Relating His Career in Atlantic Coastwise Sailing Craft from 1868–1922* (Newport News, Va 1967).
A fascinating book by a Chesapeake Bay man who commanded the three-masted schooner *City of Baltimore* for more than twenty years, mostly in the lumber trade between Jacksonville and Baltimore. Edited by Robert H Burgess, a keen student of maritime history of Chesapeake Bay.

——, *Sea, Sails and Shipwreck: Career of the Four-Masted Schooner Purnell T White* (Cambridge, Md 1970).
Another biography of a schooner. Burgess knew her very well as a young man, although he did not sail in her. He did make a long voyage in a four-master, so he knows the subject well.

——, *Coasting Schooner: the Four-Masted Albert F Paul* (Charlottesville, Va 1978).
A very thorough study of this vessel's career, much of which was spent in the southern lumber trade. It is strong on economics, and an account of one sailor's service on board is especially good.

HOWARD I CHAPELLE, *The History of American Sailing Ships* (New York 1935).
Chapelle deals briefly with the design of large schooners. Included are a number of well-executed line drawings and sail plans.

FREDERICK KAISER, *Built on Honor, Sailed with Skill: The American Coasting Schooner* (Ann Arbor, Mich 1989).
As a boy, Kaiser was infatuated with the four-master *Annie C Ross*. He made himself useful to the master while the vessel was in port in New York and eventually he made a trip or two to Georgetown, South Carolina, for lumber. His delightful reminiscences were first published about twenty years ago in *The National Fisherman*, a monthly paper devoted to the commercial fishing industry.

CHARLES S MORGAN, 'New England Coasting Schooners', *The American Neptune* XXIII 1 (January 1963).
A splendid, well-written overview by a scholar who has been immersed in schooner lore for a lifetime.

PAUL C MORRIS, *Four-Masted Schooners of the East Coast* (Orleans, Mass 1975).
A useful compendium, but should be used with caution. It is unfortunate that it did not receive a rigorous proof-reading.

SCHOONER DEVELOPMENT IN BRITAIN

CAPTAIN W J LEWIS PARKER, USCG (Ret), *The Great Coal Schooners of New England, 1870–1909* (Mystic, Conn 1948).
Perhaps the first serious effort to explain the economics of the big schooners.

——, 'To "The River", An Offshore Schooner Trade', *The American Neptune* XXXV 1 (January 1975).

Of the countless books which deal with sailing ships, relatively few concentrate on small merchant vessels. Though the literature on the British variant of the schooner is not extensive, it includes a number of highly readable and technically competent works.

HOWARD I CHAPELLE, *The Search for Speed under Sail* (London 1968).
An essential source of reference for the development of fast sailing rigs, this work includes much of interest concerning Baltimore clippers and schooner privateers.

BASIL GREENHILL, *The Merchant Schooners* (4th ed, London 1988).
Recently revised and furnished with an excellent set of illustrations, this remains the classic work on the construction, design and operations of the small merchant sailing ship in nineteenth- and early twentieth-century Britain.

——, *Schooners* (London 1980).
A history of the schooner based on 141 illustrations, each explained in detailed linking passages and captions.

HAROLD M HAHN, *The Colonial Schooner 1763–1775* (London 1981).
Though this work is primarily aimed at modelmakers, it contains some useful information on the Navy's procurement of colonial schooners in the 1760s.

TIM LATHAM, *The Ashburner Schooners: The Story of the First Shipbuilders of Barrow-in-Furness* (Manchester 1991).
This well-researched account is much more than a family history, for as well as analysing the shipbuilding and shipowning interests of the Ashburners of Barrow it offers much information on the 'Barrow flats' and the trade and shipping of the Furness district.

DAVID MACGREGOR, *Schooners in Four Centuries* (Hemel Hempstead 1982).
An excellent, well-illustrated survey of the development of the schooner rig from the early seventeenth century to the present day.

C H WARD-JACKSON, *Stephens of Fowey: A Portrait of a Cornish Merchant Fleet 1867–1939* (Greenwich 1980).
Schooners feature prominently in this account of the shipping interests of a firm which operated small wooden sailing vessels in the home and Newfoundland trades during the last third of the nineteenth century.

—— (ed), *The Last Log of the Schooner 'Isabella'* (Greenwich 1976).
Focusing on the final voyage of the *Isabella*, to Newfoundland in 1913, this work offers many insights into the continuing viability of the small merchant sailing ship on the eve of the Great War.

The Sailing Ship in the Baltic

There is nothing of direct relevance in English, but the main Swedish and Finnish sources are listed for completeness:

S ANDERSSON, *Åländskt Skärgårdsliv* (Åbo 1945).

——, Åländsk bondeseglation, *Rospiggen* (1961).
Annual Journal.

F H CHAPMAN, *Architectura Navalis Mercatoria* (Stockholm 1768; reprinted 1971).

N FRIVERG, *Stockholm i bottniska farvatten. En historisk-geografisk studie* (Stockholm 1983).

E GUSTAVSSON, 'Fartygsinventering i Roslagen 1715', *Rospiggen* (1963).
Annual Journal.

R HAUSEN, 'Kalkuförsel från Åland under äldre tid', *Skrift-serien Åland* IV (Helsinki 1916).

P O HÖGNÄS and J ÖRJANS, 'Storbåten', *Skriftserien Åland* 13 (Mariehamn 1985).

S O JANSSON, 'Om läst och lästetal', *Sjöhistorisk årsbok* (1945–46).

G KERKKONEN, 'Bondesegel på Finska viken', *Skrifter utgivna av Finska litteratursällskapet i Finland* 369 (Helsinki/Copenhagen 1959).

——, *Borgare och bondesglare* (Helsinki 1977).

G KÅHRE, *Den åländska segelsjöfartens historia* (Helsingfors 1940).

G and K KÅHRE, *Den åländska segelsjöfartens historia* (Mariehamn 1988).

K G LEINBERG, *Bidrag till kännedom af vårt land* (Jyväskylä 1885).

A LINDAHL, 'Om höskutor', *Sjöhistorisk årsbok* (1944).

D PAPP, *Åländsk allmogeseglation* (Lund 1977).

C RAMSDAHL, *Det åländska folkets historia* II:I (Mariehamn 1988).

S STEEN, 'Fartøier i Norden under middelaldern', *Nordisk kultur* XVI (Copenhagen 1933).

The Changing Problems of Shiphandling

REAR-ADMIRAL CLAUDE CUMBERLEGE, *Master Mariner* (London 1936).
For a really good read which tells a good deal about shiphandling. It is not about the Navy, but about a merchant brig, and it is written with elegance, charm and utterly unexpected knowledge of classical merchant seamanship.

R H DANA Jr, *The Seaman's Manual* (New York 1841; many later editions).
A prime source for nineteenth-century seamanship written by the author of *Two Years Before the Mast*, this is perhaps the best contemporary work for those who wish to learn in depth about sailing vessel handling and seamanship in the era when it was most highly developed.

LIEUTENANT P W HOURIGAN, *Manual of Seamanship for the Officer of the Deck: Ship Under Sail Alone* (Annapolis 1903; reprinted 1980).
Also a valuable source on practical seamanship.

VICE-ADMIRAL SIR GEORGE NARES, *Seamanship* (Portsmouth 1862; many later editions).
This is very comprehensive but has, of course, a naval slant. It was an expanded version of *The Naval Cadet's Guide*, published in 1860.

W J SLADE, *Out of Appledore* (London 1980).
Contains a mass of information, based on personal experience, of operating the last ketches and schooners; his collaboration with Basil Greenhill, *Westcountry Coasting Ketches* (London 1974), already listed, is also applicable.

ALAN VILLIERS, *The Way of a Ship* (New York 1953; and many later editions).
A modern exposition of seamanship for the general reader.

——, *Voyaging with the Wind* (London 1975).
A small handbook with an excellent bibliography.

Glossary of Terms and Abbreviations

Compiled by Robert Gardiner. This list assumes some knowledge of ships and does not include the most basic terminology. It also omits those words which are defined on the only occasions in which they occur in this book.

aback. The situation of the sails when the wind bears on the opposite surface from that which will propel the ship forwards. In a square rigged ship the sails can be intentionally backed, to slow the vessel or to hold it relatively stationary; a ship can also be taken aback by a sudden wind shift or due to the inattention of the helmsman.

Baltimore clipper. An imprecise term applied to fine-lined American schooners with an emphasis on extreme speed; not so much a specific type as a concept, their heyday was approximately 1780–1820.

barge. Originally a fine-lined ship's boat, but latterly most commonly applied to a capacious riverine or coasting vessel, usually with a simple fore and aft rig, such as the familiar Thames spritsail barge.

barque or bark. As understood in the nineteenth century, a vessel with three or more masts, square rigged on all but the aftermost, which set only fore and aft canvas. Without further qualification the term usually applied to three-masted vessels, those with more being denominated four- or five-masted barques.

barquentine or, in America, **barkentine.** A nineteenth-century term applied to a vessel with a full square rigged fore mast but fore-and-aft rigged main and mizzen; some later vessels had four or more masts.

Bermuda sloop. An extreme version of the sloop (*qv*) rig with raked aft mast, long bowsprit and relatively large main sail. In eighteenth-century Britain this was known as the **Bermudian** or **Bermudoes** rig after its supposed place of origin.

Bessemer steel. The first commercially viable process for manufacturing steel on an industrial scale, demonstrated for the first time in 1856 by the British engineer Sir Henry Bessemer (1813–98). Early steel lacked ductility, malleability and uniformity and was difficult to work, but the perfection of so-called mild steel in the 1870s led to its rapid introduction as a shipbuilding material.

bilander. A two-masted vessel with square rigged fore mast and square main topsail but a main sail set from a lateen; this latter was not triangular but had a vertically cut forward edge or luff. Most common in North Sea and Baltic traders.

billethead. A simple form of abstract decoration to the top of the stem where more sophis-
ticated vessels had a figurehead. It was often carved like the end of a violin, which was then specifically called a fiddlehead; if it turned outwards instead of inwards, it was called a scrollhead.

billy-boy. A bluff-bowed capacious coastal trader associated with the Northeast of England. Usually sloop or ketch rigged, it may have been developed from the Humber keel, which it generally resembled in overall appearance, although the billy-boy was larger and more seaworthy.

binnacle. The cabinet housing compasses, log glasses and watch glasses. Usually positioned directly before the wheel and divided into three compartments, with compasses in the outer ones (so that one was visible to the helmsman whichever side of the wheel he stood) and a light box between to illuminate them at night. Originally known as bittacle, the form became more compact in the nineteenth century, and after the introduction of iron construction, prominent metal spheres were added to either side to compensate for the magnetism of the hull.

bitts. A frame of strong upright timbers and a cross piece to which ropes and cables were made fast. The most important were the riding bitts (double in ships of any size) to which the cables were secured when at anchor but there were others associated with the rigging.

Blackwall Frigate. Large, predominantly passenger carrying, traders to the Far East; the lineal descendants of East Indiamen (*qv*), which they replaced after the East India Company's trading monopoly was revoked. So called because the majority were launched and operated from the Blackwall area of the Thames, and resembled naval cruisers in their layout, an appearance enhanced by painted gunports.

bobstay. Piece of standing rigging between the end of the bowsprit and the ship's stem, designed to counteract the upward pull of the jibs.

bolster. Any item designed as a reinforcement against chafing, such as the moulded wooden pieces under the hawse holes or the pads of tarred canvas protecting the collars of the stays from rubbing the woodwork of the masts.

boltrope. Strengthening rope sewn around the extremities of a sail; divided according to position on the sail as head-, leech- and foot-ropes (top, sides and bottom, respectively).

boom. A relatively light spar, such as a studding sail boom; most commonly applied, without qualification, to the spar that extended the foot of a spanker (*qv*).

boomkin, bomkin or **bumkin.** A small outrigger spar used to extend the corner of a sail;
if used without qualification the term usually applied to those either side of the bow for the windward corner of the fore sail.

'Bounty' ships. French vessels built and operated in response to government subsidies at the turn of the twentieth century.

bowline. Rope attached via three or four bridles to the leech (side) of the sail; led forward to hold the leech up into the wind when the ship was close-hauled (*qv*), from whence 'on a bowline' became synonymous with this point of sailing.

bowsprit. Heavy spar (in effect, a lower mast) angled forward over the bow; provided the support for the fore mast stays and allowed sail to be set far enough forward to have a significant effect on the balance of the rig.

bp. Between perpendiculars, sometimes given as pp: modern designer's measurement of length, omitting the overhang of stem and stern structures, as opposed to length overall; roughly equivalent to length on the lower deck as understood in the eighteenth century.

brace. (i) Rope used to pivot the yards; to brace up was to swing them to as sharp (*ie* smallest) an angle with the keel as feasible; bracing in was the opposite. (ii) Also applied to the gudgeons (*qv*) of the rudder.

breasthook. Curved reinforcing timber, a form of horizontal knee (*qv*), inside the bow to support the structure of the hull forward.

brig. A two-masted square rigged vessel but with a fore and aft gaff-and-boom main sail; very similar to a snow (*qv*).

brigantine. Originally more a hull form than a rig, by the nineteenth century it came to denote a two-masted rig, square on the foremast and fore and aft on the main; it was sometimes called a brig-schooner in some European countries.

bumkin. *See* boomkin.

buntline. Rope from the foot of a square sail passing over the forward surface to the yard; used to spill the wind from a sail when necessary.

burthen. A measurement of capacity in tons calculated by a formula from the dimensions of the ship. The precise formula varied over time and was different from country to country, but usually involved dividing by 94; it greatly underestimated the real displacement but may be regarded as a crude forerunner of gross tonnage (*ie* a measure of internal volume). When more sophisticated rules for tonnage calculation were introduced, tons burthen was designated old measurement (*qv*) or builder's old measurement.
caboose. A galley of a merchant ship, usually in the form of a small separate deckhouse.

certificate of competence. In the merchant service an officer's formal qualification, setting out his level of competence (Master, Mate, etc.) and the type of vessel (fore-and-aft or square rigged) he was entitled to command.

channel. (i) The navigable part of a river or stretch of water. (ii) The platforms projecting from the hull abreast each mast to spread the shrouds (*qv*) and prevent them chafing against the hull (term derived from 'chain-wales').

chasse-marée. French lug rigged coastal craft.

clew. Lower corner of square sail or after corner of a fore and aft sail; on square sails a tackle called a clewline (or clew garnets on the courses) hauled them up to the yards.

clipper. Much abused term of no real technical precision, but generally denoting a fine-lined, fast-sailing vessel. First applied to American small craft like the Baltimore clipper (*qv*), the description was widely employed in the mid nineteenth century.

close-hauled. The point of sailing as near to the direction of the wind as possible (about 70 degrees for a square rigger although fore and aft vessels can get somewhat nearer).

composite construction. A hull combining metal and wood, usually in the form of an iron frame with wood planking, but some vessels had iron plates below the waterline with an exterior sheathing of wood. The advantages were the additional strength of a metal frame (which also took up less of the cargo capacity than a timber hull of the same external dimensions), while avoiding the fouling problems of iron hulls, since wood could be sheathed in copper or yellow metal (*qv*) without electrolytic action threatening the iron fastenings.

compound engine. Machinery in which steam was expanded in at least two stages, in a high pressure cylinder and then a larger diameter low pressure one; eventually triple expansion became the norm, but quadruple expansion was also perfected. Generally compounding refers to two-stage expansion.

coppering. The process of sheathing the underwater hull of a ship with thin copper sheets (and later yellow metal alloy). This was originally intended to protect the hull from marine borers like *teredo navalis* but was found to have a very effective antifouling effect, the slow exfoliation of the metal preventing marine growths.

counter. The area of overhang at the stern, beneath the cabin windows; usually divided into upper and lower counters.

courses. The lowest, and hence largest, sail on each mast; a lateen mizzen or spanker was also considered a course.

crossjack. Pronounced 'crojack'; the lower-most mizzen square yard that extended the clews (*qv*) of the mizzen topsail. Unlike the fore and main yard it did not regularly set its own sail, the lateen mizzen, and later the spanker (*qv*), being considered the mizzen course.

cutter. (i) A ship's boat whose principal characteristic, at least initially, was its clinker construction and handiness under sail as well as oar. (ii) Sharp-lined fast-sailing coastal craft, originally clinker-built in the English Channel ports; carried a single-masted rig of large area, with a bowsprit of little steeve (*qv*). In this century there has been a tendency to differentiate between a cutter and a sloop by the multiple headsails of the former, but in the nineteenth century it was also a matter of hull form, since sloops might also carry a number of jibs.

deadeye. Used in tensioning the shrouds (*qv*), these discs of wood were set up in pairs, one attached to the shroud itself and the other, via chains, to the hull. Tensioning was achieved by a lanyard (*qv*) rove through three holes in each deadeye and bowsed tight.

deadrise. The angle of the floors in the midship section of a ship; one measure of the relative 'sharpness' of the hull lines, a vessel with a V-shaped section having much deadrise whereas one with a flat bottom had none.

Down Easters. American wooden ocean-going merchant ships, built in the northeastern states (predominantly Maine) in the latter half of the nineteenth century.

driver. A sail set on the mizzen that was originally a fine weather addition (initially a square sail but later a fore and aft extension of the mizzen) and finally a temporary replacement for a smaller gaff mizzen. Finally replaced by the spanker (*qv*) with which it is often confused.

East Indiaman. The ships of the English East India Company, and the largest and most prestigious merchant ships of their day. Known as the Honourable East India Company or colloquially as John Company, it was incorporated by royal charter in 1600 and maintained a monopoly of trade with the East until 1813, when India was opened to competition, but it retained its China monopoly until 1834. The Company was effectively the government of India from the mid eighteenth century until 1858. Its ships carried both passengers and high value cargo.

entrance. The fore part of the underwater hull; usually refers to its shape and the fineness of the lines in this area. *See also* run.

flat. Local name for various types of British sailing barge (*qv*), in the Mersey area, for example.

Flinders bars. Iron placed around the binnacle (*qv*) to compensate for the deviation caused to the compass by a metal hull. Named after Matthew Flinders, the famous navigator and explorer of the Australian coast, who developed the system.

floor. The hull bottom; floor timbers are the lowest elements in the frame (*qv*).

flush deck. One without a break or step; later applied to ships with an open weather deck, lacking quarterdeck and forecastle structures above.

flying kites. *See* kites.

fore-and-aft sails. Those carried on gaffs, sprits or stays that at rest hung in the fore and aft axis of the ship; opposite of square sails which were set from transverse yards. A vessel whose principal mode of propulsion came from such sails was said to be fore-and-aft rigged, as opposed to square rigged (*qv*).

forecastle. A structure over the forward part of the upper deck; in medieval times, a castle-like addition, but by 1650 a relatively lightweight platform useful for handling the headsails. When forecastle and quarterdeck (*qv*) were combined into a spar deck, the forward portion was still known as the forecastle.

frame. The structural ribs of a wooden ship, comprising floor timber, a number of tiers of futtocks, and toptimbers.

gaff. A short spar to extend the head of a fore and aft sail; usually hoisted with the sail, for which purpose it was equipped with jaws that fitted around the mast. A larger permanent (standing) gaff was sometimes called a half-sprit.

galeas (*plural* **galeaser**). Applied to various types of coastal traders in and around the Baltic, characteristics depending on country of origin and date: for example, the Swedish and Finnish version was a two-masted schooner for most of the nineteenth century, but a three-master developed towards the end of that period.

halyard. Rope or tackle used to hoist sail or yard; sometimes spelt haliard or halliard.

hanging knee. An L-shaped bracket fastening beam end to the ship's side; originally of naturally grown timber, iron knees became increasingly common in the nineteenth century.

hobbler. *See* hoveller.

hog. Because of their fine lines fore and aft, a ship had more buoyancy amidships, which could cause the ship to arch upwards, distorting the structure and breaking the sheer, as it was described. This propensity to hog was enhanced in longer and more lightly constructed ships and was a major problem until structural improvements like the employment of iron strapping in the early nineteenth century gradually reduced hogging to manageable proportions.

hoveller. An unlicensed pilot or boatman, particularly one who assists a ship by towing or, on land, by taking a rope. Originating on the English Channel coast, the term became widespread; at times had insalubrious connotations of smuggler and wrecker. Also occurring as hobbler.

Indiaman. Shortened form of East Indiaman (*qv*).

jaght. Dutch coastal trader (and, in earlier periods, small warship); originally a hull form rather than a rig.

jakt. Scandinavian term for type of small coastal trader, exact characteristics depending on country and date.

Jarvis brace winch. Patent geared winch much used on larger sailing vessels of the late nineteenth century to allow smaller numbers of crewmen to change the angles of the yards than the old method of hauling the braces directly.

jibboom. An extension of the bowsprit (in effect its topmast); from the end of the eighteenth century, a further extension, called the flying jibboom, was added.

Kajut-boat. Small undecked craft used by the Åland Islanders down to the mid nineteenth century.

keel. (i) The lowermost longitudinal structural member of the hull; in effect, its 'back-bone', the frames forming the 'ribs'. (ii) In the Northeast of England a type of barge (*qv*) for river use, usually propelled by one large sail.

keelson or **kelson.** Internal keel fitted above the main keel (*qv*) and serving to secure the frames.

ketch. A two-masted rig characterised by a main and mizzen (often said to be a ship without a fore mast); originally square rigged, but fore and aft versions became common later.

kites. Light good-weather occasional sails set at the extremities of the conventional sail plan; sometimes encompassing studding sails (*qv*) but more often confined to the unusual – skysails, moonsails, ringtails, etc. Sometimes called flying kites.

lanyard. Short piece of rope or line used to secure an item or act as a handle, such as the lanyard to a gunlock which allowed it to be triggered from a safe distance; lanyards between the deadeyes (*qv*) were used to tauten the shrouds.

lasts. An old Scandinavian measure of weight and bulk; of differing value in specific trades. Ships were also measured in lasts of about 2 tons.

lateen. Triangular sail set from a long yard that was slung from its mast at a 45-degree angle; any vessel whose principal driving sails were of this kind was said to be lateen rigged. The rig is ancient in origin and was employed by galleys and most kinds of Mediterranean war vessels; the sail also formed the mizzen course of square riggers until the late eighteenth century.

leeward. Downwind, or away from the direction of the wind; opposite of windward (*qv*).

Leith smack. A heavily rigged cutter used on the packet service between London and Edinburgh (for which Leith is the port).

lug. A rig characterised by a four-sided sail with a head about two-thirds the length of the foot; hoisted on a angled yard with about a quarter of its length ahead of the mast.

lugger. A lug rigged coastal craft, two- and sometimes three-masted, which could also set lug topsails; fast and weatherly, they were popular with smugglers and privateers but also with fishermen and legitimate traders. The French *chasse-marée* (*qv*) was similar.

martingale. The stay tensioning the jibboom from below, set up over a spar called the dolphin striker.

menhaden. A species of fish, much used in the manufacture of fertiliser on the Atlantic coast of America.

mizzen. The aftermost mast of a ship or ketch, and the yards, sails and rigging pertaining to it.

moonraker or **moonsail.** Light weather sail, set above skysail (*qv*); such occasional canvas was generally termed flying kites.

Moorsom's Rule tonnage. The basis of modern gross tonnage calculation was worked out by a committee set up by the British government under the chairmanship of Admiral Moorsom in 1849. It was formally adopted in the Merchant Shipping Act of 1854 and for some time was known as Moorsom's Rule tonnage.

Navigation Acts. A system of British restrictive legislation dating back to the seventeenth century (although there were even earlier precedents) which aimed at retaining British trade in British ships. Repealed in 1849 as part of Britain's new commitment to Free Trade.

new measurement. A revised version of burthen (*qv*), which for the first time took into account the depth in the hold of the ship. It was introduced in Britain in 1836 and survived until replaced by the Moorsom Rule (*qv*) in 1854.

packet or pacquet. Fast mail-carrying craft; usually government-sponsored, like British Post Office packets.

parrel. An assemblage of beads called trucks and wooden dividers called ribs strung onto a series of horizontal ropes. Forming a collar between the upper yards and their masts, and designed to allow the yards to be hoisted and lowered easily, it vaguely resembled a flexible abacus, although the beads were intended to revolve to reduce friction and the ribs stopped them moving from side to side.

polacre. Mediterranean trading vessel, originally lateen rigged; later examples acquired square topsails but set on single-piece masts (*ie* no separate upper masts) and thereafter the term came to denote pole-masted.

pole-masted. *See* polacca.

poop. Deck above the quarterdeck; often no more than the roof of the cabins below. On merchant ships with a flush weather deck, the after superstructure which might have been called the quarterdeck on a warship was usually known as the poop.

run. the after part of the underwater hull; the opposite of entrance (*qv*).

sagging. The opposite of hogging (*qv*), in which the hull distorts by drooping amidships rather than at the extremities.

sail-assist. Wind power adapted to operate in conjunction with mechanical power to increase the ship's speed or, more usually, the economy of the engines.

schooner. Gaff rigged vessel with two or more masts, originating around 1700; later examples had square topsails. *See also* tern schooner and topsail schooner.

shallop. In the early seventeenth century, a large seaworthy boat, possibly the ancestor of the sloop (*qv*); the term continued to denote a boat type, although a rather lighter and more decorative craft, down to the nineteenth century.

shelter deck. A structure above the principal deck, not regarded as part of the hull for tonnage measurement purposes.

ship rig. In the sailing era the ship, or full, rig was defined as the principal driving sails on all three masts being square (later a few four- and one five-masted full-riggers were built, but later the vast majority carried three masts; two square rigged masts made the vessel a brig). The lower sail on the mizzen usually comprised fore and aft canvas but as long as square sail was carried above it the ship was still rated as a ship.

shroud. Heavy rope supporting a mast from behind and transversely. *See also* deadeye.

Siemens-Martin process. Open hearth method of manufacturing steel which produced more consistent quality mild steel than the earlier Bessemer process.

skuta (*plural* *skutor*). Scandinavian coastal trader; early Swedish versions had one or two masts, each with a single square sail, but there are later examples with three masts.

skysail or **skyscraper.** An occasional light-weather sail set above the royals (*qv*).

slättoppare. Swedish designation dating from the 1890s for sail schooner with three or more masts of approximately the same height; known in Denmark as *slettop skonnert*.

slettop skonnert. See slättoppare.

sloop. Originally a boat designation (*see* shallop), in the merchant marine the term came to denote a rig: a single-masted gaff vessel with fixed bowsprit and jib headsails, and usually no square topsails.

smack. Small inshore fishing craft, usually cutter (*qv*) rigged.

snow. Two-masted square rigged vessel, with gaff-headed main course; in later eighteenth-century definitions, this gaff sail had to be hoisted on a rope horse or separate trysail mast (to distinguish the snow from the brig, which hoisted its gaff course directly on the main mast), the sail itself being loose-footed – not being extended by a boom. *See also* brig.

spanker. Large gaff-and-boom sail; the main course of a brig and mizzen course of ships and barques.

square rig. Any sail plan in which the principal power was derived from canvas set from yards which crossed the centreline of the ship (the yards were 'square' – at right angles – to the centreline when the wind was directly aft).

standing rigging. The permanently set up support for the masts and tops – stays, shrouds, etc.

steeve. The angle of the bowsprit relative to the waterline; the larger the angle, the more steeply steeved the bowsprit was said to be.

stiff. having a good reserve of stability and hence able to carry sufficient sail in all weathers; the opposite of crank.

stor-båtar. Small undecked craft used by the farmer-sailors of the Åland Islands.

studding sails. Additional fair weather square sails set on each side of the principal sails with removable yards and booms; pronounced stuns'ls and often written as stunsails.

sump. Scandinavian single-masted trading vessel.

tack. When sailing with the wind anywhere but aft, a rope used to extend to windward the lower corners of courses (*qv*) and staysails as sheets confined them to leeward; by extension it also applied to the parts of the sail to which it was attached. When so sailing, either the port or starboard tacks were said to be on board, from whence came the phrase port tack or starboard tack and the term *tacking* for the manoeuvre of changing course from one oblique angle to the other.

tern schooner. A three-masted schooner with masts of equal height; American in origin signifying 'three of a kind', the term deriving from a card game.

top hamper. General term for masts, spars and rigging.

topgallant. The mast, yard, sail and rigging above the topmast (*qv*).

Topmast. The portion of a mast (and its rigging) above the top, usually separate from the lower section; its sail was called the **topsail**, which gave its name to the yard and running rigging.

topsail schooner. A schooner (*qv*) with square canvas on at least one topmast.

trailboard. The timbers (usually decorated) between the cheeks and the knee of the head, below the headrails.

trenails. Wooden dowels much used in the construction of wooden ships since, unlike iron nails or bolts, they did not corrode. Also occurs as treenails, trennels, trunnells, etc.

triple expansion engine. Machinery in which the steam is subject to three stages of expansion, driving in sequence a cylinder at high pressure, then a larger one at intermediate pressure, and finally the largest at the low remaining pressure. Since the same amount of steam was made to do more work, it was far more economical than simple expansion engines and resulted in significantly increased range.

trow. British local type of sailing barge, like those associated with the river Severn.

trysail. A gaff-and-boom sail set from an auxiliary (trysail) mast or rope horse; the trysails which replaced staysails were called spencers in nineteenth-century navies. Trysail was also used of the reduced storm canvas employed by small craft in place of the regular main.

tumblehome. The curving-in of the ship's side above the waterline; this feature was abandoned in the nineteenth century, the resulting ships being described as wall-sided.

weather helm. A well balanced sailing vessel will usually have a tendency to gripe or come up into the wind, which is considered far safer in emergencies because if control is lost the ship will end up head to wind and more or less stationary. However, under sail it is necessary to offset this tendency by use of the steering, holding the helm or tiller up to windward; for this reason a vessel with this most desirable characteristic is said to carry weather helm.

wherry. A light fine-lined pulling boat mostly used on rivers for the transportation of small numbers of passengers.

windward. Towards or on the side from which the wind blows; the weather side. The opposite of leeward or lee side.

yard. Spar from which sail was set, irrespective of whether the vessel be square or fore-and-aft-rigged (*qv*).

yawl. A two-masted fore and aft rig in which the mizzen was very much smaller than that of a ketch (*qv*) and usually stepped abaft the sternpost.

yellow metal. Copper and zinc alloy used to sheath the underwater hulls against the effects of fouling; replaced genuine copper in the nineteenth century. *See also* coppering.

Index